TAKING SIDES IN PEACEKEEPING

Taking Sides in Peacekeeping

*Impartiality and the Future
of the United Nations*

EMILY PADDON RHOADS

OXFORD
UNIVERSITY PRESS

OXFORD

UNIVERSITY PRESS

Great Clarendon Street, Oxford, OX2 6DP,
United Kingdom

Oxford University Press is a department of the University of Oxford.
It furthers the University's objective of excellence in research, scholarship,
and education by publishing worldwide. Oxford is a registered trade mark of
Oxford University Press in the UK and in certain other countries

© Emily Paddon Rhoads 2016

The moral rights of the author have been asserted

First Edition published in 2016

Impression: 1

Published in the United States of America by Oxford University Press
198 Madison Avenue, New York, NY 10016, United States of America

British Library Cataloguing in Publication Data

Data available

Library of Congress Control Number: 2015958363

ISBN 978-0-19-874724-6

Printed in Great Britain by
Clays Ltd, St Ives plc

Acknowledgements

The opportunity to acknowledge the many people and institutions whose intellectual, financial, and moral support made this book possible is, in many ways, the most gratifying part of finishing it. But it is also the hardest, as it is difficult to find words to express my gratitude.

This project began nearly ten years ago as an MPhil thesis completed under the supervision of Sir Adam Roberts. It was an honour to study with him and I will forever cherish our early morning tutorials in his office at Balliol overlooking Broad Street. Adam nurtured my initial curiosity about the United Nations and the norm of impartiality, and encouraged me to continue this research at the doctoral level, first under his able tutelage, and then, after he had retired, that of Jennifer Welsh. It was an immense privilege to work with Jennifer. She has shaped this book with her measured advice and incisive questions, and has been a constant source of support and encouragement.

My ideas and arguments also benefited greatly from conversations and debate with friends, colleagues, and mentors. Three are deserving of particular thanks. My thesis examiners, Henry Shue and Mats Berdal, provided helpful comments and advice on developing the dissertation into a book. Henry, whose course in international normative theory gave me a foundation from which to explore many of the issues in this book, has been unfailingly generous with his time and advice over the years. Lord Patten gave me an opportunity first to work on the Congo. He has been a wonderful mentor, and shared invaluable insights into the way politics actually works, gleaned from his decades of experience. In addition, I am immensely grateful to Lee Jones, Iason Gabriel, Neil MacFarlane, Alex Betts, Henning Tamm, Keith Stanski, and Francesca Giovannini, all of whom read parts of this book or the entire manuscript, and provided insightful comments.

Beyond Oxford, I am indebted to the many people who helped me with my research and generously sat with me for hours and described their experiences. Robert Fowler and Larry Murray offered valuable counsel before my fieldwork and opened doors at the UN that I did not even know existed. Louise Fréchette and Jean-Marie Guéhenno, seasoned UN hands and unmatched experts in the field of peacekeeping, took time out of their busy schedules to share their insights on several occasions. In New York, I must thank Adam Smith, Edward Luck, and the staff at IPI for hosting me as a visiting scholar in 2010, as well as Michael Doyle who generously provided an institutional home for me at Columbia University while I updated the research in 2014–15. In Congo, I owe a special debt to Jason Stearns, Ida Sawyer, Koen Vlassenroot, Nick Vysny, Michael

Kavanagh, Fergus Thomas, Carlo Ontal, Tom and Maria Pravda, Eugenia Zorbas, Venetia Holland, Sofia Candeias, Günther von Billerbeck, Guillaume Lacaille, Philip Winter, Christian Manahl, and Timo Mueller—all of whom helped me find my way, offered expert advice, and the warmest of hospitality and friendship over the years.

None of this would have been possible without the generous support of several funding bodies and institutions. The research received funding from the European Research Council under the European Union's Seventh Framework Agreement (FP/2007–2013) / ERC Grant Agreement n. [340956], Overseas Research Trust, Pierre Elliott Trudeau Foundation, Canadian Department of National Defence, and Department of Politics and International Relations at the University of Oxford. In addition, St Antony's College, Wadham College, Lady Margaret Hall, and the European University Institute all served as wonderfully supportive institutional bases at various stages of writing. At Oxford University Press (OUP), I would like to give special thanks to Dominic Byatt and Olivia Wells for their enthusiasm, guidance, and patience with this project. I am also grateful to OUP for granting me permission to reproduce sections of 'Peacekeeping in the Congo: Implementation of the Protection of Civilians Norm', in Alexander Betts and Phil Orchard, *Implementation & World Politics: How International Norms Change Practice* (Oxford: Oxford University Press, 2014), pp. 160–78.

The final round of acknowledgements is reserved for those closest to me. Josie, Kelly, Lindsey, Alec, Serena, Laura, Taylor, Bici, David, Sondra, Urvashi, and Alex have been the best of friends anyone could hope for. They endured countless conversations about this project on muddy meadow walks and over endless cups of tea and dark chocolate curled up in my yellow chairs; I am eternally grateful to them. Finally, my greatest debt and deepest appreciation goes to my family: the UK contingent, for making Oxford a true home for close to ten years; Jaffa, for her limitless love and unfailing belief in me; and Tim, who deserves a medal for his unwavering support and kindness. The last, greatest and most unexpected part of this adventure was meeting my husband, Christopher Rhoads. From Congo to Cuttyhunk, he has been a source of unstinting encouragement, humour, and love as this project (and our family) grew. It is to him and baby Roscoe that I dedicate this book.

Emily Paddon Rhoads

Contents

Contents

List of Acronyms

ADF–NALU	Allied Democratic Forces—National Army for the Liberation of Uganda
AFDL	*Alliance des Forces Démocratiques pour la Libération du Congo-Zaire*
AG	Armed Group
ALiR	*Armée pour la Libération du Rwanda*
APCLS	*Alliance Patriotique pour un Congo Libre et Souverain*
AU	African Union
BDK	*Bundu dia Kongo*
CIAT	*Comité International d'Accompagnement de la Transition*
CLA	Community Liaison Advisor
CLI	Community Liaison Interpreter
CNDP	*Congrès National pour la Défense du Peuple*
COBS	Company Operating Bases
DDR	Demobilization, Disarmament, and Reintegration
DDRRR	Disarmament, Demobilization, Repatriation, Resettlement, and Reintegration
DFS	Department of Field Support, United Nations
DPA	Department of Political Affairs, United Nations
DPKO	Department of Peacekeeping Operations, United Nations
DRC	Democratic Republic of the Congo
DSRSG	Deputy Special Representative of the Secretary-General, United Nations
DSRSG/RC/HC	Deputy Special Representative of the Secretary-General/ Resident Coordinator/Humanitarian Coordinator, United Nations
FAG	Foreign Armed Group
FAPC	*Forces Armées du Peuple Congolais*
FAR	*Forces Armées Rwandaises*
FARDC	*Forces Armées de la République Démocratique du Congo*
FPDC	*Front Populaire pour la Démocratie du Congo*
FDLR	*Forces Démocratiques de Libération du Rwanda*
FIB	Force Intervention Brigade
FNI	*Front des Nationalistes et Intégrationnistes*

FRPI	*Force de Résistance Patriotique en Ituri*
GA	General Assembly
HQ	Headquarters
ICC	International Criminal Court
ICGLR	International Conference on the Great Lakes Region
ICISS	International Commission on Intervention and State Sovereignty
ICJ	International Court of Justice
ICRC	International Committee of the Red Cross
ICTR	International Criminal Tribunal for Rwanda
ICTY	International Criminal Tribunal for the Former Yugoslavia
IDP	Internally Displaced Person
IEMF	Interim Emergency Multinational Force
IHL	International Humanitarian Law
IMF	International Monetary Fund
IPI	International Peace Institute
IR	International Relations
ISAF	International Security Assistance Force
ISSSS	International Security and Stabilization Support Strategy
JMAC	Joint Mission Analysis Centre
JMC	Joint Military Commission
JOC	Joint Operations Centre
JPT	Joint Protection Team
LRA	Lord's Resistance Army
MINURCAT	*Mission des Nations Unies en République Centrafricaine et au Tchad*
M23	*Mouvement du 23-Mars*
MINUSCA	*Mission Multidimensionnelle Intégrée des Nations Unies pour la Stabilisation en Centrafrique*
MINUSMA	*Mission Multidimensionnelle Intégrée des Nations Unies pour la Stabilisation au Mali*
MINUSTAH	*Mission des Nations Unies pour la Stabilisation en Haïti*
MLC	*Mouvement de Libération du Congo*
MONUC	*Mission de l'Organisation des Nations Unies en République Démocratique du Congo*
MONUSCO	*Mission de l'Organisation des Nations Unies pour la Stabilisation en République Démocratique du Congo*
MoU	Memoranda of Understanding
NAM	Non-Aligned Movement

NATO	North Atlantic Treaty Organization
NGO	Non-Governmental Organization
OAU	Organization of African Unity
OCHA	Office for the Coordination of Humanitarian Affairs, United Nations
OHCHR	Office of the High Commissioner for Human Rights, United Nations
OIOS	Office of Internal Oversight Services, United Nations
OLA	Office of Legal Affairs, United Nations
ONUB	*Opération des Nations Unies au Burundi*
ONUC	*Opération des Nations Unies au Congo*
ONUCI	*Opération des Nations Unies en Côte d'Ivoire*
PARECO	*Patriotes Résistants Congolais*
PCC	Police-Contributing Country
PoC	Protection of Civilians
PSCF	Peace, Security, and Cooperation Framework
PUSIC	*Parti pour l'Unité et la Sauvegarde de l'Intégrité du Congo*
RBA	Rights-Based Approach
RCD	*Rassemblement Congolais pour la Démocratie*
RCD-G	*Rassemblement Congolais pour la Démocratie-Goma*
RPA	Rwandan Patriotic Army
RPF	Rwandan Patriotic Front
RoE	Rules of Engagement
RtoP	Responsibility to Protect
RUF	Revolutionary United Front
SADC	Southern African Development Community
SEA	Sexual Exploitation and Abuse
SNA	Somali National Alliance
SoFA	Status of Forces Agreement
SRSG	Special Representative of the Secretary-General
SSR	Security Sector Reform
TCC	Troop-Contributing Country
TG	Transitional Government
UN	United Nations
UNAMID	United Nations African Union/United Nations Hybrid Operation in Darfur
UNAMIR	United Nations Assistance Mission for Rwanda
UNAMSIL	United Nations Mission in Sierra Leone

UNDOF	United Nations Disengagement Observer Force
UNDP	United Nations Development Programme
UNDSS	United Nations Department for Safety and Security
UNEF	United Nations Emergency Force
UNFICYP	United Nations Peacekeeping Force in Cyprus
UNHCR	United Nations High Commissioner for Refugees
UNIFIL	United Nations Interim Force in Lebanon
UNIPOM	United Nations India Pakistan Observation Mission
UNJHRO	United Nations Joint Human Rights Office
UNMIK	United Nations Interim Administration Mission in Kosovo
UNMISS	United Nations Mission in the Republic of South Sudan
UNOSOM	United Nations Operation in Somalia
UNPROFOR	United Nations Protection Force
UNSC	United Nations Security Council
UNSSSS	United Nations Security and Stabilization Support Strategy
UNTAET	United Nations Transitional Administration in East Timor
UPC	*Union des Patriotes Congolais*
UPDF	Uganda People's Defence Force

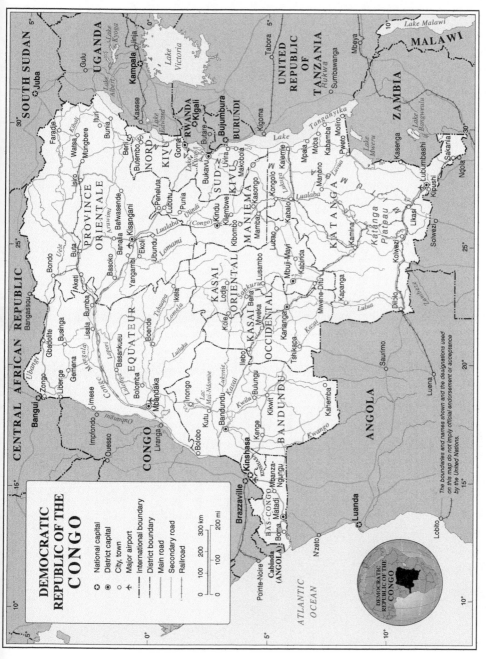

Fig.1. Map of the Democratic Republic of the Congo, reprinted with the permission of the United Nations (Map no. 4007 Rev. 10, July 2011).

Introduction

On 1 March 2005, United Nations (UN) peacekeeping forces launched an offensive in the northeast of the Democratic Republic of the Congo in order to suppress a rebellion.[1] At 08:00, commanders deployed twelve armoured personnel carriers. Ground forces cordoned off the area and asked for air support. At 11:00, the target was located and engaged. Mi-25 attack helicopters swooped in, firing sixteen rockets in eight passes. The militia camp was successfully 'neutralized' and UN troops were withdrawn from the area by 16:00. An estimated fifty rebels were killed. 'It may look like war', explained Lieutenant-General Babacar Gaye, Force Commander of the mission, 'but it is peacekeeping.'[2] 'We were impartial.'[3]

The assault, part of the UN's *Operation Djugu III*, was no aberration. Since 1999, blue helmets in places such as Sierra Leone, Haiti, Ivory Coast, and Mali have conducted military offensives to 'keep' and 'make' peace. Once limited in scope and based firmly on the consent of all parties, peacekeeping operations are now regularly authorized under Chapter VII of the UN Charter, charged with penalizing spoilers of the peace and protecting civilians from peril. Anything less amounts to what the *Report of the Panel on United Nations Peace Operations* (2000) condemned as 'complicity with evil'.[4] Peacekeepers are now expected to search for, and then side with, the victims.

Despite this more aggressive posture, UN officials such as Lt. Gen. Gaye as well as academics continue to affirm the vital importance of impartiality—a norm traditionally regarded as the 'oxygen'[5] and 'lifeblood'[6] of peacekeeping—while stating that it no longer means what it once did. They characterize the new impartiality as 'active' impartiality,[7] 'unrestrained' impartiality,[8] even 'imperial' impartiality[9]—implying that peacekeepers are, or should be, robust and assertive in carrying out their increasingly lofty and ambitious mandates.

IMPARTIAL PEACEKEEPING AND ASSERTIVE
LIBERAL INTERNATIONALISM

This book is the first scholarly attempt to analyse this transformation and its implications. It argues that the change in the understanding and practices of impartiality is significant. Because impartiality refers not only to the position of peacekeepers as an unbiased and informed third party but also to the values and norms the UN itself seeks to project, this change, which is manifest in discourse and institutionalized in doctrine and rules of engagement (RoE), signifies a radical transformation in the very nature and substance of peacekeeping, and in the UN's role as guarantor of international peace and security. Claims to impartial authority are no longer based exclusively on terms to which all parties consent. Instead, they are premised on a more ambitious and expansive set of human-rights-related norms, around which consensus is presumed but not always secured. While traditional peacekeeping mandates treated parties with moral equivalence and eschewed notions of blame and punishment, instigators of violence are often now seen as criminals—their crime a form of moral collapse to be judged and righted by peacekeepers, rather than as a symptom of a political conflict to be mediated.

What is more, this change is not limited to peacekeeping. It is an integral part of the turn towards what I refer to as a more assertive liberal internationalism, one that is transforming existing international institutions and practices, particularly the UN. The realization, promotion, and protection of human rights is at the core of this broader shift and has translated into forms of international engagement that are less consensual and more compulsory and coercive, justified by upholding human rights and constellating a new class of international crimes.[10]

Here, too, claims to impartial authority figure prominently, but they have taken on new meaning. For example, through the principle of universal jurisdiction, the International Criminal Court (ICC) is unprecedented in its claim to impartially investigate and try alleged perpetrators of international crimes independently of whether their states have given consent to the organization by ratifying the Rome Statute.[11] In the field of humanitarian assistance, many of today's aid workers no longer impartially provide emergency relief to individuals based exclusively on need. Decisions about who should receive assistance are now often influenced by whether they help or hinder the realization of rights. While claiming to be impartial, humanitarian actors frequently advocate for human-rights protections and actively seek to reform political and social structures that impinge on those rights. Similarly, the UN's *Human Rights Up Front* policy, developed in 2013, puts the imperative to protect people from serious violations of human rights and international humanitarian law at the core of the organization's strategy and operational activities, and obliges staff to speak out on an 'impartial basis' about abuses and looming crises.[12]

The legitimacy of this more assertive liberal internationalism, and associated claims by peacekeepers, judges, and aid workers that their more coercive and intrusive actions *are* impartial, rests largely on what is extolled as a newfound unity of purpose. What is the base for such a claim? Academics and practitioners alike contend that the 'internationalization of human rights' over several decades has allowed for an acceptable transformation in the foundation of certain norms that now have authority not because they are based on the consent of individual states, but rather because they are seen to reflect a collective international consensus—what scholar Ruti Teitel describes as the 'new law of humanity'.[13] At the core of this transformation is the idea that human rights and the protection of those rights, particularly for those most vulnerable in armed conflict, are no longer tied to a particular political or partisan agenda. 'Protecting civilians transcends politics', as one diplomat recently proclaimed in the Security Council.[14]

This notion has become a powerful piety, described by some as the 'new ideology', even a 'secular religion'.[15] The unassailably worthy conviction that human rights and peacekeeping in the service of those rights are above politics, and that above all, individual civilians should be protected, is potent. It allows for simple and easily comprehensible accounts of right and wrong, in what are often contexts of extreme human suffering. It differentiates victim from perpetrator, assigns innocence and guilt, and it furnishes apparently straightforward answers to questions about what must be done to bring about good, to stop the suffering. In other words, it provides something to believe in. All of which makes it very difficult indeed to argue with. Contestation, from this perspective, would appear to be a thing of the past.

This book examines this shift towards assertive liberal internationalism in the context of UN peacekeeping. This focus is important because, despite the significance of this change and the long lineage of impartiality in peacekeeping, the norm has been the subject of surprisingly little sustained analysis.[16] Whereas consent of the host state and non-use of force—the two other norms traditionally associated with peacekeeping—have been the focus of several comprehensive academic studies,[17] impartiality has received little more than passing references to its vital importance[18] and its application in specific historical cases.[19] Given that the dominant meaning of impartiality has radically changed, this omission is a glaring oversight, not least because of its implications *for* the other two norms.

Rather, in an apparent case of 'taking sides', scholars of peacekeeping have done more actively to advocate for the new more assertive conception of impartiality and applaud its institutionalization in the new millennium than they have critically to interrogate the norm and its implications from political and operational perspectives.[20] In their reflections on the peacekeeping failures of the 1990s, many academics excoriated the UN and its 'institutional ideology of impartiality' as entirely inappropriate for the post-Cold War operational environment of catastrophic mass violence.[21] They contended that 'impartiality had to be reconceived', called for clarification in both the conceptual and operational domains, and advanced their own interpretations of the norm.[22] Others imposed a distinction where none had previously existed; they redefined Cold War peacekeeping, ex post facto, as 'neutral' to denote its passive character whereas it was hoped that post-Cold War activity would, in a more dynamic sense, be 'impartial'.[23] These texts do not engage in rigorous conceptual analysis or with what one author describes as the 'broader political-strategic issues surrounding new impartiality'.[24] Lacking this wider view, our understanding of the politics and practices of contemporary peace-keeping, as well as the normative framework that underpins and is used to justify the authority of peacekeepers and the UN, is incomplete and partial.

Meanwhile, peacekeeping has descended into a state of renewed crisis. In many mission contexts, which have experienced repeated crises in recent years, peace and stability have become a mirage. In places like Darfur, South Sudan, Burundi, and Congo where the UN's political space has been restricted, mandate implementation has been thwarted by intransigent host govern-ments, freedom of movement has been curtailed, officials have been made persona non grata and missions have, at various junctures, been threatened with expulsion. What is more, an increase in attacks on and kidnappings of UN personnel has prompted troop-contributing countries (TCCs) to with-draw contingents from missions that are already notoriously under-resourced and plagued by technical difficulties.

THE POLITICS OF PEACEKEEPING

It is in this context that a closer and more critical examination of the dominant conception of impartiality as a norm of UN peacekeeping becomes essential. This book starts from the premise that claims to impartiality must be con-sidered as only that—claims. Rather than accept that consensus exists over the meaning and appropriateness of the new more assertive conception of impar-tiality, and that the decisions and actions of peacekeepers *are* impartial, I take these as assertions that require empirical investigation. History is rife with instances of closeted sectarianism and abuses of authority under the guise of impartiality. Without social validation there is a danger that impartialism becomes, as John Rawls cautioned, 'just another sectarian doctrine', except that, whereas others are up front about their sectarianism, impartialists con-ceal their predilections.[25] Indeed, it is precisely because, as Thomas Franck put it, impartiality's 'yoke is so eminently wearable', that a closer look at the norm in contemporary peacekeeping is vital.[26]

Two central and closely connected questions provide the overarching focus for this inquiry. First, how is impartiality understood as a norm of UN peacekeeping and, second, what are the effects of this understanding? To answer these questions, I conceptualize impartiality as a 'composite' norm, one that is not free-standing but is in fact an aggregate of other principles— each of which can change and is open to contestation, singly or in combination. Drawing on political and legal theory, I elucidate the core components of impartiality and provide much needed conceptual clarity.

The composite norm is then used to conduct a multi-level analysis. I trace the evolution of impartiality in peacekeeping and examine the macro-level politics surrounding institutionalization of the new, more assertive conception of the norm at the UN, as well as the micro-level politics surrounding its implementation in the Democratic Republic of the Congo, site of the largest and costliest peacekeeping mission in UN history (1999–2015).[27] I identify the various sites and sources of contestation over assertive impartiality at both levels and explicate their linkages. Multi-level analysis is crucial because impartiality is a peripatetic norm, relevant from the hallowed halls of UN headquarters in New York to the remote villages where blue helmets deploy. To understand how, amidst contestation, certain conceptions of impartiality have become dominant both in policy and practice, I analyse different institutional decision-making pathways and their power dynamics. In doing so, this book illuminates how certain actors wield greater influence than others in determining the policies and practices of UN peacekeeping, and the meaning of impartiality itself.

The Congo case is particularly salient in examining the effects of impartiality on peacekeeping practice as well as broader institutional dynamics. The *Mission de l'Organisation des Nations Unies en République Démocratique du Congo* (known by its French acronym, MONUC) was first deployed in late 1999, three years before the formal end of Congo's epic war and just as the new conception of impartiality began to take hold at the UN. It was a testament to the prevailing thinking in the Security Council. During deliberations on the creation of the mission, lessons learned from previous peacekeeping failures were recounted, and the need for robust peacekeeping affirmed by various member states.[28] Indeed, MONUC became the standard-bearer for a new era of blue-helmet intervention and represented, as South African ambassador Dumisani Kumalo opined, a 'litmus test' for the Council's commitment to peacekeeping in Africa.[29]

MONUC's decade-long deployment saw the institutionalization of the more assertive conception of impartiality manifest in Council resolutions that steadily increased the reputed robustness of the mission. Its Chapter VII mandate expanded to encompass the entire country, naming and shaming of spoilers became a recurrent feature of resolutions, and protection of civilians was designated MONUC's highest priority. In 2010, the mission was renamed the *Mission de l'Organisation des Nations Unies pour la Stabilisation en République Démocratique du Congo* (MONUSCO), a signal that the UN was willing to use force more proactively, and in 2013, the Council deployed the Force Intervention Brigade (FIB), a specialized unit within MONUSCO, authorized to take offensive military action to 'neutralize' and 'disarm' rebel groups.[30] Throughout this period, Congo became a laboratory for more assertive approaches to peacekeeping, and operational mechanisms and guidance developed by MONUC/MONUSCO in turn fed back into policymaking at UN headquarters, leading to more general innovations in doctrine.[31] In addition, Congo became a focus country for the ICC and, more broadly, the locus of numerous humanitarian reform initiatives associated with assertive liberal internationalism.

And yet, the analysis of impartiality at both macro- and micro-level in Congo reveals that despite a veneer of consensus, 'impartiality' is in fact a highly contested norm. As the collection of principles it refers to has changed and expanded to encompass human rights, contestation has increased, with deep disagreement among key UN member states and local actors in Congo as to what keeping peace impartially means and, consequently, over the purposes of contemporary peacekeeping and the UN's broader approach to conflict resolution. This is not to say that human rights in peacekeeping are irrelevant. Few would disagree that they matter deeply, arguably more so now than ever before. But, as this book demonstrates, human rights cannot be divorced from power and partisan interests, past injustices, and present inequalities. Nor can they be considered separately from the privileges still accorded to states in international relations and particularly those at the UN, given its state-centric constitution.

The contestation over assertive impartiality reveals this plurality of contending perspectives at multiple levels. The objections raised during institutionalization within the UN are varied and diverse as Chapter 3 demonstrates. They reflect fears, frequently emanating from the experiences of some states as colonial subjects, that more coercive forms of peacekeeping chip away at sovereignty and self-determination and may be used to realize more nefarious intentions. They come in the form of charges of hypocrisy, and criticisms of unequal burden-sharing in peacekeeping. They reveal concerns about the viability of and the moral hazards engendered by contemporary practices— hard lessons learned from time on the ground. And they have very real implications for the willingness of traditional troop-contributing countries to sustain these operations as well as for the UN's acceptance on the ground.

These forms of contestation have also been manifest during implementation, a process that, as I show in Chapter 4, generates its own forms of disagreement related to the historical, social, and political dynamics in

Congo. Among the many sites and sources of contestation, from tensions between troop-contributing countries to bitter divisions within the Security Council over policy towards the Congo and the wider region, I show how the dichotomies attendant in assertive impartiality often break down in practice. In Congo, there were often no clear answers to the questions of who is perpetrator and who victim, who protector and who in need of protection. And thus, attempts to pass judgment and take action by assigning such roles have, at numerous junctures, divided those involved, from the warring parties themselves to the peacekeeping mission, and more broadly, the international community.

Beyond the semantics, this disagreement has led to inconsistencies in peacekeeping practice, which further amplify perceptions of partiality and, together with the varying expectations and incentives created by the norm, have frequently resulted in perverse and unintended consequences that run contrary to the norm's original intent and undermine the UN's legitimacy. In Congo, civilians who were told that UN forces would protect them were at times emboldened to take even greater risks. Instead of fleeing to possible safety, they remained in place, or travelled in insecure conditions to UN bases. When protection was forthcoming, such risks were worthwhile. When it was not, the consequences were sometimes fatal. Similarly, armed groups and factions of the national army manipulated the mission and its mandate in order to realize strategic and political aims. The discourse of civilian protection was, for example, co-opted and instrumentalized by certain militia in an effort to change perceptions of their own legitimacy and to de-legitimate other actors, including the mission itself. This had negative consequences for peacekeepers and the UN, and crucially impeded their ability to act and be accepted as a political arbiter, as a broker of peace.

As a whole, the book shows how the transformation in impartiality has deeply politicized peacekeeping and, in some cases such as Congo, effectively converted UN forces into one warring party among many. I argue that the implications of this change are significant, not only for peacekeeping but for the UN more broadly. As several scholars have demonstrated, the legitimacy of the organization—and by extension the likelihood of its securing the resources and access so critical to its operations—derives not just from its practical effectiveness, but from whether it is seen to reflect and promote shared values.[32] This is of consequence, given that the institutional and broader geopolitical landscape have profoundly shifted. The rise of non-Western states and changes in the global balance of power mean that contestation around underlying values, as described in this book, is likely to persist and even to grow. As the Conclusion argues, this raises pressing questions about the UN's future role and its ability to act as the legitimate guarantor of international peace and security if it is perceived as partial, as having taken sides.

THEORETICAL APPROACH AND CONTRIBUTIONS

This book is designed to speak to scholars and practitioners of peacekeeping and the UN, to others interested in Congo and, more broadly, to those concerned with the challenges associated with assertive liberal internationalism. Yet it is not solely a work of policy analysis and prescription. It contributes to debates within the inter-disciplinary field of peacekeeping studies, which has undergone remarkable growth over the last decade.[33] The literature on peacekeeping has long been criticized for being apolitical and overly focused on the macro-level, skirting the importance of context and treating peacekeeping operations as technical policy tools. This trend, however, is being reversed by a body of work that does explore the political dimensions of peacekeeping operations.[34] Overlapping this research is a growing field of scholarship that has 'gone micro'.[35] Drawing on the burgeoning political science literature on the micro-foundations of conflict, as well as insights from anthropology and sociology, this diverse research agenda has drawn much needed attention to the local dimensions of peacekeeping and peacebuilding, including, the everyday practices of interveners, their interactions with local actors, and the consequences, intended and otherwise, of international engagement. These investigations affirm the importance of context, the contingency of peacekeeping practices, and offer a valuable counterpoint to macro-level analyses that have dominated the field and approached peacekeeping as a predominantly international phenomenon.

My analysis of impartiality's implementation and effects in Congo complements this scholarship. This book, however, departs from this body of work in stressing the importance of multi-level analysis. Whereas existing texts tend to look either at the global or the local dimensions of peace operations, I examine both and explore the relationship between them. As the analysis shows, this is important because the global politics of peacekeeping are not and cannot be separated from the local dimensions of peacekeeping. For example, as Chapter 3 details, the states which contribute the preponderance of peacekeepers to Congo were among those most critical of assertive impartiality during institutionalization, most notably India and Pakistan. This had a profound effect on peacekeeping in Congo, as these actors resisted the new conception of the norm and advanced their own interpretations, which in turn heightened contestation at the field level and led to inconsistencies in practice.

The multi-level analysis of impartiality also contributes to scholarly debates about the role of norms in international relations—what they are, the effects they have, and how and where they should be studied. As Chapter 1 explains, I understand impartiality as a norm in the social constructivist sense of the word, as a '*prescription*[] *for action in situations of choice*, carrying a sense of obligation, a sense that [it] *ought* to be followed'.[36] For constructivist scholars, the sense of 'oughtness' inherent in norms such as impartiality stems from their existence as 'social facts'.[37] They are beliefs or ideas that have no independent material or physical reality, and exist only because they are held intersubjectively—shared, to a certain degree, by actors in a group or community. This collective aspect is what gives norms their force.

Until recently, constructivist theorizing has been largely dominated by linear accounts of ideational change involving dichotomous outcomes, binary oppositions whereby actors either accept and institutionalize/internalize a norm, or resist and reject it. In what has been described as a series of 'waves', scholars considered norms as developed and transported by norm entrepreneurs and social networks to be institutionalized internationally through various forms of socialization (first wave).[38] They emphasized the role of socio-legal structures to explain variance in institutionalization at the regional and domestic level (second wave).[39] And they introduced the notion of localization: the adaptive processes of 'reinterpretation' and 'reconstitution' through which international norms become congruent with pre-existing local normative orders during institutionalization (third wave).[40] In other words, how international norms 'stick' if they have, or are made to have, local resonance. The importance accorded to institutionalization by these scholars is premised on their belief that it produces consensus, as actors clarify the meaning of a norm, what constitutes 'violation', and what procedures will be used to coordinate 'disapproval' and impose 'sanctions' for violations.[41] A norm's formal adoption, in other words, is considered the bellwether of behavioural change.

However, as others have argued, this focus on the structuring power of norms downplays their inherent dynamism and complexity, the role of power in changing their content and scope, and in determining when, how, and why certain norms matter more than others, and to what effect.[42] What follows a norm's institutionalization—actual practice—is for the most part left unattended in orthodox considerations of norms.[43] This assumes an improbably straight line between ideas and outcomes, and suggests a somewhat simplified view of human agency in which action is reduced to 'something that approaches stimulus-response behaviour'.[44] Moreover, it ignores the very real possibility of contestation either between two norms that do not fit together, or of conflicting interpretations of the same norm following its formal acceptance. It is precisely because norms like impartiality are not objective truths but rather intersubjectively held beliefs that they can continue to be contested and their meaning change even as they are formally adopted, shaped by practice, and by the broader social context in which they are situated.

To account for this dynamism and the inherent contestability of norms, I conceive of impartiality as a composite. The composite norm is a heuristic tool that captures the changing meaning of impartiality and provides analytical purchase for the study of contestation at both the macro- and micro-level. Rather than simply rejecting or accepting impartiality, it reveals how actors may resist particular elements of a norm and/or advance their own interpretations of these elements, shaped by both ideational and material considerations, and how, during both institutionalization and implementation, certain interpretations or group interpretations may be privileged.[45] These nuances matter precisely because they shape behaviour and social expectations of behaviour. As Martin Hollis reminds us: 'norms are no less effective for being fluid and no less real for being negotiable'.[46] Indeed, it is critical to the argument of this book that the contestability of norms like impartiality does not invalidate, or even necessarily weaken them. Rather, it brings them, vitally, into the real and present-day world.

By widening the analytical lens to examine implementation in the Congo case, this book also engages with an emerging area of research on normative practice. These scholars critique constructivism's longstanding neglect of what happens *after* a norm like impartiality is institutionalized. Understanding the actual effects of international norms, they argue, requires the study of their implementation, or what one scholar describes as their 'meaning-in-use'.[47] This body of work fully embraces the social essence of norms and highlights the practices, structures, and agents associated with norm interpretation and implementation, that, as the work rightly demonstrates, often result in norm contingency and contestation.[48]

My approach complements this research, but, similar to the peacekeeping literature, it also demonstrates the importance of accounting for *both* institutionalization and implementation as distinct, but often related, processes. To illuminate the mechanisms that incite contestation during implementation, scholars in this emerging area analytically bracket the disagreement over the meaning and/or appropriateness of norms that may have occurred during institutionalization.[49] In doing so, they overlook the effects that institutionalization dynamics may have on the very practices they seek to understand.

This omission is problematic, inasmuch as it assumes that the practice of international norms can be understood without consideration of how they are debated, drafted, and institutionalized—processes that are frequently fraught with contestation and unresolved differences. As Chapter 2 describes, the UN's formal adoption of a new conception of impartiality did not represent the moment of clarity suggested by many constructivist models. What is more, ambiguity at the macro-level over the norm's relationship to sovereignty, the result of unresolved differences, became an issue in Congo when state officials were found to be complicit in widespread human-rights abuses and the mission, in turn, was internally divided on how to respond in a manner consistent with impartiality. The implications of this for the present study are clear: if the meaning of impartiality was contested during its institutionalization and if, as a result, it is vague and ambiguous, its implementation cannot be studied in isolation from the broader politics associated with its development and formal adoption.

METHODOLOGY

The theoretical approach I adopt to analyse impartiality has methodological implications. Given my emphasis on the contextual and contingent nature of norms, I pursue an interpretivist approach, which, as Mark Bevir explains, seeks to understand actions and events by taking into account 'the intentions, concepts, and ideas constitutive of them'.[50] In doing so, I employ a number of different methods.

Since this book proceeds from the argument that there has been a shift in the dominant understanding of impartiality as a norm of UN peacekeeping, a first, key task is to demonstrate that change. To do so, in Chapter 2 I construct a historical narrative of impartiality using the composite norm.[51] Through textual analysis of a wide range of primary and secondary sources, I examine the norm's origins at the UN, trace the evolution of its components over six decades, and explicate the conceptual ambiguity surrounding the dominant understanding of impartiality that was institutionalized in the new millennium.[52] This provides the basis for my subsequent analysis of macro-level politics surrounding institutionalization, as well as micro-level politics surrounding implementation in the Congo case.

To illuminate political dynamics at both levels, the research is situated in what some have labelled the ethnographic turn in International Relations (IR).[53] Like others in this emerging area of scholarship, I use ethnographic methods, including extensive fieldwork, participant observation, and semi-structured interviews at both the global and local level—an approach referred to as 'multi-sited ethnography'. One of the advantages of this methodology is that it affords access to key institutional actors and local figures, as well as opportunities for sustained observation, both of which are necessary to study contestation directly. In the present study, this approach provided insight into critical decision-making processes surrounding peacekeeping in Congo and the effects of those processes on those responsible for and affected by the practices of UN peacekeeping. It also enabled an in-depth analysis of impartiality at the macro-level, and by extension an account of the relationship between headquarters and the mission.

Fieldwork was carried out in several locations. Research on macro-level dynamics was done primarily in New York, with supplementary interviews in Washington, Ottawa, London, Paris, Brussels, Geneva, and Nairobi. Research for the case study and micro-level politics of peacekeeping was conducted during four periods of fieldwork in Congo between 2008–15. In Congo, I worked in a diversity of locales, from remote rural bases to field offices in the country's eastern region, to the national headquarters of the mission in Kinshasa, the capital.[54] This allowed me to discern critical differences in how officials in these areas understood their role and interpreted their mandates.

Multi-sited research produced multiple types of data and sources to illuminate contestation and the effects of the norm. A significant portion of data derives from the more than 300 semi-structured interviews I conducted with individuals involved in every aspect of peacekeeping: senior UN officials, diplomats, member state representatives, civil and military field officers, armed group members, civil society actors, and conflict-affected populations. In selecting my interviewees, I aimed to gain exposure to the broadest range of perspectives. I actively sought out individuals who contested the dominant conception of the norm but who were largely excluded from decision-making during the processes of institutionalization and implementation. In New York, for example, I met with member states affiliated with the non-aligned movement (NAM), including representatives of the largest troop- and police-contributing countries. Findings from these interviews were supplemented by numerous discussions with political analysts and scholars who closely follow developments at the UN. The majority of these interviews were conducted under the condition of anonymity given political sensitivities surrounding the research and potential professional, reputational, and security ramifications.[55]

Participant observation, which entails more intensive interaction between the observer and observed, complements the interview data. Observation conducted primarily for the case research was facilitated through attendance at daily internal UN meetings,[56] field visits with UN staff, and by accompanying peacekeeper patrol sweeps in rural areas.[57] These encounters shed light on the nature of the UN's operations in Congo and assisted in understanding broader, ongoing political and security developments. This access also provided a particularly effective way of exploring the difference between formal policies and mandates, and actual practice. Lastly, I consulted a comprehensive set of primary and secondary sources. These materials were used to cross check data obtained through interviews and participant observation, to ensure accuracy and to mitigate potential bias or selectivity of information.[58]

Two final points of clarification on methods are necessary. The first concerns the extent of my claims about the effects of impartiality. In evaluating the broader repercussions of the norm, I am not suggesting that impartiality 'causes' particular action or outcomes in a constant or deterministic way, as is construed by positivist methodologies. Like other constructivists, I am interested in how norms may guide, inspire, rationalize, or justify behaviour; in other words, how understandings of impartiality and contestation over the norm enable and constrain particular actions or possible outcomes.[59] Moreover, my account of implementation notably draws particular attention to both the intended and unintended effects of norms. As discussed above, constructivists have tended to assume that, once adopted, a norm 'does what it says on the tin', i.e., induces actors either to undertake or avoid the behaviour it prescribes or enjoins. In contrast, my analysis shows how norms can also have unforeseen consequences as individuals respond strategically to the constraints and opportunities afforded by the international normative structure and by the expectations it engenders. In doing so, the book moves beyond the usual constructivist emphasis on how 'good' norms make the world better, showing that ostensibly well-intentioned norms can have harmful, even disastrous, consequences.[60]

Lastly, in order to delve deeply into the material, the analysis was focused on a single-case study. While some social scientists highlight the limitations of the single-case study approach, namely, the lack of generalizability across cases and potential selection bias, these concerns apply to scholars seeking to develop falsifiable claims, and thus do not apply to the present study. Instead, the rigorous single-case research approach chosen here allowed me to go narrow and deep, and is necessary to explicate in sufficient detail the process of impartiality's change, contestation, and effects across various levels of analysis. The Congo case, which stretched over fifteen years, serves the heuristic purpose of elucidating contextual contingencies during both institutionalization and implementation, and the implications of assertive impartiality in UN peacekeeping.[61] The length of the conflict also enabled me to look at the change over time within that context. In contrast to theory testing, the approach adopted is thus more akin to theory generation; it provides a strong empirical base, which allows for additional case research and conceptual refinements.[62] To include a second or third case would have required a sacrifice of depth for the sake of breadth. Given the paucity of conceptual analysis on impartiality as well as the intrinsic importance of the Congo case, objectives of generalizability are less applicable in this context. That said, as I discuss in the Conclusion, the analysis presented in this book opens the door to future research into how impartiality is being contested in other peacekeeping cases and, more broadly, into the practices of those institutions associated with assertive liberal internationalism.

OUTLINE OF THE BOOK

Chapter 1 outlines the book's conceptual framework. Both existing research on peacekeeping and popular discourse on UN operations are rife with conceptual confusion, exemplified by the frequent conflation of impartiality with neutrality. This confusion is not limited to scholarship on peacekeeping. Impartiality figures as a central concept in moral, political, and legal theory.[63] Yet, despite its ubiquity in the literature, impartiality is lamented by some critics as 'almost universally misdescribed',[64] 'haphazardly analyzed',[65] and as having 'stumbled its way into a series of holes, imponderables, and seeming contradictions.'[66]

Chapter 1 thus seeks in part to provide conceptual clarity regarding the norm of impartiality. It also situates this study within the constructivist approach. I introduce and develop the concept of a composite norm and elucidate the components of impartiality. This grounds the subsequent analysis of how understandings of impartiality in UN peacekeeping have changed and the ways in which the norm itself has been contested during the processes of institutionalization at the macro-level and implementation in the Congo case.

Using the composite norm, Chapter 2 traces the evolution of impartiality within the UN, explicates the reasons for and significance of the reconceptualization of impartiality in the new millennium, and situates this change in the broader shift towards a more assertive liberal internationalism. As peacekeepers and other international actors became more heavily engaged in intra-state conflict during the 1990s, in contexts where consent for their operations was tenuous, they confronted difficult questions about the sources of their own authority and how to adjudicate disputes between competing local claimants of authority. Assertive impartiality was an attempt to re-ground the authority of these actors in what was presented as a newfound unity of purpose: the culmination of the internationalization of human rights over several decades, and the supposed disassociation of rights from a particular political or partial agenda. Crucially, however, and contrary to what many constructivist theories would hold, impartiality's institutionalization has not resulted in conceptual clarity. The chapter concludes by considering the various ways in which the new dominant understanding of impartiality is in fact ambiguous and imprecise, rife with contradictions.

Through an analysis of political dynamics within the UN at the macro-organizational level, Chapter 3 calls into question the purported consensus over the dominant conception of impartiality and the purposes of contemporary peacekeeping. It demonstrates how impartiality's ambiguity is partly a reflection of contestation, and elucidates the procedural, substantive, and consequential objections of various actors. The chapter explains how, despite fierce contestation, the Security Council has continued to authorize robust mandates in accordance with the new conception of impartiality. It argues that the surmounting of this disjuncture is explained by the Council's overarching ability to determine peacekeeping policy. But, crucially, the power of Council members is not unfettered; they too face constraints due to the very nature of assertive impartiality and to their prior rhetorical affirmation of the norm. These dynamics matter, precisely because they have an impact on peacekeeping practice.

From here, my analysis turns to the process of implementation and the micro-level politics associated with peacekeeping in Congo. Chapter 4 begins with a brief historical overview of the conflict and the five phases of the UN mission (1999–2015). I examine each phase, and identify critical junctures where spoilers obstructed the peace or political process, and/or civilians faced imminent threats or were harmed: situations that, according to assertive impartiality, warrant the use of force. The chapter reveals how judgments as to who was perpetrator and who was victim, as well as to who was the protector and who the party in need of protection, were subjective, fluid and deeply contested, reflecting dynamics at both the global and local level. As a result of this contestation, implementation of the norm was inconsistent, with a host of unintended consequences.

Chapter 5 examines the effects of assertive impartiality on four specific sets of actors at the field level: civilians, armed groups, the state, and the UN mission itself. It shows how the robust role prescribed for peacekeepers raised expectations and created incentives for local actors in the Congo, engendering behaviour that would not have occurred otherwise. These effects damaged the mission and deepened local perceptions that the UN was partial. Despite these consequences, the Security Council's response to policy failure in the Congo, time and time again, was to scale up the mission's mandated 'robustness', which in turn only further tarnished its credibility and capacity to act as a broker of peace. The chapter argues that in the absence of consensus over a real strategy to resolve conflict in the Congo, without a willingness by member states to commit the necessary political capital and resources, assertive impartiality offered merely the illusion of constructive and active engagement. Ambitious mandates that aimed to save lives projected an image of consensus. They covered up deep political divisions at both the global and local level, while making scant progress to foster peace in Congo.

The Conclusion lays out the book's implications for theory and policy. It summarizes the findings, discusses their relevance for other contemporary peace operations and offers a way forward. It argues that analysis of the inherent and perhaps irreconcilable tensions and moral quandaries associated with the new conception of impartiality is critical if we are to move beyond the usual litany of 'lessons learned' studies as well as the technical solutions to peacekeeping dilemmas so frequently tabled by practitioners and academics.

Understanding contemporary peacekeeping practice as well as other liberal internationalist advances requires an acute sensitivity to context, and an appreciation of how politics—international, institutional, and local—shapes practice. More fundamentally, the way in which even the most laudable of international norms may produce grievous unintended consequences requires both practitioners and academics to be more reflective about the norms they study, defend, and even espouse. Seen from such a multiplicity of perspectives, the loud circling of the UN's helicopter gunships during *Operation Djugu III* represents a stage of evolution in international relations that this book argues is anything but impartial.

NOTES

1. MONUC, 'OP DJUGU – III', Eastern Command, Powerpoint presentation, March 2005 (internal).
2. Quoted in Marc Lacey, 'U.N. forces using tougher tactics to secure peace', *The New York Times*, 23 May 2005.
3. Interview with Lt. Gen. Gaye, Military Advisor to the UN Secretary-General; former Force Commander, MONUC/MONUSCO, New York, October 2011.
4. United Nations, A/55/305-S (2000), ix.
5. Shashi Tharoor, 'Should UN Peacekeeping Go "Back to the Basics?"', *Survival* 37/4 (1995–6), 58.
6. Alan James, 'The United Nations, Peace Keeping, and Nonalignment', in *The Nonaligned and the United Nations*, edited by M.S. Rajan et al. (New York: Oceana, 1987), 11.
7. Dominick Donald, 'Neutral is not Impartial: the Confusing Legacy of Traditional Peace Operations', *Armed Forces and Society* 29/3 (2003), 415–48; Dominick Donald, *Active Impartiality: A Survival System for 'Grey Area' Peace Support Operations* (London: King's College London, Department of War Studies, 2006).
8. Interview with Louise Fréchette, former Deputy Secretary-General of the UN, Montreal, March 2011. Donald Daniel and Bradd Hayes refer to this as 'blind impartiality', defined as the unprejudiced execution of the mandate 'regardless of the consequences to any party'. *Coercive Inducement and the Containment of International Crisis* (Washington, DC: USIP Press, 1999), 25.
9. Richard Betts, 'The Delusion of Impartial Intervention', *Foreign Affairs* 73/20 (1994), 28.
10. Chapter 2 discusses peacekeeping's relationship to assertive liberal internationalism at greater length. This broader shift has also been conceived by scholars as the 'individualization of warfare'. The term refers to the processes by which the rights and responsibilities of individuals, as opposed to those of collective political entities such as states, are transforming the theory and practice of armed conflict. See *Individualization of War Project*, European University Institute, http://iow.eui.eu/; Gabriella Blum, 'The Individualization of War: From War to Policy in the Regulation of Armed Conflicts', in *Law and War*, edited by Austin Sarat, et al. (Stanford: Stanford University Press, 2014), 48–83.
11. The Court may, for instance, prosecute nationals of states not party to the Statute if they have committed international crimes on the territory or against nationals of states party to the Statute. In addition, the Security Council may, acting under Chapter VII, refer a situation in which crimes appear to have been committed to the ICC prosecutor. According to the Statute, the conduct of all proceedings must be impartial, and agents of the Court, including judges and the prosecutor, must take a solemn oath to exercise their duties impartially. See Articles 17, 20, 36, 41, 42, 45, 64, 67 and 68 of the Rome Statute (1998).
12. United Nations, *Rights Up Front: A Plan of Action to Strengthen the UN's Role in Protecting People in Crises. Follow-up to the Report of the Secretary-General's Internal Review Panel on UN Action in Sri Lanka*, 9 July 2013, Reprinted with

the permission of the United Nations, 4. See also 'Human Rights Up Front' website, http://www.un.org/sg/rightsupfront/

13. Ruti Teitel, *Humanity's Law* (Oxford: Oxford University Press, 2011). See also Kathryn Sikkink, *The Justice Cascade: How Human Rights Prosecutions Are Changing World Politics* (New York: Norton, 2011); Bruce Cronin, 'International Consensus and the Changing Legal Authority of the UN Security Council', in *The UN Security Council and the Politics of International Authority*, edited by Bruce Cronin and Ian Hurd (London: Routledge, 2008), 57–79.

14. Statement by Ambassador Peter Wilson, Deputy Permanent Representative of the UK Mission to the UN, Security Council Open Debate on Protection of Civilians, 12 February 2014. Speech available at http://www.gov.uk/government/speeches/protecting-civilians-transcends-politics

15. For example, see Anthony Julius, 'Human rights: the new secular religion', *Guardian*, 19 April 2010; Andrew Nathan, 'How human rights became our ideology', *New Republic*, 16 November 2012; Stephen Hopgood, *The Endtimes of Human Rights* (Ithaca: Cornell University Press, 2013); Eric A. Posner, *The Twilight of Human Rights Law* (Oxford: Oxford University Press, 2014).

16. Exceptions include: Donald (2003, 2006); Jane Boulden, 'Mandates Matter: An Exploration of Impartiality in United Nations Operations', *Global Governance* 11/2 (2005), 147–60; Hikaru Yamashita, '"Impartial" Use of Force in United Nations Peacekeeping', *International Peacekeeping* 15/5 (2008), 615–30; Daniel Levine, 'Peacekeeper Impartiality: Standards, Processes, and Operations', *Journal of International Peacekeeping* 15/3 (2011), 422–50. These texts do not however address the underlying political issues associated with impartiality.

17. On the use of force, see Michael Pugh, ed., *UN, Peace and Force* (London: Frank Cass, 1997); Trevor Findlay, *Use of Force in UN Peace Operations* (Oxford: Oxford University Press, 2002); Niels Blokker and Nico Schrijver, eds., *The Security Council and the Use of Force: Theory and Reality–A Need for Change?* (Leiden: Martinus Nijhoff, 2005); Christine Gray, *International Law and the Use of Force*, 3rd ed. (Oxford: Oxford University Press, 2008); Marc Weller, ed., *The Oxford Handbook of the Use of Force in International Law* (Oxford: Oxford University Press, 2015). On consent, see Neil Fenton, *Understanding the UN Security Council: Coercion or Consent?* (London: Ashgate, 2004); Ian Johnstone, 'Managing Consent in Contemporary Peacekeeping Operations', *International Peacekeeping* 18/2 (2011), 168–82.

18. Numerous practitioners and scholars have stressed the importance of impartiality in peacekeeping. E.g., Alan James, *Peacekeeping in International Politics* (London: Macmillan, 1990), 3, 106; Virginia Fortna, *Does Peacekeeping Work? Shaping Belligerents' Choices after Civil War* (Princeton: Princeton University Press, 2008), 5; Adekeye Adebajo, *UN Peacekeeping in Africa: From the Suez Crisis to the Sudan Conflicts* (Boulder: Lynne Rienner, 2011), 9.

19. David Roberts, 'More Honoured in the Breech: Consent and Impartiality in the Cambodian Peacekeeping Operation', *International Peacekeeping* 4/1 (1997), 1–25; David Gibbs, 'The United Nations, International Peacekeeping and the Questions of "Impartiality": Revisiting the Congo Operation of 1960', *Journal of Modern African Studies* 38/3 (2000), 359–82; Anne Hughes, 'Impartiality and the UN

Observation Group in Lebanon, 1958', *International Peacekeeping* 9/4 (2004), 1–20; Yuka Hasegawa, 'The United Nations Assistance Mission in Afghanistan: Impartiality in New UN Peace Operations', *Journal of Intervention and Statebuilding* 2/2 (2008), 209–26.

20. A body of critical scholarship has developed over the last two decades that exposes and critiques the commitment of many scholars to the liberal underpinnings of contemporary peacekeeping and the literature's overwhelming focus on policy-oriented research. See, for example, Roland Paris, 'Broadening the Study of Peace Operations', *International Studies Review* 2/3 (2000); Michael Pugh, 'Peacekeeping and Critical Theory', *International Peacekeeping* 11/1 (2004), 39–58; Oliver Richmond, 'Critical Research Agendas for Peace: The Missing Link in the Study of International Relations', *Alternatives: Global, Local, Political* 32/2 (2007), 247–74. These works however give only cursory consideration to the concept of impartiality.

21. Michael Barnett and Martha Finnemore, *Rules for the World: International Organizations in Global Politics* (Ithaca: Cornell University Press, 2004), 124.

22. Jarat Chopra, John Mackinlay and Larry Minear, *Report on the Cambodian Peace Process* (Olso: Norwegian Institute of International Affairs, 1993), 93. Betts, for example, urged that the 'gentle, restrained impartiality' of the Cold War period be abandoned in favour of an 'active harsh impartiality that overpowers both sides: an imperial impartiality' (1994: 28). For Daniel and Hayes, traditional 'symbiotic impartiality' (avoidance of prejudicing the interests of the parties) had given way to a 'blind' impartiality necessary in coercive inducement (1999: 61). In the context of what he observed as the 'changing meaning of impartiality', Adam Roberts asserted that peacekeepers were not to be impartial 'between the parties to a conflict' but rather impartial 'in carrying out UN Security Council decisions'. He argued that in some cases the UN should be 'tougher with one party than another'. Roberts, 'The Crisis in UN Peacekeeping', *Survival* 36/3 (1994), 115. See also Chapter 2 for a discussion of Mary Kaldor's conception of peacekeeping as impartial 'cosmopolitan law enforcement' in *New and Old Wars: Organized Violence in a Global Era*, 2nd ed. (Cambridge: Polity Press, 2006).

23. See Donald (2003); Nicholas Tsagourias, 'Consent, Neutrality/Impartiality and the Use of Force in Peacekeeping: Their Constitutional Dimension', *Journal of Conflict and Security Law* 11/3 (2006), 465–82. As discussed in Chapter 1, this imposed distinction is problematic in two respects. First, it fails to account for the conceptual differences that exist between impartiality and neutrality. Second, it obfuscates the language people *actually* used. Impartiality has been such a staple of institutional practice that scholars have argued that there is strong evidence that the norm has formal standing in international law stemming from both custom and the instruments necessary to create specific missions. See Shyla Vohra, 'Impartiality in United Nations Peace-Keeping', *Leiden Journal of International Law* 9/1 (1996), 63–85.

24. Yamashita (2008: 619).

25. John Rawls, 'Justice as Fairness: Political not Metaphysical', *Philosophy and Public Affairs* 14/3 (1985), 246.

26. Thomas Franck, *The Structure of Impartiality: Examining the Riddle of One Law in a Fragmented World* (New York: Macmillan Company, 1968), 331.
27. I define institutionalization as the process during which the new conception of impartiality became reflected in the UN and specifically in organizational policy documents, standard operating procedures, and formal and informal agreements between members of the organization. As other scholars have demonstrated, the institutionalization of international norms occurs at various levels (local, national, regional, and international). My analysis focuses primarily on institutionalization as a macro-level, international process, although as Chapter 2 explains, the new, more assertive concept of impartiality has also been institutionalized in the national doctrine of various troop-contributing countries. Implementation is a distinct but related process during which actors interpret and follow the prescriptions associated with a norm that has been formally adopted. As a norm of peacekeeping, impartiality's implementation encompasses a variety of actors: from the Security Council, which provides the initial authorization for and ongoing guidance to a mission in consultation with the Secretariat and host country, down to the boots on the ground.
28. For example, see United Nations, S/PV.4083 (1999), 6; S/PV.4194 (2000), 6, 17; S/PV.4143.1 (2002), 22.
29. United Nations, S/PV.4083 (1999), 6.
30. United Nations, S/RES/2098 (2013), 7–8. The mandate was subsequently renewed in S/RES/2147 (2014) and S/RES/2211 (2015).
31. MONUSCO's conditionality policy (2010) provided the impetus for the UN's *Human Rights Due Diligence Policy on United Nations Support to non-United Nations Security Forces*, applicable to all peacekeeping missions and UN entities that provide assistance to non-UN security forces. United Nations, A/67/775 (2013). Additionally, protection tools developed by the mission have been incorporated into best practices and have been applied in other operational contexts. See, for example, United Nations, 'Lessons Learned: Report on the Joint Protection Team (JPT) Mechanism in MONUSCO. Strengths, Challenges, and Considerations for Replicating JPTs in Other Missions', DPKO/DFS-OHCHR, 2013.
32. See Jennifer Welsh and Dominik Zaum, 'Legitimation and the United Nations Security Council', in Dominik Zaum, ed., *Legitimating International Organizations* (Oxford: Oxford University Press, 2013); Ian Hurd, *After Anarchy: Legitimacy and Power in the United Nations Security Council* (Princeton: Princeton University Press, 2007); Allen Buchanan and Robert Keohane, 'The Legitimacy of Global Governance Institutions', *Ethics and International Affairs* 20/4 (2006), 405–37. In addition to both substantive and consequential (or output) legitimacy, scholars note the importance of procedural legitimacy, that is, legitimacy related to the character of decision-making procedures. While procedural objections over impartiality do appear, as discussed in Chapter 3, I argue that ultimately they are secondary to substantive and consequential objections. In short, reforms to address decision-making procedures are unlikely to resolve these more fundamental differences. Moreover, in the context of the UN—where enlarging participation in decision-making is usually discussed as a way to bolster legitimacy—there is a risk

that reform will come at the cost of effectiveness. Thomas Franck, *The Power of Legitimacy Among Nations* (Oxford: Oxford University Press, 1990).

33. For an overview of the literature, see contributions to 'Future Directions for Peacekeeping Research', *International Peacekeeping* 21/4 (2014), 481–538.

34. See, for example, Alex Bellamy and Paul Williams, *Providing Peacekeepers: The Politics, Challenges, and Future of United Nations Peacekeeping Contributions* (Oxford: Oxford University Press, 2013); Jeni Whalan, *How Peace Operations Work: Power, Legitimacy and Effectiveness* (Oxford: Oxford University Press, 2013); Philip Cunliffe, *Legions of Peace: UN Peacekeepers from the Global South* (New York: Hurst & Co., 2014); Jair Van Derlijn and Xenia Avezov, *The Future Peace Operations Landscape: Voices from Stakeholders around the Globe* (Stockholm: SIPRI, 2015).

35. For a comprehensive overview, see Séverine Autesserre, 'Going Micro: Emerging and Future Peacekeeping Research', *International Peacekeeping* 21/4 (2014), 492–500.

36. Abram Chayes and Antonia Handler Chayes, *The New Sovereignty* (Cambridge: Harvard University Press, 1995), 113 (emphasis in the original).

37. John Ruggie, *Constructing the World Polity: Essays on International Institutionalization* (London: Routledge, 1998), 12.

38. Finnemore and Sikkink's three-stage 'life cycle' is the most widely cited model in this area of scholarship. Martha Finnemore and Kathryn Sikkink, 'International Norm Dynamics and Political Change', *International Organization* 52/4 (1998), 887–917. In the first stage, *norm emergence*, highly motivated entrepreneurs conceive of and pursue the creation of a norm. To strengthen their position, they use platforms such as international organizations to reach a wide and diverse audience, and begin institutionalizing the norm. During institutionalization, early-adopting states socialize other states to follow them through a combination of persuasion, social, and cognitive pressures. This is a, if not *the*, critical step in the life cycle, as it is during institutionalization that the norm gains support as states 'clarify what, exactly, the norm is and what constitutes violation' (900). This contributes strongly to the potential for a *norm cascade* during which a critical mass of states embrace the norm. Once this occurs, it enters the third stage, the *internalization* of the norm. At this mature stage, norms themselves 'become more important than domestic politics for effecting norm change' (902) and achieve a 'taken for granted' status (896). See also Thomas Risse, Stephen Ropp, and Kathryn Sikkink, eds., *The Power of Human Rights: International Norms and Domestic Change* (Cambridge: Cambridge University Press, 1999).

39. See, for example, Jeffrey Legro, 'Which Norms Matter? Revisiting the "Failure" of Internationalism', *International Organization* 51/1 (1997), 31–63; Jeffrey Checkel, 'Norms, Institutions, and National Identity in Contemporary Europe', *International Studies Quarterly* 43/1 (1999), 83–114; Andrew Cortell and James Davis, 'Understanding the Domestic Impact of International Norms: A Research Agenda', *International Studies Review* 2/1 (2000), 65–87.

40. Amitav Acharya, 'How Ideas Spread: Whose Norms Matter? Norm Localization and Institutional Change in Asian Regionalism', *International Organization* 58/2 (2004), 239–75. According to Acharya, localization goes further than socialization

and is the 'active construction (through discourse, framing, grafting, and cultural selection) of foreign ideas by local actors, which results in the former developing significant congruence with local beliefs and practices', (243–5). See also Amitav Acharya, 'Norm Subsidiarity and Regional Orders: Sovereignty, Regionalism, and Rule Making in the Third World', *International Studies Quarterly* 55/1 (2011), 95–123.
41. Finnemore and Sikkink (1998: 900). Similarly, scholars in the second wave illuminate the various factors that contribute to the successful adoption of a norm in the domestic or regional context into which it is introduced. And while Acharya (third wave) ascribes greater dynamism to the notion of localization, his concern is with explaining congruence and the processes by which foreign ideas become consistent with pre-existing normative orders. Across this scholarship, institutionalization is overwhelmingly portrayed as a progressive process during which norm convergence occurs. That a dominant norm could become embedded institutionally and yet remain ambiguous and contested is not considered by these scholars.
42. Antje Wiener, *The Invisible Constitution of Politics: Contested Norms and International Encounters* (Cambridge: Cambridge University Press, 2008); Samuel Barkin, *Realist Constructivism: Rethinking International Relations Theory* (Cambridge: Cambridge University Press, 2010); Matthias Hofferberth and Christian Weber, 'Lost in Translation: A Critique of Constructivist Norm Research', *Journal of International Relations and Development* 18/1 (2015), 75–103.
43. As political philosopher James Tully writes: 'The traditional end-point of normative analysis, even when it is related to practical case studies, leaves the entire field of implementation and review to empirical social sciences, often under the false assumption that implementation is different in kind from justification, simply a technical question of applying rigid rules correctly.' 'The Unfreedom of the Moderns in Comparison to Their Ideals of Constitutional Democracy', *The Modern Law Review* 65/2 (2002), 227.
44. Stacie Goddard and Daniel Nexon, 'Paradigm Lost? Reassessing Theory of International Politics', *European Journal of International Relations* 11/1 (2005), 14.
45. I accept that actor interpretations and motivations to accept or reject the norm may reflect both 'logic of appropriateness' *and/or* 'logic of consequences'. While the separation of 'logics' remains widespread in the literature, a healthy scepticism about the professed autonomy of these logics has begun to develop, and a growing group of constructivist scholars have come to regard this distinction as spurious. They illustrate the various ways in which norm adoption and behaviour are often motivated by both social belief and strategic considerations, in ways that are difficult to separate. In line with this scholarship, I conceive of both logics as being often entwined to shape how impartiality is interpreted, contested, and enacted. See, for example, Hurd (2007: 16); Alexander Betts and Phil Orchard, eds., *Implementation and World Politics: How International Norms Change Practice* (Oxford: Oxford University Press, 2014).
46. Quoted in Andrew Hurrell and Terry MacDonald, 'Norms and Ethics in International Relations', in *Handbook of International Relations*, edited by Walter Carlsnaes, et al. (London: Sage, 2012), 72–3.

47. Wiener (2008).
48. Antje Wiener, for example, emphasizes a norm's 'cultural' validity, the less tangible 'background knowledge' or 'ways of life' that actors have accumulated through experience and social interaction about a norm's substance within a particular context, and which are distinct from its 'formal validity' (or text) resulting from institutionalization (2008: 11). She argues that contestation and thus the possibility for different meanings and practices is conditioned by the type of norm and its specificity as well as contextual changes (namely, historical contingency; changes in social practice; situations of crisis) which reduce the 'social feedback' necessary to interpret a norm (2008: 6). Alexander Betts and Phil Orchard broaden the analysis to focus on a more expansive set of structures (ideational, material and institutional) that, in combination with particular actors exerting agency on those structures, may play a constitutive role (changing the norm) or have a constraining influence (channelling the norm) during implementation. Betts and Orchard, eds., (2014). Other scholars have also used the concept of implementation, albeit with less conceptual theorizing, e.g., Carolyn Deere, *The Implementation Game: The Trips Agreement and the Global Politics of Intellectual Property Reform in Developing Countries* (New York: Oxford University Press, 2009); Séverine Autesserre, *The Trouble with the Congo: Local Violence and the Failure of International Peace Building* (New York: Cambridge University Press, 2010); *Peaceland: Conflict Resolution and the Everyday Politics of International Intervention* (New York: Cambridge University Press, 2014).
49. Wiener, for example, assumes the 'formal validity' of the fundamental norms she studies, describing them somewhat offhandedly, as having 'found their way into international treaties, conventions or agreements' (2008: 82). But she does not explain *how* they 'found their way' or perhaps are 'still finding their way' in processes of ongoing institutionalization. What is more, Wiener's theory of contestation largely omits consideration of power relations. By focusing on individual interpretations of a norm, Wiener's account of 'meaning-in-use' does not consider the relative influence of particular individuals in determining which meaning of a norm *is* enacted. Indeed, her theory would suggest that all norm contestation is among interpretations of equal standing. The relative power of actors in the negotiation, adoption, and implementation of a norm and the ways in which these processes may privilege particular outcomes is left unattended. Similarly, Betts and Orchard, eds., (2014) focus exclusively on implementation.
50. Mark Bevir, 'Introduction: Interpretive Methods', in *Interpretive Political Science* (Vol. 2), edited by Mark Bevir (London: Sage Publications, 2010), vii.
51. On historical narrative see Hidemi Suganami, 'Narrative Explanation and International Relations: Back to the Basics', *Millennium: Journal of International Studies* 37/2 (2008), 327–56; Stephen Van Evera, *Guide to Methods for Students of Political Science* (Ithaca: Cornell University Press, 1997).
52. Primary sources I consulted include: policy documents, provisional verbatim of public debates and plenary sessions, speeches, communiqués, field manuals, military doctrine and training documents, and letters and memoirs of key individuals. UN and government research reports, including draft documents, were also examined to capture institutional reflection and deliberations in the wake of

particular events or following specific operations. This research was coupled with close analysis of all Security Council resolutions authorizing the deployment of over 1,000 forces to determine the changing substance and practices associated with impartiality and called for in mission mandates. Secondary sources on peacekeeping, the UN, humanitarianism, international criminal justice, military intervention, and international history were critical in providing a broader context for impartiality's evolution at the macro-level.

53. For IR scholarship drawing on ethnographic methods, see Michael Barnett, *Eyewitness to a Genocide: The United Nations and Rwanda* (Ithaca: Cornell University Press, 2002); Stephen Hopgood, *Keepers of the Flame* (Ithaca: Cornell University Press, 2007); Autesserre (2010, 2014).

54. During my fieldwork, I was based in Goma, the capital of North Kivu province. The Kivus are the epicentre of Congo's ongoing conflict and for much of the last decade have been the priority area for the UN mission and its operations. Research was conducted throughout North Kivu in five of the province's six territories (Masisi, Rutshuru, Beni, Nyiragongo, and Lubero). I also made separate trips to Bukavu, capital of South Kivu, and Kinshasa to gain a broad spectrum of perspectives and ensure that my findings were representative of mission dynamics more generally.

55. Throughout the book I fully reference the data obtained through on-record interviews. In characterizing anonymous interviewees, I list only their official status, month, year, and location of the interview. In certain cases, location is omitted to ensure confidentiality and safety of participants.

56. From January to April 2010, I attended daily briefings at 'Forward HQ' in Goma. These meetings were roughly an hour in duration and covered security and political developments in the east (including North Kivu, South Kivu, and Province Orientale). This was particularly advantageous as it enabled me to stay informed of dynamics beyond North Kivu, and was thus a means to further ensure that my findings were representative. In addition, I attended several 'protection cluster' meetings. Hosted by OCHA, these coordination meetings draw together staff from UN agencies as well as from the wider humanitarian community to discuss protection needs and programming.

57. I visited company operating bases (COBs) of the main TCCs in North Kivu (Indian, Nepalese, South African, and Uruguayan contingents), located in five territories.

58. In addition to the primary sources cited above, in Congo I was granted access to over 1,000 internal UN documents and memos. These documents provide considerable insight into decision-making at various levels within the mission, and shed light on contestation among officials about particular decisions and courses of action.

59. Friedrich Kratochwil and John Gerard Ruggie, 'International Organization: A State of the Art on an Art of the State', *International Organization* 40/4 (1986), 767; Friedrich Kratochwil, 'How Do Norms Matter?', in *The Role of Law in International Politics: Essays in International Relations and International Law*, edited by Michael Byers (Oxford: Oxford University Press, 2000), 35–68; Martha Finnemore, *The Purpose of Intervention: Changing Beliefs about the Use of Force*

(Ithaca: Cornell University Press, 2003), 15; Nina Tannenwald, *The Nuclear Taboo: the United States and the Non-Use of Nuclear Weapons since 1945* (Cambridge: Cambridge University Press, 2007).

60. See also, Sarah Percy, *Mercenaries. The History of a Norm in International Relations* (Oxford: Oxford University Press, 2007); Richard Price, ed., *Moral Limit and Possibility in World Politics* (Cambridge: Cambridge University Press, 2008).

61. Harry Eckstein, 'Case Study and Theory in Political Science', in *Handbook of Political Science*, edited by Fred Greenstein and Nelson Polsby (Reading: Addison Wesley, 1975), 104.

62. Alexander George and Andrew Bennett, *Case Studies and Theory Development in the Social Sciences* (Cambridge: MIT Press, 2005), 19.

63. See, for example, Brian Barry, *Justice as Impartiality* (Oxford: Oxford University Press, 1995); Susan Mendus, *Impartiality in Moral and Political Philosophy* (Oxford: Oxford University Press, 2002); Pierre Rosanvallon, *Democratic Legitimacy: Impartiality, Reflexivity, Proximity* (Princeton: Princeton University Press, 2011); Ofer Raban, *Modern Legal Theory and Judicial Impartiality* (London: Routledge, 2012).

64. Bernard Gert, *Morality: Its Nature and Justification*, 2nd ed. (Oxford: Oxford University Press, 2005), 131.

65. Charles Geyh, 'The Dimensions of Judicial Impartiality', *Florida Law Review* 65/2 (2014), 495.

66. Geyh (2014: 495).

1

The Composite Norm of Impartiality

Impartiality is not new or specific to peacekeeping. It has long featured as a norm associated with certain professional roles and institutions. In the domestic realm, impartiality has been a defining feature of the judiciary dating back to antiquity. Within the Judaeo-Christian tradition, impartial judgment was God's power and prerogative, and man's eschatological reward. Similarly, within the natural law tradition, divine law and eternal verities could, through right reason, become discernible to humans beyond the confines of scriptural and other theological revelation. While elements of these traditions persist, a more secular understanding of impartiality emerged with the Enlightenment and, over time, became dominant.[1] Today, impartiality is tied to independent bodies of oversight, regulation, and administration in many Western democracies.[2] And it is associated with the exercise of judgment in such diverse fields as journalism, medicine, science, and sports refereeing. In the international realm, impartiality is closely linked with institutions and practices of adjudication and arbitration, the development of an international civil service, the role of international experts from fact-finding missions to regulatory and oversight commissions, humanitarianism, and, of course, with peacekeeping and the United Nations (UN).

In each of these areas, impartiality figures as a norm in the sense that it prescribes how actors should behave: namely, that they be unbiased and informed when making decisions or in taking action. Like the judge or police officer, the impartial peacekeeper is one that passes judgment and acts by setting aside particular preferences or interests. The decisions and actions of peacekeepers are not to be prejudged or biased—that is, influenced by whether they help or harm one person or group over another. The interests of everyone count, and, unless specified otherwise, count equally.

But impartiality is also more than that. It not only proceeds from, but is defining of these roles and the institutions with which they are so closely linked. Impartiality is integral to the identity of peacekeepers, to what peacekeeping is and what it is not (war-fighting), and to the values and principles the UN seeks to project. It is a form of authority, derived not only from a lack of bias, but, critically, from what peacekeepers—such as judges or the police—are supposed to represent and further in the absence of particular interests. It is thus a complex and changing norm, inherently bound up in claims about authority, and it is one that has been contested many times in the past, in peacekeeping and beyond.

To analyse impartiality in the context of peacekeeping this chapter conceives of it as a composite norm. The first section begins by discussing the characteristics of norms generally. I define impartiality as a norm and explain why a finer parsing of impartiality is necessary. The following two sections draw on political and legal theory to explicate the two core components of impartiality: the *mode of* decision-making (its procedural dimension) and the *basis for* decision-making (its substantive dimension). The discussion is both abstract, generally specifying the properties of the components and areas of possible tension between components, and empirical, addressing the ways in which they manifest in peacekeeping. The aim is to provide some conceptual clarity, and to outline what Thomas Franck referred to as the 'broad structure' of impartiality.[3] This frames the analysis of the changing content of impartiality and contestation over the norm during the processes of institutionalization and implementation, which are the focus of subsequent chapters.

Dispelling the notion that impartial actors are omniscient figures providing judgments of universal and objective truth, the chapter argues that impartial judgments are always subjective and socially bound—'valid' and 'true' only insofar as the *basis for* decision-making reflects shared purposes and resonates with shared values. This is a source of legitimacy but it also leaves the impartial actor in a precarious position, as its decisions must hew closely to shared purposes that may change. And yet, the very difficulties inherent in attempts to establish impartiality indicate exactly why impartiality matters in peacekeeping as in other realms. 'It matters', as the political philosopher Susan Mendus explains, 'because we must, somehow, find a way of living together despite our conflicting beliefs about the right way to live. It also matters because, in finding that way, we must at least try and go beyond mere *modus vivendi*.'[4]

IMPARTIALITY AS A NORM

That norms like impartiality have a long lineage in international relations is a widely shared observation.[5] There is, however, less agreement among scholars on what these norms are, and when and how they matter. Andrew Hurrell and Terry MacDonald's assertion that all normative analysis revolves around two classic meanings of the term 'norm' offers a helpful entry point from which to situate this study in the literature and elucidate the statement that impartiality is a norm.[6]

According to the first meaning of the term, norms are understood as descriptive and predictive. They reflect patterns of recurrent behaviour among actors, giving rise to 'expectations as to what will, in fact, be done in a particular situation'.[7] In other words, norms refer to what is 'normal'. The second meaning of the word contains a deontic element. By this account, norms prescribe patterns of behaviour that encompass a feeling of obligation on the part of the actors—a sense of 'what ought to be done' that is socially rooted.[8]

Rational choice scholars typically subscribe to the first meaning of norms.[9] Being less interested in the ideas contained in norms themselves or the possibility that people act or are expected to act in certain ways because they are understood to be legitimate and the right thing to do, these scholars analyse norms as objective facts which are functional and regulative.

Moving beyond the precepts of rationalism's methodological individualism, constructivism emerged in the late 1980s and advanced a social understanding of international politics more akin to the second meaning of norms suggested by Hurrell and MacDonald. The 'logic of the social' introduced by construct-ivists is premised on the belief that 'we can't understand people, their interests, their discourses or behaviour in isolation from their social context'.[10] For constructivists, then, norms imply a sense of obligation and expectation precisely because they are '*social* facts'.[11] They are beliefs or ideas that have no independent material, physical, or individual moral reality. They exist only because they are held intersubjectively by actors in a group or community. This emphasis on the social realm means that constructivists do not focus solely on the regulative effects of norms—how they order behaviours—but also on their constitutive effect. That is, the ways in which they define actor identities and interests, 'create . . . certain kinds of activity' and 'foster group identification' that allows for 'the coordination of . . . social power'.[12]

Impartiality in peacekeeping is a norm in this second sense of the term in that it dictates how peacekeepers *ought* to behave, thereby giving rise to social expectations of behaviour. As a social fact, impartiality is not reducible to an individual actor. While a peacekeeper, a peacekeeping mission or the UN more generally may develop a reputation for being impartial, impartiality does not exist as an absolute or intrinsic characteristic of a person or institution. Rather, it figures as an attribute of decision-making or action within a given social context. As such, the common characterization of actors *as* impartial is somewhat misleading and, as moral philosopher Bernard Gert describes, 'always elliptical'.[13] An individual peacekeeper may claim to be acting impar-tially, but what that means—the content of impartiality—and the degree of obligation that is attached to the norm are defined by the broader group or community, which judges the correctness of the behaviour. As with other norms, the importance of impartiality 'lies not in being true or false' but in the fact that it is to some degree 'shared'.[14]

It is precisely because norms are not objective truths but rather intersubjectively held beliefs, that they can change and be contested, shaped by practice and by the broader social context in which they are situated. This lends them a 'dual quality'; on the one hand they are often stable enough that actors take them as a given reference for behaviour; on the other, they are flexible, constructed through socially embedded practices and therefore able to evolve over time and according to place.[15] Impartiality both affects and is itself affected by actor interactions.

For impartiality to be rendered meaningful in a particular mission context and as a norm of UN peacekeeping more generally, actors must interpret it and determine 'its place within the broader normative order'.[16] Differences in individual interpretations or shifts in the context can thus produce changes in the content of impartiality—in how it is understood—and cause it to be strengthened or weakened. Moreover, interpretations may differ and engender disagreement over the meaning and appropriateness of the norm. In other words, a gap between the subjective and intersubjective appraisals of impartiality may open up, such that expectations of what 'norm following' entails diverge.[17] As I explain below, impartiality is particularly susceptible to contestation given its indeterminate nature and the fact that it is complex, containing more than one prescription. And yet, changes in the content of impartiality and possible differences in how it is interpreted and by whom are important precisely because they shape behaviour and social expectations of that behaviour.

To account for this dynamism and possible contestation over impartiality in peacekeeping during the distinct but related processes of institutionalization and implementation, I conceive of it as a composite norm. Rather than being discrete or a seemingly simple entity, impartiality, like other norms, is a complex ideational structure, composed of different sub-norms and normative elements, each of which can change and is open to contestation singly or in combination.

The composite norm is a heuristic tool that introduces heterogeneity and complexity, and provides analytical purchase for examining impartiality.[18] It is inspired by the work of constructivist scholars who highlight the interdependence of norms[19] and it is similar to the notion of a 'regime complex' advanced by neoliberal institutionalists.[20]

The composite norm enables and supports the analysis in three crucial ways. First, disaggregating impartiality into its component parts—the *mode of* decision-making (its procedural dimension) and *basis for* decision-making (its substantive dimension)—provides conceptual clarity. While the first component is critical to understanding the manner in which peacekeepers should behave, it tells us little about the nature of that behaviour—what peacekeepers *actually* do, are expected to do, or why the decisions and actions claimed as impartial by some may be contested by others, despite adherence to the procedural requirements of the norm. In other words, to fully grasp the meaning of impartiality we must account for both dimensions.

Second, a finer parsing of impartiality is necessary to capture changes in its meaning within and across historical and contemporary contexts. This is particularly important for analysing impartiality as a norm of peacekeeping, given that, as I explain below, the *basis for* decision-making, the mandate, may evolve significantly over the course of a mission's deployment and differ considerably across contemporary and historical peacekeeping contexts.

Finally, conceiving of impartiality as a composite norm helps to structure the analysis of contestation. It assists in revealing divergent and at times conflicting interpretations of impartiality, and allows for a nuanced account of contestation in which actors may resist particular elements of the norm and/or advance alternative interpretations of these elements. These differences matter because they help to ascertain how certain interpretations and under-standings of a norm are realized during institutionalization and implementa-tion. As scholars have recently demonstrated, not all interpretations of a norm are of equal standing. Certain actors may have greater power and influence to realize their preferred conception of a norm and thus determine particular outcomes.[21] In this way, the composite norm helps to reveal how, in the context of peacekeeping at both the macro-and micro level, particular indi-vidual and group interpretations of impartiality attain and maintain primacy.

In what follows, I examine the two core components of impartiality: the *mode of* decision-making, and the *basis for* decision-making.

FIRST COMPONENT OF THE NORM: *MODE OF* DECISION-MAKING

The first component of impartiality, the *mode of* decision-making, refers to the procedural dimension of the norm, specifically, to the manner in which decisions are made and actions taken. It prescribes that actors be unbiased and informed when passing judgment.

An impartial actor is one that passes judgment and acts by setting aside particular preferences or interests vis-à-vis a conflict or contest. The actor's decisions and actions are not prejudged or biased—that is, influenced by whether they help or harm one person or group over another—but rather are made according to a certain external standard.[22] An impartial decision, in other words, is one in which the interests of every participant count equally unless specified otherwise by the substantive *basis for* decision-making. Con-sequently, in liberal moral and political philosophy, impartiality is widely regarded as reflecting a core commitment to equality.[23]

What differentiates impartial actors from other actors is the independence of their status. They occupy a role that is distinct from that of the disputants and from those among whom they pass judgment. As a 'third party', impartial peacekeepers are supposed to be, in a sense, detached from the conflict or contest; it is this independence that is thought to safeguard their judgment from potential biases.[24]

Another necessary but not sufficient condition of the norm is that, in addition to being unbiased and independent, impartial actors must be in possession of the requisite knowledge about the issue over which they are expected to pass judgment. Impartiality, as Thomas Franck contends, entails 'the idea of an *informed* decision'.[25] There are two dimensions to this condition. First, the actor requires information about the particular conflict or contest. A judge, for example, needs to be informed of the facts of a case. Similarly, peacekeepers must have sufficient knowledge about the context of deployment, lest partial information result in faulty judgment. But this can make for tension: in some instances, information gathering may require proximity to, not detachment or distantiation from, the actors among whom peacekeepers claim impartial authority. This, in turn, may jeopardize perceptions of independence and lead to charges of bias.

Second, impartial actors must have the ability and expertise to make sense of the information they acquire in order to pass judgment. The range of competence and degree of technical expertise required by impartiality depends on the context, and may vary greatly according to the type of issue and the particularities of the case or course of action to be decided.[26] In peacekeeping, for example, troops are expected to have operational and technical competence in assessing and responding to conflict dynamics, while civilian officials must be knowledgeable about their area of thematic focus (e.g., human rights, rule of law, child protection). As peacekeeping contexts differ, there may be considerable variation across missions in terms of the types of expertise necessary.

Institutional Measures

Institutions like the UN that are tasked with operationalizing impartiality frequently adopt measures to ensure adherence to the procedural requirements of the norm. Peacekeepers must be seen to 'do it' right. These efforts may be just as much about the 'optics' of impartiality; that is, with projecting an image of impartiality, as of effecting that impartiality in practice. This imperative to be seen as impartial is vital for those who claim such authority, as they are only impartial to the extent that they are perceived as such. If peacekeepers are biased, ill-informed, or incompetent, or are seen to be so, consent for their activities or for the operation as a whole may be withdrawn.

Four measures taken by the UN to insure adherence to the procedural requirements of impartiality warrant mention. These measures are driven in large part by the UN's desire to cultivate an international outlook on the part of peacekeepers and to safeguard decision-making from national biases and undue interference by member states.

First, institutional *selection processes* for peacekeeping personnel—both civilian and military—are designed to include provisions for individual expertise, competence, and mitigation of potential biases.[27] Similar to the principle of judicial disqualification, in instances where a senior official or troop-contributing country has, or is perceived to have, a vested interest in a conflict or lacks the necessary expertise and competency, their participation may be blocked by the host state or members of the Security Council.[28]

In addition to individual selection and disqualification procedures, attention to the composition of the group is regarded as strengthening impartiality through the aggregate, preventing what legal scholar John Griffith describes as 'corporate bias'.[29] The Charter, for example, stipulates that staff of the Secretariat be drawn from as 'wide a geographical basis as possible'. Furthermore, it binds member states 'to respect the exclusively international character of the Secretary-General and his Staff' and prohibits them from trying to influence their judgment in this regard.[30] The importance of obtaining a cross-section of nationalities for a force's deployment has historically been emphasized to safeguard a mission's impartiality and project an image of international will. Since the inception of peacekeeping, over 130 states have participated in operations.

Second, the procedural requirements of the norm are manifest in *codes of conduct* for UN personnel. Before taking up an appointment, all UN staff are required to take the UN Oath of Office in which they pledge to act with impartiality and independence in the performance of their official duties, and to abide by an expansive set of rules and regulations, and standards of conduct.[31] The issue of conduct is especially relevant for field-based missions, given their proximity to and daily interaction with a host of local actors, and the potential for abuses of their authority. Consequently, the UN Conduct and Discipline Unit issues separate documentation for uniformed personnel that incorporates the UN Standards of Conduct but is tailored to the deployment context. For example, on a two-sided pocket-sized card distributed to all blue helmets, peacekeepers are reminded to '[d]ress, think, talk, act and behave in a manner befitting the dignity of a disciplined, caring, considerate, mature, respected and trusted soldier, displaying the highest integrity and impartiality'.[32] Specific guidelines concerning relations with host communities, including non-fraternization policies, are intended to safeguard independence and prevent interactions that could potentially undermine a force's acceptance and impartiality. These include restrictions on personnel movement, curfews, a requirement that soldiers must wear uniforms outside barracks, designation of certain areas as 'off-limit', and the deployment of conduct and discipline team personnel into locations with a potentially high risk of misconduct.[33]

Third, *professional immunities and privileges* are regarded as important features to foster commitment to the organization, to shelter UN staff from external influences that could lead to bias, and to allow for unimpeded access to gather information and fulfil their mandate. As a subsidiary organ of the UN, peacekeeping operations enjoy similar immunities and privileges to other UN entities.[34] These immunities and privileges, as well as provisions for the mission's safety, security, and right of freedom of movement, are enumerated in the Status of Forces Agreement (SoFA).[35] The SoFA constitutes an important legal basis for a peacekeeping operation and is signed by the host state and the UN in consultation with troop-contributing countries (TCCs).

UN peacekeeping personnel, including military personnel, are entitled to further protection as civilians under international humanitarian law.[36] They are accorded such protections in part because of their impartiality. 'They are not members of a party to the conflict', as the International Committee of the Red Cross (ICRC) stipulates, and thus are granted protection 'as long as they do not directly participate in hostilities'.[37] As will be discussed in Chapter 3, recent Security Council resolutions authorizing robust operations against particular armed groups and/or in support of the host state have prompted debate over the legal basis of contemporary operations and whether military personnel, particular contingents actively engaged in hostile operations, and/or mission staff more generally, including civilian personnel, should continue to benefit from such protections.[38]

Lastly, the *use of symbols* and *rituals* also aims to buttress 'in-group' loyalty, and effect an outward projection of impartiality. In this respect, the iconic blue beret and white armoured vehicle not only distinguish peacekeepers from enemy forces clad in camouflage, they also strengthen the fidelity that national contingents have towards a mission and the UN. They project an image that links those contingents to what political anthropologist Robert Rubinstein describes as the 'larger metaphorical space' that the UN occupies.[39] Similarly, routine tasks and rituals such as manning observation posts or conducting patrols—activities which were part of the original observer mission—'create a shared sense of meaning among the mission members' that ties them to a larger collective and embeds them in the history of peacekeeping.[40] While these symbols may also be used to project an image of impartiality, differentiating and distancing peacekeepers from local combatants, they are effective only to the extent that the target audience understands them as such. As Ian Hurd explains, '[a] symbol is a valued good—one it makes sense to attempt to acquire—by virtue of the process of legitimation that surrounds it'.[41] At the same time as they may be esteemed, white trucks and blue helmets make peacekeepers stand out as targets in an operational landscape where the UN may be seen as partial, as just one more enemy combatant.

The Subjective Dimension of Impartial Judgment

While these four institutional measures seek to ensure that peacekeepers are informed and unbiased in their decision-making, the impartial actor does not have the complete objectivity of judgment that some characterizations and theories would hold.[42] In making decisions or in taking action claimed to be impartial, a peacekeeper such as a judge or police officer interprets the information available to them in light of how they understand their role and mandate—a process that is inherently subjective. As Franck explains, '[l]ike the parties to a dispute' the impartial actors' perceptions 'are grounded in the senses, and are thus subjective . . . Where he differs from the parties . . . is that *his* subjectivity is *not that of the disputant*'.[43] In other words, the independent status of peacekeepers affords them an opportunity to make informed subjective determinations with 'the greatest possible openness, sensitivity, and receptivity'.[44]

That judgments considered to be impartial have a subjective dimension is an observation long since made in legal thought, which recognizes that juridical judgments invariably entail subjective determinations. As Theodor Meron writes, 'judges are not empty vessels that litigants fill with content'.[45] Recent research in the social sciences has expanded on the ways in which human commitments affect the administration of justice both domestically and internationally.[46] Scholars contend that without such commitments, '[t]he beings then judging us would know nothing at all of what standard human lives look and feel like or, knowing something, would completely ignore it'.[47] If King Solomon cannot feel for the human frailty of those who come before him, how can he make a wise determination?

Dispelling the notion that impartial actors are omniscient is important in several respects. First, it allows for the possibility of differential outcomes. While one would expect a certain degree of consistency in decisions and actions that are claimed to be impartial, consistency, as Gert explains, is neither a necessary nor sufficient condition of impartiality.[48] 'Consistency', said Oscar Wilde, 'is the last refuge of the unimaginative.' Like other actors for whom impartiality is a core norm, peacekeepers do not, nor can they reasonably be expected to, always make the same decisions or follow the same course of action even if presented with the same facts or information. Interpretations will invariably differ, leading to variation in judgment and action. In some instances, for example, interpretations may clash as actors reasonably disagree on what constitutes an appropriate decision or course of action (i.e., differences over what action most faithfully adheres to impartiality). Second, the inherent subjectivity of judgment suggests that a degree of social unity must exist among the impartial peacekeeper and other actors in the wider social context where decision-making takes place. This unity, as Hegel explained, enables 'the confidence which the parties feel in the subjectivity of those who give the verdict'.[49] As I discuss further below, agreement on the substantive basis for decision-making is critical in this respect, as it sets boundaries on what can legitimately be claimed *as* impartial, as a subjective but nonetheless authoritative interpretation. And yet, it is precisely because agreement is often elusive, that impartiality is frequently subject to contestation.

SECOND COMPONENT OF THE NORM: *BASIS FOR* DECISION-MAKING

Impartial judgments rest explicitly or implicitly on a foundation of values, on what Charles Taylor describes as the 'background of valuation'. It is from this that an impartial actor 'selects what is relevant to the judgment'.[50] Whereas the procedural requirements of the norm remain relatively constant across contexts and roles, the background of valuation may differ significantly according to the type of actor and the social context. Judges, for example, administer justice according to the law, while also making subjective assessments of the facts. Civil servants take guidance from their constitutional mandate. Peacekeepers look to the mission mandate. For each of these actors, it is the *basis for* decision-making—the background of valuation—that animates the substantive content of decisions and actions.

The authority of impartial actors is premised to a large extent on whether the *basis for* decision-making is acknowledged as legitimate by disputants and other actors within the wider social context in which decision-making takes place. Where does the background of valuation come from? Is the base on which an 'impartial' actor makes a judgment absolute? What determines its validity and legitimacy as the foundation of values for judgment? Who judges the judges?

Agreement, Consent, and the Mandate

Impartiality has historically been linked to notions of divine and natural law. While elements of these absolutist traditions persist, in contemporary political and legal theory the *basis for* decision-making is commonly associated with contractarianism, which borrows from the social contract tradition the notion that morality and political authority are 'the result of an agreement between those who are to be bound by its dictates'.[51] Impartiality, as Mendus put it, is 'best made manifest through [the concept of] agreement'.[52]

The concept of agreement, however, is not entirely straightforward. Agreements come in different shapes and sizes, and exist on a spectrum with varying levels of political obligation. In liberal political philosophy, consent is generally regarded as 'the gold standard', the most powerful basis for creating political obligations, and thus impartial authority.[53] The appeal and prominence of consent theory, as Allen Buchanan explains, stems from its ability to reconcile the exercise of political power with two core values of liberal philosophy: 'the idea that liberty is the proper condition of human beings and the idea of the fundamental moral equality of persons'.[54] As Mendus states, '[i]f we hope that the moral and legal rules of our society will be impartial in the sense that they will show equal concern for everyone, then we can best ensure that by asking what the rules are that everyone could agree to'.[55] However, in modern societies—both national and international—agreement is often difficult to obtain, and, given the inherent diversity and complexity of social relations, the conditions for securing explicit consent are often lacking.

Notwithstanding these challenges, expressions of agreement, often in the form of consent, have been central to attempts to establish the impartial authority of peacekeepers and, more broadly, of the UN itself. In signing the UN Charter, a document that has the legal status of a multilateral treaty, states give their consent, and in doing so delegate specific power to the Security Council on matters related to international peace and security.[56] Peacekeeping was not an endeavour foreseen by the UN's founders, but developed in a manner consistent with the spirit of the Charter.[57] The deployment of peace-keepers has historically been contingent on securing the consent for a mission and its mandate from parties in the context of operation. Typically, this has been the host government, but in a number of instances this has broadened to include other actors. Parties may approach the UN and request the deploy-ment of peacekeepers, or may be enjoined to do so by members of the Security Council or the Secretariat.

As the background of valuation for peacekeepers, the mandate is far from fixed; the content of mandates varies across and within contexts of deploy-ment. This variation is partly because the Security Council, the principal authorizing body for peacekeeping missions, formulates mandates in relation to particular circumstances of conflict or potential conflict, and/or as a com-plement to a broader peace or political process. As a result, mandates frequent-ly encompass details of specific ceasefire and/or peace agreements that parties to the dispute have agreed upon and which peacekeepers are entrusted to oversee and assist in implementing.

The renewal of peacekeeping mission mandates takes place on a semi-annual or annual basis, or when changes in circumstances are such that reconsideration of the *basis for* decision-making is warranted. As the mandate for a particular mission may evolve significantly over the course of its deployment, the renewal of mandates becomes a means to actively manage continuing consent.[58] Further to the mandate, legal consent for a mission is established in the SoFA, which outlines the rights and responsibility of both the UN and host country. SoFAs are usually complemented by a number of issue-specific Memoranda of Understanding (MoUs) with the government.

In addition to representing the consent of the parties, peacekeeping mandates, and the variation in mandates, are also thought to reflect broader agreement; an international consensus on norms related to international peace and security. Here, the 'power of consent' is held 'collectively by the international community, rather than an individual state'.[59] Inis Claude referred to this as the 'collective legitimization' offered by UN decisions and Security Council authorizations.[60] Writing in the 1960s, Claude maintained that statesmen had 'by general consent' recognized the UN as 'the most impressive and authoritative instrument for the expression of a global version of the general will' and that, by virtue of its universal membership, the UN could act as 'custodian of the seals of international approval and disapproval'.[61] More recently, practitioners and scholars have argued, not without controversy, that the Security Council's internal structure, relationship to the general UN membership and deliberative process of decision-making allows for it to legitimately play the role of arbiter of what constitutes a consensus on the course of action that would best further international peace and security. As Bruce Cronin explains:

> Since the five permanent members represent the most powerful states in the world, a consensu among them provides the means for implementing commonly held standards . . . Moreover, the rotating members act as a check against a great power cabal, since any binding decision requires that a majority of these smaller states adhere to the consensus, at least in theory.[62]

As I describe in Chapter 3, the shift in the understanding of impartiality reflects a change in the *basis for* decision-making and, critically, how the authority of peacekeepers is justified and legitimated. The judgments which contemporary peacekeepers claim *as* impartial are no longer based exclusively on terms consented to by parties to a dispute; rather, they are premised on a more ambitious and expansive set of norms relating largely to human rights, and their relationship to international peace and security, over which many proclaim there is international consensus. Implicit in this change is the belief that 'collective agreement' on these norms can 'override an individual objection'.[63]

Impartial Judgment as Partial Judgment

That there must be some agreement on the *basis for* decision-making is critical, in part because—though it would in surface consideration seem profoundly paradoxical—impartial judgment may lead to differential treatment of disputants or parties to a conflict. While the procedural requirements of impartiality dictate that parties to a dispute be treated as equal, this treatment is only in relation to the *basis for* decision-making. In certain instances, the *basis for* decision-making may contain injunctions for differential treatment, even for coercive action against particular individuals or groups.[64]

Judges, for example, are expected to consider individuals equally without prejudice or prejudgment, but this is only insofar as the law regards these individuals as warranting equal treatment. In most countries, convicted murderers are not viewed as equal to other citizens before the law insofar as the crime committed is seen to warrant differentiated punishment (e.g., imprisonment, withdrawal of voting rights). This results in judgments which may be widely accepted as impartial but which treat these individuals differently. While judgments may be criticized—a murderer, for example, may disagree with his sentencing or whether, according to the law, his actions constitute murder at all—the credibility of the judge and the meaningfulness of his or her role are rooted in a broader social acceptance of the law and confidence in the judge's ability to administer it. Furthermore, what constitutes 'murder' and thereby justifies differential treatment under the rubric of impartiality may differ across social, religious and legal, and even circumstantial contexts. Consequently, judgment regarded as impartial in one context may be admonished as deeply partial in another.

This example raises a fundamental issue. It underscores that while peacekeepers can be impartial in their *application* of the mandate, they cannot, like the judge, be impartial *about* the mandate itself. They are committed—'*partial*' in a sense—to the background valuation implicit in the mandate that provides the basis for their judgment. This is encapsulated in Jeremy Bentham's seemingly paradoxical proclamation that 'it is the duty of the judge to be impartial, therefore it is his duty to be partial'.[65]

It is this commitment and fidelity to the substantive *basis for* decision-making that differentiates impartiality from neutrality, the concept with which it is so often confused and conflated. Simply put: impartiality allows a person to be judgmental so long as their judgment adheres to the values that are generally agreed upon within that particular social context. Neutrality, by contrast, requires *withholding* judgment. It refers to the apolitical and nonactive character of a person's role and thus entails negative limitations such as the prohibition of taking a policy position or making public statements and denunciations. The Swiss jurist and expert on International Humanitarian Law (IHL), Jean Pictet, captured this distinction well when he wrote that 'the neutral man [*sic*] refuses to make judgments whereas the one who is impartial judges a situation in accordance with pre-established rules'.[66]

Recognizing that impartial judgments rest on 'pre-established rules', on a background of valuation that is, in a sense, partial, is important. It suggests, as Franck argued, that impartial judgments are '*intruths* that are valid or invalid, effective or ineffective, "true" and "good", or "false" and "bad" only within the context of a given value system'.[67] And it serves as a cautionary reminder that when an individual or institution like the UN attempts to make an impartial judgment outside the particular social sphere in which such agreement or 'intruths' obtain—that is, in contexts in which the 'values are *not* commonly shared'—they face as an impossible task: the 'invention of a decision that is universally valid—an *extruth*'.[68]

Furthermore, making such judgment requires that those claiming impartial authority be open and willing to re-appraise the basis upon which their decisions are made, so that they hew closely to shared purposes that may change. Mandates must be updated to reflect the specifics of new peace agreements or political processes, as well as evolving norms related to international peace and security. As Franck aptly describes:

> The impartiality of the judge is his ability to perceive, and then work with, hypotheses that, like sets of numbers, have no provable external validity but are the hypothetical shorthand of group communication used to communicate group-values. Moreover, he must be able to sense when the hypotheses have shifted, and if the shift is clear and non-aberrational, he should be able and willing to find the midpoint of a new line or work with a new set of figures.[69]

In this respect, impartiality is not a consequence of detachment, distantiation, or aloofness, of being set apart from society. Instead, it results from what Rosanvallon calls 'reflective immersion'. It necessitates 'vigilance and an active presence in the world, a determination to represent social reality as faithfully as possible'.[70] Drawing on Kant, Hannah Arendt maintained that this requires an 'enlargement of the mind'—a broadening of one's own thinking in order to take into account the viewpoints of others, thereby working towards a greater level of generality.[71] However, this also leaves the impartial actor in a precarious position. The very fact that the *basis for* decision-making may change—the hypothesis or 'the numbers' may shift—means that the legitimacy of the peacekeeper is never secure. The 'impartial institution' is, as Rosanvallon notes, 'by its very nature subject to constant testing. The legitimacy of impartiality needs to be fought for at all times.'[72]

CONCLUSION

Despite impartiality's ubiquity in both policy and scholarly discourse on peacekeeping, the norm is insufficiently studied and largely misunderstood. Impartiality is widely invoked but rarely accompanied by rigorous conceptual analysis. This chapter has sought to provide some clarity on impartiality. However, providing an objective definition is incompatible with the focus of this book, which seeks to analyse how understandings of the norm in UN peacekeeping have changed and the ways in which impartiality itself has been contested during the processes of institutionalization and implementation. Thus, instead of working from a limiting or fixed definition, this chapter has sketched and expanded upon what Franck has referred to as the broad 'structure of impartiality'. Drawing on constructivist approaches as well as moral, political and legal theory, it has presented impartiality as a composite norm. It has elucidated the core components of the norm, and outlined the ways in which they manifest in the context of peacekeeping. As a social belief, impartiality cannot be presumed. Like other norms, it exists only as a matter of shared assessments. This collective aspect is what gives impartiality its force, while also making it so challenging, particularly in the international realm.

NOTES

1. For a historical overview of impartiality, see Thomas Franck, *The Structure of Impartiality: Examining the Riddle of One Law in a Fragmented World* (New York: The Macmillan Company, 1968); Kathryn Murphy and Anita Traninger, eds., *The Emergence of Impartiality* (Leiden: Brill Publishers, 2013); Charles Geyh, 'The Dimensions of Judicial Impartiality', *Florida Law Review* 65/2 (2014). On divine impartiality, for example, see Jouette M. Bassler, *Divine Impartiality: Paul and a Theological Axiom* (Chico, CA: Scholars Press, 1982).
2. See for example, Bo Rothstein and Jan Teorell, 'What is Quality of Government? A Theory of Impartial Government Institutions', *Governance* 2/2 (2008), 165–90; Pierre Rosanvallon, *Democratic Legitimacy: Impartiality, Reflexivity, Proximity* (Princeton: Princeton University Press, 2011).
3. Franck (1968).
4. Susan Mendus, 'Impartiality', in *The Oxford Handbook of Political Theory*, edited by John S. Dryzek, Bonnie Honig, and Anne Phillips (Oxford: Oxford University Press, 2008), 434.
5. Edward H. Carr, *Twenty Years' Crisis, 1919–1939* (New York: Harper and Row, 1946); Hedley Bull, *The Anarchical Society: A Study of Order in World Politics*, 2nd edition, (New York: Columbia University Press, 1977); Nicholas Onuf, *World of Our Making: Rules and Rule in Social Theory and International Relations* (Columbia: University of South Carolina Press, 1989).
6. Andrew Hurrell and Terry MacDonald, 'Norms and Ethics in International Relations', in *Handbook of International Relations*, edited by Walter Carlsnaes, Thomas Risse-Kappen, and Beth Simmons (London: Sage, 2012), 67.
7. Hurrell and MacDonald (2012: 67).
8. Hurrell and MacDonald (2012: 67).
9. Rational choice scholars assume that individuals act to maximize their utility according to a set of exogenously given interests. This leads neorealists and

neoliberals to view norms either as epiphenomenal, inconsequential window-dressings of the powerful for the former (e.g., Stephen Krasner, *Sovereignty: Organized Hypocrisy* (Princeton: Princeton University Press, 1999)) or helpful 'road maps' in certain 'strategic situations' for the latter (e.g., Judith Goldstein and Robert Keohane, eds., *Ideas & Foreign Policy: Beliefs, Institutions, and Political Change* (Ithaca, NY: Cornell University Press, 1996)). For both sets of scholars, however, norms are regulative and functional; they do not shape individual interests, which are viewed as ontologically prior to social institutions.

10. Samuel Barkin, *Realist Constructivism: Rethinking International Relations Theory* (Cambridge: Cambridge University Press, 2010), 58.

11. John Ruggie, *Constructing the World Polity: Essays on International Institutionalization* (London: Routledge, 1998), 12. Constructivists distinguish between social and material facts. Social facts ' . . . are facts only by human agreement . . . [They] differ from rocks and flowers, because . . . their existence depends on human consciousness and language'. Emanuel Adler, 'Constructivism in International Relations: Sources, Contributions and Debates', in *Handbook of International Relations*, edited by Walter Carlsnaes, Thomas Risse-Kappen, and Beth Simmons (London: Sage, 2012), 119.

12. Hurrell (2002: 145).

13. Bernard Gert, *Morality: Its Nature and Justification* (Oxford: Oxford University Press, 2005), 136.

14. Peter Katzenstein, 'Coping with Terrorism: Norms and Internal Security in Germany and Japan', in *Ideas & Foreign Policy*, edited by Goldstein and Keohane 1996: 268.

15. Audie Klotz, 'Can We Speak a Common Language?', in *Constructing International Relations: The Next Generation*, edited by K.M. Fierke and K.E. Jorgensen (Armonk, NY: M.E. Sharpe, 2001), 229; Antje Wiener, 'The Dual Quality of Norms and Governance beyond the State: Sociological and Normative Approaches to "Interaction"', *Critical Review of International Social and Political Philosophy* 10/1 (2007), 47–69.

16. Hurrell and Macdonald (2012: 70).

17. Nicola Contessi, 'Multilateralism, Intervention and Norm Contestation: China's Stance on Darfur in the UN Security Council', *Security Dialogue* 41/3 (2010), 325.

18. The composite norm is a heuristic tool in the sense that it serves 'to find out or discover something', *New Shorter Oxford English Dictionary* (1993: 1228). The designation of an idea as 'heuristic' implies, as Humphreys notes, 'only that the idea helps us to understand that to which it is applied'. Adam Humphreys, 'The Heuristic Application of Explanatory Theories in International Relations', *European Journal of International Relations* 17/2 (2011), 262.

19. Scholars have demonstrated how the meaning of a particular norm within a particular context may be constituted by other adjacent relevant norms. For example, in her history of mercenaries, Sarah Percy chronicles the intimate ties between the anti-mercenary norm and other norms and ideas as varied as the belief that the 'state ought to have control over the use of force' and 'the norm against prostitution' to reveal 'what particular states find dangerous about mercenaries at particular times'. Percy, *Mercenaries: The History of a Norm in*

International Relations (Oxford: Oxford University Press, 2007), 30. Similarly, Richard Price explains how components of the chemical weapons taboo shed light on international practices of violence. Price, *Chemical Weapons Taboo* (Ithaca: Cornell University Press, 1997), 9. Finally, Dominik Zaum elucidates the changing and unchanging tenets of sovereignty in his analyses of international statebuilding efforts over time. Zaum defines sovereignty not as a single norm, but rather 'an institution comprising several sometimes conflicting norms'. Zaum, *The Sovereignty Paradox: The Norms and Politics of International Statebuilding* (Oxford: Oxford University Press, 2007), 4.

20. For an overview of the literature on regime complexity, see Karen Alter and Sophie Meunier, 'The Politics of International Regime Complexity', *Perspectives on Politics* 7/1 (2009), 13–24; Robert Keohane and David Victor, 'The Regime Complex for Climate Change', *The Harvard Project on International Climate Agreements* (Cambridge, MA: Harvard University, 2010). While the notions are similar, several key differences between 'regime complexes' and 'composite norms' are worth noting. Regime complexes are concerned with entire, and potentially overlapping, issue areas and are thus more expansive in terms of their object of study. Furthermore, they consist only of formal institutions such as agreements and treaties, which, given the rationalist approach adopted by regime theorists, are treated as objective facts with fixed meaning. In contrast, the composite norm is more specific in focus and may encompass informal norm associations that are flexible and made meaningful by actor interpretation. These components may at times form a coherent structure or, as I describe, they may be characterized by ambiguity and dissonance.

21. Barkin (2010); Alexander Betts and Phil Orchard, eds., *Implementation and World Politics: How International Norms Change Practice* (Oxford: Oxford University Press, 2014).

22. Bernard Gert's formal conception of impartiality captures this basic understanding. He stipulates that 'A is impartial in respect R with regard to group G if and only if A's actions in respect R are not influenced by which member(s) of G benefit or are harmed by these actions.' Gert (2005: 132).

23. Ronald Dworkin, *Taking Rights Seriously* (Cambridge: Harvard University Press, 1977), 227. See also Thomas Nagel, *Equality and Partiality* (Oxford: Oxford University Press, 1990); Susan Mendus, *Impartiality in Moral and Political Philosophy* (Oxford: Oxford University Press, 2002).

24. While independence and impartiality are inextricably linked, they are not the same thing. A peacekeeper can be an independent third party, distinct from the parties to a conflict, and yet still be biased in their decision-making and actions. Simply put: impartiality requires independence, but as Pierre Rosanvallon explains, 'independence by itself is not enough to achieve impartiality.' Rosanvallon (2011: 94–5).

25. Franck (1968: 307).

26. Franck (1968: 208).

27. Appointments to the Secretariat, including the selection of civilian peacekeeping personnel, fall under the remit of the Secretary-General and his staff. The selection of military personnel differs slightly. Absent a standing army of its own, the UN

recruits military personnel for each individual mission fielded. The selection of and solicitations for forces from member states is the primary responsibility of the Secretariat unless otherwise specified in the mandate. Once selected by the Secretariat, both the Council and host state are consulted on the force composition and the Force Commander is appointed. Unlike the procedure with civilian personnel, it is the troop-contributing country that decides which specific individuals are deployed. However, if military personnel are found to be incompetent, unskilled or otherwise unable to implement the mandate, the UN may terminate the contract of employment and, with the cost assumed by the mission, return individual military personnel to their country of origin.

28. Judicial disqualification is a fundamental principle in law, dating back to the Roman Code of Justinian, which maintains that litigants who believe a judge to be biased or unfair are permitted to recuse the judge, so long as this is done before the issue is joined. See for example, Grant Hammond, *Judicial Recusal: Principles, Process and Problems* (Oxford: Hart Publishing, 2009); Hirad Abtahi, Odo Ogwuma, and Rebecca Young, 'The Composition of Judicial Benches, Disqualification and Excusal of Judges at the International Criminal Court: A Survey', *Journal of International Criminal Justice* 11/2 (2013), 379–98.

29. Griffith identifies two forms of bias: personal bias and corporate bias in which actors as 'a corpus decides certain types of cases in a biased way'. While the issue of judicial disqualification speaks to the former, judicial representation seeks to address the latter form of bias. It reflects the view that judges as well as juries should represent a fair cross-section of the community (e.g., gender, cultural, ethnic, and religious diversity). Conversely, a court's impartiality may be threatened if it appears to lack an understanding of the broad range of people who come before it because of its own narrow membership. John Griffith, *The Politics of the Judiciary*, 5th edition (London: HarperCollins Publishers, 1997), 290.

30. United Nations, *Charter of the United Nations* (1945), Articles 101 and 100, http://www.un.org/en/documents/charter/index.shtml

31. Staff are reminded that they 'do not have the freedom that private persons have to take sides' and are prohibited from acting in ways 'that unjustifiably could lead to actual or perceived preferential treatment for or against particular individuals, groups or interests'. Secretary-General's Bulletin, *Staff Regulations*, ST/SGB/2003/5, 7. For documentation on UN Standards of Conduct, see https://cdu.unlb.org/UNStandardsofConduct/PolicyDocuments.aspx. To avoid possible conflicts of interests, personnel are provided with detailed guidance on a wide range of issues, including: personal relationships; gifts, hospitability, awards and honours; outside employment; political activities; and financial disclosure.

32. United Nations, 'Ten Rules: Code of Personal Conduct For Blue Helmets' (1998) https://cdu.unlb.org/UNStandardsofConduct/TenRulesCodeofPersonalConductForBlueHelmets.aspx

33. United Nations, https://cdu.unlb.org/UNStrategy/Prevention.aspx

34. These are prescribed in the 1946 Convention on the *Privileges and Immunities of the United Nations*, A/RES/22 A(I). The specific level of privileges and immunity accorded to individuals depends on the category and rank of personnel; however,

UN officials generally enjoy immunities 'in respect of words spoken and written, and all acts performed by them in their official capacity'. Ibid., *Section 18(a)*. For an overview of the application of law to peace operations, see Guglielmo Verdirame, *The UN and Human Rights: Who Guards the Guardians?* (Cambridge: Cambridge University Press, 2011), Chapter 5.

35. SoFAs have been concluded for the majority of peacekeeping operations. The UN's Model SoFA was written by the Secretary-General in 1990 and serves as a template for drafting individual agreements. The Model SoFA was based on 'established practice' and drew 'extensively upon earlier and current agreements'. United Nations, A/45/594, *Model Status-of-Forces Agreement for Peacekeeping Operations*, 9 October 1990, paras. 59–60. According to Bowett, SoFAs 'represent compromises and shifts between the law of visiting forces on the one hand and the law of international privileges and immunities on the other, against the background of functional necessity'. D. W. Bowett, *United Nations Forces: A Legal Study of United Nations Practice* (London: Stevens & Sons, 1964), 434. See also University of Essex, *UN Peacekeeping and The Model Status of Forces Agreement*, University of Essex, School of Law, United Nations Peacekeeping Law Reform Project, 2011.

36. State practice establishes this rule as a norm of customary international law applicable in both international and non-international armed conflicts. Intentional direct attack against personnel and objects involved in a peacekeeping mission is considered a war crime under the Rome Statute, Article 8(2)(b)(ii), and numerous states have adopted the Convention on the Safety of United Nations and Associated Personnel (1994) and the subsequent, Optional Protocol (2005). Host states that are not party to the Rome Statute have been required to apply these provisions under the SoFA. See 'Rule 33', in *Customary International Humanitarian Law*, edited by Jean-Marie Henckaerts and Louise Doswald-Beck (Cambridge: Cambridge University Press, 2005).

37. The UN takes a similar position. See, United Nations, Secretary-General's Bulletin, *Observance of United Nations Forces of International Humanitarian Law*, ST/SGB/1999/13 (1999).

38. See Nils Melzer, *Interpretive Guidance on the Notion of Direct Participation in Hostilities Under International Humanitarian Law* (Geneva: ICRC, May 2009).

39. Robert Rubinstein, 'Intervention and Culture: An Anthropological Approach to Peace Operations', *Security Dialogue* 36/4 (2005), 535. See also, Séverine Autesserre, *Peaceland: Conflict Resolution and the Everyday Politics of International Intervention* (Cambridge: Cambridge University Press, 2014).

40. Rubinstein (2005: 535).

41. Ian Hurd, *After Anarchy* (Princeton: Princeton University Press, 2007), 16.

42. In Western thought, the 'impartial view' has long been portrayed as a higher standpoint, God's perspective, transcending human understanding, but nevertheless invoked to judge human disputes. For an overview and critique of characterizations of the impartial actor as 'godlike judge' and 'foreign prince' as well as the image of impartiality as an 'invisible hand', see Rosanvallon (2011: 107–9).

43. Franck (1968: 307).

44. Franck (1968: 307).

45. Theodor Meron, 'Judicial Independence and Impartiality in International Criminal Tribunals', *American Journal of International Law* 99/2 (2005), 365.
46. Researchers describe how judges are influenced by ideological predilections (Jeffrey Segal, et al., 'Ideological Values and the Votes of US Supreme Court Justices Revisited', *The Journal of Politics* 57/3 (1995), 812–23), policy preferences (Lee Epstein and Jack Knight, *The Choices Justices Make* (Washington: Jack Knight, 1998)), and may draw upon subconscious biases (Chris Guthrie et al., 'Blinking on the Bench: How Judges Decide Cases', *Cornell Law Review* 13/1 (2007)). See also Erik Voeten, 'The Impartiality of International Judges: Evidence from the European Court of Human Rights', *American Political Science Review* 102/4 (2008), 417–32.
47. William Lucy, 'The Possibility of Impartiality', *Oxford Journal of Legal Studies* 25/1 (2005), 15. Renowned legal scholar, Martha Minow, expands eloquently on this point: 'None of us can know anything except by building upon, challenging, responding to what we already have known, what we see from where we stand. But we can insist on seeing what we are used to seeing, or else we can try to see something new and fresh. The latter is the open mind we hope for from those who judge, but not the mind as a sieve without prior reference points and commitments. We want judges and juries to be objective about the facts and the questions of guilt and innocence but committed to building upon what they already know about the world, human beings, and each person's own implication in the lives of others. Pretending not to know risks leaving unexamined the very assumptions that deserve reconsideration.' Martha Minow, 'Stripped Down Like a Runner or Enriched by Experience: Bias and Impartiality of Judges and Jurors', *William and Mary Law Review* 33/4 (1992), 1217.
48. Gert (2005: 133).
49. Georg Hegel, *Philosophy of Right*, Translated by T.M. Knox (Oxford: Clarendon Press, 1952), 144–5.
50. Charles Taylor, 'Neutrality in the University', in *Neutrality and Impartiality: The University and Political Commitment*, edited by Alan Montefiore (Cambridge: Cambridge University Press, 1975), 131.
51. Troy Jollimore, 'Impartiality', in *The Stanford Encyclopedia of Philosophy* (Spring 2014 edition), edited by Edward N. Zalta, available at http://plato.stanford.edu/cgi-bin/encyclopedia/archinfo.cgi?entry=impartiality
52. Mendus (2008: 434).
53. Allen Buchanan, 'Political Legitimacy and Democracy', *Ethics* 112/4 (2002), 699.
54. Buchanan (2002: 697).
55. Mendus (2008: 434).
56. Article 25 requires that members 'accept and carry out the decisions of the Security Council in accordance with the present Charter'. Chapter VI and VII detail the types of mandates which the Council may issue to the membership.
57. As discussed in Chapter 2, peacekeeping was not foreseen in the Charter. It initially emerged through the actions of the General Assembly in the creation of the First United Nations Emergency Force (UNEF I). However, the Security Council assumed control of peacekeeping following the controversy surrounding the United Nations Operation in Congo (*Opération des Nations Unies au Congo,*

or ONUC) and has since retained it. The legal basis upon which either the General Assembly or the Security Council can organize peacekeeping operations is provided for by the theory of implied powers. On the constitutionality of peacekeeping operations, see International Court Justice, *Certain Expenses of the United Nations (Article 17, Paragraph 2, of the Charter)*, Advisory Opinion, (1962), 151, 163–8.

58. Ian Johnstone, 'Managing Consent in Contemporary Peacekeeping Operations', *International Peacekeeping* 18/2 (2011), 168–82.

59. Bruce Cronin, 'International Consensus and the Changing Legal Authority of the UN Security Council', in *The UN Security Council and the Politics of International Authority*, edited by Bruce Cronin and Ian Hurd (London: Routledge, 2008), 67.

60. Inis Claude, 'Collective Legitimization as a Political Function of the United Nations', *International Organization* 20/3 (1966), 367–79.

61. Claude (1966: 371–2).

62. Cronin (2008: 70–1).

63. Cronin (2008: 67).

64. Impartiality, as Dworkin notes, requires not that everyone receive equal treatment, but rather that 'everyone be treated as an equal'. Dworkin (1977: 227).

65. Jeremy Bentham, *Rationale of Judicial Evidence. Vol. VI.* (1843), 350.

66. Jean Pictet, *The Fundamental Principles of the Red Cross* (Geneva: Henry Dunant Institute, 1979), 3.

67. Franck (1968: 306).

68. Franck (1968: 306).

69. Franck (1968: 87).

70. Rosanvallon (2011: 89).

71. Reflecting on Kant, Arendt writes: 'You see that *impartiality* is obtained by taking the viewpoints of others into account; impartiality is not the result of some higher standpoint that would then actually settle the dispute by being altogether above the melée.' Hannah Arendt, *Lectures on Kant's Political Philosophy* (Chicago: University of Chicago Press, 1982), 42 (emphasis in the original).

72. Rosanvallon (2011: 95).

2

From Passive to Assertive Impartiality

The Irish statesman and writer, Conor Cruise O'Brien once characterized the United Nations (UN) as 'sacred drama'—a theatrical construction with a profoundly theological content. He said that the creation of the UN in 1945 following the ravages of two world wars represented nothing less than 'humanity's prayer to itself to be saved from itself'.[1]

In the name of 'we the peoples of the United Nations', the famous opening words of the Charter offer this sacred prayer, reaffirming 'faith in fundamental human rights' and expressing its members' commitment to renounce the use of 'armed force . . . save in the common interest'.[2] The power and promise of this post-war exhortation lay in the universality of the UN's membership and the belief that for the first time all peoples would be governed by the same rules.

The Charter's idealism is tempered, however, by a good dose of realism, reflecting the desire of the UN's founders to overcome the structural weaknesses of its predecessor, the League of Nations. While the Charter develops an ambitious framework for collective action, it also contains a number of provisions which mean that it falls short of a genuine collective security system among equal states and peoples.[3] The creation of the Security Council and the powers of the veto, conferred on its five permanent members by Article 27, are most notable in this respect.[4] The Council is empowered to identify those who threaten peace, and to mobilize member states' responses. It is demonstrably a pragmatic system of collective action founded on the primacy of the strong—what Franklin Roosevelt referred to as a 'trustee of the powerful'—expected to manage peace and security through a modicum of political consensus.[5] Action may happen if enough arms can be twisted, or votes obtained.

The Cold War laid bare these tensions and impeded implementation of the Charter's more ambitious collective goals.[6] The global divide meant that international conflict was invariably cast in terms of opposing ideologies, and consensus on the rights and wrongs of particular crises was a rarity. The UN remained on the side-lines of the main theatres of the Cold War and the Council rarely made use of its 'finger-pointing' power.

The global schism did not, however, lead to the institution's obsolescence. Under the leadership of Dag Hammarskjöld, the second Secretary-General of the UN, the organization carved out a limited role in the area of peace and security. Beginning with the Suez Crisis in 1956, lightly armed peacekeepers were deployed to assist states in creating the conditions for peace with the consent of those directly involved. Unforeseen by the UN's founders, peace-keeping was situated at the interstices of the Charter—beyond the Security Council's procedures for conciliation and yet distinct from the type of force envisaged under Chapter VII. Hammarskjöld famously referred to it as a 'Chapter 6 ½' activity—a 'fictive' category that, as Franck asserts, illustrated the Charter's adaptation to practice.[7] Peacekeeping, like its institutional pro-genitor, was a 'radical . . . experiment in international cooperation'.[8] Military forces, whose national loyalties had long epitomized the essence of partiality, were expected in their capacity as peacekeepers to act impartially in support of peace.

Over the past six decades, the deployment of blue helmets has become the UN's flagship activity and the norm of impartiality, the 'bedrock' of peace-keeping.[9] The political and normative context in which peacekeeping emerged has, however, changed dramatically since the Cold War, and thus so too has the dominant understanding of what it means to 'keep' the peace impartially. No longer passively impartial—tasked with observing frontiers and ceasefire agreements based on terms directly consented to by those parties in dispute—peacekeepers regularly operate with Chapter VII mandates and are now expected to be assertive: the vanguard of human-rights protection.

This chapter analyses the change in the dominant understanding of the composite norm of impartiality as institutionalized in UN policy documents and peacekeeping doctrine. This change, I argue, is significant not only because it marks a radical shift in the practices and purposes of peacekeeping, and values projected by the UN, but also because it represents an evolution in how the authority of peacekeepers is constituted, justified, and practised. The judgments which contemporary peacekeepers claim *as* impartial are no longer based exclusively on terms consented to by all parties to a dispute. Rather, they are premised on a more ambitious and expansive set of norms relating largely to human rights, over which it is claimed there is now international consensus.

The chapter proceeds chronologically. The first section provides an over-view of peacekeeping's inception and conceptual development during the Cold War. The next section examines peacekeeping during the 1990s, a decade ushered in with high hopes, but which quickly became mired in crises, prompting the reconceptualization of impartiality. The third section, which focuses on peace operations in the new millennium, analyses the new conception of impartiality and situates this change in a broader shift towards a more assertive liberal international order. The fourth section concludes by illuminating ambiguities inherent in the now dominant conception of the norm. I argue that these ambiguities point to an enduring tension within the UN as an organization, which, though composed of and founded on the sanctity of sovereign states, has since its inception aspired to more collective purposes, including those that promote individual rights. Moreover, as Chapter 3 argues, ambiguity over impartiality and the substantive *basis for* decision-making reflects the more fundamental contestation over the dominant understanding of the norm and the politics of contemporary peacekeeping.

PEACEKEEPING'S INCEPTION AND DEVELOPMENT DURING THE COLD WAR

In October 1956, the UN faced two crises. Within the span of a few days, the Soviet suppression of the Hungarian uprising and Israel's attack on the Sinai Peninsula threatened to deepen the Cold War divide. While both cases were brought before the General Assembly, the responses they elicited were noticeably different: inaction and comparatively muted criticisms over the former; direct moves to develop a system of international peacekeeping in the latter.

Israel's invasion had been backed by Britain and France and was part of a covert, tripartite plan to control the Suez Canal, which Egyptian President Gamel Abdel Nasser had nationalized. As Anglo-French involvement became plainly apparent, the attack incurred international opprobrium.[10] The United States, which had been kept in the dark about the plan, was trenchant in condemning the behaviour of its erstwhile allies.[11] Western solidarity began to fray at precisely the moment when violence on the streets of Budapest signalled it might be most needed.

Sidestepping Anglo-French vetoes in the Council, the Suez Crisis was transferred to the General Assembly under the 'Uniting for Peace' procedure and Resolution 998 was passed, requesting that the Secretary-General submit to the Assembly 'a plan for the setting up, with the consent of the nations concerned, of an emergency international United Nations Force to secure and supervise the cessation of hostilities'.[12]

With a commitment from Britain and France to withdraw their troops if such a force were deployed, Hammarskjöld quickly developed a plan. Within days, he presented two reports on the formation of the UN Emergency Force (UNEF), both of which were endorsed by the Assembly.[13] While the concept of peacekeeping and its core principles would subsequently be refined, these reports laid the foundations for what Brian Urquhart, senior advisor to the Secretary-General, described as 'an entirely new kind of international activity'.[14]

In his reports, Hammarskjöld differentiated UNEF from previous UN observer missions by specifying that it was to be paramilitary in character. However, unlike combat operations, the force, he explained, was not to be deployed with the aim of 'controlling the territory in which it [was] stationed'.[15] UNEF was to operate with the consent of Egypt—in accordance with what would later be referred to as the Good Faith agreements. Peacekeepers were to abstain from political involvement in the crisis and were prohibited from using force, save in self-defence. UNEF's role, as a scholar at the time submitted, was 'passive and pacific'.[16]

In assembling the force, Hammarskjöld rejected an initial proposal to subsume Anglo-French troops under the UN flag, expressing concern that it would merely legitimate their aggressive actions.[17] UNEF was to have an international character and contributions from permanent members of the Council were prohibited.[18] To differentiate UNEF from Anglo-French troops, the Secretariat purchased stocks of American army helmets and spray-painted them UN blue.

On 15 November 1956, advance units of the force arrived in Cairo. Within six months, UNEF, which comprised ten national contingents and totalled roughly 6,000 forces at its peak, had fulfilled the majority of its mandated tasks. These included: oversight of British and French withdrawal; clearing the Suez Canal; maintenance of minimum order through patrols and monitoring; and, through interposition, the separation of Egyptian and Israeli combatants.[19]

The virtue of the force's design, as Norrie MacQueen argues, was that 'most of the protagonists of the crisis could interpret some aspect of UNEF's deployment as benefiting their own national interest'.[20] The authorization for UNEF, which came from the General Assembly, did not assign blame or explicitly identify an aggressor. In this way, its deployment enabled Britain and France to retreat with minimal loss of face while vindicating Nasser's claim of imperial interference and the increasingly popular view, as Roger Louis notes, that 'colonialism was an anachronism'.[21] The mission was initially heralded as a success.

Soldiers without Enemies: Passive Impartiality in Theory and Practice

While UNEF was an ad hoc and temporary solution to the Suez Crisis, peacekeeping quickly became a core UN activity and an important signal that the UN could play a role in international security during the Cold War. Unlike UNEF, most of the other thirteen missions fielded during this period were authorized by the Council. Peacekeeping was thus invariably limited and only took place within what Macqueen describes as 'permitted areas'. Its perimeters were 'fixed by tacit agreement between East and West, and excluded issues and regions where core national interests were in play'.[22] As the strategic interests of the superpowers were fluid, peacekeeping's prevalence paralleled the wax and wane of Cold War relations.[23]

In addition to serving as a *via media* between East and West, peacekeeping was a valuable instrument during the process of decolonization, commensurate with Hammarskjöld's conception of the UN as the 'main protector' of newly minted states.[24] In Cyprus, Palestine, and Congo, peacekeepers were deployed to buttress the often-abrupt ending of empire and to safeguard independence. In other cases, such as Kashmir, Gaza, and Lebanon, peacekeepers were sent to quell the 'conflicted aftermath of partition stemming from imperial practices of divide-and-rule'.[25]

In both respects—as handmaiden to Cold War and Third World politics—the form and content of peacekeeping reflected the Charter's statist commitments. With little consensus on how states—new or old—should be governed, and in the absence, as R.J. Vincent opined, of a 'coherent and pervasive morality which transcends international frontiers and which might then inform and justify particular acts of intervention',[26] the principles of sovereignty, non-intervention, and self-determination became 'the cornerstone of the UN system' and peacekeeping's foundation during the Cold War.[27] As missions deployed to safeguard the process of decolonization, the Council dared not trespass into the domestic realm, and resolutions rarely passed judgment on the character of the 'self' whose self-determination they assisted. Discussion of human rights was stymied by lack of consensus on what exactly constituted a human right and which rights to prioritize. In this context, peacekeeping figured as a buffer force or stopgap measure deployed to defuse tensions *between* sovereign states. Forces were passively impartial, beholden to the wishes and policies of parties to a dispute in areas permitted by the superpowers. Peacekeepers, as the title of a training manual from the period aptly put it, were expected to be *Soldiers Without Enemies*.[28]

The Master Texts of Peacekeeping

The 'basic principles and rules' of Cold War peacekeeping were inscribed in what Hammarskjöld referred to as the 'master texts'.[29] Buoyed by UNEF's initial success and with decolonization gathering pace, in 1957 Hammarskjöld established a study group to distil UNEF's experience and discourage future improvisation. The group's work, coupled with the Final Report from November 1956, formed the basis for the Secretary-General's own Summary Report, which he delivered to the General Assembly in October 1958.[30] Guidelines for the Second UN Emergency Force to the Middle East (UNEF II), written by Secretary-General Kurt Waldheim in 1973, supplemented these initial texts.[31]

At the core of these documents was what became known as the 'holy trinity' of peacekeeping norms: impartiality, consent, and non-use of force (except in self-defence). While no formal doctrine was developed during the Cold War, these norms came to be regarded as the bedrock of peacekeeping, and were closely associated with, if not always adhered to by, the missions fielded during this period.[32] As Herbert Nicholas noted in 1963: '[t]hese three principles ... are merely in the present state of the world indispensable. They may be stretched, modified, even conceivably bypassed; they cannot within the framework of the present United Nations be replaced by any positive alternatives'.[33]

With respect to impartiality, the master texts contained a number of specifications to ensure that the procedural requirements of the norm were met: principally that peacekeepers should be informed and unbiased when making decisions and taking action. Underscoring the necessity of access to information, Hammarskjöld dictated that peacekeepers enjoy freedom of movement within the operational area consented to by the parties and deploy with the communications necessary to carry out their mandate.[34] Likewise, to prevent potential biases, the composition of missions was scrutinized. Forces were to be 'exclusively international in character'[35] and were 'not to include units from any of the permanent members of the Security Council' or 'from any country which, because of its geographical position or for other reasons, might be considered as possibly having a special interest in the situation'.[36] Moreover, the consensual nature of peacekeeping meant that troop contributions by member states were voluntary and, as with UNEF, subject to host-state approval.[37]

In accordance with these requirements, during the Cold War peacekeepers were frequently selected from 'middle power' states like Canada, Denmark, Sweden, and Norway.[38] These countries were considered acceptable because they did not have colonial legacies and were regarded as having less at stake in any given conflict. Third World states—most of which were newly independent—were also looked to for troop contributions. Many of these former colonies had large armies of available forces. Crucially, their involvement also carried symbolic significance. Their participation alone was regarded by many as distinguishing peacekeeping from the imperial conquests they had endured, and the Cold War ideologies in opposition to which they defined themselves. In the initial decade of peacekeeping, many soldiers from the Third World transitioned seamlessly 'from military service in support of a global empire to service in support of an international organisation'.[39]

For example, in 1960 when, as Cunliffe recounts, the Nigeria regiment of the Royal West African Frontier Force became the army of independent Nigeria, it was re-deployed to the UN peacekeeping mission in newly independent Belgian Congo. There, forces from Nigeria were joined by 'their erstwhile comrades-in-arms of empire'—soldiers from independent Ghana, the Federation of Malaya, Ceylon, India, and Pakistan.[40]

In addition to the procedural requirements, the impartiality of peacekeepers during the Cold War was predicated on consent for a mission and its mandate. Security Council resolutions reflected the peace or ceasefire agreement that parties had reached prior to a mission's deployment, and provided peacekeepers with the basis for their decisions and actions. In this way, the peacekeeper's role was akin to that of a mediator whose authority is limited to that which is conferred on it by parties to a dispute. To ensure that consent was firm and comprehensive, the master texts advised that peacekeepers be prohibited from involvement in conflicts internal to sovereign states, as non-state actors were less likely to be reliable partners, and domestic disputes risked embroiling them in local politics.[41]

By adhering to those terms directly consented to by states party to a dispute, Hammarskjöld maintained that peacekeepers were unlikely to be 'used to enforce any special political solution of pending problems or to influence the political balance decisive to such a solution'.[42] Peacekeepers, he asserted, were to be 'impartial, in the sense that [they] would not serve as a means to force settlement in the interest of one party, of political conflicts or legal issues regarded as controversial'.[43] That the actions of peacekeepers could be without controversy—their decisions perceived as impartial—was contingent on the consent of the parties and tacit acquiescence of the superpowers and their allies.

The impartiality of, and consent for, a mission were in turn thought to obviate the need for more forceful action, since it was assumed that parties would comply with the agreement that provided the basis for deployment and subsequent action. If force were used, it risked being seen as partial, thereby jeopardizing consent and potentially dragging UN forces into a fight for which they were ill-equipped. Peacekeepers, being comprised mainly of infantry units, had limited defensive capabilities and were not trained for enforcement action.[44] Self-defence, the only exception to the non-use of force requirement, was, according to Hammarskjöld, to be exercised 'under strictly defined conditions' for fear that it might 'blur the distinction between [peacekeeping] operations and combat operations'.[45]

While the next Secretary-General, Kurt Waldheim, expanded the conditions under which force could be used to include 'force in defense of the mandate', this change was of little consequence during the Cold War, given that the tasks outlined in mandates were limited to and based on prior agreement among the parties.[46] Were an agreement to disintegrate, were consent to be formally withdrawn, or political consensus in the Council to deteriorate, peacekeepers had little recourse to defend their mandate. UNEF was a case in point. On 16 May 1967, the mission closed amid much controversy, Secretary-General U Thant having unsuccessfully attempted to persuade Nasser to rescind his request for the mission's withdrawal.[47] Following UNEF's expulsion, Egypt increased its military activity near the border and blocked the Straits of Tiran to Israeli ships, causing Israel to launch a pre-emptive attack on Egypt's air force, thus precipitating the cataclysmic 1967 war. A temporary force that aimed to foster conditions conducive to conflict resolution by the parties themselves, UNEF, like other Cold War missions, was not intended as a substitute to a parallel or separate peace process. The authority of a peacekeeping mission was limited to that which the parties conferred on it; peacekeepers were passive to their demands.

The Limits of Passive Impartiality: Cold War Peacekeeping in Congo

The model of peacekeeping developed in the master texts was based largely on the UNEF experience. It assumed a modicum of agreement among the superpowers, firm consent, and provision of a clear mandate from the Council—conditions that did not always materialize during the Cold War. Peacekeeping missions in Congo (1960), Cyprus (1963), and Lebanon (1978) were aberrations from this model and involved the deployment of UN forces into civil conflicts where assuming a passive posture was challenging, if not untenable. Of the three missions, the UN Operation in Congo (*Opération des Nations Unies au Congo*, or ONUC) was most notable in this respect, and presaged many of the issues with which peacekeepers in the post-Cold War context would grapple.

ONUC was a milestone in peacekeeping, unparalleled both in its size—nearly 20,000 troops at its peak—and its cost, which nearly bankrupted the UN. The mission was deployed in July 1960, shortly after the country was granted independence from Belgium. It was created at the request of the newly elected Prime Minister, Patrice Lumumba, who sought assistance in preventing Congo's ex-colonial power from meddling in its internal affairs.[48] Belgium had re-entered the country without the consent of the Congolese government, ostensibly to protect foreign nationals, and sent paratroopers to support Moise Tshombe's secessionist movement in the mineral-rich province of Katanga.

From its inception, ONUC had to walk a fine political line. In the Council, Britain and France were sympathetic to Belgian concerns, while in the General Assembly Belgium's actions were criticized as an assault on sovereignty.[49] Consequently, Security Council Resolution 143 established ONUC under the pretence of responding to international aggression, but without explicitly naming Belgium's actions as such.[50] Moreover, the mission was issued with the contradictory mandates of both assisting the fledgling government *and* abstaining from involvement in conflict internal to the country. The challenges of such a mission operating at cross-purposes quickly became apparent. Hammarskjöld's refusal to assist the central government in suppressing the secessionist movement in Katanga provoked a fiery response from Lumumba who, in an irate letter to the Secretary-General, 'question[ed] his impartiality . . . [and] challeng[ed] his interpretation of the resolutions'.[51] According to Lumumba, the UN had 'reneged on the original terms on which its assistance had been sought and offered'.[52]

Tensions were further inflamed by the constitutional crisis of September 1960, which pitted Prime Minister Lumumba against President Kasavubu.[53] Faced with competing claimants of lawful authority, UN officials attempted to maintain a pretence of impartiality, but, in fact, sided with the pro-Western Kasavubu and his Army Chief of Staff, Colonel Mobutu, amidst rumours that Lumumba had accepted military and financial support from the Soviets to put down the Katanga rebellion.

On 14 September, Lumumba was unseated from power and placed under house arrest by Mobutu in a CIA-backed coup. In public, Hammarskjöld called for Lumumba to be treated according to due process of law; in private, the Secretary-General told senior diplomats that 'Lumumba must be "broken"'.[54] Appeals by Lumumba to local UN forces for protection following his escape from arrest came to no avail. On 17 January 1961, the country's first elected prime minister was tortured and killed—an act still viewed by many Congolese as 'the country's original sin'.[55]

Following Lumumba's death, ONUC's original policy was overturned and the Council authorized military operations in support of the government in Katanga.[56] The mission's complete abandonment of its passive stance and the forcing of Tshombe's surrender suggested to some that robust action was effective. However, the death of 249 UN peacekeepers—the largest number of fatalities of any UN mission, before and since—meant that even to those in support of an assertive role for ONUC, it was a pyrrhic victory.

The political fallout of ONUC's policy was tremendous. Lumumba's toppling, and enforcement activities in Katanga, led several Third World states to withdraw their contingents in protest over what they saw as the UN's distinctly partial role.[57] Similarly, the Soviet delegation in New York condemned Hammarskjöld for failing 'to display the minimum impartiality' and for 'functioning most unashamedly on the side of the colonialists, thus compromising the United Nations in the eyes of the world'.[58] These accusations eventually led the Soviet Union to propose the abolition of the position of Secretary-General, to be replaced by a 'troika,' representing Western, Socialist, and Non-Aligned Movement (NAM) countries.

While the Soviet proposal was ultimately rejected, the UN's involvement in Congo exposed the perils of deploying peacekeepers *within* a state and the challenges of passive impartiality. Political developments following the mission's arrival in Congo indicated the ephemeral nature of the initial consent secured for the mission and the fragility of what little authority ONUC may have had. In the context of the Cold War, in which competing visions of social and political order were precisely what the superpowers believed to be at stake, decisions by senior UN officials to liaise with one set of internal actors over another were invariably controversial, and were seen by some as indisputably partial.

The chastening experience in Congo resulted in a retrenchment to those few peacekeeping missions in which it was believed the holy trinity could be unquestionably upheld. Blue berets were deployed in Cyprus (UNFICYP) and again along the Egyptian–Israeli border (UNEF II), and observer missions were sent to monitor hostilities between India and Pakistan (UNIPOM), and Israel and Syria (UNDOF). With the exception of UNIFIL in Lebanon, which was the last mission to be deployed during the Cold War, these assignments generally consisted of lengthy monitoring missions in which forces could simply toe a blue line.[59]

PEACEKEEPING DURING THE 1990s

The easing of Cold War tensions resulted in newfound optimism over the UN's potential role in maintaining international peace. Renewed interest in peacekeeping, particularly on the part of the Soviets, indicated a growing receptivity towards multilateralism.[60] Following a decade-long hiatus, ten new UN missions were fielded between 1988 and 1991. In places like Namibia, El Salvador, and Cambodia, peacekeepers, as discussed below, played an active role in managing the transition from war to peace.

While these missions foreshadowed a new era of peacekeeping, the UN-authorized enforcement action against Iraq over Kuwait in 1990 was critical in re-energizing the doctrine of liberal internationalism that would fundamentally alter peacekeeping, its purposes, and the dominant understanding of impartiality at the end of the decade. The US-led coalition garnered an unprecedented degree of international support, signifying to many the beginning of what President George H.W. Bush exalted as the 'new world order', in which the UN 'was poised to fulfil the historic vision of its founders'.[61] With the sound and fury of the Cold War over, and its ideological cleavages erased, it was believed that a sort of 'natural contract' between states would once again characterize international relations and forge collective purposes.[62] To that end, on 31 January 1992, following the first-ever Security Council summit at the level of heads of state, the leaders in attendance issued a strongly worded statement asserting 'their commitment to the collective security of the charter'.[63]

An expanded definition of security and its concomitant threats was at the core of this new vision for managing global order. 'Human security', which shifted the referent from state to individual, became an increasing concern of the Council during the 1990s, prompting, in certain instances, authorization to use force for humanitarian ends under Chapter VII.[64] This change in Council practice was not solely attributable to the advent of a more complex world of heightened insecurity, as some suggested.[65] The Cold War was rife with threats to human life. Extreme violence against civilians—including genocide and crimes against humanity—occurred in such places as Cambodia, Bangladesh, and Uganda. However, collective action to protect and promote human rights was hindered by tensions between the superpowers and con- testation over the inherent meaning of these values.[66] That these sources of human vulnerability had *become* 'threats to international peace and security' was due perhaps less to an exogenous change, than to the fact that the Council now regarded them as such.[67]

Liberal Peacekeeping and the New World Order

This shift in the political and normative landscape had a significant impact on peacekeeping and its purposes. From December 1990 to July 1993, the number of UN personnel deployed surged from roughly 10,000 to over 78,000. In response to the flurry of activity, the Department of Peacekeeping Operations (DPKO) was created in 1992. Overnight, peacekeeping became a global activity. Missions were fielded in areas, including Europe, that previously would have been unthinkable, given the strategic stakes. The face of peace- keeping drastically changed as well. Britain, France, and the US—states that had been barred from contributing forces during the Cold War—became stalwart supporters of peacekeeping in the early 1990s.[68] The implicit assump- tion was that these troops could now be accepted both locally and internation- ally as unbiased actors, impartial in their decision-making and actions.

No longer principally confined to interposition *between* states or to observer tasks, deployment of peacekeepers *within* states began in the late 1980s to become the norm rather than the exception. In this new context, the 'peace' that blue helmets were tasked with 'keeping' and, in many cases, 'making' and 'building' fundamentally changed.[69] Peace was no longer the by-product of a debate between two competing visions of social and political order. With the end of the Cold War, peace became synonymous with the West's conception of peace and good government, and its concomitant revulsion against illegitimate forms of violence. The peace of the new world order was a liberal peace and peacekeepers were tasked with promul- gating 'a particular vision of how states should organize themselves intern- ally'. This vision was based, as Roland Paris notes, on 'the principles of liberal democracy and market-oriented economics'.[70]

The practices associated with liberal peacekeeping were a far cry from those undertaken during the Cold War. Operations in the late 1980s and early 1990s comprised a range of specialized elements, including military and civilian police, election monitors, and rule of law, human-rights, and gender experts, who sought to realize this more ambitious peace by assisting with constitution-drafting, election-monitoring, disarmament-programming, protection of humanitarian assistance, and implementation of agreements—what British Foreign Minister Douglas Hurd aptly called 'painting a country blue'.[71]

An Agenda for Peace

The seismic shift in the form and content of peacekeeping was rapid and unforeseen, and developed largely in the absence of an overarching UN security framework. Recognizing this deficiency and with a view to 'strengthening' and 'making more efficient' its engagement, the Security Council in 1992 commissioned a report from newly appointed Secretary-General, Boutros Boutros-Ghali. Buoyed by early successes in places like Cambodia and Namibia, the Secretary-General's *Agenda for Peace* presented an ambitious and proactive vision for realizing the liberal peace. Yet for all its zeal and alacrity, the Secretary-General's conceptual analysis of peacekeeping lacked rigour and clarity, raising more questions than it answered.

The Secretary-General acknowledged that the nature of peacekeeping operations had fundamentally changed. Nonetheless, he maintained that the traditional principles of peacekeeping and 'basic conditions for success remain[ed] unchanged'. What seemed to be an affirmation of the holy trinity outlined in the master texts was, however, at odds with his definition of peacekeeping as the 'deployment of a United Nations presence in the field, *hitherto* with the consent of all the parties concerned'.[72] The Secretary-General's proposal to create specialized 'peace enforcement units' further muddied the conceptual terrain, as the distinction between these units and peacekeeping forces deployed with or without consent, was not specified. Impartiality was mentioned only as a principle of humanitarian assistance.

The Secretary-General's qualification of the traditional requirement of consent was a significant departure from the 'tried-and true principles of UN peacekeeping' and was presented, as Adam Roberts lamented, without 'full discussion of all the implications'.[73] The challenges of attempting to engage as an impartial actor in contexts where one was not invited—the security and reputational risks, as well as sheer commitment such engagement required in places that now were often of marginal strategic interest to Council members—were given cursory consideration at best. The Secretary-General's report was, in sum, far from a clear and actionable agenda for peacekeeping in the post-Cold War world. As explained below, it provided little guidance in dealing with the tumultuous circumstances in which peacekeepers would soon become embroiled.

The Nadir of UN Peacekeeping and the Crisis
in Liberal Internationalism

The optimism pervasive in the early post-Cold War period was quickly curtailed by a string of peacekeeping failures that laid bare the difficulties of realizing a more ambitious liberal peace and the deficiencies of existing conceptual frameworks. If UN-authorized action in Iraq had been the harbinger of a 'new world order', the violence that engulfed the places in which peacekeepers were deployed in the mid-1990s suggested instead a world plagued by disorder. These conflicts were often a direct outgrowth of the Cold War—the breakup of empire, withdrawal of proxy patronage, and decades of economic dependency and stagnant development. Multiple competing factions vied for political and social authority in places choked with weapons and landmines. The toll on civilians was dire.

In such contexts, UN personnel were not alone in the challenges they faced. Indeed, the morass in which peacekeeping became mired pointed to a deeper crisis of liberal internationalism.[74] Humanitarian organizations also grappled with uncertainty over their role as third parties. Impartiality and neutrality—core norms of humanitarian action which traditionally meant that aid workers abstained from passing judgment on the cause or conduct of war in order to safeguard access and liaise with local authorities—came under sustained attack.[75] Scholars and practitioners warned of the dangers of 'supping with the devil' and media headlines shouted of 'militarised aid' and the 'well-fed dead' in places like eastern Zaire and Bosnia.[76]

At the crux of this crisis was the issue of authority, giving rise to what Anne Orford identifies as two sets of inter-related questions for humanitarians and peacekeepers alike.[77] The first set of questions concerned the authority of international actors as they engaged in contexts where consent was qualified. Without the consent of all parties and firm commitment to their objectives, on what basis could their decisions and actions be legitimate and impartial? From where and whom did their authority derive? Moreover, why should UN officials, rather than domestic or local authorities, have the power to use force and temporarily govern societies?

Inextricably linked to these concerns was a second set of questions concerning the relationship between international actors and local claimants to authority. How were international actors to decide with whom to coordinate and work in places where social divisions ran deep and authority was virulently contested? Whose acceptance, if any, was necessary for their presence? Could dialogue with all parties to a conflict, including those responsible for committing grievous suffering, be justified?

Without a clear conceptualization of their own authority and background of valuation on which to base their decisions and actions, peacekeepers and aid workers had no coherent answers to these questions. Nor could they justify, as

Orford explains, 'the political choices they were inevitably making by treating *génocidaires* in the same way as insurgents, or by liaising with warlords as well as parliamentarians'.[78]

Somalia, Rwanda, and the former Yugoslavia

The UN's engagement in Somalia, Rwanda, and the former Yugoslavia brought these questions to the fore and nearly led to peacekeeping's collapse. In each context, peace proved to be elusive and consent for the mission and its mandate was difficult, if not impossible, to obtain and maintain. Ceasefire and peace agreements, which frequently lacked buy-in, broke down and were suspended.

The first UN Operation in Somalia (UNOSOM) was deployed in 1992 to 'provide protection for humanitarian operations' and monitor a shaky cease-fire arrangement.[79] Without a sovereign government to offer its consent, however, the mission's deployment had only the temporary acquiescence of the main two factions.[80] That same year, after failed attempts by the European Community to negotiate peace, the UN Protection Force (UNPROFOR) was authorized as 'interim arrangement for the negotiation of an overall settlement of the Yugoslav crisis'.[81] While several groups agreed to the mission's deployment, others withheld their consent. In recommending the force, the Secretary-General gambled that the consequences of deployment without full consent were 'less grievous' than the danger of delay.[82] Finally, even the UN Assistance Mission for Rwanda (UNAMIR), which was based on the Arusha Peace Accords—an agreement that took years to negotiate and was signed by all the main parties—had dim prospects. The multiparty transition outlined in the Accords raised the stakes of peace and exacerbated tensions by creating a framework for democratization through which the Rwandan Patriotic Front (RPF) would come out as the strongest political force.[83]

The absence of a strong commitment to peace and the vagaries of consent in these contexts meant that the decisions and actions of peacekeepers were invariably viewed as partial: activities regarded as legitimate by one faction were criticized by others as furthering the war effort of their enemies. The myriad tasks which peacekeepers were authorized to carry out further widened the scope for criticism and instrumentalization by warring parties. Mandated to disarm militia, protect humanitarian assistance, and document human-rights violations, peacekeepers became either obstacles to the realization of war aims or pawns with which to achieve them.

In addition to these challenges, the issue of a mission's composition was still of consequence to its actual and perceived impartiality. With empire a seem-ingly distant memory, and fears of superpower meddling abated, the once delicate and contentious process of selecting troops for particular missions became a perfunctory exercise of matching supply with ever increasing demand. The assumption, however, that most soldiers could now serve as impartial peacekeepers, and be accepted as such, was flawed in two respects.

First, it assumed that history was of little consequence in shaping local perceptions of peacekeepers and their ability to be impartial. Reactions on the ground, however, suggested otherwise. In Rwanda, violent demonstrations took place when Belgium, the country's former colonial power, sent forces to join UNAMIR in 1994.[84] Colonial rule had entrenched ethnic divisionism and supported the Tutsi minority as the ruling class. Consequently, as Roméo Dallaire, Force Commander of UNAMIR, acerbically notes, it was hardly surprising that Belgium's involvement would deepen animosity towards the mission, particularly by radical Hutu factions.[85] On the first day of the genocide, ten Belgian troops assigned to guard the prime minister were killed and mutilated. In response, Belgium withdrew its forces. A report by the Belgian Senate following the genocide deplored the decision to deploy forces, arguing that in such circumstances there could be no question—or very little—of 'impartiality, a condition essential to the success of a peacekeeping operation'.[86]

Second, the lack of attention to troop selection and procedural requirements of impartiality disregarded the motivations compelling states to contribute forces to these more demanding missions. It discounted the possibility that peacekeeping in the name of the international community could mask more nefarious and partial interests of particular states. The French *Opération Turquoise*, deployed in the wake of the Rwandan genocide to set up 'safe zones', an operation which the Council specified should be 'conducted in an *impartial* and *neutral* fashion', provided jarring evidence to the contrary.[87] The French were long-time allies of Hutu President Juvénal Habyarimana and, until the start of the genocide, had provided military support to his government, making its subsequent involvement highly questionable.[88] While French forces managed to stem some violence by establishing a 'safe zone' in the Cyangugu-Kibuye-Gikongoro triangle, by refusing to detain *génocidaires* and by staving off RPF advancement by their very presence, *Opération Turquoise* opened the way for members of the Rwandan Armed Forces (FAR) and leaders of the *Interahamwe* to flee to neighbouring countries, causing conflict in the region for years to come, as detailed in Chapter 4.

In Somalia, it was not the involvement or motivations of particular troop-contributing countries that called into question the mission's impartiality, but rather the perceived bias of the Secretary-General. As Egypt's foreign minister from 1977 to 1991, Boutros-Ghali fostered close relations with former Somali President Siad Barre, the long-time foe of Mohamad Farah Aideed, leader of the Somali National Alliance (SNA), and a main faction leader with whom the UN had direct relations throughout the early 1990s.[89] When the Secretary-General visited the country in early 1993 he was met with large hostile demonstrations.[90] As discussed below, tensions between the UN and Aideed's faction eventually escalated to the point of all out battle.

The Delusion of Impartial Peacekeeping during War Time

The challenges of peacekeeping in contexts where consent was illusory and the impartiality of UN forces was questioned bore down on the Secretariat. Despite the odd veteran who remembered the tribulations of ONUC, the peacekeeping landscape that UN officials confronted was largely uncharted terrain. As Louise Fréchette, Canadian Permanent Representative to the UN from 1992–94 and later Deputy Secretary-General, recounts: 'In the 1990s, none of the member states nor the Secretariat really had any experience in what they were attempting to do... there was a lot of naiveté. They really thought that if you deployed lots of troops with a UN mandate that would do the trick... Well it didn't... There was improvisation every day.'[91]

The Council lurched from crisis to crisis, displaying an acute lack of strategic foresight. As the situation in a country would deteriorate, the Council was wont to issue new mandates and a slew of tasks; a piling up of purposes that critics argued was often a substitute for meaningful political engagement. Improvisation in New York led to chaos on the ground, as field officials grappled with increasingly complex, and often contradictory, mandates that were grossly under-resourced.

Peacekeeper responses to local actors that threatened civilians and challenged their mandate varied greatly both within and across missions. In some instances, peacekeepers were passive; in other instances, they used force to target specific intransigent groups and, more indiscriminately, in an effort to maintain an image of impartiality. The perceived failures of one mission shaped approaches in the next, and confusion over the meaning of impartiality was rife.

In Somalia, the UN mission abandoned all pretence of being passively impartial, following the killing of twenty-four Pakistani peacekeepers in June 1993. Resolution 837 authorized the mission to take 'all necessary measures' against those responsible for the attack, and explicitly named the party at fault—the SNA.[92] The change in mandate transformed the mission and local perceptions of it.[93] Confrontations between UN forces and the SNA escalated, culminating on 3 October 1993 in the attempted capture of Aideed's cabinet members in the Olympic Hotel and the shooting-down of three US Black Hawk helicopters which had been deployed to reinforce UN troops. Images of dead US personnel, pulled from the wreckage and dragged through the streets of Mogadishu by a Somali mob, were broadcast around the world.

Somalia cast a long shadow over peacekeeping. By crossing what became known as the 'Mogadishu line,' US–UN forces had, it was argued, steered peacekeeping into dangerous waters.[94] The loss of impartiality, combined with the absence of consent, was understood as the determining factor in crossing that line. Senior UN officials emphasized that any action that jeopardized a mission's impartiality, thereby dragging its forces into a potential conflict was to be avoided at all costs.[95] However, as Michael Barnett remembers, the UN's adherence to 'the rules' meant that they 'became ends in themselves'.[96]

The 'lessons' of Somalia were felt most acutely in Rwanda. That Kigali could become another Mogadishu was a pervasive concern in the Secretariat and Western capitals. For example, Dallaire's request for authorization from headquarters to raid a major weapons cache was denied for fear of losing the consent of the government, thereby jeopardizing UNAMIR's impartiality. The cache went untouched, and when the killing began shortly thereafter, UN forces were, as Colonel Marchal notes, left in the excruciating position of having to 'just stay and watch without reaction'.[97] Between April and July 1994, in what was one of the UN's darkest hours, Hutu extremists, largely unopposed by peacekeepers, systematically murdered over 800,000 Tutsis and Hutu moderates.

Impartiality was also an issue in the former Yugoslavia, where, by the end of 1992, UNPROFOR's remit extended to Croatia, Bosnia and Herzegovina, Macedonia, Montenegro, and Serbia. Through successive UN resolutions, the mission was authorized to undertake a broad range of contradictory tasks.[98] In practice, these tasks amounted to a 'limited but impartial involvement' for the UN, but one that, as Richard Betts noted bitingly, 'abetted slow-motion savagery'.[99] Measures that helped one side were offset by actions that helped the other. This duplicity, Betts notes, 'alienated [parties] and enabled them to keep fighting the other'.[100]

In Sarajevo where, among other tasks, UNPROFOR was in charge of maintaining security of the 'neutral airport', the force's ostensible commitment to impartiality resulted in action that directly imperilled civilians. Placed between the besieged city and Bosnian Serbs, the UN-controlled airport became an ever more dangerous barrier to those attempting to flee Sarajevo. 'UNPROFOR troops patrolling the area were determined to upkeep UN impartiality, often at a terrible expense.'[101] As Nedzad Brankovic, an engineer who designed a tunnel that was eventually dug underneath the airport, recalls: 'As we ran across the airport the UN troops tried to stop us. They would chase us and shine big lights in our direction. The [Serb] snipers would lie in wait and shoot many of those left defenceless in the glare of the spotlights...'[102] An estimated 250 people were killed trying to flee across the tarmac, leading the population to charge that UNPROFOR was, indeed, a misnomer for a force that provided little in the way of protection.[103]

It was, however, the tragedies in the UN 'safe areas' in Bosnia which were most damning and had the greatest impact on the reinterpretation of impartiality. Peacekeepers deployed to protect the six designated enclaves had few means to enforce their mandate on the ground and, according to Resolution 836, were to rely on air power supplied by NATO forces to deter attacks committed predominantly by Bosnian Serbs.[104] This arrangement was even more problematic given the mission's mandate to disarm the enclaves and enforce an arms embargo. 'Pinprick' air raids provoked Serb retaliation without deterring aggression or neutralizing the threat, thereby making populations inside the safe zones more vulnerable. When the safe area of Srebrenica was attacked in 1995, having been demilitarized by UNPROFOR, the Bosnians were largely unable to defend themselves, and UNPROFOR troops, themselves only lightly armed, merely fired warning shots over the attacking Serbs, lest aiming more directly engulf them in the fray. When two bombs were eventually dropped by NATO on the Bosnian Serbs' armoury, General Ratko Mladic responded by threatening to kill UNPROFOR troops and, as predicted by Serbian forces, the UN and NATO withdrew. UNPROFOR abandoned the city on foot and NATO ceased its bombing. With Srebrenica under their control, the Serbs moved in to ethnically cleanse the area, 'evacuating women and children to Tuzla, but drawing aside men' for mass execution.[105]

Operational Retrenchment and Conceptual Confusion

These harrowing experiences resulted in the UN's retreat from peacekeeping. Many within the Secretariat believed peacekeeping should 'go back to the basics' and deployments were limited to contexts where the traditional trinity could be upheld.[106] The boom was followed by a resounding bust. In 1992 roughly 70,000 peacekeepers were deployed under the auspices of the UN. By 1996, the number had been reduced to fewer than 20,000 worldwide. From late 1993 to 1998, the organization fielded only one new large mission, in Eastern Slovenia.[107]

In 1995, Boutros-Ghali issued a *Supplement to the Agenda for Peace*. More modest and cautious than his previous report, it was an attempt to reflect on recent tragedies and take stock of what he labelled as the 'new kind of UN operation'.[108] However, similar to his initial agenda, the supplement provided little conceptual clarity. The Secretary-General simply reasserted that consent, impartiality, and non-use of force were 'essential' to a mission's success and constitution.[109] Moreover, recalling the controversial *Opération Turquoise* in Rwanda, the supplement confusingly characterized the 'new kind' of operation as one in which forces, authorized under Chapter VII, should be 'neutral *and* impartial'.[110]

The supplement's inherent confusion over the meaning of impartiality and, by extension, the role of peacekeepers, was further compounded by the proliferation of national peacekeeping manuals and doctrines published in the mid-to-late 1990s.[111] These documents reflected the increasing reluctance of many Western states to participate in UN-led missions, the growing tendency of the Council to authorize peacekeeping under the auspices of regional organizations or lead-states, and an attempt by those participating in these alternative institutional arrangements to professionalize multilateral peace exercises. The resulting texts displayed an array of interpretations of the traditional trinity, leading Stephen Stedman to note in 1996 that 'when different armies speak of consent, neutrality, and impartiality, they now mean different things'.[112] Conceptual confusion persisted, and grew.

PEACEKEEPING IN THE NEW MILLENNIUM

The advent of several new conflicts in 1999 brought the crisis of liberal internationalism and attendant questions about authority to a head. After a five-year lull, the Council authorized the creation of four new peacekeeping missions within six months (UNTAET in East Timor, MONUC in the Democratic Republic of the Congo, UNAMSIL in Sierra Leone, and UNMIK in Kosovo), nearly doubling the number of peacekeepers deployed worldwide. These missions were quickly followed by several other large missions—UNMIL in Liberia, UNOCI in Ivory Coast, ONUB in Burundi, and MINUSTAH in Haiti—all unparalleled in their complexity and range of activities.

As new missions deployed, old tensions resurfaced. In late 1999, two lessons-learned reports on the UN's experience in Rwanda and Srebrenica were released, which highlighted, in particular, the 'problem of impartiality'.[113] Sobering and unsparing reminders of the challenges confronted by peacekeepers, they reopened old wounds, not least in the Secretariat, where Kofi Annan, who had been in charge of peacekeeping from 1993 to 1995, now served as Secretary-General. 'There was a deep embarrassment with what happened' as Jean-Marie Guéhenno, the newly appointed head of DPKO, remembers: 'a sense of shame amongst the Secretariat and member states—amongst everybody really—and so you had to reconceptualize [peacekeeping]'.[114] With the Council once again keen on deploying blue helmets, the time had come to forge a more coherent organizational identity and clearer purpose for peacekeeping in the new millennium.

A New Understanding of Impartiality

In March 2000, Secretary-General Annan convened a high-level panel of experts, led by Algerian diplomat Lakhdar Brahimi, to review the organization's activities in the area of peace and security. Published in August 2000, the *Brahimi Report* provided an in-depth critique of peacekeeping and identified areas for reform.

The *Brahimi Report* was first to articulate what is now the prevailing understanding of impartiality as a norm of UN peacekeeping. This conception was further institutionalized in other UN policy documents, including the 2003 *Peacekeeping Handbook* and 2008 *Principles and Guidelines* (otherwise referred to as the '*Capstone Doctrine*').[115] The latter is notable in that it is the first and only attempt by the UN to develop a comprehensive peacekeeping doctrine. It continues to serve as a touchstone for contemporary practice.

Rather than representing a novel departure, the understanding of impartiality that is institutionalized in the *Brahimi Report* 'expressed and codified a change that was already underway', as one official involved with the panel recounts.[116] The new formulation of impartiality reflected the evolving content of Council mandates at the end of the 1990s, it converged with Western doctrine and, as I describe below, was an integral part of the turn towards a more assertive liberal internationalism.

The understanding of impartiality institutionalized at the UN since 2000 differs from previous conceptions of what I have termed the composite norm. Under the new conception, the procedural requirements remain largely the same—that is, the condition that peacekeepers be unbiased and informed, and implement their mandate without 'favour or prejudice to any party', as the *Capstone Doctrine* states.[117] Rather, the transformation is in the *basis for* decision-making, which is now significantly broader than those terms set by parties to a particular dispute and agreed to by the Council. In other words, the background of valuation from which actors are expected to make decisions and take action, and from which they derive much of their authority *as* impartial actors, has fundamentally changed. The content and objectives of mandates are radically different than those authorized previously by the Council. They represent a more expansive and normatively ambitious basis for judgment that extends beyond the peace agreement to which parties may or may not have consented.

The *Brahimi Report*, *Peacekeeping Handbook*, and *Capstone Doctrine*, as well as UN official statements, are somewhat inconsistent and vague in specifying the precise source of this more expansive background of valuation, citing international humanitarian law, human-rights law, the UN Charter, and international norms more generally.[118] They are, however, unified by the idea that peacekeeper impartiality should no longer be contingent upon, or constrained by, securing the continual consent of all parties within a specific context, particularly when civilians are in peril. As a background report for the *Capstone Doctrine* asserts:

> Impartiality... is about ensuring that what is supposed to happen does happen... that international laws and norms are respected, that UN mandates are fulfilled, and that agreements concluded between contending parties and endorsed by the UN are honoured both in spirit and in practice... It is about ensuring that this all happens regardless of what some might have preferred or some might now prefer.[119]

Impartiality, as the *Brahimi Report* states, means 'adherence to the principles of the Charter and to the objectives of a mandate that is rooted in those

Charter principles'.[120] In contrast to the passive conception of the norm inscribed in the master texts during the Cold War, peacekeepers, according to the *Handbook*, must now 'actively pursue the implementation of their mandate even if doing so goes against the interests of one or more of the parties'.[121] Peacekeeping missions, as the *Capstone Doctrine* emphasizes, should not 'condone actions by the parties that violate the undertakings of the peace process or the international norms and principles that a UN peacekeeping operation upholds'.[122]

By expanding the *basis for* judgment to encompass conditions that may not be agreed to by all parties to a dispute, the new conception of impartiality calls into question the very notion of consent. While the condition of consent has not been completely abandoned and is in theory required at the strategic level, as discussed below, its significance has been dramatically reduced. That most missions since 1999 have been authorized through invocation of Chapter VII and thus do not formally require consent as a legal prerequisite for deployment or to undertake particular actions, is testament to the established dominance of the new understanding of the norm and, relatedly, to a new role for UN peacekeepers.

No longer commensurate with the impartial mediator whose judgments are based on terms set by those parties consenting to mediation, the blue helmets of today are more akin to police officers that enforce the law and 'penalize infractions'.[123] As Professor Michael Doyle, who closely followed the panel's work and was involved with the Secretary-General's follow-up report *No Exit No Strategy*, remembers:

> The analogy that was often used was the cop on the beat who is impartial in the enforcement of the law—who stops the criminal activity—who shoots and/or arrests the criminal . . . Impartiality, the right doctrine, means that without fear or favour—whoever is the victim will be supported to stop victimization more widely.[124]

The characterization of peacekeeping as policing which finds expression in the *Brahimi Report* and *Capstone Doctrine*, resonates with the scholarship of Mary Kaldor and others who in the late 1990s called for a new genre of peacekeeping as 'cosmopolitan law enforcement'.[125] A reconceptualization of impartiality was at the core of Kaldor's vision in which peacekeeping forces would uphold 'the rules' and ensure compliance with 'international humanitarian and human rights law'.[126] Enforcement of 'the rules' and 'law' was legitimate insofar as they reflected 'universal principles' and a common commitment to human values. 'The point', Kaldor underscored, was for peacekeepers 'to retain impartiality from the point of view of the victims.'[127]

While not framed explicitly as such, peacekeeping in the new millennium hews closely to this law-enforcement vision, perceivable in the proliferation of tasks mandated by the Council and the increasing number of police and rule-of-law experts that are regularly deployed in contemporary UN missions.[128]

This shift in thinking about the role of peacekeepers is premised to a large extent on a particular understanding of violence as illegitimate and criminal—a notion that captured headlines in the West and was promulgated by scholars and practitioners in the late 1990s.[129] As Kaldor asserts: 'these wars are not football matches; the various parties do not accept the rules. On the contrary, the nature of these wars is rule-breaking. The point is rather to persuade ordinary people of the advantages of rules so as to isolate and marginalise those who break them'.[130]

According to this view, conflict in the post-Cold War era is less about politics and ideology than about profit and plunder, or atavistic and ancient enmities. A distinction is drawn between the 'old' wars, which are considered 'ideological, political, collective, even noble', and the 'new' wars, characterized principally as 'criminal, depoliticized, private and predatory'.[131] For some, the utter 'barbarism' of conflict in the post-Cold War era even signalled that it is 'about *nothing at all*'.[132]

With violence now understood as a form of moral collapse, the new understanding of impartiality is an attempt to address the conceptual morass of the 1990s, confusion over the position and posture of peacekeepers, and their relations with local actors. As police forces maintain order in general, peacekeepers now also claim an impartial authority over parties within the context of deployment, without bias or commitment to any side. Contemporary peacekeepers, vested with the authority of the 'law', are tasked with deciding what constitutes 'right' and 'wrong', and distinguishing 'victim' from 'aggressor' or 'perpetrator'. Concomitantly, from acting impartially *between* or among parties, the authority of peacekeeping missions has transformed into claiming authority *over* parties based on a more expansive background of valuation that concerns itself first and foremost with human rights. This change cements peacekeeping as a seemingly more virtuous activity, albeit one that is significantly militarized.

'Robust' Peace Operations

The use of force is inextricably linked to this role transformation. In marked contrast to the strong aversion to the use of force during the Cold War and the vicissitudes of peacekeeper responses to violence during the 1990s for fear of being perceived as partial, the *Brahimi Report* is unequivocal in countenancing that peacekeepers be given authority to use force. Blue helmets must be prepared to 'confront lingering forces of war and violence with the ability and determination to defeat them'.[133] In certain cases where 'local parties consist not of moral equals but of obvious aggressors and victims', the *Report* affirms, peacekeepers are not only 'operationally justified in using force but morally compelled to do so'.[134] Peacekeepers must at times 'oppose obvious evil'.[135]

In this way, the reformulation of impartiality has been closely tied to 'robust' peacekeeping—a concept that first figured in the *Brahimi Report* and has since taken hold.[136] The Council has developed what scholars describe as a 'vocabulary of robustness' in authorizing resolutions, and missions have frequently been buttressed with unambiguously muscular 'rules of engagement' (RoE) that include provisions for pre-emptive and proactive uses of force against likely attackers.[137] 'My RoE', as a military advisor deployed in Congo offered, 'is not very different from the one I had in Afghanistan.'[138] A study comparing the *Capstone Doctrine* and *US Army Counterinsurgency Field Manual* found much convergence in the concepts and operational modalities of both documents.[139] In addition, DPKO has incorporated the use of new technologies such as aerial surveillance drones and developed intelligence and analysis capabilities.[140]

This more robust and militarized approach has emphasized two related purposes to which peacekeepers should impartially use force: to protect civilians and confront 'spoilers' of the peace. I discuss each of these below, before considering how this change is embedded in the emergence of a more assertive liberal internationalism.

Protection of Civilians

At the core of the new understanding of impartiality and robust peacekeeping is the assertion that peacekeepers have a responsibility to protect civilians.[141] This is a direct response to the failures of peacekeepers in the preceding decade to shield civilians from slaughter, including mass atrocities and genocide. Echoing the Rwanda study, the *Brahimi Report* is forthright in arguing that peacekeepers 'who witness violence against civilians should be presumed to be authorized to stop it, within their means, in support of basic UN principles'.[142] Similarly, the *Capstone Doctrine* designates protection of civilians as a 'cross-cutting' responsibility that peacekeepers are expected to fulfil, even when it is not explicitly in their mandate.[143] As a joint DPKO and OCHA study on protection explains:

> There is no more compelling or credible stance for a mission than to advocate for the most vulnerable ... That role is the basis of the UN's moral authority, and a powerful tool ... [T]his apolitical but firm stance will help deliver credence to the mission's authority and determination to use its impartiality against those who challenge its efforts.[144]

While many peacekeeping missions in the 1990s were involved in human-rights monitoring, the safeguarding of assistance corridors, and escort of humanitarian convoys, explicit authorization to protect civilians under Chapter VII was first mandated by the Council in 1999 with respect to the situation in Sierra Leone. According to Resolution 1270, the UN Mission in Sierra Leone (UNAMSIL) was 'to afford protection to civilians under imminent threat of physical violence'.[145] UNAMSIL's landmark mandate was authorized on the heels of Resolution 1265—the first of many thematic resolutions passed by the Council on the protection of civilians in armed conflict.[146]

Since 1999 the protection of civilians (PoC) has become a central item on the Council's agenda, a critical component of peacekeeping mandates and, arguably, the most important determinant of mission success.[147] No armed UN mission has been newly deployed without a PoC mandate and, as of October 2015, 98 per cent of uniformed personnel deployed under the aegis of DPKO are explicitly mandated to protect civilians.[148] According to Resolution 1894 (2009), mission resources are to be prioritized for PoC during mandate implementation and specific protection strategies have been authorized in several contexts.[149] Additionally, the Council has delegated authority to regional peacekeeping arrangements to protect civilians in contexts such as Somalia, Central African Republic, and Congo.[150]

These developments are part of a broader trend in which civilian protection has risen to the forefront of international concern and become a consistent aim of responses to the worst of today's crises by a range of actors that claim to act impartially on behalf of victims. Within the UN system, Ban Ki-moon's *Human Rights Up Front* policy, puts the imperative to protect people from serious violations of human rights and international humanitarian law at the core of the organization's strategy and operational activity, and obligates all staff to speak out on an 'impartial basis' about human-rights abuses and looming crises.[151]

The UN's emphasis on protection as a collective responsibility (and not merely a discretionary right) is an extension of the Responsibility to Protect (RtoP) principle.[152] Pioneered by the work of the International Commission on Intervention and State Sovereignty (ICISS) in 2001 and adopted by the General Assembly in 2005, RtoP maintains: that states have a responsibility to protect their populations; that the international community has a duty to assist states to fulfil this responsibility; and that, should a state 'manifestly fail' to protect its populations, the international community should take 'timely and decisive' action to safeguard civilians.[153] The prioritization of PoC in peacekeeping has developed alongside and, at times, been closely associated with RtoP. Ban Ki-moon has, for example, referred to peacekeeping as a core area in which RtoP must be 'mainstreamed' as a goal.[154]

Despite sharing similar legal and normative underpinnings, PoC and RtoP differ in several respects that, as the following chapter examines, are politically salient.[155] While RtoP addresses a specific set of extreme situations in which any of four crimes have been committed (genocide, war crimes, ethnic cleansing, and crimes against humanity), PoC tackles a broader set of threats and is concerned with violence that is directed at civilians in conflict and post-conflict settings more generally. In addition to differences in scope, the central assertion of RtoP that a state's right to non-intervention is conditional on meeting minimal standards of behaviour is controversial in that it potentially allows the international community to use force against a state. In this respect, NATO's campaign against the Libyan Armed Forces of President Gaddafi in 2011, which was authorized by the Council with the explicit aim of protecting civilians, signalled to many a deep commitment to RtoP and humanitarian intervention's 'coming of age'.[156]

In contrast, peacekeeping missions still require, in theory, consent at the strategic level, including, critically, that of the host state. Moreover, to allay concerns over possible infringements to sovereignty and manage expectations both locally and globally, peacekeeping resolutions have at times stipulated that peacekeepers protect civilians 'within their capabilities and areas of deployment' and with 'respect to the responsibilities' of the host state. These caveats notwithstanding, the distinction between the two norms is at times exceptionally fine, revealing, as I will explain, ambiguities inherent in the new understanding of the norm and, specifically, what it means for peacekeepers to 'impartially' protect civilians.

Dealing with 'Spoilers'

Closely related to protection of civilians is the assertion that peacekeepers should take action against so-called 'spoilers' of peace. The term 'spoiler' was introduced in the late 1990s, largely through the work of Stephen Stedman. According to Stedman, this expansive category of actor encompasses individuals and groups who derail peace agreements or obstruct law and order more generally, including those who imperil civilians. Stedman maintained that with a nuanced understanding of spoilers, 'custodians of the peace', such as peacekeepers, could be more effective in developing strategies to remove, reduce, or contain threats.[157]

While the term is relatively new, confronting spoilers per se is not. As I described, in the early 1990s peacekeepers in Somalia and Bosnia were authorized to use force against recalcitrant actors. Of critical importance, however, is the fact that such action was cast as a departure from impartial peacekeeping. Conversely, according to the new understanding of the norm, peacekeepers are permitted to take forcible action against spoilers without siding with a party to the conflict; indeed, it suggests that peacekeepers have a moral obligation to do so. As the *Brahimi Report* states in no uncertain terms: 'where one party to a peace agreement clearly and incontrovertibly is violating its terms, continued equal treatment of all parties by the UN can in the best case result in ineffectiveness and in the worst may amount to complicity with evil'.[158]

In addition to the moral imperative, dealing with spoilers is viewed as necessary for operational effectiveness, a signal that the UN 'means business'.[159]

Brahimi and other officials highlight, in particular, how their reconceptualization of impartiality was influenced by what they perceived as the successful expansion of UNAMSIL's mandate in early 2000.[160] Following attacks on and the hostage taking of UN personnel by the Revolutionary United Front (RUF), the Council called for enforcement action by peacekeepers against the RUF and authorized the deployment of British rapid reaction forces. The RUF's actions were in breach of the Lomé Peace Agreement, of which it was a main signatory, and, according to the Council, constituted 'a breakdown of the prior, generally permissive environment based on the Agreement'.[161] The release of the hostages and forced submission of the RUF was an example of how, by dealing with spoilers, peacekeepers could bring about peace. As Louise Fréchette, then Deputy Secretary-General explains: 'it was a critical indication that robust peacekeeping could work'.[162]

Since 2000, the Council has continued to authorize the use of force to confront spoilers. However, in contrast to UNAMSIL, operations conducted against spoilers have not been confined to those who signed, but subsequently reneged on, a peace agreement; or similarly those who consented to the deployment of a peacekeeping mission and its mandate. In contexts such as Haiti, Congo, Mali, and CAR, the use of force has been authorized against groups deemed to pose a threat to peace and order, more generally. Moreover, resolutions that include specifications to take action against spoilers have often been passed in conjunction with economic and commodity sanctions intended to restrict their access to resources. The broadening of what constitutes spoiling activity to include, for example, domestic and transnational organized crime, further substantiates the parallel between contemporary peacekeeping and law enforcement.[163] As described below, it is also characteristic of what scholars describe as the increasing legalization of the international sphere, criminalization of certain behaviours within conflict and post-conflict settings, and a shift from a consent-based paradigm to a more compulsory paradigm of international adjudication.[164]

Assertive Liberal Internationalism

The transformation I have described in peacekeeping must be understood as an integral part of a broader shift towards a more assertive liberal internationalism. Just as peacekeepers and UN officials sought to clarify their role and justify their authority, so too did other international actors engaged in conflict and post-conflict settings at the end of 1990s. The promotion and protection of human rights is at the core of this broader change and has translated into forms of international engagement that are less consensual and more compulsory and coercive. Simply put, liberal internationalism packs a lot more punch.

The shift has been most pronounced in two areas of international engagement where impartiality also figures as a core norm: humanitarianism and international criminal justice. Understanding developments in each of these areas is important to grasp the broader context of the change in peacekeeping, but also because a defining feature of assertive liberal internationalism has been the emphasis on strengthening and deepening cooperation and integration between areas of engagement. This has prompted significant bureaucratic, conceptual, and operational restructuring both internal and external to the UN system.[165]

What underpins this new approach? How can the demonstrably more conditional and coercive practices of humanitarians and prosecutors as well as robust peacekeepers be justified *as* impartial?

The legitimacy of this more assertive approach rests largely on what is extolled as a newfound unity of purpose. Academics and practitioners contend that the 'internationalization of human rights'[166] over several decades has allowed for an acceptable transformation in the foundation of certain norms that now have authority not because they are based strictly on the consent of states, but rather because they are seen to reflect a collective international consensus—what scholar Ruti Teitel describes as 'humanity's law'.[167]

For Teitel, humanity law constitutes a 'dynamic unwritten constitution' of the contemporary international legal order, reflected in customary international law, the merging of IHL and IHRL, and aimed at 'the recognition and preservation of humankind in global politics'.[168] According to Teitel, humanity law's real power is constitutive: it is defined by the activity of locating some basis for common norms in the international realm, a context traditionally marked by the absence of community. Through this process, as she explains: '[t]he otherwise elusive world community comes to recognize itself in the act of judging that someone is outside the bounds, beyond its normative limits. The universalizable recognition or judgment recognition of the offender implies a dynamic basis for evaluation that goes to the human being and his/her/their status and treatment, a shared subject that appeals to common values and, hence, to universality.'[169]

In this way, cooperation and integration figure as important features of assertive liberal internationalism in part because they are regarded as springing from the same source. No longer distinct or completely separate areas of engagement, robust peacekeeping, humanitarianism, and international criminal justice are, as I explain below, regarded as complementary and constitutive tools in what practitioners and scholars describe as the 'growing tool kit of conflict management strategies' that seek to realize common, indeed, universal values.[170]

Humanitarian Action

In the humanitarian sphere, this change has become manifest in the transition that many organizations, and in particular UN humanitarian agencies, made in the late 1990s from a 'needs-based' assistance delivery model, to one that more explicitly encompasses a concern for human rights.[171] The 'rights-based approach' (RBA), as it is widely called, is premised on the notion that humanitarian needs arise to a large extent from violations of rights, and that consequently actors should address the underlying structural causes of vulnerability in addition to and in support of meeting basic needs. This has introduced new parameters around and, conditionality for, aid. Decisions about who should receive assistance are now partly based on whether they help or hinder the realization of human rights, and assistance that is likely to fuel conflict or legitimize certain factions may be withheld. Critics charge that the RBA has created a hierarchy of 'deserving' aid recipients in which those in greatest need are sometimes deprived of relief because of their direct or indirect affiliation with parties accused of human-rights abuses.[172]

In addition to influencing who receives assistance, the RBA has altered the types of assistance delivered. Beginning in the late 1990s, many humanitarian organizations became multi-mandated institutions that work along a relief–development continuum. Along this continuum, the realization and promotion of rights is commonly framed as 'protection'.[173] Indeed 'protection', no longer the sole purview of ICRC and UNHCR, has become an overarching priority for many humanitarians across their expanded remit of programming.[174] This is a notable departure. Whereas in the past humanitarians restricted their activities to the delivery of emergency assistance and were reluctant to pass judgment on warring parties to ensure access to those most in need, today many aim to protect civilians by speaking out against abuses, and by actively seeking to reform political and social structures that impinge on human rights.

As the role of humanitarians has evolved, so too has their relationship with peacekeepers. During the 1990s, humanitarians and peacekeepers frequently operated in the same context and in several instances coordinated activities, including the safeguarding of humanitarian access to vulnerable populations by peacekeeping forces. In the last decade, these partnerships have deepened and intensified, particularly within the UN system. The integration of 'all activities aimed at consolidating peace' is a formal UN policy, applicable to conflict and post-conflict settings where the organization has a country team and multi-dimensional peacekeeping operation or country-specific political mission.[175]

In peacekeeping, this has prompted numerous reforms, including the development of integrated planning mechanisms and creation of the post of Deputy Special Representative of the Secretary-General (DSRSG/RC/HC)—

'triple-hat role' that encompasses the humanitarian coordinator (HC) and resident coordinator (RC) of the development agencies within a particular country. In addition to facilitating integration across the UN family, in some contexts the offices of the DSRSG and OCHA serve as the focal point for co-ordination with the wider humanitarian community. They work closely with the UN Department for Safety and Security (UNDSS), which was established in 2005 following the bombing of the UN's compound in Baghdad, to monitor, assess, and ensure security as part of an integrated UN presence. Consequently, in some contexts, decisions about who is to receive assistance, where and how, are more closely aligned with broader peacekeeping policy.

International Justice and Crimes of International Concern

The second area where this shift has been prominent is in the field of international criminal justice, which has evolved rapidly in the last two decades, building in large part on the international legal framework for human rights developed following the Second World War. During the 1990s, the ICTR and ICTY were created to prosecute war crimes committed in Rwanda and the former Yugoslavia respectively.[176] Established by the Security Council under Chapter VII, both ad hoc tribunals had primacy over national domestic agents and did not require explicit consent for their operation from the states concerned.

These temporary international tribunals, as well as the establishment of several hybrid courts, laid the groundwork for the International Criminal Court (ICC) in 2002—what many regarded as a watershed moment in the global fight against impunity. Founded by the 1998 Rome Statute, to which over 123 states are now signatories, the ICC is unprecedented in that it is the first *permanent* international judicial body mandated to impartially investigate international crimes and try alleged perpetrators.[177] While the ICC's treaty would suggest to some a more consensual model of adjudication than that of the tribunals, the Court's reach extends beyond those states that have consented to the organization by ratifying the Statute. The Court may, for instance, prosecute nationals of states not party to the Statute if they have committed international crimes on the territory or against nationals of states party to the Statute.[178] Additionally, the Security Council may, acting under Chapter VII, refer a situation in which crimes appear to have been committed to the ICC prosecutor. To date, the Council has referred two situations— Sudan (2005) and Libya (2011)—to the Court. In both instances, the states under investigation were not party to the Statute.

To carry out its functions, the ICC relies heavily on cooperation with signatory states. However, since its inception, various organizations have rendered assistance to the Court through the provision of documentation and expert testimony. It is perhaps testament to the significance of the

Congo case that the first witness to appear before the Court was a child protection advisor from MONUC.[179] Part 9 of the Rome Statute provides the legal basis for such assistance by allowing the Court to invite cooperation from international organizations and non-state parties. In addition to providing information, peacekeeping missions have provided logistical support to investigation teams, and assisted with security of suspects and witnesses. These arrangements fall outside the legal parameters of Part 9 and have required, according to Article 54, that the Prosecutor enter into separate agreements. In 2004, the ICC–UN Relationship Agreement was signed, committing the UN to a general 'obligation of cooperation and coordination' with the Court.[180] The Office of the Prosecutor has also signed separate memoranda of understanding (MoU) with specific peacekeeping missions such as that in Congo.[181] The Court emphasizes the necessity of such cooperative arrangements, not least because access is precarious in many of the situations under investigation.[182] Humanitarians and peacekeepers are esteemed by the Office of the Prosecutor as 'crucial partners' in the fight against impunity.[183]

INSTITUTIONALIZED AND AMBIGUOUS

Yet despite its appearance of coherence, the new dominant conception of impartiality—institutionalized at the UN and situated in this broader turn towards assertive liberal internationalism—remains ambiguous. In what follows, I highlight three ways in which the norm continues to be imprecise in the context of peacekeeping. This discussion sets the stage for the following chapter, which calls into question the purported consensus over the meaning of impartiality in peacekeeping (particularly the *basis for* impartial decision-making). It elucidates the ways in which this ambiguity reflects contestation over the new understanding of impartiality and in doing so sheds light on the politics of contemporary peacekeeping and assertive liberal internationalism at the macro-level.

Whither Consent? Whose Consent?

The first area of ambiguity concerns the *basis for* decision-making and limits to the authority of peacekeepers, specifically as to when and in relation to whom peacekeepers should impartially implement their mandate. The documents institutionalizing the new understanding of impartiality recognize that consent for a mission is no longer absolute or fixed; that it will frequently be 'manipulated',[184] 'uncertain and unreliable'.[185] Nonetheless, the requirement of consent has not been abandoned. Consent for a mission and more broadly some form of commitment to a political process continues to be a prerequisite for the deployment of most missions.

A 'fundamental premise' of the *Brahimi Report* is that peacekeepers have authority to respond to deteriorating consent or challenges to the mission by impartially 'carry[ing] out their mandate' and by 'adhering to the principles of the charter'.[186] Thus, according to the *Report*, it would seem that consent is to be obtained as a 'one off' either through the initial consent given for a mission's deployment or by accession to the UN through the adoption of the Charter, and that subsequent to this initial offering, action may be taken without concern that parties will retract their consent.[187] The basis for such action is, however, somewhat opaquely defined. Reference to the Charter, which under Article 2 includes norms of sovereign equality and non-interference, complicates the scope of loyalty for peacekeepers and introduces ambiguity over whether they may take action against *all* parties to a particular dispute, including state actors. This ambiguity is further compounded by the authorization of most missions in part or full under Chapter VII.

The *Capstone Doctrine* presents a more nuanced treatment of consent. It differentiates between consent at the strategic level (obtained from the main parties, including the host state) and tactical level (obtained from non-state actors, including local groups or factions on the fringe of a peace or political process). The former is stated as a requirement of any peacekeeping mission and must not be jeopardized. The latter is no longer deemed necessary— forceful action should be carried out at the tactical level against those who challenge the mandate. This distinction, according to the *Doctrine*, is what separates peace*keeping* from peace *enforcement*.[188]

The *Capstone Doctrine*'s differentiation between levels is, however, mired in confusion and contradiction. The selectivity of response inherent in drawing such a distinction is fundamentally at odds with the *Doctrine*'s stipulation that impartiality requires that peacekeepers 'must implement their mandate without favour or prejudice to *any* party', particularly when civilians are imperilled. Moreover, it is incongruent with the Chapter VII authorization under which most missions operate. Furthermore, even if such contradictions are left aside, the distinction is unclear, as the *Doctrine* leaves ill-defined the actors and groups associated with each level. No additional information on what constitutes a 'main party' is provided, other than the specification that it includes the host state. By this account, it is not clear whether the assertive action undertaken by peacekeepers against the RUF in Sierra Leone, which, for many, was an indication of robust peacekeeping's effectiveness, would have been allowed; the RUF was a 'main party', a signatory to the Lomé Agreement. Moreover, the possibility that actors may be internally fragmented, operate simultaneously at both the strategic and tactical level, or use proxy forces receives little consideration.

Last, the assertion that strategic consent must be safeguarded raises a separate but related issue concerning impartiality. The doctrine's unequivocal inclusion of host state consent in the otherwise vague category of 'main party' attests to the privileged role enjoyed by states in peacekeeping. This privileging is illustrated by the proliferation of statebuilding activities undertaken by peacekeepers. These activities are not new in any sense. Statebuilding tasks such as demobilization, disarmament, and reintegration (DDR) of combatants and security sector reform (SSR) were standard practices in the 1990s. However, a mission's obligation to support and participate in such activities depended on implementation of the peace agreement in which they were stipulated. In contrast, as many contemporary missions have extended their deployments over longer periods—during which peace agreements frequently fall apart leading to renewed violence—there has been a shift in focus from statebuilding as a function of peace-agreement implementation to the more overt tasks of strengthening and extending state authority, even in the absence of agreement, and in cases where the state is weak or lacks legitimacy. For several missions, this expansion has taken place under the rubric of 'stabilization' and has entailed robust uses of force in direct support of the state.[189]

In this way, statebuilding and PoC are often closely linked; assistance to domestic institutions aims to develop the ability of the state to tackle a spectrum of civilian protection needs over the long term.[190] Crucially, however, peacekeepers have in a number of cases also engaged in military and policing action in direct support of states to address more immediate internal and external security threats. Such support marks a double broadening of the use of force: robust action is taken to rein in those who seek to 'spoil' an established peace agreement and against those actors who pose a threat to the state. The privileged role enjoyed by the state is hardly surprising given the state-centric constitution of the UN itself. However, as I discuss below, it nonetheless raises a number of issues for impartiality, particularly in contexts such as Congo and South Sudan where elements of the state pose a threat to civilians or in Ivory Coast where election results were disputed.

What Decision? What Action?

The second area of ambiguity also relates to the *basis for* decision-making and concerns the specific actions required of peacekeepers, including, critically, the use of force during the process of impartially implementing a mandate.

The robust form of peacekeeping developed in the *Brahimi Report* and *Capstone Doctrine* is confounded by the assertion in both documents that *non-use* of force (except in self-defence and defence of the mandate) remains a core principle of peacekeeping. This disjuncture stems from qualifications on the non-use of force, which serve as a gateway to robust operations and the new more assertive role for peacekeepers. It is, however, a source of considerable ambiguity. As Guéhenno notes:

> *Brahimi* and *Capstone* allow for use of force in self-defence and in defence of the mandate—which is linked to this notion of impartiality . . . Now if you think through that sentence, it's a meaningless sentence . . . You could have a mandate that allows [peacekeepers] to crush a country . . . I mean, depending on how you write the mandate, 'defence of the mandate' can open [a mission] up to anything.[191]

Confusion also arises over when and to what degree force can and should be used by peacekeepers to 'defend' their mandate either pre-emptively or when provoked. This confusion is exacerbated by the profusion of potentially contradictory tasks that are often contained in mandates. As resolutions have come to encompass a broader set of tasks related both to overseeing peace agreements as well as to other activities separate to an agreement such as PoC, the likelihood that tensions will arise between tasks has increased, and ambiguity persists over the sequencing of tasks as well as the potential trade-offs between particular courses of action. Simultaneously, peacekeepers may be expected to build and back a state, protect civilians, confront spoilers (that may or may not include the state or proxy forces of the state), as well as a number of other activities such as DDR. A mission's involvement in peacebuilding—actions to negotiate, consolidate, and steer peace processes when they have been derailed—may only further complicate mandate implementation. Can UN officials shoot at parties one day and be accepted as impartial brokers of peace the next?

Decision and Action by Whom? And with what Information?

Finally, ambiguity persists over the procedural requirements of impartiality—namely, that peacekeepers be unbiased and informed when making decisions and taking action. During the Cold War, the master texts called for the mitigation of potential biases by outlining which states were precluded from contributing forces and by advising that TCCs be selected cautiously and in a consultative process. In addition, the texts emphasized the importance of access to information and freedom of movement for mission staff. By contrast, the documents institutionalizing the new conception of the norm pay little heed to issues surrounding mission composition and are vague about the information requirements for decision-making in contemporary operations.

These omissions are of particular consequence given that the expanded background of valuation, and attendant tasks which peacekeepers are now expected to carry out, may call into question their ability to meet the procedural requirements of the norm. For example, can peacekeepers support state institutions and still be accepted as unbiased? Similarly, does the UN's involvement or the involvement of particular troop-contributing countries in peacebuilding impede a mission's ability to be unbiased, particularly if an agreement is regarded by some as illegitimate or unfair? Moreover, what constitutes an informed decision or action, and how might this vary across an expanded remit of activities? How might an absence of consent, at the tactical level or otherwise, affect the information that is available to peace-keepers? And what degree of information must be obtained before undertaking forceful action that may result in casualties?

Peacekeeping partnerships are a further source of ambiguity. That the UN should pursue regional and sub-regional partnerships was a core recommendation of the *Brahimi Report* and a priority for the *New Horizons* process (2009–11), an attempt by DPKO/DFS to develop a future agenda for peace-keeping. Over the last decade, in contexts such as Sierra Leone, Haiti, Congo, Sudan, and the Central African Republic, the Council has authorized missions involving regional or sub-regional organizations, security alliances, and ad hoc member-state coalitions. These missions have displayed 'variable geometry' with UN-led forces, including sequential deployment; parallel or co-deployment; hybrid or full integration, and standalone missions.[192]

Alternative institutional arrangements are sought for a variety of reasons. In some situations, regional partners are well placed to be quick and early responders, given their physical proximity as well as incentives to contain a conflict that threatens to destabilize their own area.[193] They may also have valuable knowledge of local conditions, and heightened awareness of cultural sensitivities, engendering greater acceptance by local parties. Similarly, security alliances or 'coalitions of the willing' may be in a position to provide force-generation capacity that UN-led missions lack. However, whether peacekeeping partners are expected to, or indeed able to fulfil the procedural requirements of impartiality is unclear and contentious. Simply put, the very characteristics that render certain actors suited to rapid and robust response may make their lack of bias—real or perceived—all the more questionable. As such, through its association with such actors, partnerships may also jeopardize the UN's ability to act and be accepted as an unbiased actor.

Last, a similar form of ambiguity stems from cooperation with humanitarians and the ICC. While these actors all claim to act impartially, their activities and short-term objectives may be markedly different, as may be the degree of consent with which they operate. These dissimilarities may, in the context of partnership, compromise an actor's acceptance. Cooperation, for example, between the ICC and a peacekeeping mission in a context of ongoing violence where peacekeepers are deployed may jeopardize the mission's ability to be perceived as unbiased. Similarly, for humanitarians, integration with particular peacekeeping missions may be problematic and, as the *Capstone Doctrine* acknowledges, weaken acceptance and access, leading to a contraction in

'humanitarian space'. In such circumstances, where the 'intensity of cooperation' may necessarily be 'limited', the *Doctrine* nonetheless advises that actors
be 'proactive [in] sharing' information.[194] However, it is conceivable that even
information sharing, which potentially raises issues of source confidentiality
and security, could impinge on an actor's ability to be accepted as unbiased.
Consequently, ambiguity persists over whether peacekeepers may enter into
cooperative and integrated partnership arrangements and still claim to be
impartial.

Taken together, these three areas of ambiguity challenge what I highlighted
in the Introduction as constructivism's tendency to see institutionalization as a
process that leads to clarification and greater norm precision. The dominant
understanding of impartiality now embedded within the UN is far from
precise. Instead, beneath the veneer of convergence and clarity, ambiguity
persists over the substantive and procedural components of impartiality, and
its relationship with other norms, such as sovereignty. This ambiguity persists
despite the fact that conceptual confusion was precisely what prompted
impartiality's reformulation in the new millennium. As Guéhenno, looking
back on reform efforts, opines: 'To be honest, I don't think we can say there
was a period of confusion and then came clarity . . . I don't think there is any
clarity over impartiality.'[195]

CONCLUSION

This chapter has analysed the change in the understanding of impartiality in
UN peacekeeping from a passive conception during the Cold War to a more
assertive conception in recent years. Claims to impartial authority, as I have
demonstrated, are no longer based solely on terms consented to by all parties
to a dispute. Rather, the *basis for* impartial decision-making—the background
of valuation—has expanded to encompass a more ambitious set of human-
rights-related norms, such as the protection of civilians, and has implied, as a
result, more coercive and exacting practices. Hitherto deployed primarily to
address intra-state conflict, contemporary peacekeeping missions frequently
aspire to nothing short of the total social transformation of the host country.
They have become, in the process, unparalleled in their organizational complexity and the sheer extent of their ambition.

The change in peacekeeping must be understood as an integral part of a wider
shift in liberal internationalism, engendering new partnerships within and
outside the UN system. Cooperation and integration across areas of engagement
is premised on the belief that despite differences in focus, actors are guided by
similar broad objectives, and, crucially, that wider agreement exists over these
objectives. The legitimacy of assertive liberal internationalism and claims by

actors that their more coercive and intrusive actions *are* impartial rests largely on what is heralded as a newfound unity of purpose—the culmination, over several decades, of the internationalization of human rights, and the disassociation of rights from a particular political or partial agenda. Proponents contend that this internationalization of human rights has allowed for an acceptable transformation in the foundation of certain legal norms that now have authority not because they are based on individual states' consent, but rather because they are seen to reflect a collective international consensus—Teitel's 'humanity's law'. The Council, by this account, plays the role of 'arbiter of what constitutes a universal legal norm'.[196] And by extension, through the mandates Council members authorize, peacekeepers are endowed, individually and collectively, with an authority to protect and promote that which is pre-political and universal. An authority which, recalling the earnest characterization of the UN's purpose by Conor Cruise O'Brien, might well be construed as 'sacred'.

NOTES

1. Conor Cruise O'Brien with Feliks Topolski, *The United Nations: Sacred Drama* (New York: Simon and Schuster, 1968), 19.
2. United Nations, *Charter of the United Nations* (New York: 1945).
3. A collective security system is one in which 'each state in the system accepts that the security of one is the concern of all, and agrees to join in a collective response to threats to, and breaches of, the peace'. Vaughan Lowe et al., eds., *The United Nations Security Council and War: The Evolution of Thought and Practice Since 1945* (Oxford: Oxford University Press, 2008), 13.
4. UN Charter, Articles 27 and 39. Other departures include the 'inherent right of individual and collective self-defence' (Article 51) and specifications for regional security arrangements (Article 57).
5. United Nations, 'History of the UN', www.un.org/en/history. See Mark Mazower, *No Enchanted Palace: The End of Empire and the Ideological Origins of the United Nations* (Princeton: Princeton University Press, 2009).
6. UN Charter Article 43–45 calls for armed forces to be made available to the Security Council. Articles 46 and 47 outlined details for Military Staff Committee. These provisions of the Charter were never implemented. See Adam Roberts, 'Proposals for UN Standing Forces: A Critical History' in Vaughan Lowe et al. (2008: 99–129).
7. Thomas Franck, *Recourse to Force* (Cambridge: Cambridge University Press, 2002), 40.
8. Dag Hammarskjöld, *To Speak for the World: Speeches and Statements by Dag Hammarskjöld, Secretary-General of the United Nations 1953–1961* (Stockholm: Atlantis, 2005), 68.
9. Shashi Tharoor, 'Should UN Peacekeeping Go "Back to the Basics?"', *Survival* 37/4 (1995–6), 58.

10. William Roger Louis, *Ends of British Imperialism: The Scramble for Empire, Suez, and Decolonization* (London: IB Tauris & Co., 2007).
11. See remarks of US Secretary of State Dulles, United Nations, A/562 A (1956).
12. United Nations, A/RES/998 (1956). The 'Uniting for Peace' resolution (A/RES/ 377A), adopted on 3 November 1950, allows the GA to issue recommendations to restore international peace and security if the Council fails to act because of a lack of unanimity among its permanent members. See Dominik Zaum, 'The Uniting for Peace Resolution', in *The United Nations Security Council and War*, edited by Lowe et al. (2008: 154–75).
13. United Nations, A/RES/1000 (1956) established UN command for the force. United Nations, A/RES/1002 (1956) asked the Secretary-General to report to the Assembly on Israeli, British and French withdrawal.
14. Brian Urquhart, *Hammarskjöld* (New York: W.W. Norton & Company, 1994), 180.
15. United Nations, A/3302 (1956).
16. Herbert Nicholas, 'UN Peace Forces and the Changing Globe: The Lessons of Suez and Congo', *International Organization* 17/2 (1963), 326.
17. Urquhart (1994: 178).
18. United Nations, A/3302 (1956).
19. See Rosalyn Higgins, *United Nations Peacekeeping 1946–1967: Documents and Commentary* (Oxford: Oxford University Press, 1980), 250–60.
20. Norrie Macqueen, *Peacekeeping and the International System* (Abingdon: Routledge, 2006), 72.
21. Louis, in Lowe et al. (2008: 297).
22. Macqueen (2006: 112).
23. Until the late 1960s, several new missions were deployed to the Middle East, reflecting a desire on the part of both superpowers to contain conflict in the region. As tensions deepened in the 1970s, peacekeeping activity all but ceased and no new missions were authorized between 1978 and 1988.
24. Brian Urquhart, 'International Peace and Security: Thoughts on the Twentieth Anniversary of Dag Hammarskjold's Death', *Foreign Affairs* (Fall 1981), 2–3.
25. Philip Cunliffe, *Legions of Peace: UN Peacekeepers from the Global South* (New York: Hurst & Co. Publishers, 2014), 249.
26. R.J. Vincent, *Nonintervention and International Order* (Princeton: Princeton University Press, 1974), 345–6.
27. United Nations, A/5746 (1964).
28. Larry Fabian, *Soldiers Without Enemies: Preparing the United Nations for Peacekeeping* (Washington: Brookings Institution, 1971).
29. Dag Hammarskjöld, 'The Uses of Private Diplomacy', in *The Servant of Peace: A Selection of the Speeches and Statements of Dag Hammarskjöld*, edited by Wilder Foote (London: The Bodley Head, 1962), 170.
30. United Nations, A/3943 (1958).
31. United Nations, S/11052/Rev.1 (1973).
32. United Nations, A/32/394/AnnII/App.I (1977).
33. Nicholas (1963: 336).
34. United Nations, A/3943 (1958).
35. United Nations, A/3943 (1958), para 14.

36. United Nations, A/3943 (1958), para 160.

37. Negotiations on mission composition were at times contentious. See Urquhart (1994: 188); Arthur Cox, *Prospects for Peacekeeping* (Washington: The Brookings Institution, 1967).

38. These states were repeatedly selected for missions from contingents specifically earmarked for UN use. The Netherlands, Austria, Italy, Iran, and New Zealand also maintained dedicated forces for UN service. See Alex Bellamy and Paul Williams, 'The West and Contemporary Peace Operations', *Journal of Peace Research* 46/1 (2009), 39–57.

39. Cunliffe (2014: 140).

40. Cunliffe (2014: 141).

41. United Nations, A/3943 (1958), para 166.

42. United Nations, A/3943 (1958), para 166.

43. United Nations, A/3512 (1972), para 4.

44. United Nations, A/3943 (1958), para 178.

45. United Nations, A/3943 (1958), para 179.

46. United Nations, S/5653 (1964); S/5950 (1964); S/11052/Rev.1 (1973). The omission of this expanded notion from the *Peacekeeper's Handbook* attests to lack of controversy over this change during the Cold War period. International Peace Academy, *Peacekeeper's Handbook* (New York: Pergamon Press, 1984).

47. United Nations, 'Middle East—UNEF I: Background', http://www.un.org/en/peacekeeping/missions/past/unef1backgr2.html

48. United Nations, S/4382 (1960).

49. For a vivid account of these dynamics, see O'Brien with Topolski (1968).

50. United Nations, S/RES/143 (1960).

51. Georges Abi-Saab, *The United Nations Operation in the Congo 1960–1965* (Oxford: Oxford University Press, 1978), 46.

52. Norrie MacQueen, *United Nations Peacekeeping in Africa since 1960* (Abingdon: Routledge, 2014), 44.

53. Under a controversial article of the interim constitution, President Kasavabu dismissed Lumumba and six other ministers. Parliament responded by nullifying Kasavubu's dismissal and Lumumba responded by dismissing Kasavubu. Georges Nzongola-Ntalaja, *The Congo from Leopold to Kabila: A People's History* (London: Zed Books, 2002), 108.

54. *Foreign Relations of the United States (FRUS), 1958–1960: Africa* (Washington, DC: US Government Printing Office, 1992), 444.

55. Georges Nzongola-Ntalaja, 'Patrice Lumumba: the most important assassination of the 20th century', *The Guardian*, 17 January 2011.

56. United Nations, S/RES/161(1961) and United Nations, S/RES/169(1961).

57. A total of more than 6,000 troops were withdrawn by the United Arab Republic, Indonesia, Mali, Guinea, Yugoslavia, and Morocco. Cox (1967: 92). Perceptions of ONUC's partiality were compounded by the presence of several senior Americans within the mission.

58. United Nations, S/4497 (1960).

59. UNIFIL was deployed at the end of détente in 1978. The mission was hastily cobbled together, largely at the behest of the US to supervise Israel's withdrawal from Southern Lebanon. Deployed into an area of ongoing hostilities, UNIFIL

suffered from poor planning, absence of a viable political process and agreement by the parties on UNIFIL's role, and retraction of consent from belligerents. The myriad problems that beset UNIFIL were a bellwether of the issues peacekeepers would confront in the 1990s.

60. Robert Legvold, 'The Revolution in Soviet Foreign Policy', *Foreign Affairs* 68/1 (1988), 82–98; Thomas Weiss and Meryl Kessler, 'Moscow's UN Policy', *Foreign Policy* 79 (1990), 94–112.
61. President George Bush, *Address Before a Joint Session of the Congress on the Cessation of the Persian Gulf Conflict*, 6 March 1991.
62. Adam Roberts and Benedict Kingsbury, 'Introduction: The UN's Roles in a Divided World', in *United Nations Divided World: The UN's Role in International Relations*, 2nd edition (Oxford: Oxford University Press, 1993), 4.
63. United Nations, S/23500 (1992), 3.
64. Neil MacFarlane and Yuen Foong Khong, *Human Security and the United Nations* (Bloomington: Indiana University Press, 2006).
65. See for example United Nations, A/47/277-S/24111 (1992), *An Agenda for Peace: Preventive Diplomacy, Peacemaking and Peace-Keeping*, para 17 (Henceforth 'Agenda for Peace').
66. The Security Council's authorization of enforcement action over Rhodesia and South Africa were notable exceptions.
67. Nicholas Wheeler, *Saving Strangers: Humanitarian Intervention in International Society* (Oxford: Oxford University Press, 2002).
68. The two main exceptions were Britain's provision of forces to UNFICYP and France to UNIFIL during the Cold War.
69. Michael Doyle, Ian Johnstone, and Robert Orr, *Keeping the Peace: Multidimensional UN Operations in Cambodia and El Salvador* (Cambridge: Cambridge University Press, 1997).
70. Roland Paris, 'International Peacebuilding and the "Mission Civilisatrice"', *Review of International Studies* 28 (2002), 637.
71. Quoted in Adam Roberts, 'The United Nations and International Security', *Survival* 35/2 (1993), 21.
72. *Agenda for Peace* (1992: para 20).
73. Adam Roberts, 'The Crisis in UN Peacekeeping', *Survival* 36/3 (1994), 100.
74. Stanley Hoffmann, 'The Crisis of Liberal Internationalism', *Foreign Policy* 98 (1995), 159–77.
75. Mary Anderson, *Do No Harm: How Aid can Support Peace—or War* (Boulder: Lynne Rienner, 1998); Fiona Terry, *Condemned to Repeat? The Paradox of Humanitarian Action* (Ithaca: Cornell University Press, 2002).
76. Nicholas Leader, 'Proliferating Principles, or How to Sup with the Devil Without Getting Eaten', *International Journal of Human Rights* 2/4 (1998), 1–27; *New York Times*, 'The well-fed dead in Bosnia', 15 July 1992.
77. Anne Orford, *International Authority and the Responsibility to Protect* (New York: Cambridge University Press, 2011), 10.
78. Orford (2011: 10).
79. United Nations, S/RES/751 (1992).

80. The Somali National Alliance and United Somali Congress provided the initial consent for UNOSOM.
81. United Nations, S/RES/713 (1991).
82. United Nations, 'Former Yugoslavia – UNPROFOR' (New York: Department of Public Information, 1996), http://www.un.org/en/peacekeeping/missions/past/un prof_b.htm
83. Catherine Newbury, 'Background to Genocide: Rwanda', *Issue: A Journal of Opinion* 23/2 (1995), 15.
84. Roméo Dallaire, *Shake Hands with the Devil: The Failure of Humanity in Rwanda* (New York: Carroll & Graff Publishers, 2003), 144.
85. Dallaire (2003: 144).
86. Commission of Inquiry by Mr. Mahoux and Mr. Verhofstadt, *Belgian Senate Report* (Brussels: 1997). Available at http://www.senate.be/english/rwanda
87. United Nations, S/1994/728 (1994).
88. Daniela Kroslak, *The Role of France in the Rwandan Genocide* (London: Hurst & Co., 2007).
89. John Hirsch and Robert Oakley, *Somalia and Operation Restore Hope: Reflections on Peacemaking and Peacekeeping* (Washington: United States Institute of Peace Press, 1995), 9.
90. Interview with Ambassador John Hirsch, Senior Fellow, International Peace Institute; former Political Advisor to the Commander of Unified Task Force (UNITAF), New York, March 2010.
91. Interview with Louise Fréchette, former Deputy Secretary General of the UN, Montreal, March 2011.
92. United Nations, S/RES/837 (1993).
93. Mohamed Sahnoun, former UN Special Representative to Somalia, remarked that Somalis came to perceive the mission as an 'occupation force'. Quoted in Ramesh Thakur, 'From Peacekeeping to Peace Enforcement: The UN Operation in Somalia', *Journal of Modern African Studies* 32/3(1994), 399.
94. Lt. Gen. Sir Michael Rose reportedly coined the expression 'crossing the Mogadishu line' to describe the dilemma faced by his troops in Bosnia, which entailed the choice of maintaining the appearance of impartiality while simultaneously attempting to achieve the mission's political objectives.
95. Thakur (1994: 399).
96. Michael Barnett and Martha Finnemore, *Rules for the World: International Organizations in Global Politics* (Ithaca: Cornell University Press, 2004), 123. See also Michael Barnett, *Eyewitness to a Genocide: The United Nations and Rwanda* (Ithaca: Cornell University Press, 2002).
97. Quoted in interview for *Frontline: The Triumph of Evil*. PBS television broadcast, 1999. Transcript available at http://www.pbs.org/wgbh/pages/frontline/shows/evil/interviews/marchal.html
98. Between 1991 and 1995, the Council issued more than 140 resolutions and presidential statements on the former Yugoslavia. Mats Berdal, 'The Security Council and Peacekeeping', in *The United Nations Security Council and War*, edited by Lowe, et al. (2008: 194).

99. Richard Betts, 'The Delusion of Impartial Intervention', *Foreign Affairs* 73/20 (1994), 24. See also, Edward Luttwak, 'Give war a chance', *Foreign Affairs* 78/4 (1999), 36–44.
100. Betts (1994: 24).
101. 'The Tunnel' (http://www.hadzic.org/secret-tunnel/tunnel.htm). Accessed through web archive (http://web.archive.org/web) on 15 October 2015.
102. 'The Tunnel' (http://www.hadzic.org/secret-tunnel/tunnel.htm). Accessed through web archive (http://web.archive.org/web) on 15 October 2015.
103. Adam Lebor, *'Complicity with Evil.' The United Nations in the Age of Modern Genocide* (New Haven: Yale University Press, 2007), 37.
104. United Nations, S/RES/836 (1993).
105. United Nations, A/54/549 (1999). *Report of the Secretary-General Pursuant to General Assembly Resolution 53/35, The Fall of Srebrenica*, para 79 (Henceforth *'Srebrenica Report'*).
106. Shashi Tharoor, 'Should UN Peacekeeping Go 'Back to the Basics?', *Survival* 37/4 (Winter 1995–6), 60.
107. The other missions authorized (e.g., UNSMIH, UNTMH, MINUGUA) during this period lacked the scale, size, or scope of previous missions.
108. United Nations, A/50/60 (1995), *Supplement to An Agenda for Peace: Position Paper of the Secretary-General on the Occasion of the Fiftieth Anniversary of the United Nations.*
109. United Nations, A/50/60 (1995), para 32.
110. United Nations, A/50/60 (1995), para 19 (emphasis added).
111. UK Ministry of Defence, *Peace Support Operations: Joint Warfare Publication 3–50 Joint Warfare Publication* (London, 1997); French Ministry of Defence, *Principles for the Employment of the Armed Forces under UN Auspices* (Paris, 1995); NATO, *Bi-MNC Directive for NATO Doctrine for Peace Support Operations* (Brussels, 1998).
112. Stephen Stedman, 'Consent, Neutrality, and Impartiality in the Tower of Babel and on the Frontlines: United Nations Peacekeeping in the 1990s', in *Managing Arms in Peace Process: The Issues, Disarmament and Conflict Resolution Project* (New York: UNIDIR, 1996), 35.
113. *Srebrenica Report*, para 129. United Nations, S/1999/1257, *Report of the independent inquiry into the actions of the United Nations during the 1994 genocide in Rwanda.*
114. Interview with Jean-Marie Guéhenno, former Under-Secretary-General of UN Peacekeeping, New York, June 2011. Cited in Emily Paddon, 'Peacekeeping in the Congo: Implementation of the Protection of Civilians Norm', in Alexander Betts and Phil Orchard, *Implementation & World Politics: How International Norms Change Practice* (Oxford: Oxford University Press, 2014), 162. Reprinted with permission of Oxford University Press.
115. United Nations, *Handbook on United Nations Multidimensional Peacekeeping Operations* (New York: Department of Peacekeeping Operations, 2003) (Henceforth *'Handbook'*); United Nations, *United Nations Peacekeeping Operations: Principles and Guidelines* (New York: Department of Peacekeeping Operations, 2008) (Henceforth *'Capstone Doctrine'*).

116. Interview with former UN official, New York, October 2011.

117. *Capstone Doctrine* (2008: 32).

118. For example, see the following UN Press Releases: United Nations, SG/SM/6870 (1999); SG/SM/6901 (1999); and DSG/SM/96 (2000).

119. United Nations, *Background Note: Workshop on Fundamental Principles of UN Peacekeeping. Stockholm, 26–28 September 2006* (New York: Department of Peacekeeping Operations, 2006), reprinted with the permission of the United Nations.

120. *Brahimi Report* (2000: para 50).

121. *Handbook* (2003: 56).

122. *Capstone Doctrine* (2008: 33).

123. *Capstone Doctrine* (2008: 33).

124. Interview with Professor Michael Doyle, New York, June 2011.

125. Mary Kaldor, 'A Cosmopolitan Response to New Wars', *Peace Review* 8/4 (1996), 505–14; *New and Old Wars: Organized Violence in a Global Era*, 2nd edition (Cambridge: Polity Press, 2006). See also, Tom Woodhouse and Oliver Ramsbotham, 'Cosmopolitan Peacekeeping and the Globalization of Security', *International Peacekeeping* 12/2 (2005), 139–56; James Pattison, 'Humanitarian Intervention and a Cosmopolitan UN Force', *Journal of International Political Theory* 4/1 (2008), 126–45.

126. Kaldor (2006: 128).

127. Kaldor (2006: 123, 212).

128. On the policing character of contemporary peacekeeping operations, see Cunliffe (2014). See also, William Durch and Michelle Ker, *Police in UN Peacekeeping: Improving Selection, Recruitment and Deployment* (New York: International Peace Institute, 2013).

129. Mainstream accounts of violence in the 1990s include: Hans Magnus Enzensberger, *Civil Wars: From LA to Bosnia* (New York: The New Press, 1994); Robert Kaplan, *Balkan Ghosts: A Journey Through History* (New York: Vintage, 1994); Michael Ignatieff, *The Warrior's Honor: Ethnic War and the Modern Conscience* (New York: Henry Holt & Co., 1998). For scholarly analysis see, Kalevi Holsti, *The State, War, and the State of War* (Cambridge: Cambridge University Press, 1996); Mats Berdal and David Malone, *Greed and Grievance: Economic Agendas in Civil Wars* (Boulder: Lynne Rienner, 2000).

130. Kaldor (2006: 136–7).

131. Stathis Kalyvas, '"New" and "Old" Civil Wars: A Valid Distinction?', *World Politics* 54/1 (2001), 100.

132. Enzensberger (1994: 22).

133. *Brahimi Report* (2000: viii).

134. *Brahimi Report* (2000: 9).

135. *Brahimi Report* (2000: 9).

136. United Nations, *Draft Concept Note on Robust Peacekeeping* (New York: Department of Peacekeeping Operations 2010).

137. GCSP, 'Annual Report 2010', *Conflict and Peacebuilding Program (COPE)*, 5. See also James Sloan, *The Militarisation of Peacekeeping in the Twenty-first Century* (Oxford: Hart Publishing, 2011); John Karlsrud, 'The UN at War', *Third World Quarterly* 36/1 (2015), 40–54.

138. Interview with senior MONUC official, Goma, January 2009. Similarly, during an interview in June 2015, a military advisor to MONUSCO stated that the mission's RoE was 'no less robust' than that which he had in a previous deployment to Iraq.
139. Karsten Friis, 'Peacekeeping and Counter-insurgency: Two of a Kind?', *International Peacekeeping* 17/1 (2010), 49–66.
140. United Nations, *Final Report of the Expert Panel on Technology and Innovation in UN Peacekeeping* (New York: 2015); Elodie Convergne and Michael Synder, *Geospatial Technology as a Conflict Prevention and Management Tool in UN Peacekeeping* (New York: International Peace Institute, 2015).
141. For an overview, see Siobhán Wills, *Protecting Civilians: The Obligations of Peacekeepers* (Oxford: Oxford University Press, 2009).
142. *Brahimi Report* (2000: x).
143. *Capstone Doctrine* (2008: 16).
144. Victoria Holt and Glyn Taylor, *Protecting Civilians in the Context of UN Peacekeeping Operations: Successes, Setbacks and Remaining Challenges* (New York: United Nations, 2009), 12.
145. United Nations, S/RES/1270 (1999).
146. United Nations, S/RES/1265 (1999).
147. The Council has adopted multiple thematic resolutions on PoC, holds biannual open debates on PoC, and regularly consults the Council Expert Group on PoC. For an overview of UN PoC activities, see United Nations, http://www.un.org/en/peacekeeping/issues/civilian.shtml
148. Calculation based on United Nations, *Peacekeeping Factsheet: 31 October 2015* (New York: Department of Peacekeeping Operations) available at http://www.un.org/en/peacekeeping/resources/statistics/factsheet.shtml
149. MONUSCO, UNMISS, MINUSCA, UNAMID, and UNMIL have all been directed by the Council to develop comprehensive PoC strategies.
150. Consequently, national and regional doctrine has developed to incorporate PoC. E.g., *Guidelines for the Protection of Civilians in AU Peace Operations* (Addis Ababa: African Union, 2013); Council of Europe, *Guidelines on the Protection of Civilians in CSDP Missions and Operations* (Brussels: Council of Europe, 2010).
151. United Nations, *Rights Up Front: A Plan of Action to Strengthen the UN's role in Protecting People in Crises. Follow-up to the Report of the Secretary-General's Internal Review Panel on UN Action in Sri Lanka,* 9 July 2013, Reprinted with the permission of the United Nations, 4. See also 'Human Rights Up Front' website http://www.un.org/sg/rightsupfront/. The initiative was a direct response to the assessment of the UN's 'systemic failure' to protect populations in the final phase of the Sri Lankan conflict in 2009. See United Nations, *Report of the Secretary-General's Internal Review Panel on United Nations Action in Sri Lanka,* November 2012.
152. Andrew Gilmour, 'The Future of Human Rights: A View from the United Nations', *Ethics & International Affairs* 28/2 (2014), 239–50.
153. ICISS, *The Responsibility to Protect: Research, Bibliography, Background. Supplementary Volume* (Ottawa: International Development Research Council, 2001); United Nations, A/60/2005, paras 138–9.

154. United Nations, A/63/677 (2009). The link between RtoP and PoC has also been made explicit in specific peacekeeping resolutions (e.g., United Nations, S/RES/ 1706, which established the mission in Darfur).
155. On the relationship between both norms, see Hugh Breakey et al. *Enhancing Protection Capacity: Policy Guide to the Responsibility to Protect and the Protection of Civilians in Armed Conflicts* (Queensland, Australia: Institute for Ethics, Governance and Law, Griffith University, 2012).
156. See Jon Western and Joshua Goldstein, 'Humanitarian Intervention Comes of Age: Lessons from Somalia to Libya', *Foreign Affairs* 90/6 (2011); Gareth Evans, 'Responsibility While Protecting', *Project Syndicate*, 27 January 2012.
157. Stephen Stedman, 'Spoiler Problems in Peace Processes', *International Security* 22/2 (1997), 53. For an overview of spoiler theory, see Edward Newman and Oliver Richmond, *Challenges to Peacebuilding: Managing Spoilers during Conflict Resolution* (New York: United Nations University Press, 2006). For a critique, see Kelly Greenhill and Solomon Major, 'The Perils of Profiling: Civil War Spoilers and the Collapse of Intrastate Peace Accords', *International Security* 31/3 (2007), 7–40.
158. *Brahimi Report* (2000: ix). Similarly, the Report states that in certain situations where 'local parties consist not of moral equals but of obvious aggressors and victims . . . peacekeepers may not only be operationally justified in using force but morally compelled to do so' (9).
159. Interview with DPKO official, New York, June 2011.
160. Interview with Lakhdar Brahimi, Algerian UN Envoy and Advisor; former Chairperson of the Independent Panel on UN Peace Operations, Paris, July 2011; Interview with Fréchette, 2011. Interviewees also mentioned *Operation Deliberate Force*—a two-week UN-authorized NATO air-strike campaign against Bosnian Serb military targets in the wake of the Srebrenica massacre.
161. United Nations, S/RES/1313 (2000), para 2.
162. Interview with Fréchette, 2011.
163. Mark Shaw and Walter Kemp, *Spotting the Spoilers: A Guide to Analyzing Organized Crime* (New York: International Peace Institute, 2012).
164. Judith Goldstein et al., 'Introduction: Legalization and world politics', *International Organization* 54/3 (2000), 385–99; Cesare Romano, 'Shift from the Consensual to the Compulsory Paradigm in International Adjudication: Elements for a Theory of Consent', *NYU Journal of International Law and Politics* 39 (2006); Cesare Romano, Karen Alter, and Yuval Shany, eds., *The Oxford Handbook of International Adjudication* (Oxford: Oxford University Press, 2013); Nico Krisch, 'The Decay of Consent: International Law in an Age of Global Public Goods', *American Journal of International Law* 108/1 (2014), 1–40.
165. E.g., United Nations, A/59 (2005).
166. Thomas Buergenthal, 'The Normative and Institutional Evolution of International Human Rights', *Human Rights Quarterly* 19/4 (1997), 703–23: 706; David Forsythe, *The Internationalization of Human Rights* (Lexington: Lexington Books, 1991); David Forsythe, *Human Rights in International Relations* (Cambridge: Cambridge University Press, 2012).

167. Ruti Teitel, *Humanity's Law* (Oxford: Oxford University Press, 2011). See also Martha Finnemore, *The Purpose of Intervention: Changing Beliefs about the Use of Force* (Ithaca: Cornell University Press, 2003), 78, 129; Kaldor (2006: 212); Bruce Cronin, 'International Consensus and the Changing Legal Authority of the UN Security Council' in *The UN Security Council and the Politics of International Authority*, edited by Bruce Cronin and Ian Hurd (London: Routledge, 2008); Kathryn Sikkink, *The Justice Cascade: How Human Rights Prosecutions Are Changing World Politics* (New York: Norton, 2011).

168. Teitel (2011: 203).

169. Teitel (2011: 199–200).

170. Western and Goldstein (2011: 49).

171. See James Darcy, *Human Rights and Humanitarian Action: A Review of the Issues* (London: Humanitarian Policy Group, Overseas Development Institute, 2004); Michael Barnett and Thomas Weiss, *Humanitarianism in Question: Politics, Power, Ethics* (Ithaca: Cornell University Press, 2008).

172. Fiona Fox, 'New Humanitarianism: Does it Provide a Moral Banner for the 21st Century?', *Disasters* 25/4 (2001), 275; David Rieff, *A Bed for the Night: Humanitarianism in Crisis* (New York: Simon & Schuster, 2002).

173. ICRC, *Professional Standards for Protection Work: Carried out by Humanitarian and Human Rights Actors in Armed Conflict and Other Situations of Violence* (Geneva: 2009); IASC, *Operational Guidelines: On the Protection of Persons in Situations of Natural Disasters* (2011).

174. Moreover, how these organizations understand protection has also changed. For example, UNHCR has expanded the remit of protection to include IDPs. See Elizabeth Ferris, *The Politics of Protection: The Limits of Humanitarian Action* (Washington: Brookings Institution Press, 2011).

175. Victoria Metcalfe, Alison Giffen, and Samir Elhawary, *UN Integration and Humanitarian Space: An Independent Study Commissioned by the UN Integration Steering Group* (London: Humanitarian Policy Group, Overseas Development Institute, 2011), 14.

176. The jurisdictions of both the ICTY and ICTR were limited geographically to crimes committed within those respective states and to specific time periods.

177. Rome Statute of the International Criminal Court, 1998. Available at https://www.icc-cpi.int/nr/rdonlyres/ea9aeff7-5752-4f84-be94-0a655eb30e16/0/rome_statute_english.pdf

178. For an overview, see William Schabas, *An Introduction to the International Criminal Court* (Cambridge: Cambridge University Press, 2011).

179. Olivia Swaak-Goldman (Office of the Prosecutor, ICC), 'Peacekeeping Operations and the International Criminal Court: Presentation at the International Institute for International Law', Sanremo, Italy, 6 September 2008, http://tableronde08.blogspot.co.uk/2008/03/peacekeeping-operations-and.html

180. United Nations, A/58/874 (2004).

181. United Nations, S/RES/1565 (2004).

182. Cooperation was a focus of the Review Conference on the Rome Statute of the ICC, Kampala, 2010. Documents available at http://www.iccnow.org/?mod=review

183. Swaak-Goldman (2008) http://tableronde08.blogspot.co.uk/2008/03/peacekeeping-operations-and.html

184. *Brahimi Report* (2000: ix).

185. *Capstone Doctrine* (2008: 32).

186. *Brahimi Report* (2000: ix).

187. This point was emphasized during the drafting of the *Capstone Doctrine*. As one official stated: 'The true strength of impartiality . . . arises from the fact that, at some prior point, the parties involved gave their consent, either explicitly or implicitly. This was accomplished when: 1) States became members of the UN and agreed to uphold the principles of the Charter; 2) They also agreed to be bound by the decisions of the UN Security Council . . . ; 3) They may even have signed a peace agreement or other settlement promising to behave in a certain way; and 4) In some cases, non-state parties may also have been accorded standing, participated in negotiations, and agreed to abide by certain understandings.' *Background Paper* (2006: 4), reprinted with the permission of the United Nations.

188. *Capstone Doctrine* (2008: 34).

189. As of April 2015, MINUSTAH, MONUSCO, MINUSMA, and MINUSCA were designated specifically as stabilization missions. However, other missions, such as UNMISS have stabilization functions in their mandates.

190. For example, the third tier of DPKO/DFS' Operational Concept for PoC is 'establishment of a protective environment'. This includes a wide range of activities (e.g., DDR and SSR). United Nations, *DPKO/DFS Policy on the Protection of Civilians in United Nations Peacekeeping* (2015). For a critique of such a broad definition of PoC, see Fairlie Chappuis and Aditi Gorur, *Reconciling Security Sector Reform and the Protection of Civilians in Peacekeeping Contexts* (Washington: Stimson Center, 2015).

191. Interview with Guéhenno, New York, March 2010.

192. For a discussion of hybrid deployment configurations, see A. Sarjoh Bah and Bruce Jones, *Peace Operations Partnerships: Lessons and Issues from Coordination to Hybrid Arrangements* (New York: Center on International Cooperation, May 2008).

193. Emily Paddon, 'Partnering for Peace: Implications and Dilemmas', *International Peacekeeping* 18/5 (2011), 523.

194. *Capstone Doctrine* (2008: 73).

195. Interview with Guéhenno, 2010.

196. Cronin (2008: 71).

3

Institutionalization and the Global Politics of Peacekeeping

On 1 October 2000, a group of top-drawer international civil servants gathered at Greentree, a 400-acre estate on Long Island, New York. Jean-Marie Gué-henno, a former French diplomat, was among the luminaries in attendance. It was his first day on the job as Under-Secretary-General for United Nations (UN) Peacekeeping.

The group had assembled at the request of Secretary-General Kofi Annan to consider the *Brahimi Report*, published a few weeks beforehand, and the new roles that the UN had been given by the Security Council in places like Kosovo, East Timor, and Congo. The discussion 'ranged from mundane issues to grand visions' as the participants tussled with the difficulties and challenges posed by such ambitious mandates.[1] However, as Guéhenno laments in his recent memoir *Fog of Peace*: 'we did not ask whether there was a consensus among member states . . . And yet, without their support there is no hope of success.'[2]

The 'grand vision', the new, more assertive conception of impartiality, insti-tutionalized in the *Brahimi Report*, was an attempt to re-ground the authority of peacekeepers and forge a more coherent organizational identity—a clearer purpose for UN missions in the new millennium, based on a presumed con-sensus over human rights. It reflected the evolving content of Council mandates at the end of the 1990s and sought to bring the UN's general membership in line with emerging Council practice.

Institutionalization of the norm did not produce clarity, however, as the previous chapter showed. Despite the appearance of coherence, the new dominant conception of impartiality—institutionalized at the UN and situated in a broader shift towards assertive liberal internationalism—remains ambigu-ous to this day. What is more, it did not reflect, nor has it brought about, the consensus highlighted by Guéhenno as necessary. Deep political fissures exist over the nature and purposes of contemporary UN peacekeeping. Although most member states readily use the same vocabulary and largely agree that impartiality must remain a bedrock norm, significant differences and diver-gent understandings persist over what keeping peace impartially should mean. Contestation remains the norm, as it were.

This chapter considers dynamics related to impartiality's institutionalization at the macro-organizational level of the UN. It seeks to both account for and analyse the contestation that surrounds the composite norm of impartiality and the robust action now expected of peacekeepers. In doing so, it portrays peacekeeping in the new millennium as a politically fragmented practice that has descended into a state of renewed crisis. Those states that have provided the bulk of blue helmets are not the same as those who control and finance their operations. Moreover, the former are among the fiercest critics of the more assertive approach. And yet, pervasive contestation has not impeded the Security Council's authorization of ever more robust peacekeeping operations.

That conflicting conceptions of impartial peacekeeping exist alongside the increasingly robust role for peacekeepers regularly stipulated in mission mandates since 2000, attests to the Council's unprecedented power to determine the content of peacekeeping policy and the increasing marginalization of other institutional actors and bodies. Critically, however, the power of the Council is not unbridled. Rather, it too must be seen as operating within a larger context of constraints and pressures. Institutionalization of assertive impartiality has, I argue, been accompanied by instances of 'norm entrapment' in which the policy choices of the Council have been constrained because of that body's prior statements supporting the norm and, more broadly, its pronouncements regarding human rights.[3] This has generated expectations that, along with the forms of contestation outlined in this chapter, have troubling implications for the process of implementation as well as for the sustainability of peacekeeping over the long term.

This chapter proceeds in five sections. In the first section, I introduce those actors who have contested the norm at the macro-level. In the second, third, and fourth sections, I illuminate in detail the specific content of contestation over the new conception of impartiality, and explicate respectively the procedural, substantive, and consequential objections raised at the organizational level. While mandates vary across deployment contexts and may be contested individually, the focus in this chapter is on broader policy developments since 2000, such as the increasing prominence of the protection of civilians as a core task of peacekeeping, which have fundamentally altered the *basis for* decision-making. Specific mandates and missions are discussed insofar as they bear importantly on wider conceptual and doctrinal development. The final section considers the role of the Security Council.

MACRO-LEVEL CONTESTATION

States from the global South, many of which include the largest troop- and police contributing countries (TCCs/PCCs), comprise the first group of actors that have contested the more assertive interpretation of the norm. The criticisms of these states tend to be aired in the General Assembly (GA) and in the Special Committee on Peacekeeping Operations (otherwise known as the C-34), which is the main forum in which TCCs/PCCs consider issues related to peacekeeping.

Established by the General Assembly in 1965, the C-34 reports annually to the GA through the Fourth Committee (Special Political and Decolonization) and operates on a consensus model.[4] It is comprised of 147 member states, many of which are past or current contributors to peacekeeping operations. In addition, various intergovernmental organizations and entities, including the African Union (AU) and the International Committee of the Red Cross (ICRC) participate as observers.

Within the C-34, most TCCs/PCCs are affiliated with the non-aligned movement (NAM). A relic of Third World solidarity during the Cold War, the NAM has maintained a certain degree of institutional coherence and continues to be formally represented in UN debates on peacekeeping. While differences exist among its 120 members, it functions as an 'intergovernmental caucus group' that, as Mats Berdal observes, broadly 'articulat[es] the views of the "global South"'.[5] States within this group tend to subscribe to the traditional, passive conception of impartiality—what Thierry Tardy describes as a 'strict' definition of the 'holy trinity'—as opposed to the 'expansive' understanding favoured by the West and manifested in Council practice.[6]

In contrast to the Council, which enthusiastically 'welcomed' the *Brahimi Report* in early September 2000,[7] the *Millennium Declaration* issued by the General Assembly later that same month merely 'took note'[8] of the report— what analysts at the time described as 'a polite but noncommittal acknowledgment' of the panel's work.[9] Subsequent discussions within the C-34 and deliberations among member states regarding various follow-on reform initiatives brought to light numerous differences. In particular, several states from the global South criticized the report's call for 'robust' capabilities and mandates, and adamantly opposed the Council's request for further development of peacekeeping doctrine.[10] India, then the largest contributor of troops to UN missions, decried the more assertive role prescribed for peacekeepers and charged that the Council was being invited back into the 'misty evangelism' of the early 1990s.[11]

Similarly, debate in the C-34 following the *Capstone Doctrine's* release in 2008 clearly reflected the dissatisfaction of many member states. While for some, such as Britain, the doctrine was not robust enough, for many NAM countries, the language on impartiality, the use of force, and the protection of civilians was *too* assertive.[12] According to one senior NAM official, the movement's 'official position is that peacekeeping should adhere to the three core principles and by the three core principles I do not mean the Capstone . . . the NAM never agreed to it'.[13]

Indeed, contestation was such that even the title, *Capstone Doctrine*, which had been used to refer to the document throughout its development and which is still widely in use today, was formally revised. 'Doctrine', it was argued, had connotations of being 'binding' and 'immutable'—characteristics that the NAM and the TCCs/PCCs in particular rejected.[14] Instead, the document was formally entitled *UN Peacekeeping Operations: Principles and Guidelines* and, at the request of the NAM, designated an internal 'paper' of the Secretariat, thus having no legal standing.[15]

The second group that has resisted the more assertive role prescribed for peacekeepers consists of current and former officials in the Secretariat. My characterization of the Secretariat as being sceptical may seem at odds with its active involvement in the very initiatives that further institutionalized the new conception of the norm. Members of the Secretariat and, in particular, Deputy Secretary-General Louise Fréchette and Iqbal Riza, chief of staff to Secretary-General Kofi Annan, were closely involved in the *Brahimi Report*'s research.[16] Similarly, the two-year consultative process that culminated in the *Capstone Doctrine* was managed by the Department of Peacekeeping Operations (DPKO) with high-level oversight.[17]

The Secretariat's involvement in the process of institutionalization was motivated, however, precisely by its members' concerns about the new conception of the norm and the expanded *basis for* decision-making—specifically, as I discuss below, the potential consequences for the instrument of peacekeeping and the institution of the UN more broadly.

The tribulations of peacekeeping in the mid-1990s left an indelible mark on Annan who, at the time, served as Under-Secretary-General of peacekeeping. Driven by great personal conviction, Annan played a formative role in drawing attention to the issue of civilian protection and was something of a 'norm entrepreneur' with regard to Responsibility to Protect (RtoP).[18] His principled activism was balanced, however, by a good deal of pragmatism, and the hard-learnt recognition that the Council's stated ambitions do not always translate into tangible commitments in practice. These concerns were widely shared among members of the Secretariat during Annan's tenure as Secretary-General (2000–07) and, particularly by Guéhenno, who headed peacekeeping from 2000–08.

Institutionalization was, in this way, partly an attempt by the Secretariat under the leadership by Annan to foster greater consensus between the institution's mandating body and the general membership, particularly with respect to those tasked with implementation of the more assertive conception of the norm. However, in both the case of the *Brahimi Report* and the *Capstone Doctrine,* the Secretariat's aim of formulating a report that would be acceptable to all meant that contentious issues and objections raised during consultations with member states were subsequently either omitted altogether[19] or couched in ways that sought to minimize dissent and prevent the process from being derailed.[20] The conception of impartiality as assertive was left purposefully vague and ambiguous. Thus, institutionalization did not lead to consensus. Instead, it generated ever greater disagreement over the norm of impartiality and the broader purposes of contemporary peacekeeping.

While certain officials remain sceptical, the Secretariat's stance has changed considerably under Annan's successor, Ban Ki-moon. Described by peacekeeping expert Richard Gowan as America's 'poodle', Ban Ki-moon's appointment in 2007 was, according to Gowan, engineered by the Bush administration because it 'wanted someone pliable to replace the occasionally difficult Kofi Annan'.[21] In contrast to Annan, Ban Ki-moon had little exposure to peacekeeping prior to assuming his post. While he entered the office with what Gowan describes as an 'ambivalent' attitude toward the effectiveness of peacekeeping, the Secretary-General became a champion of robust peacekeeping, an 'apostle of force', speaking forthrightly about crises in Ivory Coast, Libya, and Congo.[22] Critics charge that the Secretary-General's less critical and cautious stance has alienated certain member states that have come to regard the Secretariat as distinctly partial.

In the three sections that follow I present the objections and concerns of both sets of actors, classified according to whether they critique the procedural, substantive, or consequential dimensions of the assertive conception of impartiality.

PROCEDURAL OBJECTIONS

The first type of objection to assertive impartiality is procedural. It concerns the process by which the new understanding of impartiality and associated norms that inform peacekeeping mandates have 'come into being', and raises questions about whether they derive from a 'rightful source of authority'.[23] These criticisms are rooted in inequalities of power that have emerged due to the new 'division of labour' characteristic of contemporary peacekeeping.[24]

The crux of this issue is the fact that the Security Council's resurgent activism in peacekeeping has not been matched by an increased deployment of its members' personnel. In other words, even though the Council has driven the process of norm development and mandating of robust missions, its constituent states have been peripheral to the process of implementation and execution. This is particularly true of the P3 (United States, United Kingdom, and France), which spearheaded the more assertive approach.[25] But it is also true of so-called 'middle powers' like Canada and Australia, which at the end of the 1990s championed the issue of civilian protection and robust peacekeeping, while dramatically reducing their ground presence.[26] Apart from a few 'token' forces, Western powers have been largely absent from UN-led missions in the new millennium.[27] Moreover, their financial contribution to peacekeeping has been curtailed.[28]

In the absence of Western involvement, developing countries and emerging powers have contributed the majority of uniformed personnel fielded globally since 2000.[29] Driven by a diversity of motivations, relative newcomers like Rwanda and Burundi have joined veteran peacekeepers such as India, Pakistan, and Ghana in filling out the ranks of ever growing deployments.[30]

Burden Sharing

The dramatic reduction in Western deployments to and financial support of UN peacekeeping has created tensions. TCCs/PCCs argue that the Council 'shouldn't be allowed to make the rules if they won't play the game'.[31] There is animosity, as one diplomat recounts, that the West 'talks the talk, but won't walk the walk'.[32] To many developing countries, the West's absence is all the more reprehensible given that it overwhelmingly possesses the specialized military capacities and infrastructure-enabling assets required for most contemporary missions.

Tensions over burden-sharing emerged as early as 2000 when, in Sierra Leone, India and Jordan, two of the largest TCCs/PCCs, announced their intention to withdraw their forces from UNAMSIL, threatening its complete collapse. This was partly motivated, Guéhenno explains, by their contention that it was 'untenable that they would have to pay in blood while members of the Security Council and Western nations were only willing to pay in dollars at best, or through lip-service at worst'.[33] As mission mandates have become more ambitious and exacting, criticisms of the West's absence in the field have escalated and TCCs/PCCs have demanded higher compensation.[34]

Attempts in the first decade of the new millennium by some Western governments to justify their decreased support to UN-led peacekeeping missions by citing other military commitments, particularly in Afghanistan and Iraq, did not pass muster with the TCCs/PCCs; if anything, they worsened relations.[35] The missions in Afghanistan and Iraq entailed many of the same tasks and objectives as contemporary peacekeeping operations, including civilian protection, electoral support, and stabilization. Some of the more conservative and dogmatic critics within the NAM tended to see the global 'war on terror' and robust peacekeeping prescribed by the Council (and advocated strongly by the US) as ideologically one and the same.[36] Tensions in this respect were exacerbated by the fact that states such as Germany and Canada, which were concerned about maintaining domestic legitimacy for their involvement in Afghanistan as part of the International Security Assistance Force (ISAF), at times glossed over the distinction between mission types to claim, controversially, that their participation in ISAF made them one of the largest contributors to peacekeeping.[37]

In addition to military commitments related to the global 'war on terror', Western contributions to hybrid missions such as *Opération Artemis, Opération Licorne* or *Opération Serval* have also been regarded by TCCs/PCCs with a certain scepticism. In some of these missions, Western forces have operated in the same context as blue helmets and/or a UN peacebuilding mission, but not fully as a part of UN political and command structures.[38] Deployments are often short term and limited to particular geographic areas. Partly because of this, Western hybridization is seen by some TCCs/PCCs to exemplify what Martin Shaw refers to as 'risk transfer'—outside the designated area of operation or following withdrawal, the risk shifts from Western forces onto UN elements of the mission, which are often comparatively less well equipped.[39]

Concerns that hybridization leads to burden-shirking and shifting rather than burden-sharing were also reiterated by members of the Secretariat, who cautioned against the emergence of 'peacekeeping apartheid'[40] and 'à la carte' engagement'[41]—what analysts more recently have described as the 'blue helmet caste system'[42] and 'imperial multilateralism'.[43] In such a scenario, Western member states engage selectively when it is in their interest, and developing countries are left to deal with areas of marginal strategic relevance, shouldering Sisyphean tasks while remaining woefully under-resourced.

Marginalization from Policymaking

The West's selective military engagement and marked absence from UN-led peacekeeping has, in turn, led TCCs/PCCs to demand a seat at the table and greater say in the development of peacekeeping policy. However, the profusion of peacekeepers from the global South has not translated individually or collectively into greater influence. In contrast to the 1950s and 1960s, when the global South wielded considerable clout and the superpowers, intent on currying favour with them, were more receptive and amenable to their demands, the political relevance of the General Assembly and the C-34 as well as the non-permanent membership influence in the Council have declined dramatically over the last two decades.[44]

Specifically, many TCCs/PCCs condemn what they see as the Council's gross neglect of their right to participate meaningfully in the process of mandate formulation and renewal, as stipulated under Article 44 of the UN Charter.[45] Honouring this right, they argue, is both a matter of respect—if they are willing to put their lives at risk, they should have a say—and operational effectiveness, their knowledge of ground realities means that they have a more accurate understanding of what is and is not operationally feasible.

The *Brahimi Report* anticipated this very issue and called for a new three-way relationship between the Security Council, the Secretariat, and TCCs/PCCs. More than a record of mere consultation, the panel's report recommended the creation of an ad hoc subsidiary organ of the Council, as provided for by the Charter (Article 29), to formalize participatory decision-making and institutionalize experience gleaned from TCCs/PCCs.[46] The C-34 greeted the panel's recommendation enthusiastically. The Council's response was more tepid.[47] While agreeing to strengthen consultations, the P5 were unwilling to consider the establishment of formal mechanisms, stressing that the power of the Council was not to be undermined.[48]

But consultations on peacekeeping, as on other policy areas, which have increased significantly since 2000, are seen by some to be part of the problem—a means by which the Council has extended and consolidated its authority, marginalizing the non-permanent membership's room to manoeuvre in the Council while appearing to be more open to a variety of 'constituents' without necessarily giving the latter more influence over policy.[49] As Ian Hurd explains:

> Increasingly the real work of the Council takes place among the Permanent Five in 'informal sessions' (which, because they are not official Council meetings, do not need to be open to the non-permanent members or to the public). Almost every formal Council meeting now is a pro forma affair, scripted in these advance informal consultations. The President of the Council almost invariably notes in opening an official meeting that 'the Security Council is meeting in accordance with the understanding reached in its prior consultations'.[50]

With little sway over the P5, member states and Secretariat officials variously lament that the C-34 has become 'a silly exercise',[51] an 'irrelevant body'[52] that figures more as an 'echo chamber'[53] for Council policy than as a locus of constructive and meaningful dialogue on peacekeeping. As one senior official put it to me: 'The C-34 has become a forum in which member states try and chase after a train which has already left the station.'[54] As another frustrated TCC/PCC representative explains, the C-34 has become 'the only outlet for certain members to vent against the P5 and many NAM want to use the C-34 to limit Council policy, but this is pointless. It is a case of the Lilliputians trying to tie up Gulliver when Gulliver can always do what he wants.'[55]

The disconnect between what the Security Council mandates and what is debated in the C-34 is perhaps one of the clearest indications of the latter body's marginalization—what the Indian delegation describes as the 'distortion' of peacekeeping's 'policy universe'.[56] Despite the prevalence of mandates to protect civilians since 1999, the issue of PoC first featured on the C-34 agenda only in 2008, to much consternation, and appeared in the text of the committee's annual report only in 2009.[57] What's more, those involved in the C-34 negotiations contend that the inclusion of PoC reflected an ex post facto recognition of and resignation to what the Security Council had already been authorizing, rather than consensus on the issue.[58]

SUBSTANTIVE OBJECTIONS

To understand why PoC continues to be one of the most contentious issues on the C-34's annual agenda, we turn to the second type of objection, concerning the substantive content of the newly institutionalized conception of impartiality: that is, the actions peacekeepers are expected to undertake as part of the mandate and the degree to which consent is required for those actions.

Substantive objections manifest in two areas: the implications of assertive peacekeeping for state sovereignty and self-determination; and the potential demotion of political engagement in favour of a more technical approach to peacekeeping in which impartiality is seen to be above politics. The former figures as a core concern for the NAM and for what I describe as the more conservative TCCs/PCCs; the latter is an issue raised by moderate TCCs/PCCs and members of the Secretariat.

Sovereignty and Self-determination

The lack of shared understanding on the scope and function of contemporary peacekeeping reflects in part an uneasiness some states have with the encroachment of human rights on the principles of state sovereignty, non-intervention, and self-determination. Similar concerns relate to claims to impartial authority that are no longer based on firm consent. According to this perspective, defended most vocally by certain members of the NAM, contemporary peacekeeping represents an abrogation of these sacred principles and opens the door to potential abuses of power. In this view, it is an intrusive activity that imposes a particular normative order reminiscent of the 'standard of civilization' to which many in the global South were subject under colonial and international administration and which, by extension, interfered with their right as a people to determine their 'collective self'.[59] That foreign administrators also claimed to be 'impartial, above politics'—guided by an 'ameliorative and protective' agenda, when history manifestly proved them to be otherwise—only deepens such scepticisms.[60]

Contention over peacekeeping practices that are perceived to undermine state sovereignty and self-determination, and that may mask more nefarious interests, is far from new. The NAM was founded upon the sanctity of these principles. By continually affirming them during the Cold War, the movement sought to limit external scrutiny of, and interference in, state–society relations within the developing world.[61] As I described in Chapter 2, peacekeeping during this period was permissible, even desirable, so long as it respected these principles and provided space for the creation of viable political communities on terms decided by those directly concerned. Consequently, transgressions of this model, such as the assertive action undertaken by peacekeepers in the Congo during the 1960s, were vehemently denounced by the NAM, and several countries withdrew their troops from the mission.

In the post-Cold War era, the NAM has continued its effort to safeguard these principles.[62] In particular, it has viewed with great trepidation the increased uses of force by peacekeepers and qualifications on the requirement of consent. In the General Assembly, many states expressed grave concern over Boutros-Ghali's *Agenda for Peace* and criticized it for downgrading sovereignty.[63] The new understanding of impartiality and more coercive mandates authorized for robust peacekeeping missions since 2000 have exacerbated tensions. Furthermore, the Council's reference to RtoP in the context of particular peacekeeping missions as well as its authorization of enforcement action in Libya to protect civilians without an explicit reference to RtoP has blurred the lines between PoC and RtoP, and deepened anxieties at various junctures.

While this first set of substantive objections are of general concern to the NAM, the movement is far from homogenous, and countries' positions vary considerably.[64] In other words, tensions do not reflect a simple dichotomy of 'Western interventionists' versus 'non-Western' advocates of sovereignty. Instead, member states and Secretariat officials assert that over the last fifteen years a spectrum of positions has emerged and evolved within the C-34. For much of this period, Venezuela and Cuba were firmly situated at the conservative end of the spectrum, described by some as 'dogmatic',[65] 'intractable',[66] and 'uncompromising'.[67] As one more moderate member of the NAM lamented to me in 2010, 'They refuse to even have a conversation about PoC for fear of legitimizing the Council. It is all about Western imperialism and US hegemony.'[68]

In the middle of the spectrum are the big traditional TCCs/PCCs such as India, Pakistan, and Bangladesh. While sceptical of robust peacekeeping and PoC, they are less hostile in their approach and increasingly more amenable to discussing developments in Council practice. They tend to emphasize that PoC is the primary responsibility of the state, to affirm the importance of consent, and to underscore the political necessity of self-determination.[69] Their concerns are often entwined with issues of efficacy. India and Pakistan, one official notes, 'don't think robust peacekeeping and protection will work. They are painfully aware of what it takes to "statebuild"... They know that sometimes it has to be, and usually is, a violent process.'[70] China, which as I describe below has emerged as a significant TCC but one that has been relatively reticent to engage within the C-34, falls in line with this middle position.

Finally, at the other end of the spectrum are those more moderate critics, states such as Indonesia and Costa Rica, as well as a number of African countries that in recent years have emerged as proponents of robust peace-keeping. Frustrated by the many failed attempts by external actors to foster peace on the African continent, and motivated by a diversity of regional interests, these states increasingly show a willingness to field their own forces. They demand and support the use of military force to protect civilians.[71] It is with such actors that the P3 and countries like Canada and Australia frequently engage, as they are more amenable to discussions about PoC and robust peacekeeping.[72]

As one moves away from the conservative end of the spectrum, objections to more robust forms of peacekeeping are less focused on sovereignty and self-determination. Rather, their concerns are about resourcing and which tasks are prioritized, at what cost and to whose benefit. These objections, as I explain below, have also been cause for concern within the Secretariat.

Protection, Politics, and the Council's Priorities

A second substantive objection is that the moral discourse around robust peacekeeping and the new conception of impartiality—particularly its focus on PoC and action against spoilers—obscures the political nature of violence and the tough compromises that are often required when peace agreements are torn asunder and political processes are derailed.

The concern in this case is not that sovereignty and self-determination are jeopardized by the more assertive approach, but rather that the purposes which peacekeepers are now expected to serve, such as civilian protection, are conceived of as apolitical, as *impartial*, and may be pursued at the expense of meaningful political engagement to address the root causes of conflict. As a representative from a large TCC explains, '[m]any of the NAM states are not against PoC *per se*. Our problem is that PoC is predominantly defined in military terms and not really as a political problem—which it is. The fear is that by making PoC the focus of the conversation, it will dominate at the expense of other core peacekeeping issues'.[73]

Similar concerns have been raised by officials within the Secretariat and, in particular, by DPKO officials under the leadership of Guéhenno. As protection became a mandated priority for peacekeepers, Guéhenno emerged as a self-proclaimed 'sceptic' of PoC.[74] Like most members of the NAM, Guéhenno does not deny the intrinsic value of protection or that the norm should be afforded a place of prominence within the UN. As he remarks, 'being against PoC is like being against Mama and her apple pie . . . Protection is at the core of the Charter. If it's not about protecting the people then what is it about?' Instead, his concern is that 'the PoC discussion forgets that peacekeeping is about politics'. 'Peacekeeping', he maintains, 'is not the SWAT team of the world sent in to clean up the bad neighbourhoods of the world.'[75]

Underlying the concerns of both sets of actors is the contention that violence is profoundly political and not a simple moral wrong that impartial peacekeepers—either as SWAT teams or, as Doyle described, 'cops on the beat'—can make right. Their worry is that robust peacekeeping and the prioritization of protection renders peacekeeping reactive and palliative, a technical response to what are deeply political problems. And that by extension, political dialogue and other efforts to address the more intractable sources of insecurity become peripheral to peacekeeping's core purposes. In other words, they maintain that there is a risk of forgetting the old adage that peacekeeping operations can never be a substitute for an effective political process—a point that the *Brahimi Report* was at pains to remind the Security Council of.[76]

The deployment of the UN Mission in the Central African Republic and Chad (MINURCAT) in 2007 gave credence to these concerns. Tasked with protecting refugees from Sudan's Darfur region and Chadian civilians displaced by violence within the country, MINURCAT was unprecedented in that its initial mandate did not include any provisions to nurture or support a parallel peace or political process.[77] Indeed, Chadian President Deby's consent for the mission was contingent on these very limitations, lest such a process involve the opposition groups who threatened to topple his presidency.

While no other mission to date has so blatantly marginalized political engagement, MINURCAT was, to some critics, merely the clearest instantiation of what they regard as a worrying trend in this direction.[78] In this context, critics charge that robust peacekeeping is becoming a strategy of political expediency—a way for actors both local and global to be seen to do something without meaningful political engagement. PoC is used 'strategically', a form of what scholars have described as 'cheap talk'[79] and 'rhetorical action'.[80] As one UN official admonishes: '[PoC] is like the refugee issue—it's easier to have warehouses of refugees in Kenya and Palestine for decades than to actually address the politics behind their being there ... No one wants to deal with the *real* issues'.[81] Guéhenno makes a similar point about the PoC agenda, and in doing so problematizes the analogy of the contemporary peacekeeper as a cop on the international beat.

> You can say you have to protect the people of New York, but New York is a solid state ... In the case of the United Nations ... there is no such thing as a world government. There is no such thing as a world police force. And so PoC is a trap ... it is a diversion from what is the real issue: that is, how to create accountable governments that people can trust, so that they will feel protected in a real way, because they own it ... This is precisely the reason why people focus on protection of civilians; because it transforms what is a highly political and divisive issue—'what kind of government do you want'—where there is no substantive agreement into a kind of technical issue.[82]

As the mandating body for peacekeeping, the Security Council is the main target of such substantive criticisms. Sceptics charge that international grandstanding by the P5 is a means of papering over political apathy. The resolutions authorized by the Council become a reflection of and alibi for its lack of engagement, political or otherwise. During interviews, Secretariat officials spoke of the Council's 'preoccupation', indeed, 'obsession' with 'the microphone'—that is, with conveying to outsiders an image of activism and engagement. These characterizations are not wholly unwarranted, and are given credence by members of the Council openly acknowledging the pressures exerted on the decision-making body to be seen—and heard—to respond to crises. As a former representative to the Council concedes:

> PoC and ambitious mandates are about giving the Security Council something to walk out to the microphone with. We spent hours and hours to produce something for that microphone. It was all about the microphone. It was about being seen to do something. At the end of the day, it is for 'show' and not really about 'reality'. It is about staving off real political engagement in places of minor strategic importance . . . It is so the Human Rights Watches of the world don't finger point.[83]

In this way, member states and Secretariat officials also lament that robust mandates may serve as a substitute not only for the Council's political engagement, but also for more forceful military action. PoC is seen to 'top the agenda' because RtoP, and in particular its third pillar, are, as one official chides, 'too demanding'.[84] The assertion implicit in this comparison is that because peacekeeping still requires, at least in theory, a degree of consent, it limits the possible coercive uses of force and is thus less exacting and arguably less controversial than RtoP. By this account, even though Western states no longer contribute blue helmets, their authorization of a peacekeeping mission creates an illusion of their 'doing something', including in those cases that some may argue warrant a more coercive intervention, without having 'to do' anything. Looking back, Annan highlighted this as a core concern of the *Brahimi Report* and cautioned against the deployment of peacekeeping forces that serve as a 'fig leaf . . . designed to conceal [the Council's] unwillingness to intervene with the true commitment necessary, as a means of appeasing demands for forceful humanitarian intervention'.[85]

In the absence of real political commitment or willingness to meet the demands of more forceful engagement, critics charge that the Council—'distant and disengaged' at the field level—has little incentive to ensure the feasibility of mandates it authorizes and the viability of the missions it deploys.[86] In levelling such complaints, TCCs/PCCs and members of the Secretariat point to the paltry resourcing of contemporary peacekeeping missions as evidence—the absence of military technology, equipment and training—as well as the inappropriately low troop numbers relative to mandated tasks.[87] In the words of one official: 'The Council doesn't think about "how"—they just authorize mandates. Newsflash: 100 civilians are killed. The Council thinks, "right, we need to protect civilians". You only have to look at our equipment and numbers to see that very little attention is paid to "how", whether it's possible or the potential consequences.'[88]

CONSEQUENTIAL OBJECTIONS

The substantive concerns of TCCs/PCCs and the Secretariat give rise to a final and closely related area of contention: namely, objections regarding the consequences of the new conception of impartiality and robust role prescribed for peacekeepers.

Expectations and Reputational Risks

As prescriptions for action that have an element of moral or ethical duty, norms invariably engender expectations. It is thus of little surprise that the normative shift which altered the nature and purposes of peacekeeping over the last fifteen years would engender new and higher expectations both locally and globally.[89] As missions have become more complex and multi-dimensional, peacekeepers have been expected to undertake a plethora of tasks including protection, maintenance of law and order, and supervision of elections.

Critics assert that expectations, when unmet, can diminish the effectiveness of peacekeeping as a tool, sully the reputation of the UN and, crucially, have dire consequences for those on the ground. These concerns have been particularly acute within the Secretariat, which has historically resisted the Council's authorization of impossible mandates.[90] As Louise Fréchette explains:

> The UN is not an NGO, [the Secretariat] cannot call for a dream world, because it knows that it will get stuck with an impossible mandate and insufficient resources. So the Secretariat tends not to separate the aspiration and the vision from the practicalities; otherwise it is suicide. It cannot afford just to be an advocate—an advocate of a rigorous response because it will be the one who is going to have to do the job. It must be clear that whatever is crafted is possible.[91]

Moreover, the Secretariat's relative incapacity to defend itself against its critics when handed impossible mandates deepens these concerns. As Fréchette continues:

> The UN cannot defend itself. You cannot defend yourself without attacking your member states. If you want the UN to defend itself as an institution, it would have to point the finger precisely at the failure of member states and not just on the

resource issue but also the ways in which [member states] at times undermine security . . . The UN and the Secretariat have to be diplomatic. We are the servant of the member states.[92]

Given these constraints and limitations, Secretariat officials were initially more reticent to endorse the more assertive conception of peacekeeping than is often acknowledged. However, senior officials were constrained in the way they could voice their concerns. As former UN Ambassador Robert Fowler, who was instrumental in advancing the PoC agenda during Canada's tenure on the Council, explains: 'Kofi was in a tough position. He couldn't come out publicly and say "don't include provisions in mandates to protect civilians" when certain key members were calling for such specifications. Instead, he did it through negatives—"if you don't give us the tools to be able to carry out such mandates then you can't criticise us when we can't implement them".'[93]

Behind closed doors, Annan was more forthright in expressing his 'grave concern' about the inclusion of an injunction to protect civilians in peace-keeping mandates. 'Stern words' were exchanged between Annan and Fowler during the drafting of Resolution 1265 for the mission in Sierra Leone.[94] The Secretary-General's disquiet extended downward through the Secretariat, which gave significant 'kickback' to the Council. The resounding message from the Secretariat was, as Fowler explains:

> Don't design to fail. Just because you have a nice idea, just because it is informed by goodness doesn't mean it will work. If you set up a mandate like this and we fail, it will be catastrophic for the institution. The UN will be besmirched; we will look flaccid and weak . . . We risk that the instrument will become ever more blunt.[95]

These appeals did not fall on deaf ears. The Council responded to these concerns and inserted caveats with what Fowler describes as 'weasel words'.[96] UNAMSIL was authorized '*within its capabilities and areas of deployment,* to afford protection to civilians under imminent threat of physical violence, taking into account the responsibilities of the Government of Sierra Leone'.[97] These specifications were intended to moderate expectations and have persisted in various forms over the last decade. Nonetheless, members of the Secretariat question the extent to which expectations for protection and assertive action against spoilers really can be moderated. 'Civilians', Guéhenno states acerbically, 'don't read the fine print of Council mandates.'[98] Beyond providing a nebulous sense of hope, the very presence of UN forces may, as the *Brahimi Report* cautioned, instil expectations of material assistance and phys-ical safety for people on the ground and particularly for those in peril. Critics assert that this holds even truer when the mandate explicitly entrusts a mission with specific protection tasks.

Faced with these hard dilemmas, some Secretariat officials have argued for an approach that more assiduously protects the instrument of peacekeeping and, by extension, the UN's organizational reputation in general. They advocate that the UN must be more pragmatic and realistic. As a senior advisor in the Secretariat argues powerfully:

> We need to be honest about the institution's weakness and capabilities. There is a certain power in weakness, which we seem to have forgotten. We need people who say 'we can't do it'—people who are realistic about what is achievable. The worst thing at the end of the day is to make empty promises and create false hope. If people are going to need to run, then let them run. Let them run fast.[99]

Accountability and Liability

The repercussions of raising expectations and dashing hopes give rise to a final set of *consequential* objections. These concerns pertain to questions about accountability and the potential liability of peacekeepers for their actions (or lack thereof). This issue has taken on greater significance as peacekeepers have been held to higher moral and legal standards, given their more overt and visible role in human-rights-related activities such as PoC. Scholars note, for example, how the issue of sexual exploitation and abuse (SEA) by peace-keepers, which sullied operations in the past, 'came to a head in the early 2000s' and was explicitly linked to the new understanding of impartiality.[100] As one official notes,'[i]f impartiality implies adherence to human rights, reports of sexual abuses or illegal activity by UN peacekeepers compromise its core principles and legitimacy'.[101] Such sentiments have also been reflected in training and guidance material produced as a response to the more intense scrutiny of peacekeeper conduct.[102]

While reprehensible behaviour by peacekeepers is in no way new, the deployment of UN missions over the last two decades into states where functioning institutions of governance are lacking is such that the potential for abuse by members of national contingents is significant. In this context, it is reasonable to ask 'Who guards the guardians?' as the title of a recent book does plainly.[103] While various attempts to clarify the legal obligations of peacekeepers have been made over the last two decades, the diversity of command and control structures that characterize contemporary peacekeeping missions problematizes the issue, as does the UN's lack of jurisdiction to prosecute instances of abuse.[104] Ambiguities remain.

Alongside these general concerns regarding conduct, TCCs/PCCs have focused on their potential culpability related to impartiality's expanded scope for the use of force. Their concerns are twofold. First, they fear the possible penalties and legal implications for uses of force that may, at the time, have been regarded as acting in accordance with the mandate, but which post facto may be deemed excessive.[105] This issue has come up in several mission contexts. When Brazilian peacekeepers, using automatic weapons, conducted operations in Cité-Soleil, Haiti in 2005, formal complaints of excessive force were made by several human-rights organizations and an investigation was conducted by the UN Commission of Human Rights' Special Rapporteur on Extrajudicial, Summary, or Arbitrary Executions.[106] Similar investigations have been conducted in eastern Congo, Ivory Coast, and Mali.[107]

But just as TCCs/PCCs have expressed concerns about the potential penalties associated with taking action, they have also feared the possible consequences of inaction—that is, for failing to use force that is authorized for protection. Once again, precedent fuels these concerns. In 2013, the Dutch Supreme Court ruled that peacekeepers acted unlawfully in failing to protect the Bosnian population that sought refuge in the Srebrenica 'safe area', and specifically in evicting three Bosnian Muslim men who later were killed.[108]

While the UN has been reluctant to acknowledge a more general legal responsibility for failure to use force that is authorized, some scholars maintain that PoC mandates do create an affirmative obligation to act under international law.[109] Others note that the International Court of Justice (ICJ)'s 2007 judgment on Serbia's failure to prevent genocide set a legal precedent that could potentially be applied to peacekeeping missions. Under such a scenario, as legal scholar Guglielmo Verdirame explains, a mission would incur responsibility if, according to the ICJ judgment, it 'manifestly failed to take all measures to prevent genocide which were within its powers'.[110]

This potential source of liability, scholars argue, is new. Traditional peacekeeping missions would likely be exempt from liability given the legal limit on their uses of force. Robust peacekeeping, however, is 'different' as Verdirame notes, in that it is given both Chapter VII authorization and RoE that unequivocally permit the use of force.[111] This potential source of liability is particularly worrisome for TCCs given that, in addressing the issue of capacity, the ICJ concluded that the obligation is one of conduct rather than result and thus the scope of duty is to 'employ all means reasonably available . . . so as to prevent genocide so far as possible'.[112] Simply put, peacekeepers may be 'on the hook' regardless of whether or not they are adequately resourced.

This final point is particularly salient for TCCs/PCCs, given the procedural and substantive objections discussed above. If peacekeepers have little involvement in the process of mandate formulation, and if the P5 are unwilling to shoulder the burdens of implementation or furnish the necessary hardware, why should TCCs/PCCs take the blame?

THE POWER OF THE SECURITY COUNCIL

The objections raised by the UN's broader membership did not prevent the institutionalization of the new conception of impartiality, nor did they impede the Council's authorization of ever more robust peacekeeping operations. Instead, as the previous chapter explained, the new understanding of the norm of impartiality and the advent of a more robust role for peacekeepers coincided with a dramatic surge in blue-helmet activity. What explains the Council's activism and the general membership's lack of influence over the agenda? And what are the implications?

Largely unencumbered by the prospect of the veto and with the changes, discussed above, to Security Council working procedures, the Council has in the post-Cold War period amassed an unprecedented ability to determine peacekeeping policy and to hold the Council on a very different course from that of the general membership. What is more, a division of labour has emerged among members of the P5, which shapes dynamics in the Council and has enabled this activism. Peacekeeping policy is generally viewed as the domain of the P3; they take the lead, drafting mandates, advancing reforms, and actively engaging in the C-34. China and Russia for their part are visibly less involved and, despite their attachment to the principles of sovereignty and non-intervention, have been relatively restrained in their use of the veto over peacekeeping mandates. As one official stated, 'Russia picks and chooses its battles, and peacekeeping isn't usually seen as an issue worth fighting for.'[113] Similarly, analysts in New York remark that an increase in Chinese troop contributions in recent years has not translated into greater policy engagement or a more critical stance on peacekeeping.[114]

This is not to diminish or downplay the competing interests at play in the Council itself. Particular crises have certainly engendered discord. As the next chapter explains, divisions among P5 states over Great Lakes policy had a pronounced effect on the Council's approach towards the region and MONUC's mandate, particularly during the first phase of its deployment (1999–2002). And Congo is not an anomaly in this respect. The point, rather, is that since 2000, such differences have not impeded the Council from consistently authorizing robust mandates in line with the new conception of impartiality. In other words, the general pattern with respect to peacekeeping has overwhelmingly been one of restraint and limited cooperation.

To explain this activism, scholars observe that missions authorized by the Council tend to be deployed to countries and regions that, following the end of the Cold War, are of comparatively less strategic importance or where competing interests are not sufficient to thwart engagement.[115] In addition, acrimonious relations over areas of great strategic relevance and on policy issues other than peacekeeping have not dimmed the Council's enthusiasm for deploying blue helmets. In 2004, Berdal, for example, observed that the 'deep divisions' among member states over Iraq did not have the 'lasting and paralysing effect on the Security Council' that many predicted. In fact, the opposite was true. Following the invasion of Iraq, new peacekeeping missions were authorized and existing ones like MONUC were 'substantially expanded' at 'an unprecedented rate.'[116] More recently, deadlock over Syria has coincided with new deployments to CAR and Mali as well as the creation of the Force Intervention Brigade in Congo. Diplomats maintain that this is not mere coincidence.[117] During periods of great discord, the permanent members looked to reconcile their differences and deepen cooperation where and when they could. Contexts such as Congo *appeared* to provide such an opportunity.

These observations echo the substantive objections discussed above. But they are also a reminder of the broader context within which the Council is situated, and the constraints and competing pressures under which it operates. In an age of hyper connectivity, the Council and specifically the P5 are subject to unprecedented scrutiny and intense pressure by the media, human-rights organizations, and civil society to respond to crises.[118] Failure to do so risks undermining the body's legitimacy and its standing as guarantor of international peace and security. And yet, its capacity is limited. As a former P5 Ambassador explains:

> The Council tries very hard to deal with the demands in the area of peace and security with words. The Council can't say a crisis is not relevant. Its members can never say that they don't trust the UN to deal with the problem or that they only deal with an issue on a smaller scale . . . There is a ceiling [on the resources needed for and complexity of] on each particular context—however, the Council can't publicly acknowledge that ceiling.[119]

This compulsion to respond, even if only by passing resolutions, is partly what explains the Council's activism and continued activism on peacekeeping since the late 1990s. Following the failures of Rwanda and Bosnia and on the heels of NATO's unilateral intervention Kosovo in 1999, observers and member states openly questioned both the Council's effectiveness and legitimacy with regard to authorizing (and withholding authorization) of force for protection purposes. And yet, the Council's response—the new assertive missions mandated at the turn of the new millennium—set an even higher standard for how it would be expected to respond in the face of future crises.

In this respect, early proponents of the more assertive approach to impartiality may not have fully appreciated the extent and nature of the transformation they brought about, or the power of the various pressures, which would make returning to a more passive approach difficult. Looking back, Brahimi somewhat exasperatedly states: 'we didn't express enough caution around protection in the report. We didn't see what it would become in the 2000s. On this issue, sometimes the Security Council acts like a student union— meting out resolutions, bold sweeping statements . . . You know, when a Council resolution says the UN is to protect the civilian population in Darfur, how serious is that? It is ridiculous, totally ridiculous to expect a relatively small mission to provide protection to the population of a territory as big as Texas or France'.[120] Or as Ambassador Fowler laments: 'Once humanitarian INGOs got a taste of these mandates and their ambitious aims, there was no going back... The Permanent Five believed that they could be on the side of [the] angels and not do anything beyond their mandated financial contributions. They believed they could manage the spin when it all went wrong.'[121] In other words, once members of the Council proclaimed that peacekeepers should protect civilians in places like Congo, it was difficult, no matter what the circumstances or prospects for success, to go back on their word.

CONCLUSION

The analysis in this chapter demonstrates that the process of institutionalization of a norm—particularly in the form of a codified text—does not necessarily affect consensus nor does it result in clarity, as much constructivist theorizing would suggest. Assertive impartiality remains ambiguous and deeply contested at the macro-organizational level, despite being manifest in doctrine and Security Council resolutions over the last fifteen years.

And yet, without member states' support there is, as Guéhenno laments, little hope of success. The legitimacy of the UN—and by extension the likelihood of its securing the resources and access so critical to its operations—derives in large part from whether it is seen to reflect and promote shared values, as well as from its effectiveness. Absent a standing force of its own, UN peacekeeping depends completely on the willingness of states to offer troops and police for operations. However, as this chapter has demonstrated, many of those countries that contribute large numbers of forces to contemporary UN operations are critical of assertive impartiality. In this context, analysis of contestation is important because it raises pressing questions about the viability and sustainability of peacekeeping and the UN's legitimacy in the years to come. In the nearer term, understanding these political fault lines is crucial because, as we shall see in the following chapter, it offers insight into contemporary practices, and the much-criticized discrepancy between what is mandated and what is practiced on the ground.

NOTES

1. Jean-Marie Guéhenno, *Fog of Peace: A Memoir of International Peacekeeping in the 21st Century* (Washington: Brookings Institution Press, 2015), 291.
2. Guéhenno (2015: 292).

3. Loren Cass, 'Norm Entrapment and Preference Change: the Evolution of the European Union position on International Emissions Trading', *Global Environmental Politics* 5/2 (2005), 38–60.

4. United Nations, A/2006/19 (1965). On the C-34 see Michael Hanrahan, 'The United Nations Special committee on Peacekeeping Operations: From 1965 to 2005', *International Peacekeeping: The Yearbook of International Peace Operations* (Leiden: Brill, 2007), 29–45.

5. Mats Berdal, *Building Peace after War* (Abingdon: Routledge, 2009), 150.

6. Thierry Tardy, 'Emerging Powers and Peacekeeping: an Unlikely Normative Clash' (Geneva: GCSP Policy Paper, 2012/13), 2.

7. The US, France, and UK were particularly positive and issued separate statements in support. See for example, US Department of State, Factsheet, 23 August 2000, http://www.state.gov/www/issues/fs-peacekp_reform_000823.html

8. United Nations, A/RES/55/2 (2000).

9. William Durch et al., *The Brahimi Report and the Future of UN Peace Operations* (Washington: Stimson Center, 2003), 7.

10. United Nations, A/C.4/55/6 (2000), 45.

11. United Nations, 'No Exit without Strategies' Statement by Mr. Kamalesh Sharma, 15 November 2000, http://www.un.int/india/ind420.htm. See also United Nations, A/54/670 (2000); United Nations, A/RES/55/2 (2000); United Nations, A/RES/55/135 (2000).

12. Interviews with DPKO officials and government officials, New York, March 2010.

13. Interview with government official, New York, March 2010.

14. Interview with DPKO official, New York, March 2010.

15. Interview with government official, New York, March 2010.

16. *Brahimi Report* (2000: x).

17. Interviews with DPKO official, New York, March 2010.

18. United Nations, S/1999/957 (1999). For his own reflections on these issues see Kofi Annan with Nader Mousavizadeh, *Interventions: A Life in War and Peace* (New York: Penguin Press, 2012).

19. For example, the Brahimi panel deliberately left to one side the issues of Security Council reform, the remuneration of peacekeepers, the use of *gratis* military officers and, more broadly, the distinction between peacekeeping and humanitarian intervention. See Silke Weinlich, '(Re)generating Peacekeeping Authority: The Brahimi Process', *Journal of Intervention and Statebuilding* 6/3 (2012), 257–77; Salman Ahmed, Paul Keating, and Ugo Solinas, 'Shaping the Future of UN Peace Operations: is there a Doctrine in the House?', *Cambridge Review of International Affairs* 20/1 (2007), 11–28.

20. For example, the issue of defining a doctrine, which was particularly contentious, and when raised during the research phase of the *Brahimi Report*, prompted 'several delegations to question the intent and appropriateness of the [panel's] exercise', was left purposely vague. The report's treatment of the core norms of peacekeeping, including the reformulation of impartiality, was seen to be 'pushing the edge of the envelope' such that any additional detail or specification risked provoking even greater consternation. Ahmed, et al. (2007: 18); Interview with Lakhdar Brahimi, Algerian UN Envoy and Advisor; former Chairperson of the

Independent Panel on UN Peace Operations, Paris, July 2011. Similarly, the consultative process for the *Capstone Doctrine* revealed a number of divisive issues that influenced the wording of the text. For example, the formulation of the use of force and the impartial implementation of mission mandates reflected disagreements aired during the process—disagreements that became particularly visible at a workshop in Jordan in 2007. During the workshop, the five largest TCCs in attendance were vocal in their reluctance to endorse the language of protecting civilians and the use of force. Given this opposition, the final decision to sanction 'non-use of force except in self-defence and in defence of the mandate' was, as one participant described, a last-ditch effort to strengthen covertly the robustness of the doctrine under the guise of a seemingly benign and passive principle: 'We pulled the wool over their eyes as mandates include almost everything under the sun, including most importantly the protection of civilians.' Phone interview with government official, October 2009.

21. Richard Gowan, 'Yes, Ban Ki-moon is America's Poodle. And no, that's not a good thing', *Politico Magazine*, 22 January 2014, http://www.politico.com/magazine/story/2014/01/ban-ki-moon-united-nations-united-states-102491

22. Richard Gowan, 'Floating Down the River of History: Ban Ki-moon and Peace-keeping, 2007–2011', *Global Governance* 17/4 (2011), 401. Ban Ki-moon's stance on peacekeeping shifted visibly in 2011 over the electoral crisis in Ivory Coast and was sustained thereafter. The robust response mounted by the UN and championed by his office became a key part of his bid for a second term as Secretary-General. The change may in part have been a reflection of timing and existing practice. In particular, the concern of setting a precedent was no longer a relevant issue, as the Council had been authorizing robust mandates for over a decade. This accumulated practice may also have engendered a certain degree of confidence that the institution could weather criticisms over such missions. In addition, the development of both the PoC agenda and an implementation plan for RtoP (the 2005 Summit Declaration and the subsequent appointment of a Special Advisor to the Secretary-General) may have led Ban Ki-moon and others to believe—however inaccurately—that greater consensus and commitment existed amongst the membership for more coercive forms of engagement to protect civilians.

23. Arthur Isak Applbaum, 'Culture, Identity, and Legitimacy', in *Governance in a Globalizing World*, edited by Joseph Nye and John Donohue (Washington, DC: Brookings Institution Press, 2000), 326. See also Hurd (2002).

24. Jane Boulden, 'Double Standards, Distance and Disengagement: Collective Legitimization in the Post-Cold War Security Council', *Security Dialogue* 37/3 (2006), 409.

25. US contributions, which peaked at 28,000 uniformed personnel under UNITAF, ceased entirely after the losses incurred in Somalia. Presidential Decision Directive 25, issued by the Clinton administration in 1994, constrained American participation in UN peace operations throughout the 1990s. See Samantha Power, *A Problem from Hell: America and the Age of Genocide* (New York: Basic Books, 2002), Ch. 10. Britain and France, which, respectively, had roughly 9,000 and 8,000 forces deployed in 1995, pulled back their field presence. By the end of 2000, both countries had only a few hundred personnel deployed globally,

26. Similarly, Sweden, Norway, Denmark, Finland, and Ireland—countries that combined contributed more than 25 per cent of UN troops deployed during the Cold War—limited their total global commitment to 1.6 per cent by the end of 2001. Alex J. Bellamy and Paul D. Williams, 'The West and Contemporary Peace Operations', *Journal of Peace Research* 46/1 (2009), 43.

27. Katharina Coleman, 'Token Troop Contributions to United Nations Peacekeeping Operations', in *Providing Peacekeepers: The Politics, Challenges, and Future of United Nations Peacekeeping Contributions*, edited by Alex J. Bellamy and Paul D. Williams (Oxford: Oxford University Press, 2013).

28. While Western nations are still the largest financial backers of peacekeeping, reforms to the apportionment scheme since 2000 have meant that Western funding has gradually decreased (notable exceptions include the UK, Canada, and South Korea). Under the new system, P5 states have been relieved of approximately 2 per cent of their allotted dues to UN peacekeeping. In addition, Western states have accumulated significant arrears on their contributions. Bellamy and Williams (2009: 46). For an overview of peacekeeping financing, see Katharina Coleman, 'The Political Economy of UN Peacekeeping: Incentivizing Effective Participation', *Providing for Peacekeeping Thematic Study No.7* (New York: International Peace Institute, May 2014).

29. See Bellamy and Williams, eds. (2013).

30. Contributions to peacekeeping are explained by myriad motivations. Indeed, the typical assumption that developing states and emerging powers are driven by profit and prestige is a gross oversimplification that obfuscates the complexity of motives that compel states to contribute personnel. A state, for example, may see peacekeeping as a profile enhancement tool on the international stage, as a way to spread democracy and promote liberal norms, as a form of espionage, personnel training, or even as a means to keep the military distracted and engaged so as to avoid their meddling in the state's domestic affairs. Moreover, as Bellamy and Williams aptly note, the 'general *predisposition*' of a particular state towards the UN and peacekeeping, may vary over time and be distinct from 'specific *decisions*' taken by its government with regards to particular missions. Alex Bellamy and Paul Williams, *Broadening the Base of United Nations Troop- and Police Contributing Countries* (New York: International Peace Institute, 2012).

31. Interview with senior military officer, United Kingdom, November 2009.

32. Phone interview with senior military officer, United States, November 2009.

33. Jean-Marie Guéhenno, 'On the Challenges and Achievements of Reforming the UN Peace Operations', *International Peacekeeping* 9/2 (2002), 76.

34. In July 2014, the fifth committee reached agreement on increasing personnel reimbursement and important steps were taken towards reimbursement of contingency-owned equipment. However, for large TCCs/PCCs, particularly India and Pakistan, these commitments are still regarded as inadequate. See United Nations, S/PV.7228 (2014).

35. While over-commitment in other operational contexts was the public rationale given for their reduced support, in private many diplomats I interviewed conceded that the real reason for the West's disengagement is a deep distrust of the UN's command capabilities. As one diplomat asserted: '[n]o first-world nation wants to

devote forces to a UN mission. The UN doesn't match up to their training and they don't respect DPKO like [a defence department]'. The fact that Western governments have not re-engaged in UN peacekeeping in recent years following the drawdown of their forces in Afghanistan and Iraq would support this view.

36. Karsten Friis, 'Peacekeeping and Counter-insurgency: Two of a Kind?', *International Peacekeeping* 17/1 (2010). Interview with DPKO official, New York, March 2010.

37. Bellamy and Williams (2009).

38. See A. Sarjoh Bah and Bruce Jones, 'Peace Operations Partnerships: Lessons and Issues from Coordination to Hybrid Arrangements' (New York: Center on International Cooperation, New York University, May 2008). Bellamy and Williams also distinguish between 'tightly-coupled' and 'loosely-coupled' hybrid missions. In 'tightly-coupled' hybrid missions, such as KFOR/UNMIK in Kosovo, the UN and non-UN components are jointly mandated and share some common command or political decision-making structure. 'Loosely-coupled' hybrids, in contrast, are ad hoc and the different components do not share formal legal or institutional structures, though the UN and non-UN components may cooperate very closely, as in the British operation in Sierra Leone (2000–05) which ran parallel to UNAMSIL.

39. Martin Shaw, *The New Western Way of War: Risk-transfer War and its Crisis in Iraq* (Cambridge: Polity Press, 2005).

40. In 2005, Jean-Marie Guéhenno argued: 'We cannot support what has been called peacekeeping apartheid—the logic that keeps a larger force of the world's best troops in tiny Kosovo than is kept in Congo, where millions have died.' Guéhenno, Address to the Challenges Project, London, March 2005. Available at http://www.un.org/en/peacekeeping/articles/article020305.htm

41. Interview with senior government official, London, December 2011.

42. Colum Lynch, 'The Blue Helmet Caste System', *Foreign Policy*, 11 April 2013.

43. Philip Cunliffe, *Legions of Peace: UN Peacekeepers from the Global South* (New York: Hurst & Co., 2014), 20.

44. In the Council, the need to ensure an equitable geographic representation across non-permanent seats results in a disadvantage for the majority of TCCs/PCCs which, drawn from Africa and Asia, count as one region each during biennial council elections. Even when they are represented on the Council, the influence of non-permanent members has been circumscribed by changes to the Council's working procedures, such as expanded consultations, which have contributed to the growing lack of transparency in recent years.

45. Article 44 of the UN Charter stipulates that '[w]hen the Security Council has decided to use force it shall, before calling upon a Member not represented on it to provide armed forces in fulfilment of the obligations assumed under Article 43, invite that Member, if the Member so desires, to participate in the decisions of the Security Council concerning the employment of contingents of that Member's armed forces'.

46. *Brahimi Report* (2000: 11).

47. United Nations, A/54/839. The Council considered the issue on two occasions, including during an open debate organized by Singapore on the issue. See United Nations, S/1327 (2000), S/2001/21, S/PV/4257.

48. United Nations, S/PRST/2001/3.
49. Susan Hulton, 'Council Working Methods and Procedures', in *The UN Security Council. From the Cold War to the 21st Century*, edited by David Malone (Boulder, CO: Lynne Rienner, 2004), 240–1; Cunliffe (2014).
50. Ian Hurd, 'Legitimacy, Power, and the Symbolic Life of the UN Security Council', *Global Governance* 8/1(2002), 42–3. Various reform initiatives advanced by the General Assembly and, specifically, the Accountability, Coherence, and Transparency Group, to address the issue of Council working methods have had little traction. For example, in 2012 the so-called S5 (Costa Rica, Jordan, Liechtenstein, Singapore, and Switzerland) put forward a draft General Assembly resolution to ensure that the Council honour its own commitments for transparency. The proposal was however withdrawn, as the P5 regarded the initiative as undue interference in its working methods. Jennifer Welsh and Dominik Zaum, 'Legitimation and the United Nations Security Council', in *Legitimating International Organizations*, edited by Dominik Zaum (Oxford: Oxford University Press, 2013), 75; see also United Nations, GA/11590, *Considering Security Council's Annual Report, General Assembly Calls for Continued Reforms, Greater Transparency in Working Methods of 15-Nation body*, 21 November 2014.
51. Interview with DPKO official, New York, March 2010.
52. Interview with government official, New York, March 2010.
53. Interview with military official, New York, March 2010.
54. Interview with senior Secretariat official, New York, March 2010.
55. Phone interview with government official, April 2010.
56. Statement by Mr. Mohammed Adeep, Honorable Member of Parliament and Member of the Indian Delegation, on Agenda Item 53: Comprehensive Review of the Whole Question of Peacekeeping Operations in all their Aspects, 30th October 2013, https://papersmart.unmeetings.org/media2/703760/item-53-india.pdf
57. United Nations, A/61/19/Rev. 1 (2008); United Nations, A/63/19 (2009).
58. Similarly, the C-34 first discussed robust peacekeeping in 2010, a decade following the *Brahimi Report*'s introduction of the concept.
59. Antonio Cassese, 'Self-Determination' in *The Oxford Companion to Politics of the World*, edited by Joel Krieger (New York: Oxford University Press, 1993), 822–3.
60. For example, international administrators for the League of Nations were expected to be 'impartial' in adjudicating colonial claims. See Howard Ellis, *The Origin Structure & Working of the League of Nations* (London: George Allen & Unwin, 1928).
61. United Nations, A/RES/2131 (1966).
62. See for example, Non-Aligned Movement, *The Jakarta Message: A Call For Collective Action and the Democratization of International Relations. Tenth Conference of Heads of State or Government of Non-aligned Countries* (Jakarta: 6 September 1992); Non-Aligned Movement, *Final Document of the Sixteenth Conference of Heads of State or Government of Non-Aligned Nations* (Tehran: 31 August 2012).
63. United Nations, A/47/120A (1992) and 47/120 B (1993).
64. In addition to variation within the group, several interviewees noted that the rotating leadership of the NAM plays a critical role in determining how productive

the C-34 is from year to year. Several officials remarked that under the leadership of Prince Zeid of Jordan there was less bickering among its members than in more recent years when the group has been led by representatives of Morocco, Pakistan, and Egypt.

65. Interview with DPKO official, New York, March 2010.
66. Interview with government official, New York June 2011.
67. Interview with senior DPKO official, New York, March 2010.
68. Interview with government official, New York, April 2010. See for example the remarks of Cuba, United Nations, S/PV.6531 (2011).
69. See remarks of Uruguay, United Nations S/PV.6513 (2011) and India S/PV.6917 (2013); United Nations, GA/SPD/568 (2014).
70. Interview with research analyst, New York, September 2010.
71. Thorsten Benner, et al., *Effective and Responsible Protection from Atrocity Crimes: Toward Global Action* (Berlin: Global Public Policy Institute, 2015); Interview with diplomat, New York, May 2015.
72. Interviews with government officials, New York, March 2010. States within the Community of Latin American and Caribbean States (CELAC), a grouping that overlaps with the NAM, are also regarded as being more moderate. Interview with diplomat, New York, May 2015.
73. Interview with government official, New York, March 2010.
74. Interview with Jean-Marie Guéhenno, former Under-Secretary-General of UN Peacekeeping, New York, March 2010; June 2011.
75. Interview with Guéhenno, 2010.
76. *Brahimi Report* (2000:1).
77. The UN made several other concessions to President Deby, including construction of an airport, which led several analysts to charge that MINURCAT had become 'impotent' and partial to the government. The mission was asked by the government to withdraw in 2010. Interview with DPKO official, New York, March 2010. See also Chrysantus Ayangafac, *Resolving the Chadian Political Epilepsy: An Assessment of Intervention Efforts* (South Africa: ISS, 2009); John Karlsrud and Randi Solhjell, 'An Honourable Exit for MINURCAT?', *NUPI Policy Brief* 3 (2010).
78. Interviews with DPKO officials and government officials, New York, March 2010.
79. Thomas Risse, '"Let's Argue!" Communicative Action in World Politics', *International Organization* 54/1 (2000), 22.
80. Frank Schimmelfennig, 'The Community Trap: Liberal Norms, Rhetorical Action, and the Eastern Enlargement of the European Union', *International Organization* 55/1 (2001), 63.
81. Interview with UN official, New York, March 2010.
82. Interview with Guéhenno, 2011.
83. Interview with Robert Fowler, former Permanent Representative of Canada to the United Nations (1995–2000); former personal representative for Africa for Prime Ministers Jean Chrétien, Paul Martin, and Stephen Harper; former Canadian Deputy Minister of National Defence, Ottawa, May 2011.
84. Interview with government official, New York, June 2011.
85. Annan with Mousavizadeh (2012: 77).

86. Boulden (2006); Philip Cunliffe, 'The Politics of Global Governance in UN Peacekeeping', *International Peacekeeping* 16/3 (2009), 323–36.
87. See, for example, the remarks of India and Uruguay, United Nations, S/PV.6917 (2013).
88. Interview with UN official, New York, March 2010.
89. *Capstone Doctrine* (2008: 38).
90. Interview with Louise Fréchette, former Deputy-Secretary-General of the UN, Montreal, March 2011. These concerns are also echoed by member states. For example, Uruguay notes that 'the UN has valuable capital' which it does not have the 'luxury of squandering', noting that it is 'easier to destroy' the trust necessary for political mediation than it is 'to build'. United Nations, S/PV.6531 (2011).
91. Interview with Fréchette, 2011.
92. Interview with Fréchette, 2011.
93. Interview with Fowler, 2011.
94. Interview with Fowler, 2011.
95. Interview with Fowler, 2011.
96. Interview with Fowler, 2011.
97. United Nations, S/RES/1270 (1999).
98. Interview with Guéhenno, 2011.
99. Interview with senior UN official, New York, March 2010.
100. Kate Grady, 'Sexual Exploitation and Abuse by UN Peacekeepers: A Threat to Impartiality', *International Peacekeeping* 17/2 (2010), 215–28.
101. Interview with senior Secretariat official, New York, October 2011.
102. For example, training guidance states that peacekeepers should 'never become involved in sexual liaisons which could affect [their] impartiality'. United Nations, *Standards of Conduct: We are United Nations Peacekeeping Personnel*, https://cdu.unlb.org/UNStandardsofConduct/WeAreUnitedNationsPeacekee-pingPersonnel.aspx. This point was also reiterated by Prince Raad bin Zeid in United Nations, A/59/710 (2005), para 6.
103. Guglielmo Verdirame, *The UN and Human Rights: Who Guards the Guardians?* (Cambridge: Cambridge University Press, 2011), 229. On peacekeeper enmesh-ment in illicit activity, see Peter Andreas, *Blue Helmets and Black Markets: The Business of Survival in the Siege of Sarajevo* (Ithaca: Cornell University Press, 2008).
104. States contributing peacekeepers retain exclusive disciplinary and criminal jur-isdiction. The Office of Internal Oversight Services (OIOS) and the Conduct and Discipline Unit are only empowered to conduct internal investigations. See the 'Peacekeeping Law Reform Project' at the University of Essex, http://www.essex.ac.uk/plrp/documents/default.aspx
105. A confidential survey by the DPKO/DFS in 2013 found that 'court martial, repatriation, loss of financial benefits or even prosecution by the International Criminal Court were among [the] consequences reportedly feared by troops'. Quoted in United Nations, OIOS, A/68/787 (2014), 16.
106. The Special Rapporteur described MINUSTAH's response as 'broadly satisfac-tory'. See United Nations, *Report of the Special Rapporteur, Commission on Human Rights*, E/CN.4/2006/53/Add.1 (2006); *United Nations, Report of the*

Secretary-General on the UN Stabilization Mission in Haiti, S/2006/592 (2006). A complaint against Brazil was submitted to the Inter-American Commission on Human Rights by human-rights activists, but was eventually rejected by the Commission.

107. For example, internal reviews were conducted into MONUC's operations against the LRA in Garambe National Park (2006), UNOCI's operations in Ivory Coast (2011), and regarding the use of force by MINUSMA contingents in Mali (2015).

108. Marlise Simons, 'Dutch peacekeepers are found responsible for deaths', *New York Times*, 6 September 2013. The UN's impunity was also challenged in relation to Srebrenica when a case was brought against both the UN and the Dutch state by the Mothers of Srebrenica on behalf of 6,000 Bosnian Muslim men and boys. However, the Court's ruling determined that UN immunity prevailed and an appeals court ruling stated that the Court did not have the jurisdiction to hear the case against the UN. On treating the UN as a moral agent, see Toni Erskine, 'Blood on the UN's Hands? Assigning Duties and Apportioning Blame to an Intergovernmental Organisation', *Global Society* 18/1 (2004), 21–42.

109. See, for example, Siobhán Wills, *Protecting Civilians: The Obligations of Peacekeepers* (Oxford: Oxford University Press 2009), 266–7.

110. Verdirame (2011: 222).

111. Verdirame (2011: 223).

112. Cited in Verdirame (2011: 223).

113. Interview with government official, New York, June 2011. Since attempting to undertake regional peacekeeping in places like Georgia, Moldavia, and Tajikistan in the mid-1990s—operations derided by critics as mere cover ups for Russia's own aggressive ambitions—Moscow has disengaged from peacekeeping and rarely contributes to mission deployments. Russia's lack of engagement may be partly explained by the fact that the country has few political and economic stakes in Africa where, as of May 2015, 80 per cent of all peacekeepers were currently deployed.

114. Interviews with diplomats, New York, 2011 and 2015. See Miwa Hirono and Marc Lanteigne, 'Introduction: China and UN Peacekeeping', *International Peacekeeping* 18/3 (2011), 243–56.

115. MacQueen (2006: 158); Boulden (2006).

116. Mats Berdal, 'The UN after Iraq', *Survival* 46/3 (2004), 88.

117. Interview with former Permanent Representative to the Security Council, December 2011; interview with diplomat, New York, May 2015.

118. On the role of NGOs in norm diffusion and in shaping and influencing international policymaking, see Margaret Keck and Kathryn Sikkink, *Activists Beyond Borders: Advocacy Networks in International Politics* (Ithaca: Cornell University Press, 1998); Thomas Weiss, Tatiana Carayannis, and Richard Jolly, 'The "Third" United Nations', *Global Governance* 15/1 (2009), 123–42.

119. Interview with former Permanent Representative to the Security Council, December 2011.

120. Interview with Brahimi, 2011.

121. Interview with Fowler, 2011.

4

Implementation and the Local Politics of Peacekeeping in the Congo

During an interview in 2010, I asked a senior Congolese official whether the United Nations (UN) was being impartial in keeping peace in Congo. His response was telling. 'Impartial about whose peace?' he asked me. 'Peace is political. Peace is always somebody's peace . . . peace is very controversial and that's why it often doesn't happen in Congo.'[1]

Tragically, that official's observation is as true today as it was then. After fifteen years of attempts by the UN to impartially keep peace in Congo as one of the most 'robustly' mandated peacekeeping mission's in the organization's history, violence in the east of the country continues unabated. Human-rights protection is illusory for many, if not most, Congolese. And since holding landmark elections in 2006, the country has dropped nineteen places in the UNDP development rankings to claim the dubious distinction of being the world's second least-developed state.[2] What might be the connection between these obvious, distressing and demoralizing failures, and changes in the very way that peacekeeping—indeed impartiality itself—is construed and understood?

In the following two chapters I analyse implementation of the dominant conception of assertive impartiality and its effects in the specific case of the Congo mission (MONUC/MONUSCO). Consideration of implementation is crucial because it sheds light on what norms actually do: that is, how they function and shape behaviour. Given the social nature of norms, we cannot assume that the institutionalization of a norm such as impartiality will translate automatically into practice or that it will hold similar meaning for actors across and within peacekeeping contexts such as Congo. While this is true of all norms, it is particularly the case with impartiality given that the *basis for* decision-making—peacekeeping mandates—frequently change.

This chapter analyses implementation of the assertive conception of impartiality over the course of the mission's decade-and-a-half long deployment. It demonstrates how actors within the mission and the Security Council vehemently contested the very meaning and appropriateness of the norm itself.

Judgments about who was a 'spoiler' and what constituted 'spoiling activity' were subjective, fluid, controversial and reflective of political dynamics at both the macro- and micro-levels. Violence was no longer considered to be an unquestionable wrong that peacekeepers, as pseudo-law enforcers, could right, or eliminate. Rather, like its opposite, peace, violence in the Congo was deeply political.

That the ethical and the political are not easily disentangled—a key contention of this book—runs counter to the epistemology implied in the assertive conception of impartiality presented in Chapter 2: the belief that the Security Council and the peacekeeping missions it authorizes can be and in fact are above particular political interests, that 'impartial' judgments are beyond reproach because they are rooted in human rights and therefore in the interest of every individual regardless of whether he or she is Congolese, Rwandan or, for that matter, Canadian. Examination of peacekeeping in Congo amply demonstrates that this has never been the case—that it has never been possible *not* to take sides in some fashion.

The chapter proceeds in five substantive sections that take the form of a historical analysis. Each section covers a core phase of the mission, delineated by significant political developments that altered the mandate and *basis for* decision-making: 1) Lusaka Ceasefire Agreement (1999–2002); 2) Transitional Government (2003–06); 3) Post-Election Period (2007–08); 4) Regional Rapprochement and 23 March Agreement (2009–11); and 5) The Fall of Goma and a 'Framework of Hope' (2012–15).

For each phase, I begin by reviewing the roles prescribed for the mission by the Security Council, and provide background on the peace agreement or political process that it was tasked with overseeing. I then explain how local actors obstructed the mission and transgressed its mandate, and how peacekeepers responded. I focus specifically on instances in which 'spoilers' were in contravention of the peace agreement or political process, and where civilians either faced imminent threats or were actually harmed: in other words, situations that according to an assertive conception of the norm of impartiality would warrant the use of force and robust intervention. Finally, I recount how the posture assumed by the mission and its responses to specific instances of miscreant and violent behaviour were, in a kind of vicious circle, both produced by and further contributed to contestation over impartiality at both the macro- and micro-level. The conclusion explores the linkages between the levels in greater detail.

I begin, however, by introducing the Congo case. Congo has a long and tragic history of conflict, plunder, and predation, first under Belgian colonial rule and then under President Mobutu. While a comprehensive study of this complex history is beyond the scope of this book, the following section provides a sketch of Congo's more recent history of violence.[3] It begins in the aftermath of the Rwandan genocide an event that seasoned analysts contend acted as the trigger for the Congo Wars (1996–97; 1998–2003) and which continues to be a critical factor in the region's instability. In this way, as this chapter demonstrates, the very case of peacekeeping inaction that arguably did most to prompt impartiality's reconceptualization at the end of the 1990s figured prominently throughout the mission's deployment. An account of this history is therefore crucial to understanding the content of and contestation over the various roles assumed by the mission, and claims by peacekeepers that their actions and decisions were impartial.

A SHORT HISTORY OF A CONTINENTAL WAR

During the Rwandan genocide, roughly two million Hutus fled their country for fear of retaliation when the largely Tutsi Rwandan Patriotic Front (RPF) took power and ended the slaughter. More than a million settled in the east of what was then Zaire, becoming what Sarah Lischer has termed 'state-in-exile refugees'.[4] These refugees congregated in sprawling camps around the cities of Goma and Bukavu, where they were mixed with members of former Rwandan President Habyarimana's government, ex-*Forces Armées Rwandaises* (FAR) and others who had perpetrated the genocide.

Between 1994 and 1996, international donors spent $1.3 billion on humanitarian assistance to address the refugee crisis in eastern Zaire. Beyond providing sustenance, this aid was a critical 'building block' in the remilitarization of the ex-FAR who were shielded by the protection of the camps.[5] After the camps were dispersed and abandoned in 1996, documents, including the contents of a filing cabinet belonging to Major General Augustin Bizimungu, chief of staff of the ex-FAR, revealed how humanitarian aid was integral to the military strategy and planning of the genocidal government in exile.[6] Moreover, non-governmental organizations (NGOs) recounted how the aid they delivered was used against actual refugees, increasing their vulnerability. This massive misuse of assistance prompted several international NGOs to withdraw and spurred a flurry of criticisms on the harmful consequences of aid. UN agencies working in the area made numerous appeals to member states to demilitarize the camps, but carried on working in them though the appeals went unanswered.[7]

First Congo War (1996–97)

The presence of both genuine refugees and militia exacerbated existing interethnic tensions over citizenship and land. In the face of mounting domestic opposition, Zairian President Mobutu supported the Hutu extremists in the camps, supplying arms and military training in a bid to shore up his own power. The proximate cause for the First Congo War—which led the Rwandan leadership to attack Zaire—was the threatening presence of these large militarized camps on its border. In the fall of 1996, Rwanda intervened and forcibly closed the camps. Within days, approximately 500,000 refugees returned to Rwanda, while an estimated 200,000 people fled further westward into the dense Congolese forest. During the invasion, several thousand Hutu refugees and local Hutu civilians were killed in a series of massacres.[8]

Rwanda's security concerns were, however, only part of the rationale for invading and only go so far in explaining what ensued after the camps were attacked and many of the refugees returned home. Years of President Mobutu's inequitable 'Zairianization' campaign, buttressed by successive Western governments willing to fill his coffers during the Cold War, meant that by the late 1980s the Congolese state was in decay, teetering on the edge of total economic collapse. By 1996 Gerard Prunier writes, 'the Zairean core of the continent had become a hologram flickering on the brink of its own destruction'.[9]

For those regional statesmen at the helm of what they hoped would be an African renaissance, Mobutu's kleptocratic rule personified the worst of the continent's Cold War leadership, and his overthrow was increasingly seen as Africa's *Kulembeka* ('our duty, our task').[10] To that end, Rwanda and Uganda played an instrumental role in creating the *Alliance des Forces Démocratiques pour la Libération du Congo-Zaire* (AFDL), an alliance of Zairian rebel groups that—supported by Angolan, Rwandan, and Ugandan armies—marched on Kinshasa, ousting Mobutu's government in May 1997.[11]

Second Congo War (1998–2003)

The installation of Laurent Kabila as President by the AFDL was lauded as the harbinger of a new era, of a new *Democratic* Republic of the Congo (DRC), as it was now named. Kabila, however, fearful of losing favour as people across the country became alarmed by the number of Rwandan strongmen around him, and by what they saw as their neighbour's potentially expansionist aims, in July 1998 made the fateful move of expelling the Rwandans from the country, thereby turning the 'kingmakers', as René Lemarchand notes, against their newly crowned king. Twelve days later, in an event which marked the start of the second, more lengthy and brutal Congo war, the Rwandan army re-entered the country, hijacked a plane to the Western city of Kitona, aligned themselves with local forces and began encroaching on the capital and on what was viewed as Kabila's unworthy regime. Shortly thereafter, this newly formed Rwandan and Ugandan-backed Congolese rebel group was named the *Rassemblement Congolais pour la Démocratie* (RCD).[12]

The RCD's attack on Kinshasa was foiled by Angola and Zimbabwe, who entered the war on the side of Kabila. The war quickly escalated, drawing in no fewer than ten African states in gradations of conflict (*Core conflict*: Congo, Rwanda and Uganda; *second layer*: Angola, Zimbabwe, and Namibia; *third layer*: Libya, Chad, and Sudan; and *fourth layer*: Burundi and Central African Republic).[13] The largest war in modern African history, the conflict continued for five years and, in the making and unmaking of alliances, eventually even pitted Rwanda against Uganda, as these erstwhile allies fought, in part, over control of minerals in the East. By the time Joseph Kabila took over after his father's assassination in 2001, the country-wide war, which had by then claimed some three million lives, had begun to run out of steam, formally ending in 2003, as Prunier describes, not with a bang but with a whimper.[14] In effect, the war wound down because no one could win it.

It was into this cauldron of conflicts that MONUC was first deployed in 1999 as an observer mission to oversee the Lusaka Ceasefire Agreement, three years before the formal end of hostilities. While the trappings of a sovereign state became visible with the establishment of a Transitional Government in 2003 and national elections in 2006 and 2011, Congolese political space continued, and still continues, to be defined by those who bear arms and have money, and conflict plagues much of the country's eastern region.

Rather than a 'simple binary conflict neatly arrayed along a single issue dimension', persistent violence in Congo is the result of what political scientist Stathis Kalyvas describes as 'welters of complex struggles' that have local, national, and regional dimensions, giving rise to conflicts within conflicts.[15] Factors contributing to the country's endemic instability and ongoing suffering include, in particular, the prevalence of weak and corrupt state institutions; tensions over land and citizenship, which are inextricably bound to issues of identity and belonging; and meddling by Congo's neighbours, particularly Rwanda. In what follows, I analyse the mission's contested role in the five phases of its deployment, each delineated by political advents in the country.

LUSAKA TO SUN CITY (1999–2002)

Signed on 10 July 1999, the Lusaka Ceasefire Agreement was the culmination of multiple international peace initiatives, brokered under the auspices of the Southern African Development Community (SADC) and Organization of African Unity (OAU).[16] Angola, Namibia, Uganda, Rwanda, Congo, and Zimbabwe were initially parties to the agreement with the RCD and MLC rebel groups signing later in August 1999.

The ceasefire called for the respect of international humanitarian law (IHL) by all parties, definitive withdrawal of all foreign forces from Congo, and establishment of an 'all inclusive' National Dialogue.[17] To oversee the agreement and safeguard the peace process, the signatories requested the deployment of an 'appropriate UN force', outlined mandates for both a peacekeeping and peace-enforcement operation, and drafted a calendar for deployment.[18] The more robust mission was to be a 15,000-strong force designated to 'track down', disarm, and rehabilitate members of the various 'negative' militia that were not signatories to the agreement.[19] Moreover, the withdrawal of foreign forces from Congo was to be premised on the successful 'neutralization' of these forces. Critically, this included ex-FAR and *Interahamwe* militia who had participated in the Rwandan genocide and were still at large in Congo. Until 2001, the militia operated under the rubric of the *Armée pour la Libération du Rwanda* (ALiR). It later rebranded itself as the *Forces Démocratiques de Libération du Rwanda* (FDLR).

The Security Council welcomed the Lusaka Agreement, extolling it as a 'viable basis' for ending the conflict in Congo.[20] On 6 August, the Council passed Resolution 1258 authorizing the deployment of ninety military personnel to liaise with the signatories and lay the groundwork for the larger mission specified in the agreement.[21] In November, the mission was named MONUC[22] and in February 2000 the Council adopted Resolution 1291, which expanded the UN's presence to include 500 observers and a protection force of 5,037 soldiers.[23] Authored by the US delegation, Resolution 1291 detailed a three-phase concept of operations: MONUC was to deploy UN liaison officers, verify the ceasefire and ascertain troop positions, and then facilitate the demobilization, disarmament, and reintegration (DDR) of all armed groups while overseeing the withdrawal of foreign forces.[24] Phase III was made conditional on adequate security guarantees and cooperation by the parties. In addition, the mission was instructed to support humanitarian operations, and cooperate with the facilitator of the National Dialogue. Based on the IHL provisions of Lusaka and the precedent of the UN mission to Sierra Leone, the Council authorized the force, acting under Chapter VII, to 'take the necessary action, in the areas of deployment . . . and as it deems it within its capabilities . . . to protect civilians under imminent threat of physical violence'.[25]

Passive Peacekeeping as War Continues

That the Lusaka Agreement was signed under intense international pressure meant that most of the belligerents had little intention of fulfilling the commitments detailed therein.[26] For Rwanda and Uganda, which at the time controlled roughly two-thirds of Congo, Lusaka provided recognition of their territorial gains and legitimated their proxies as parties with which to be negotiated. For Kabila, who faced the prospect of defeat, the ceasefire provided a convenient respite to mitigate further territorial losses. Consequently, the agreement did not hold and the Second Congo War continued unabated on every front, as the signatories 'held out for a return on their investment' in the conflict.[27] Serious violations of human rights and IHL were committed by all parties.[28]

Given this background of often hidden and conflicting agendas, the consent for MONUC that was formally given both in Kinshasa's initial request for the mission and by the parties in their adoption of the Lusaka Agreement proved in practice to be a chimera. Throughout this phase, hostility towards the mission was visceral and widespread. All of the signatories at one time or another impeded the force from carrying out its mandate. While on the face of it this intransigence reflected the unwillingness of the signatories to abide by the terms of the agreement, it also demonstrated a deeper and more pervasive anti-UN sentiment, tied to the institution's history in the region.

The role prescribed for the UN in the ceasefire agreement was both duplicitous and impracticable; the signatories knew that the Council would be reluctant to meet their demands, for reasons I discuss further below. Brokered primarily by African leaders, Lusaka was seen by many of those involved as a testament to an emerging 'renaissance' of leadership on the continent—a leadership that was quick to highlight the West's meddling during the Cold War, failed interventions of the 1990s, and comparatively meagre attention paid to the Congo Wars, in contrast to those in the Balkans. According to the International Crisis Group, the signatories' request for a Chapter VII force had been a way to set up Western powers, to expose their reluctance to commit to the troubled region, and reveal their 'double standards when it came to the African continent'.[29] At the signing in Lusaka, Rwandan Vice President Paul Kagame, whose lieutenants had authored much of the agreement, publicly derided the UN's capabilities. Citing both the genocide in Rwanda and subsequent arming of Hutu refugees in eastern Zaire 'under the eyes of UN observers', Kagame noted: 'I know how to fight insurgents. Does the UN also know?'[30]

Such animus towards and deep distrust of the UN meant that the signatories were a priori unlikely to accept the UN as an unbiased and legitimate actor, regardless of the contents of the agreement or mandate. In Kinshasa, President Laurent Kabila, who had been a staunch supporter of Lumumba during ONUC's deployment in the 1960s, was outwardly hostile toward the UN. He initially refused to meet Kamel Morjane, the mission's first Special Representative of the Secretary-General (SRSG), placed severe restrictions on MONUC's freedom of movement, and did little to quell demonstrations against the mission or stop the circulation of inflammatory anti-UN propaganda in the capital.[31] The government's obstruction of the mission continued until Kabila's death in January 2001.[32]

The mission encountered similar issues with the various parties to the conflict.[33] Of these, MONUC's relationship with the Rwandan-backed RCD was particularly acrimonious. The RCD held deep-seated grievances against the UN, in particular, for UNAMIR's failure to halt the genocide and the organization's support to the militarized camps in eastern Zaire. The irony was not lost on many that the refugee crisis, which the international community failed to contain, had instigated the very conflict that peacekeepers were now deployed to address. As one former officer recounts, 'The UN fed, clothed and housed the killers, and [then] returned to "get them". *C'est la folie!*'[34] In addition to historical enmities, the RCD charged that the UN was inherently biased towards a unified Congo with a capital in Kinshasa—this despite RCD's control of roughly two-thirds of the country.[35] The RCD's resentment and profound distrust of the UN meant that for much of the Second War, access to areas they held was blocked or frustrated.

Amid this hostility, peacekeepers overwhelmingly adopted a passive posture in relation to the belligerents, including when confronted with aggression that threatened civilians. The 2002 massacre in Kisangani, the capital of Province Orientale, was the most egregious instance of such inaction. On 14 May, following a suspected mutiny, RCD loyalists 'went on a rampage' that killed roughly 180 people and injured many more.[36] Young women were rounded up and raped, and hundreds of homes were pillaged. The 1,000 or so peacekeepers stationed in the area, who had knowledge of the violence underway, did not use force to halt the massacre or patrol to deter abuses. Throughout this phase, as one official observed, MONUC remained 'little more than a shadow over the horizon'.[37]

Contestation: Divisions over Great Lakes Policy

Implementation during the first phase of the mission's deployment was shaped largely by contestation within the Security Council over Great Lakes policy. This in turn had operational consequences for MONUC and its ability to adopt a robust posture.

The Rwandan genocide prompted a recalibration of donor relations with the region. Overnight, the small east African state was catapulted onto the international policy agenda to become an aid darling of the West, particularly Anglophone donors. Plagued by both collective and, in some instances, personal guilt over international inaction, senior officials in both the second Clinton administration in Washington[38] and the new Labour government in London fostered and maintained strong links to Kigali, and committed millions of dollars in direct long-term budgetary support to the government.[39] By contrast, France—its legitimacy in Rwanda shot—shifted its gaze from its erstwhile ally to neighbouring Congo. In an attempt to maintain regional influence and preserve the Francophone *précarré* (private domain), French development and military assistance flowed into Congo and in January 1997 France was involved in the covert levying of 300 mercenaries in a failed attempt to save Mobutu.[40]

This division of loyalties meant that from the mid-1990s until 2002, US–UK and French interests on the Council remained at odds.[41] France inveighed against Uganda and Rwanda's presence in Congo, was a 'driving force' behind the UN Panel of Experts which investigated Kigali and Kampala's wartime profiteering, and repeatedly called for sanctions against senior officials in both states.[42] In contrast, the US and UK denied, downplayed, and at times ardently defended Rwanda's involvement even as Kigali's reach extended beyond the Kivus, thereby weakening the justification that it was simply taking defensive precautions along its borders. Information and analysis presented to the Council that implicated Rwanda and illuminated abuses by its forces or those it backed was frustrated or swept aside by its Anglophone allies.[43] These differences undermined a common international approach to addressing the conflict in Congo, and crippled Council proceedings on the region. It in part explains why members of the Council were averse to acknowledging the 'reality gap' inherent in the Lusaka Agreement, the role prescribed for the UN by the signatories, and, indeed, their own mandates for the mission.

Contestation within the Council, in turn, had implications for the mission and its operations, which gave rise to additional forms of contestation. Senior officials questioned whether, despite their Chapter VII mandate, forceful action would actually have the backing of their authorizing body. Moreover, divisions within the Council meant that, in addition to the belligerence of the parties, member states were wary of committing the resources and personnel necessary for a more assertive role. By February 2001, only 200 UN military personnel had arrived in Congo, and an additional two years passed before the original size of the force authorized by the Council was realized.[44] This impacted the force's posture. For example, Deputy Force Commander General Martinelli explicitly stated at the time that his decision not to deploy forces during the 2002 massacre in Kisangani was largely out of concern for the casualties that MONUC would likely incur given that peacekeepers were ill-equipped to deal with the threat posed by the RCD and its Rwandan backers.[45] 'The RPA was the strongest army in the region and possibly in Africa' as one analyst recounts. 'The RCD were ruthless and very powerful and the UN was in way, way above its head.'[46]

The inherent challenges of peacekeeping in such a context engendered further contestation between the Council and senior officials in the mission as well as the Secretariat. The objections put forward by the latter mirrored those raised during impartiality's institutionalization at the macro-level. Specifically, members of the Secretariat expressed doubt about the viability of the mission and its assertive mandate. In a draft of the first-ever UN report on the DRC, senior officials recommended a delay in sending the mission until the environment proved more hospitable for deployment,[47] and in January 2000, Secretary-General Annan advised against making protection of civilians (PoC) a core task of the mission.[48] This was consistent with Annan's position on the mandate for Sierra Leone, as described in Chapter 3.

These tensions persisted throughout the first phase of the mission's deployment. Following the Kisangani massacre, SRSG Ngongi came to the defence of his personnel and, contradicting the mission's mandate, stated that 'MONUC did what it could at the time . . . [the mission] was not created to ensure the security of the population'.[49] In New York, when, in the wake of the massacre, the Council reaffirmed MONUC's responsibility to promote PoC, Annan issued cautionary words and called for the Council to adjust the strength of MONUC.[50] In the same vein, Jean-Marie Guéhenno, Under-Secretary-General for UN Peacekeeping, drew attention to the mission's lack of capacity. He warned that the mission was too small to 'present a credible military deterrent . . . The risks are tremendous. We are taking a gamble'.[51]

The Kisangani massacre became a symbol of the mission's passivity during its first phase and was also a key turning point. Behind closed doors, Western donors increased pressure on Rwanda and Uganda, and in the months following the massacre both states signed bilateral accords with Kinshasa, leading to the formal withdrawal of their forces.[52] These accords paved the way for the Global and Inclusive Agreement, signed in Sun City, South Africa, and the formation of the Transitional Government of national unity, headed by Joseph Kabila.

Moreover, in the Council, tensions over Great Lakes policy softened. No longer the *bête noir* of Kigali, Chirac's government welcomed the 2003 Rwanda elections as 'an encouraging sign of progress'; in Washington, those senior officials closest to Kigali—including Susan Rice and Madeleine Albright—were replaced under the Bush administration; and in London, Clare Short—the chief architect of the UK's partnership with Rwanda—resigned from her post as Secretary of State for International Development over Tony Blair's handling of the Iraq war. Galvanized by the prospect of peace in Congo, member states increased the resources available to the mission, and a deluge of development assistance flowed into the country. The great powers adopted broadly similar policies to ensure that the Transition stayed on course for elections.

This confluence of factors, as the following section explains, enabled peacekeepers to adopt an assertive posture at several junctures. Differences, however, in how officials within the mission perceived the legitimacy of and threat posed by particular actors in abrogation of the Transition and/or who imperilled civilians led to operational inconsistencies.

THE TRANSITION (2003–06)

The establishment of the Transitional Government (TG), based on a 'one-plus-four' power-sharing model, marked the formal end to the war and prompted a radical shift in the mission's focus.[53] Details of MONUC's plans for the Transition period were outlined in a new concept of operations issued in July 2003.[54] Peacekeepers, as William Swing, the newly appointed SRSG and former US Ambassador to Congo, explained were 'to provide support to the [TG], leading to the country's first free and fair elections in four decades'.[55] In addition, following the Kisangani massacre, PoC was reaffirmed in every subsequent resolution relating to the mission.

Increased international commitment and unity among donors brought about new coordination bodies and security arrangements in Congo. Of these, the creation of the *Comité International d'Accompagnement de la Transition* (CIAT) in late 2002 was particularly significant. Chaired by MONUC, the CIAT was the international community's main liaison mechanism with the TG.[56] It met regularly and played an important role in preventing the Transition from derailing at several critical junctures, including during the elections. These new institutions were accompanied by a dramatic expansion in the mission's size and resourcing. Beginning in 2002, the number of uniformed personnel increased from roughly 4,000 to over 18,000 by mid-2006.[57]

As elections drew near and political impasse on several issues central to the Transition led to violence, the Council also issued a series of increasingly robust mandates that propelled what UN officials described as the mission's 'quantum leap' into a more 'active phase'.[58] Resolution 1565 of October 2004 authorized MONUC to 'use all necessary means, within its capacity and in the areas where its units are deployed', to build confidence and 'discourage violence' that threatened civilians and the stability of the Transition.[59] Six months later, in Resolution 1592, MONUC's mandate was further strengthened with the specification that the mission 'with all necessary means ... may use cordon and search tactics to prevent attacks on civilians and disrupt the military capability of illegal armed groups that continue to use violence in those areas'.[60]

To translate the mandate into practice, Secretary-General Annan requested that the Council allow his military advisor, Major General Patrick Cammaert, to develop an operational plan that he would then oversee as Division Commander in eastern Congo.[61] Of Dutch origin, Cammaert had served with the UN mission in Srebrenica, where inaction in the face of violence came to inform the approach to peacekeeping he would later take in Congo. A reconceptualization of impartiality as assertive was at the crux of this vision. As Cammaert writes:

> The UN is impartial and thus is obliged to act when directly confronted with any force attacking/threatening civilians—even if the perpetrators represent the

government...Impartiality means literally 'to give a fair share' of something...it involves the repeated exercise of personal judgment, the application of fairness and principle to a given situation. Impartiality is a quality used at the tip of your toe; neutrality on the heel of your foot. Neutrality cedes opportunity, initiative and advantage to others. Impartiality allows seizing all three.[62]

Throughout the Transition, many expatriates and Congolese officials espoused a similar view to Cammaert's, and saw greater possibility for MONUC to be impartial, 'equidistant between the various belligerent actors'.[63] As a European diplomat stationed in Kinshasa during this period reflected: '[t]he UN could be more independent and impartial when there wasn't an elected government whose consent was critical. During the Transition, MONUC supported a process, shepherding the country to elections...It tried to be partial to the principles of the Transition with the aim of bringing peace and democracy to the Congo.'[64]

With Cammaert at the helm, peacekeepers, as I describe below, undertook some of the most combative military operations in the UN's history. This action was far from consistent, however; the mission's responses to actors in abrogation of the Transition and who threatened civilians varied significantly.

Threats to the Transition

While the Sun City Agreement succeeded in reuniting the country under the TG, it did not bring an end to violence. Armed actors and their domestic and foreign backers proved reluctant to cede power, the economic and political benefits of peace outweighing the illusory gains of further fighting. Those that did lay down their weapons left power vacuums in which others vied for control. Rebellious factions of former rebel groups adopted a strategy of holding out for a possible resort to force if the elections did not turn out in their favour. Parallel chains of command persisted in the army, limiting control of those brigades which were said to be 'integrated', and competing authorities sprang up simultaneously in the administrative and financial structures of the capital and provinces.[65]

During the Transition period, flashpoints of instability were seen across the country. The Ituri district of north-eastern Province Orientale, and the Provinces of North and South Kivu were particularly wracked by violence. As such, they became priority areas for the UN.

In Ituri, the formal withdrawal of Ugandan troops in 2003 left a gap of authority. During the war, neighbouring Uganda played a formative role as 'both arsonist and fire-fighter', enflaming and containing violence between groups linked to rival Hema and Lendu communities.[66] From 2003–04, ethnically based attacks and wanton destruction escalated as groups viciously competed for control over mining areas and commercial zones—often supported and sustained by Congolese and regional (especially Ugandan) actors who sought to profit from the gold and timber trade.[67]

Unlike the situation in Ituri, where actors outside the TG were the principal cause of the area's instability, violence in the Kivus was fomented by both parties and non-parties to the Transition.[68] In particular, the Global Accords were a source of deep disquietude for the RCD and its Rwandan backers. After years of expansive control in Congo, they faced a precipitous decline in power during the Transition. Fissures opened up within the RCD as members debated whether their interests were better protected through positions of power in Kinshasa or through more localized and violent resistance. Sceptical of where the RCD's loyalties now lay, Rwanda formally abandoned the group and threw its weight behind those dissident elements in abrogation of the Global Accord, in an effort to safeguard its economic and political interests in the region.[69]

In North Kivu, Kigali sided with Eugène Serufuli, a founding member of the RCD and Governor of the province, who maintained a personal militia of 3,000 Hutu throughout the Transition.[70] In addition, Laurent Nkunda (ex-RCD and RPA) enjoyed Rwanda's support and was said to have been instrumental to Kigali's 'plan B' should the Transition not work out in its favour.[71] Based in the highlands of Masisi (North Kivu), Nkunda recruited militia from refugee camps in Rwanda and mobilized thousands of supporters. He drew on deep-seated grievances surrounding land and ethnicity, and claimed to offer succour as protector of minorities, particularly of the Congolese Tutsi from the FDLR, which, although diminished in strength, continued to be active in the Kivus.

Inconsistent Implementation of the Mandate

The mission's responses to the sources of Congo's instability during this period were varied. It undertook robust action against those groups that were not party to the Global Accords and thus were outside the TG. While assertive action occurred across the east—including in the Kivus where MONUC launched operations against such groups as the FDLR, Rastas, and Allied Democratic Forces (ADF)—Ituri district was the centre of enforcement activity.[72]

Combat operations in Ituri began in 2003 following a surge of violence in and around the city of Bunia. Vicious attacks on civilians as well as on the small contingent of blue helmets deployed for guard duty elicited international attention and prompted the Security Council to authorize the deployment of a three-month Interim Emergency Multinational Force (IEMF) to the district, carried out under the auspices of the EU and spearheaded by France.[73] During

Operation Artemis, the 1,400-strong force provided a modicum of peace in Bunia, and thousands of IDPs returned to the city.

Operation Artemis paved the way for a more sustained and farther-reaching campaign launched by MONUC forces in December 2004 in conjunction with the national army, *Forces Armées de la République Démocratique du Congo* (FARDC), to root out the remaining armed groups in the wider area. The campaign's primary objective was to pacify the region so that elections could take place and, second, to protect civilians.[74] Employing a carrot-and-stick approach, peacekeepers coerced militias to disarm and used considerable force if they failed to do so. Efforts intensified in the lead up to the elections and with the expiration of an ultimatum that SRSG Swing issued in 2005, calling on all armed groups in Ituri to disarm.[75] At the peak of this activity, the mission conducted an average of fifteen operations per day, most of which were supported by attack helicopters.[76] By late 2006, operations began to wind down as the leaders of the various remaining armed groups in Ituri were arrested, entered DDR, or were integrated into the FARDC. Without these key individuals at the helm, many of the groups dissolved and roughly 18,000 militia members were demobilized during this period.[77] The campaign was widely heralded a success.

Such shows of force were, however, in marked contrast to the mission's pusillanimous and passive posture towards those groups that were party to or were backed by parties to the Global Accords. In Ituri, for example, MONUC's campaign, which was conducted jointly with the FARDC, revealed that the national army was often a greater risk to civilians than the very militia they were pursuing. In 2005, UN officials estimated that more than 75 per cent of the total human-rights offences documented in Ituri for that year were committed by FARDC.[78] While Cammaert reports having cancelled operations where FARDC forces appeared ill-equipped, and on occasion instructed the brigade to arrest miscreant officers, force was never used against the FARDC, and abuses by the army continued.[79]

More damning was MONUC's inaction vis-à-vis ex-RCD members in the Kivus, and, especially, Nkunda. The renegade General's May/June 2004 siege of Bukavu, provincial capital of South Kivu, was of particular consequence, dubbed by some as the start of Congo's 'Third War'.[80] For months, tensions within the city had been running high as RCD officers and government loyalists disputed the terms of army integration. Nkunda's attack in support of dissident RCD Colonel Mutebutsi was allegedly aimed at preventing genocide against the city's Tutsi community and was backed by Rwanda. While the Tutsi had certainly been persecuted at the hands of the FARDC, Nkunda's claims of genocide were wildly exaggerated and, as UN field staff reported, were inflamed by Rwanda.[81]

As Nkunda's militia approached Bukavu, the contingent of Uruguayan peacekeepers stationed at the airport handed over the facility after consulting with their superiors in Montevideo and despite orders from MONUC's military command to defend the airport with force if necessary.[82] The following day, Nkunda continued his march as FARDC troops fled, unprepared to defend the city from his better-equipped force. Emboldened by their absence, Nkunda's militia took Bukavu without resistance on 2 June. MONUC evacuated inhabitants of the city and provided assistance to IDPs. However, for reasons I discuss below, the 400–600 peacekeepers stationed in Bukavu did not use force to confront Mutebutsi or Nkunda's militia—both of which acted in clear violation of the Transition agreement and posed a threat to civilians.[83] Members of the militia raped civilians and pillaged the city, killing more than 100 people and displacing an estimated 24,800 civilians in the region before retreating to North Kivu under international pressure.[84] Back in Masisi, where he continued to be unopposed by blue helmets, Nkunda stepped up recruitment, set up parallel police and intelligence services, and carried out attacks on those who did not support him.[85]

Contestation: How to Safeguard the Transition

Manifest inconsistencies in the response of MONUC forces in these circumstances prompt several key questions: Why did peacekeepers undertake robust action against some armed actors and not others? And how did this both reflect and give rise to additional contestation?

The armed groups in Ituri and the Kivus against whom the mission used force were not what the *Capstone Doctrine* would later call 'main' parties. Specifically, they were party neither to the Global Accords nor the TG. Taking action against them did not pose a threat to the stability of the Transition; if anything, officials asserted that it guaranteed that the Transition stayed on course.[86] Moreover, the withdrawal of consent was not an issue since these armed groups had not consented to the mission's deployment or the peace agreement it was tasked with overseeing.

Critically, action against these actors had the full support of the Security Council. None of the groups targeted were allies or backed by allies of Council members. Most were widely regarded by international actors as 'negative', 'illegal', and 'criminal'. Indeed, individuals at the helm of several groups against which MONUC launched operations were targeted with international sanctions and were wanted for international prosecution. What is more, analysts contend that contestation in the Council over other policy issues actually had diplomatic dividends that made assertive action in Congo possible. Specifically, they maintain that the Anglo-French rift over the Iraq war compelled both sides to look for opportunities to 'play nice' when and where they could.[87] With comparatively less at stake strategically in Ituri than in Baghdad, they could agree on robust action against the armed groups there.

As in the Council, there was relatively little disagreement within the mission about robust engagement in Ituri and against non-signatories elsewhere. UN officials contend that the Council's backing of these operations was critical in this respect. Mission resources increased exponentially and the deployment of Cammaert, the Secretary-General's own military advisor, to oversee the campaign conveyed the seriousness of the Council's intent, and, according to some officials, was instrumental in the willingness of troop-contributing countries to sustain casualties in Ituri. In addition, officials note that these groups were widely seen within the mission to be illegitimate—a fact that was regularly emphasized to peacekeepers. The scaling up of the mission's use of force was accompanied by a dehumanization of the 'target'. A standard Powerpoint presentation slide shown to peacekeepers in Ituri, entitled 'What they are capable of' featured photos of militia jovially holding up severed heads and limbs.[88] According to an officer deployed to the region during this period, these images were meant to 'provoke fear and incite action'. And instil fear they did—tales of cannibalism were rumoured to keep MONUC soldiers up at night and were also said to have been a key factor in their willingness to use force.[89]

While there was broad agreement within the Council and mission on assertive action against non-signatories, MONUC's stance towards signatories of the Global Accords, and in particular, towards former RCD members, was a different matter. Unlike the previous phase, this contestation was primarily within the mission.

The political leadership of MONUC was most averse to a robust stance vis-à-vis those party to or allied to parties of the Global Accords, and in particular Nkunda. Their reluctance stemmed from a concern that aggressive action would jeopardize commitment to the Transition, cause an intensification of conflict, and prompt retaliation by actors and their domestic or foreign allies.[90] Closely related, some officials perceived a possible risk of MONUC's expulsion, given that it was through the Transition agreement that the parties had conferred consent on the mission.[91] Others assert that a 'pervasive pro-Rwandan sentiment' among the mission's political leadership influenced decision-making, a sentiment which partly explains their reluctance to confront Rwandan-backed belligerents who, in addition to representing local grievances, safeguarded Kigali's economic and political interests in Congo. This favouritism was said to be the result of both a more general 'institutional guilt' over the genocide, and personal ties between certain senior officials and Rwandan elites/ex-RCD elements. For example, several UN officials condemned what one described as the 'wildly inappropriate relationship' between the head of MONUC's North Kivu office, and Governor Serufuli.[92]

In addition, critics charged that a more robust approach towards renegade ex-RCD members was undermined by the passive posture adopted by TCCs/PCCs. The reluctance of peacekeepers to use force, they argued, was out of fear over the potential implications for their own personal safety. Rwandan-trained and battle-hardened, both Nkunda and Serufuli's militias were thought to be fearsome fighting forces. Furthermore, the mountainous jungle terrain of North Kivu was described as less conducive to military operations than the 'rolling hills' of Ituri where, as one officer described, '[y]ou could see the guys you were going after'.[93] While security concerns may have contributed to TCC passivity in certain instances, the strength of this explanation is diminished by the fact that during the Transition period peacekeepers *did* use force, despite considerable risks. Indeed, during Cammaert's time as Commander in the East, twenty-six peacekeepers lost their lives during active combat.

This line of reasoning is further undermined by the fact that MONUC's military command was, at times, among the most vocal advocates of robust action against ex-RCD elements in general, and Nkunda in particular. At various points during the Transition, MONUC's military commanders advocated robust responses in line with their mandate and the more assertive conception of impartiality. Their interpretations of the mandate were 'literal' and 'matter of fact', as one official explained. Nkunda and others in abrogation of the Transition were regarded as sources of instability that needed to be tackled. This desire to reel in recalcitrant actors was also shared by field officials in the political affairs and human-rights sections who saw the effects of such bellicosity on the local population.

Tensions within the mission and particularly between the military and political leadership came to a head during the Bukavu crisis. Throughout the crisis, MONUC's military commanders advocated a forceful response. With access to attack helicopters and heavy weaponry, they believed that peacekeepers 'could contain Mutebutsi' and 'stare down Nkunda's forces'.[94] To that end, on 28 May the brigade commander presented Mutebutsi with an ultimatum threatening the use of force should he fail to contain his troops.[95] In addition, as Nkunda's men approached South Kivu, the Force Commander issued a directive reminding peacekeepers in the area that the mission was operating under a Chapter VII mandate and that they would be expected to defend the city from renegade militias. Accordingly, orders were issued for the deployment of MI-25 and MI-17 attack helicopters.[96]

The military command's plans to defend Bukavu were, however, rapidly thwarted by the political leadership in Kinshasa who explicitly ordered the retraction of the ultimatum issued to Mutebutsi.[97] Without consulting the Force Commander, who was travelling at the time, and in direct contradiction of his directive, civilian leaders transmitted a message to the brigade commander that force was not to be used against Nkunda.[98] An internal UN post-event report on the crisis found that the leadership was unduly concerned for the safety of the Tutsi community, giving credence to Nkunda's alleged fears of genocide. The report surmised that this was likely the result of the leadership's direct communication with Nkunda during the crisis as well as their disregard of field reports showing that his claims of genocide were unfounded.[99] Contradictory orders coming from the leadership were also identified as an important reason for peacekeepers' lack of action against Nkunda; for example, one official suggested that the mixed signals from Kinshasa in part explained why the Uruguayan commander sought direction from Montevideo and, having been advised not to take action that would imperil the forces, handed over control of the airport.[100]

MONUC's inaction during the Bukavu crisis provoked fierce criticism from UN headquarters in New York, which had been given little warning of the crisis in the daily reports sent by the political leadership.[101] The post-event report on the crisis censured the mission's political leadership for having 'undermined the military chain of command' and 'concept of operations', and condemned MONUC for failing to uphold its Chapter VII mandate.[102] The report questioned 'how the senior leadership in Kinshasa had come to the conclusion that a well-armed attack by mutinous FARDC officers, supported by Rwanda, did not constitute a security threat to the Congolese population in Bukavu?'[103] It argued that the threat Nkunda posed to the Transition government was precisely the reason *for* an assertive response. It further charged that the mission's leadership 'appeared to confuse impartiality with neutrality and was reluctant to confront individuals or groups who were clearly working to undermine the Transition process'.[104] 'MONUC's failure actively to condemn the mutineers Mutebutsi and Nkunda for their acts of treason', it concluded, 'left the Congolese people with the impression that MONUC was favouring its enemies'.[105]

And yet despite these trenchant criticisms, following the Bukavu crisis the mission did not undertake offensive action against Nkunda or other renegade elements of the Transition. In 2004, SRSG Swing circulated an edict forbidding all contact with Nkunda. His decree did not allow for military action.[106] When in 2006 Nkunda debuted his new militia, the *Congrès National pour la Défense du Peuple* (CNDP), senior UN officials in Kinshasa authored a policy document on the 'Nkunda problématique'. The official line adopted by the mission and allowed for by the Council was clear, as one official recounts: '"Do not confront. Contain". And the logic was simple: "Keep the Transition functioning, hold elections, and hope that he disappears after the polls."'[107] As during the Bukavu crisis, the military command, as well as numerous civilian officials in the east, opposed the policy. Such dissenting views, however, were 'marginalized' by the political leadership, as one official described; others, like Cammaert, left the mission in frustration.[108]

MONUC's policy proved to be wishful thinking; 'disappear', Nkunda did not. The CNDP was to wreak ever-greater havoc on the population of North Kivu after the elections, spawning several counter-militias in opposition to the foreign-backed general.

THE POST-ELECTION PERIOD (2007–08)

On 6 December 2006 Joseph Kabila was sworn in as the country's first democratically elected president in more than four decades. Thousands of guests gathered at the State House in Kinshasa, sheltered from the rain under a sea of umbrellas in the national colours of red, blue, and yellow. They listened sanguinely as Kabila proclaimed 'a new page' was opening up before them, and pledged to combat the corruption and violence that had devastated his war-battered country. His administration, he exclaimed, would be based on 'the trilogy of good governance, democracy and respect for human rights'.[109] To the delight of the donors in attendance, the thirty-five-year-old president paid homage to the 'remarkable solidarity' of the international community during the Transition.[110]

Following the elections, the Security Council and UN Secretariat reviewed MONUC's role. In his 23rd report, the Secretary-General asserted that the central focus of the mission was to support the government in order to consolidate democracy and extend state authority. In support of this over-arching aim, he recommended that the Council continue to authorize the mission to protect civilians 'under imminent threat of violence'.[111]

Support to the nascent government was an integral part of the UN and donor community's exit strategy. No sooner had the ballots been counted than discussions about drawdown plans began. In late 2006, Lise Grande, the DSRSG and Humanitarian Coordinator, developed the UN Security and Stabilization Support Strategy (UNSSSS) and a package of interlinked humanitarian reforms was introduced, intended to shepherd the Transition from crisis to development, and strengthen humanitarian coordination.[112] However, for many within the mission, the appointment of Alan Doss as Swing's successor to the position of SRSG was the clearest indication of the direction in which the UN 'thought things *should* be going'.[113] Although he had a strong background in development, Doss was, as one official described, 'simply not a political animal'.[114] He was widely seen as a 'mission closer'[115]—a 'shadow SRSG'[116] that would 'pack the UN up and leave the Congo mid-way through Kabila's term'.[117] As one senior official told me: '[w]e planned for the election, after which we thought our job was largely done'.[118]

The mission plans for withdrawal were, however, soon shelved as security conditions deteriorated in various parts of the country and particularly in the east, where, as discussed below, the CNDP rebellion gained force. The Council responded by reiterating its support of the government and in increasingly strong language admonished those who challenged Kabila's authority. In December 2007, the Council reaffirmed MONUC's mandate under Chapter VII to 'use all available means . . . to support the FARDC integrated brigades with a view to disarming the recalcitrant domestic and foreign armed groups'.[119] The Force Commander's Directive of March 2008 further clarified that the mandate allowed for pre-emptive action, calling upon the forces to be more 'proactive and seek to prevent incidents from taking place rather than reacting to them'. The Directive also highlighted MONUC's robust RoE, which authorized peacekeepers 'to use all means, up to and including lethal force, to guarantee protection of the population'.[120]

However, as I explain below, during this period, the two core tasks assigned to the mission—protection of civilians and support of the government—came into tension with one another, and brought to light ambiguities over assertive impartiality and consent. For all the president's international posturing, signs of resurgent authoritarianism in Congo soon followed the elections, suggesting that rather than turning a 'new page', Kabila was in fact taking a leaf from the book of his predecessors.

La Pagaille and Rebellion in the East

Deprived of what he had expected to be a landslide victory, President Kabila saw his election as the chance to end all political opposition.[121] He acted swiftly and brutally. In early 2007, government forces clamped down on opposition supporters in the west and centre of the country where Bemba had won 75 per cent of the vote in the run-off election. Protests by groups such as the *Bundu dia Kongo* (BDK), which sought greater provincial autonomy, were put down by state agents using excessive force. And in Kinshasa, Kabila launched an all out military offensive to 'eliminate Bemba' and his guards.[122] Hundreds of civilians were killed in the crossfire.

Kabila's violent clampdown directly following the elections set a precedent. It presaged the president's ongoing attempt to crush all opposition at the expense of democratic and equitable peacebuilding for the benefit of the country's population. Throughout the remainder of the mission's deployment, governance in Congo continued to be structured around power dynamics similar to those that existed at the peak of the war—defined by a lack of accountable leadership at both local and national level, and the extreme centralization of formal power in Kinshasa. The decentralization reforms stipulated by the Constitution were ignored and the local elections, scheduled to follow general elections, were never held. This created a shortage of local and representative governance, and ensured that community tensions and grievances remained unaddressed. Moreover, with security sector reform largely stagnant, the national army persisted as a venal and weak institution, a rag-tag team of numerous rebel groups incorporated but not unified under a single chain of command that preyed on civilians and continued to form temporary and opportunistic alliances with various militias, including the FDLR. Resurrecting a term from the Congo of the 1960s, scholars questioned whether the period should be referred to as *la pagaille*—

a time of uncertainty, wayward morality, and chaos brought about by a weak yet brutal government.[123]

Nowhere were the challenges for MONUC in supporting such a government more acute than in eastern Congo where the authority of Kabila was most contested. Developments in this region not only demonstrated discord over the mission's relationship with Kabila's regime and the FARDC, they also engendered their own forms of contestation over MONUC's response to groups that took up arms against, and in the absence of, state institutions. Of these, the CNDP was most significant.

The elections were a resounding disappointment for the RCD, which after years of controlling the Kivus failed to inspire popular support in the polls.[124] Their defeat was unsettling for Nkunda, and for those on both sides of the border whose interests he sought to safeguard. The General responded by redoubling his efforts to expand the CNDP's sphere of influence in direct challenge to the government's authority and in the name of protecting the Tutsi minority from, among others, the FDLR.

Beginning in 2006, Nkunda launched a series of offensives in North Kivu, which the FARDC proved unable to defeat. A pattern emerged: bursts of violence in and around urban centres were accompanied by an expansion of CNDP power in rural areas, which would then compel the government to negotiate with the General. This produced several 'peace agreements', brokered largely by the parties themselves, including a failed attempt in 2007 to integrate the CNDP into the FARDC—a process known as 'mixage'. In most instances, however, parties had barely signed on the dotted line and shaken hands before forces on one side or the other would launch an attack thereby nullifying the so-called peace. Alongside this deadly game of cat and mouse, Nkunda gained control of huge swaths of territory, committed widespread human-rights abuses, and brutally terrorized the local population.[125]

These hostilities provoked a groundswell of local opposition and the rapid mobilization of at least a dozen or more armed groups in the east. This increased mobilization was driven by insecurity, as communities sought to defend themselves against the CNDP and an increasingly rapacious government. The region, which, as Stearns notes 'had been on the mend for the several years following the 2002 peace deal . . . plunged into a downward spiral of violence'.[126]

From Assertive to Passive Peacekeeping

MONUC's initial response was robust. In the early post-election period, MONUC's earlier aversion to confronting the CNDP was briefly overturned. On two occasions, the mission adopted an aggressive posture against Nkunda in support of the government. In August 2006, MONUC used force to repel the militia from taking the strategic town of Sake, located a mere 17 kilometres from Goma. Similarly, when in November of that same year Nkunda proceeded with his advance on Goma after repeated warnings from the mission, Indian peacekeepers gunned down over 150 CNDP men in a single day.

The mission's willingness to use force against Nkunda in support of the government and to protect civilians more generally was, however, not sustained. An internal military evaluation conducted for the Secretary-General by General Maurice Baril in 2008 noted a precipitous decline in firing engagements by UN contingents starting in 2006.[127] The reticence of peacekeepers to use force was most striking in the autumn of 2008. With the latest peace agreement in tatters, renewed hostilities between the CNDP and FARDC plunged North Kivu into crisis. In one month alone 250,000 people were displaced, raising the total number of IDPs in the province to one million (or 25 per cent of the population).

In addition to atrocities committed by the CNDP, it was during this period that the extent of FARDC's miscreant behaviour and predatory nature was revealed. While MONUC's frustrations with the FARDC were longstanding, they reached new levels. As the Congolese army abandoned their posts, they ransacked towns and villages, and raped and pillaged, terrorizing the local population.[128] Moreover, incensed by MONUC's unwillingness to fight the CNDP *for* them, FARDC stirred up local opposition to the mission and in certain instances attacked peacekeepers. Indeed, MONUC officials have documented proof that during the crisis the UN suffered more attacks from 'friendly fire' (FARDC) than from the CNDP.[129] Peacekeepers did not respond forcefully.

During this spate of violence—what became widely known as the 'Goma crisis'—the CNDP greatly expanded its zone of control and threatened to take the provincial capital, as Nkunda also began expressing national ambitions.[130] As the FARDC fled most urban centres, MONUC publicly pledged to defend the towns of Goma, Sake, Masisi, and Rutshuru. When the CNDP encroached on Goma, the mission fired on Nkunda's positions and, along with international pressure, succeeded in averting an attack on the provincial capital.

However, while MONUC tried to defend Goma, Nkunda's men took the neighbouring towns of Kiwanja and Rutshuru with no resistance from the 120 Indian peacekeepers stationed in the area. Upon entering the towns, the CNDP ordered the local population to destroy the IDP camps that housed 27,000 people and announced to MONUC that they had taken control.[131] In the days that followed, the militia summarily executed an estimated 150 people. The blue helmets stayed at their base. As one woman I interviewed recounted:

[The CNDP] broke down doors and killed. When they entered they would look for young people because they said they were Mai Mai because we speak the same language we negotiated with them—tried to tell them we weren't Mai-Mai. They asked us to lie down on the ground and they started to fire. Lots of bullets into bodies. When it stopped there was the dead. My two sons died... The FARDC and MONUC did nothing.[132]

The attacks elicited international attention, and were widely condemned. The possibility of an EU Rapid Reaction Force to protect civilians was briefly discussed in New York and Brussels, but gained little traction. The CNDP maintained control of Rutshuru and Kiwanja, and expanded its territorial reach, unopposed by the peacekeeping contingent stationed in the area.

Contestation: Shifts in Legitimacy

What explains the mission's increasingly passive stance towards Nkunda, and its unwillingness to confront elements of the FARDC that threatened civilians? And how might this have reflected and engendered contestation? To understand implementation during this period requires analysis of donor relations with Kabila's government following the elections, as well as dynamics internal to the mission.

The elections ushered in a new phase in donor engagement, as Kabila sought to quash all outside criticisms of his government. During conversations, the president made it clear 'that anyone who dared so much as question his authority was not welcome'.[133] In January 2007, the CIAT was disbanded at Kabila's order and shortly thereafter his staff informed donors that bilateral relations would be prioritized over multilateral engagement 'to avoid interference in domestic affairs'.[134] This afforded the president greater control over policy and the allocation of resources.

Kabila's increasing intransigence met little resistance. Appearances of donor unity and commitment that characterized the Transition fell by the wayside. The semblance of peace and democracy in Congo brought new opportunities for investment and profit, and states now competed for lucrative mining and oil contracts. As one official noted wryly: 'You didn't need to be particularly brilliant to see that everyone wanted to curry favour with Kabila. They were all scrambling to gain their own national advantage.'[135] Competition only increased as Kabila looked east and deepened economic ties with non-traditional donors willing to build much-needed infrastructure in return for natural resources, without good governance conditions.[136]

As a result, the Security Council and international donors were slow to react to the crisis in the east. When they did engage, officials in the mission argued that the approach was contradictory and misguided. While calling for robust action in support of the state against Nkunda, beginning in July 2007, the Council was also increasingly in favour of direct political negotiations with the CNDP.[137] In September 2007, key members of the international community, including senior representatives from the US, UK, France, Belgium, and South Africa, met in New York to develop a 'road map' for the east. Shortly thereafter, an American diplomat was appointed as a high-level dialogue facilitator.

This sent contradictory signals to the mission about what position it was expected to assume, and gave rise to contestation about the mission at the macro-political level. Civilian staff deployed in the east complained that 'the countless delegations of diplomatic officials that trekked up to see Nkunda only further legitimized him', exclaiming sarcastically that 'during the Goma crisis the only person not to visit was the Pope!'[138] Moreover, as evidence of Kigali's support to the CNDP and meddling in North Kivu mounted, officials criticized what they perceived as the 'hypocrisy' of the Council and particularly the US and UK—who took the lead on Great Lakes policy and yet remained uncritical of Rwanda.[139] While member states were prepared to engage Rwanda as a stakeholder in Congo's future stability, they refused to acknowledge and put pressure on Kigali for its culpability in fomenting instability in the Kivus.[140]

These broader macro-level political dynamics had an impact on the micro-level operations of the mission that without doubt fomented contestation. No longer at the helm of the CIAT, MONUC 'struggled to assert itself' while supporting the government.[141] As a senior UN official recounted, '[t]he hissing sound that you heard after the elections was the sound of leverage leaking away from the Mission . . . MONUC, without backing, was weak'.[142]

In this context, MONUC's political leadership adopted an approach that mirrored the Council's and Doss took a pliant attitude towards the government and then towards Nkunda. Few criticisms were made of Kabila's brutal clampdown in 2006 and 2007. Moreover, as the government's true colours came to light and as the Council urged engagement with Nkunda, the political leadership proved less willing to confront Nkunda militarily. As one civilian official explained: 'many in the mission were initially willing to give the government a chance, but as the shambolic nature of Kabila's administration became apparent and the FARDC failed to deal decisively with the CNDP, Nkunda and his men didn't look so bad'.[143] What's more, officials stressed that the mission's mandate was to support FARDC, not wage war on its behalf. As a result, when the national army proved unwilling or incapable to fight, peacekeepers did not assume responsibility for 'holding down the fort', save in instances where civilians were imperilled. When asked to explain why MONUC adopted this position, one senior official replied:

We felt as though the government had not exhausted all peaceful means. The CNDP had genuine issues in need of address. We felt as though the use of force to neutralize the CNDP would have done little to take those issues off the table and would have meant very little in terms of long-term stability . . . However, at the same time, the UN didn't question the FARDC's right to deal with the CNDP with force.[144]

These political and strategic reasons for MONUC's passive stance were related to micro-level operational challenges and contestation on the ground. As the CNDP grew in strength and increasingly resorted to guerrilla warfare tactics, the risks of confronting the militia increased. As during the previous two phases, peacekeepers were concerned about their own security, particularly given their inadequate resourcing. This material fact explains in part the robust posture adopted in 2006 but not in 2008.[145] Despite MONUC's pronouncements during the Goma crisis that peacekeepers would defend key urban centres, the mission simply lacked the capabilities to do so. In private, UN officials confessed to diplomats that if challenged 'they would only have been able to defend two pockets around the main MONUC bases in Goma'.[146] Similarly, investigations into the Kiwanja massacre found that inaction by the nearby Indian contingent was partly due to mobility constraints as well as the absence of an interpreter to inform the peacekeepers as the crisis unfolded.[147] With only 6,000 blue helmets deployed in North Kivu (approximately one peacekeeper for every 60 square kilometres), the mission was grossly overstretched.[148]

As peacekeepers found themselves ill-equipped to deal with the deterioration in security and were frustrated by having to work alongside FARDC, TCCs were said to have increased communication with their respective capitals and, following the direction of their superiors that they were 'not to come home in body bags', assumed a passive stance.[149] Some argued that TCCs actually developed close relations with CNDP in an attempt to ensure their own security. Peacekeepers were reportedly seen drinking and socializing with the militia on numerous occasions and, in 2007, a video surfaced which contained footage of Nkunda being decorated by a departing Indian Brigadier General.[150]

Others argued that such instances of fraternization by the forces reflected a more essential bias towards Nkunda and his men. Specifically, UN officials maintained that the Indian contingent supplying the majority of troops to North Kivu had an affinity for the CNDP based on an inherent cultural bias, which stymied a more aggressive approach. As one official explained: '[c]oming from a caste system at home, the Indians see the Tutsi as more cultivated and advanced, and therefore deserving of respect. Also, they are much easier to deal with than the FARDC. Some speak English. Many are Rwandan trained and unlike the other [armed groups] they have a clear hierarchy and are organized. They show up on time and in suits . . . and, most importantly, they know what to say.'[151]

This more passive approach towards the CNDP, the result of both macro- and micro-level factors, was deeply contested within the mission. It was opposed at various times by the military command. In a highly publicized incident at the height of the Goma crisis, General Vicente Diaz de Villegas, the newly appointed Force Commander, resigned after just three weeks on the job. Echoing the frustrations of Cammaert, de Villegas charged that the mission's policy regarding Nkunda was misguided and 'dangerous', and underscored the urgent need for 'impartial' peace enforcement in the east with adequate resources.[152] Other officials, particularly civilians stationed in the east, were also critical of the unwillingness of peacekeepers to confront the CNDP.[153] They argued that UN forces had a responsibility to take action given their Chapter VII mandate to disarm combatants and protect civilians.

However, while the military command, was bullish on confronting the CNDP, like the political leadership, it was unwilling to undertake robust action against miscreant elements of the FARDC. Here, the perceived risks were both an escalation in hostilities as well as the mission's possible expulsion. As one former official explained: '[O]ur mandate was to support the government, which had been democratically elected. Using force against the army seemed like a step beyond peacekeeping.'[154] Moreover, given the broader, more solicitous approach of donors towards the government, such action, many argued, would not have had Council backing. Suggestions to both the military command and political leadership that force be used to address FARDC violations, particularly given the mission's mandate to protect civilians, provoked fiery responses.[155] As one senior official later exclaimed, that 'would never have been possible. The UN hierarchy would never have allowed it'.[156]

It therefore came as a surprise to many when, in the wake of the Goma crisis, the Council authorized Resolution 1856, which was unprecedented in two respects: it was the first resolution to designate PoC as a mission's highest priority; and, controversially, it specifically authorized the use of force to protect civilians 'under imminent threat of physical violence . . . from *any* of the parties engaged in the conflict'.[157] While the importance of protection relative to other mission tasks was implicit and action against miscreant FARDC forces legal under the mission's previous Chapter VII mandate, the explicit injunction added important emphasis. As a senior official involved with drafting the resolution explained in early January 2009: 'After the crisis, the threat of the FARDC to the population could no longer be ignored.' He added, however, that '[w]hether it will be implemented in practice is another issue altogether'.[158]

As the next two sections explain, protection continued to be a primary concern for the mission. But a seismic shift in regional relations, unforeseen by the Council and by the senior official in Goma, gave new meaning to Resolution 1856, resulting in significant contestation over its implementation and the mission's impartiality.

REGIONAL RAPPROCHEMENT AND THE 23 MARCH AGREEMENT (2009–11)

The Goma crisis precipitated what many Western diplomats praised as a historic rapprochement between the erstwhile enemies of Congo and Rwanda.[159] For Kinshasa, the crisis revealed the strength of the CNDP, the impotence of the FARDC, and the international community's unwillingness to rein in Nkunda. The CNDP was proving to be the greatest threat to Kabila's presidency and had become emblematic of the government's lack of control. For Kigali, Nkunda's liability quotient increased as collusion between the CNDP and the Rwandan leadership was widely exposed. Moreover, as Nkunda began to express national ambitions, he was seen by his backers to be 'getting too big for his own boots'.[160]

Talks began in December 2008 and concluded in the 23 March 2009 Agreement signed in Goma between the CNDP and Kabila's government. Under the agreement, the CNDP committed to transform itself from a military to a political entity and dismantle their parallel administrations. The government agreed to the integration of combatants into the FARDC, the police, and institutions of national and local administration. Overnight, the renegade enemies of yesterday became members of the national army. The agreement was rolled out under the rubric of disarming the FDLR.

But the 23 March Agreement was in reality only a front for an earlier back-room deal reached by Kinshasa and Kigali in late 2008. While the details of the secret pact are still unknown, it is widely believed that the agreement balanced Rwandan actions to depose Nkunda with tacit acceptance by the Congolese authorities of Rwanda's ongoing political and economic control over important areas of eastern Congo (facilitated by the CNDP's integration into the FARDC).[161] Events preceding the formal March agreement provided evidence that this was the case. In early January, Nkunda was 'arrested' by Rwandan authorities in the border town of Gisenyi. This was followed by the launch of *Umoja Wetu* ('Our Unity')—a one-month military campaign conducted jointly by Rwandan and Congolese forces, ostensibly to target the FDLR, but which, in actual fact, sought to consolidate CNDP control of mineral-rich areas and prevent an uprising within the group. In mid-February, CNDP forces were 'integrated' by the thousands into the FARDC. All of this occurred before the peace agreement was even signed.

MONUC was kept in the dark about the negotiations that led to the rapprochement and was side-lined from any involvement in the military campaign or the integration process.[162] However, when the RPA withdrew from Congo in late February, the government turned to the mission and secured its support for future operations. At the closing ceremony for *Umoja Wetu,* Congo's Foreign Minister Alexis Thambwe Mwamba proclaimed to the cheers of many Congolese that the primary responsibility for the follow-up operations lay with MONUC, which was now tasked with implementing Resolution 1856 by continuing operations against FDLR and protecting civilians. As one observer noted, it was almost as an 'afterthought that [Mwamba] added that, of course, the FARDC would also be involved in operations against the FDLR'.[163] Very quickly, in the words of one official, 'MONUC became the punchbag of the secret pact between Kagame and Kabila without knowing the contents of the deal.'[164]

Joint Operations

Operation Kimia II commenced in North and South Kivu in March 2009. Initially the operations were against the FDLR. However, they expanded to target other armed groups following the government's decree on 3 July 2009 that the integration process was complete and that all remaining armed groups would henceforth be considered enemies of the state. During *Kimia II*, MONUC provided significant material, logistical, and operational support to FARDC and the newly integrated CNDP. This included intelligence gathering and operations planning, air strikes, transportation, provision of rations, fire support, joint patrolling, and medical evacuations.

Kimia II led to an immediate increase in FDLR defections and succeeded in removing a number of the group's temporary bases.[165] However, whatever short-term gains were made against the FDLR were quickly overshadowed by the political and humanitarian consequences of the operations, which, in the words of Philip Alston, UN Special Rapporteur on Extrajudicial, Summary, or Arbitrary Executions, were 'catastrophic'.[166] During the first nine months, UNHCR reported an increase of over 500,000 IDPs. Retaliatory massacres and rampant rape were committed by members of the FDLR. As well, ex-CNDP units within the FARDC—MONUC's partners in the operations—killed 732 civilians, including 143 Rwandan Hutu refugees.[167] As one military officer noted: 'the CNDP is the same nasty CNDP as in Kiwanja. They are just playing dress-up in FARDC clothes'.[168]

While the stated goal of the operations was to reduce the threat posed by the FDLR and other armed groups, *Kimia II* provided a successful vehicle for the CNDP to greatly increase its military, political, and economic power within the Kivus under the guise of the FARDC. CNDP killings were largely about securing broad control of fertile grazing land and taxable roads, mines, and other sources of revenue. Many communities were displaced to make way for Congolese Tutsi refugees from Rwanda as well as Rwandan settlers and their cattle. The rise in CNDP power deepened resentment among non-Rwandophone indigenous communities. New armed groups such as *Mai-Mai Cheka* sprang up in reaction to CNDP control and aggression, and others, like the *Alliance Patriotique pour un Congo Libre et Souverain* (APCLS), garnered increased public support.[169] When the deadline for integration expired, these groups were deemed enemies of the state and possible targets for military operations by the FARDC and MONUC.

Contestation: Challenges within MONUC

MONUC's involvement in *Kimia II* was strongly encouraged by the Council and Western diplomats in Kinshasa, who praised the rapprochement between Congo and Rwanda, and anti-FDLR operations.[170] To senior UN officials, MONUC's participation was commensurate with its mandate. In addition to outlining the mission's protection function, Resolution 1856 affirmed MONUC's commitment to assisting the government, including providing support to the FARDC in operations aimed at disarming foreign and domestic armed groups. And it specifically highlighted the FDLR as a 'major obstacle to peace'.[171] Moreover, senior MONUC officials such as SRSG Doss claimed that the mission's protection mandate was precisely why peacekeepers should be involved in the operations, as they would be better placed to ensure that civilians were protected. As one senior official insisted: 'It would have been morally and ethically untenable *not* to support the operations.'[172]

MONUC's participation in *Kimia II*, particularly without conditions on the support given to the FARDC, was virulently contested within the mission. Officials working within the Civil Affairs and Human Rights Divisions opposed their superiors' decision to engage in joint operations from their very inception.[173] They cited the FARDC track record of civilian abuse, and argued that the potential backlash and retaliatory measures by the FDLR and non-Rwandophones in the region were likely to be significant, and the humanitarian consequences dire. In March 2009, Civil Affairs staff brought forward concerns about the mission's possible complicity in human-rights violations by the FARDC and called for conditionality measures. These concerns echoed formal legal advice given to the mission by the UN Office of Legal Affairs (OLA).[174]

The initial objections of a few within the mission became more widespread as the humanitarian consequences of *Kimia II* came to light. Civilian and military staff in the field and close to the frontline were among the most ardent critics. However, MONUC's leadership in Kinshasa gave little weight to their concerns. Officials complained that their field analyses of the humanitarian and political implications of the operations were regularly dismissed by Kinshasa, and that they were side-lined from decision-making forums in which their objections could be raised.[175] Tense relations between field offices and mission headquarters developed, with field officers expected to toe the line. As two civilian UN officials recounted:

[W]e'd send info up to Kinshasa and they would say 'confirmed or speculative?' and the evidence would get shot down without a request for clarification ... Doss refused to have any analysis in sitreps [situation reports]. We were only allowed to recount the details. Triangulation of sources was not valued—there was no space to say I believe in my sources—in order to make the information more credible. He found ways to dismiss information.[176]

The SRSG kept us out of meetings ... he didn't want to hear from [us] ... He wanted to hear what he wanted to hear. The mission in Kinshasa is not open to criticism on policy decisions, and many UN officials were sidelined during *Kimia II* ... The SRSG says that the Human Rights division of MONUC can't do what it wants to because of the sovereignty issue.[177]

Military officials within the mission voiced similar frustrations. TCC anxieties—and in particular those of the Indian, Pakistani, and South African contingents—about partnering with members of FARDC, including well-known human-rights violators, were regularly dismissed. As a military adviser in the North Kivu brigade explained: '[d]uring *Kimia II* there was a taboo about talking about the CNDP and abuses committed during the operations'.[178] Moreover, concerns about the legitimacy of the operations, particularly as they expanded to include attacks against groups other than the FDLR, surfaced. Peacekeepers argued that these groups, portrayed as indictable, were perhaps otherwise. As the same official recounted: 'Not all the armed groups align with the FDLR. Some are working to provide protection to their own people in a place where there is simply no law and order, and where the state is a big part of the problem. How can supporting operations against such groups be a good idea? No one in Kinshasa is willing to listen to or address these concerns.'[179] In this context, NGOs charged that 'Kimia'—which can be translated roughly as 'keep quiet'—had become disturbingly appropriate given the efforts undertaken by the leadership of MONUC to play down the negative impact of the operations and to silence reports of abuses.[180]

In December 2009, after nine months of operations, the UN attempted to mitigate the potential legal and moral liability of continuing to support the FARDC. The Council renewed MONUC's mandate in Resolution 1906 and introduced the UN's first-ever conditionality policy in which the mission's assistance to Congolese army units was to be contingent on human-rights verification and respect for IHL. *Kimia II* operations were terminated and, in what many criticized as largely a rebranding exercise, were replaced by a new set of operations—*Amani Leo* ('Peace Today'). *Amani Leo* incorporated the conditionality policy, reiterated PoC as a key objective of the operations, and laid greater emphasis on operations against *all* armed groups in eastern Congo.[181]

Some UN officials saw Resolution 1906 as the harbinger of a new phase of peacekeeping. They argued that the conditionality policy—coupled with the strong mandate to protect civilians—provided the necessary framework for peacekeepers to be 'truly impartial' in an assertive manner.[182] Such optimism, however, was tempered by the frustrations of UN military officers on the ground, who maintained that the policy was difficult to enforce. The vetting process, which fewer than 10 per cent of screened FARDC officers were able to pass, was cumbersome, and the UN lacked oversight over key parts of the operations.[183]

In a damning interview with the *Washington Post*, Colonel Innocent Zimurinda, FARDC commander with one of the worst records of human-rights abuses, claimed to have benefited from MONUC support during operations in 2010—that is, following the adoption of the conditionality policy.[184] 'We cannot say we are happy with the level of support', Zimurinda said in the interview. 'But anyway, we want to say "thank you" to the UN.'[185] Months later, it was reported that General Bosco Ntaganda, an ICC-indicted war criminal also known as the 'Terminator', was deputy coordinator of the joint operations despite government and MONUC assurances to the contrary.[186]

Kabila's government felt aggrieved by the negative attention. With the country's fiftieth anniversary of independence later that year and national elections scheduled for 2011, the president grew increasingly concerned that it would reflect poorly on its leadership, which was already greatly contested. MONUC's support was beginning to come at a higher cost. In March 2010, during a visit to Congo by Alain Le Roy, Under-Secretary-General for Peace-keeping, the president forcefully called for the mission's complete withdrawal by mid-2011.[187]

In response, the Security Council intervened and negotiated a deal: the number of blue helmets would be scaled down but the force could remain, in return for the UN's continued support of FARDC in joint operations. In May 2011, the mission was relabelled the UN Organization Stabilization Mission in the Democratic Republic of the Congo (MONUSCO), which, through its emphasis on stabiliza-tion, aligned the UN even more closely, compromisingly, and invidiously with the Congolese state.[188] Military operations continued. Roads were paved. Buildings were erected. And the security situation in the east continued to deteriorate. Reflecting on the mission during this period, Guéhenno, Le Roy's predecessor, damningly charged that it had 'lost its way' and become a 'kind of gun for hire . . . President Kabila's own private military company'.[189]

THE FALL OF GOMA AND A 'FRAMEWORK OF HOPE' (2012–15)

In December 2011, Congolese once again headed to the polls. Kabila was re-elected as president. However, unlike the 2006 elections, the country's second attempt at democracy was rigged, marred by frequent irregularities and deadly violence. His legitimacy greatly weakened, the president in early 2012 announced his intention to arrest Ntaganda and made explicit his plans to dismantle ex-CNDP networks by transferring regiments of the army away from the Kivus, thereby reneging on his secret pact with Kigali. A wave of defections soon followed.

On 6 May 2012, the mutineers announced the creation of the *Mouvement du 23-Mars* (M23), a successor to the CNDP; its name was a reference to the failed 23 March 2009 Agreement. Colonel Makenga, a close associate of Ntaganda, became the public face of the movement.

The M23 rebellion, backed by Rwanda and, to a lesser extent, Uganda, rapidly gained ground.[190] To the shock of many, on 20 November 2012, the militia captured Goma. FARDC units fled, retreating to the town of Minova where they carried out mass rapes.[191] UN forces stayed put, but watched from their armoured personnel carriers as M23 strolled into the city and proceeded to control it for ten days before retreating after the government, battered and bruised, agreed to negotiations with them.[192] The mission was condemned as a failure in what was arguably the nadir of its legitimacy. Critics railed that it had little to show for the billions upon billions of dollars that had been spent.[193]

The fall of Goma prompted a flurry of diplomatic activity—what analysts heralded as the most significant political re-engagement by regional actors and the UN since the Transition period.[194] In Addis Ababa, the African Union (AU) and the UN hosted peace talks, which culminated in the Peace, Security, and Cooperation Framework (PSCF), signed on 24 February 2013 by Congo and eleven other neighbouring countries, with mechanisms for considerable international oversight.[195]

Described as a 'Framework of Hope' by Mary Robinson, the newly-appointed UN special envoy to the region, the PSCF had high aims indeed.[196] It sought to tackle the root causes of violence in the region: namely, the absence of strong, accountable institutions in Congo and the persistent interference of neighbouring states, particularly in the east of the country.

In support of the PSCF and to address the ongoing threat posed by the M23, MONUSCO was revamped. In March 2013, the Council authorized a new mandate for the mission. Resolution 2098 laid out an ambitious programme to bolster Congolese state reform and called for the creation of a 'force intervention brigade' (FIB) to undertake offensive military action to 'neutralize' and 'disarm' rebel groups either unilaterally or in support of the FARDC, and subject to vetting.[197] Originally proposed by the ICGLR and supported by SADC as an entirely separate regional force, the FIB was authorized as a specialized unit within MONUSCO. However, it kept its regional dimension and was comprised of roughly 3,000 troops from South Africa, Tanzania, and Malawi.

To oversee implementation of Resolution 2098, the Secretary-General appointed as SRSG Martin Kobler, a German diplomat who had worked in Iraq and Afghanistan, and had a reputation for activism; a 'dark horse' in the UN system, as described by one senior official.[198] Carlos dos Santos Cruz, a Brazilian Lt. General who had led robust peacekeeping operations in Haiti, was made Force Commander. Under their direction, a more proactive approach was devised for the mission. The aim was to create 'a dynamic and agile force oriented towards the main source of insecurity—the armed groups'.[199] The approach, which was laid out in a new mission concept entitled 'Peace It!', was characterized as a 'shape-clear-hold-build' strategy, loosely inspired by counter-insurgency doctrine.[200] While the FIB was to provide added teeth, the entire mission was implicated in the new strategy. All forces were subject to the same robust RoE and unity of command was emphasized under the slogan 'one mandate, one mission, one force'.[201] To focus on operations, the bulk of MONUSCO's staff was moved to the east.

Partial Implementation of 'Peace It!'

The FIB deployed into eastern Congo in July 2013, equipped with long-range artillery, special forces, snipers, and drones. The mission set up a security perimeter around Goma and Sake, and armed groups in the area were given a 48-hour ultimatum to disarm.[202]

The M23 was the first armed group to be targeted in a series of robust offensive operations jointly planned and conducted by the FARDC and MONUSCO. In late October 2013, after four days of intense battle, the group announced defeat and Makenga surrendered. FIB attack helicopters, artillery, and mortar units provided critical tactical support to the FARDC, which carried out the bulk of the fighting, its performance dramatically improved by a reshuffle in its command and control structures, and the provision of adequate equipment. In addition, small teams of South African Special Forces operated behind M23 lines, disrupting the group's supply routes from Rwanda and killing enemy combatants with long-range sniper shots.[203] Beyond enabling the M23's defeat, the FIB's brazen show of force served as a particularly effective deterrent to other armed groups in the area. In the months that followed, a reported 4,000 combatants came out of the bush to surrender. As one senior official recounted: 'We went in Rambo style and scared the shit out of them. The M23's defeat sent a strong message to other armed groups . . . We're coming to get you.'[204]

In the wake of the M23's defeat, the FARDC launched an offensive against the ADF, a Ugandan Islamist militia in north-eastern Congo, as well as a series of operations targeting groups such as the APCLS and NDC/Cheka. As before, MONUSCO provided support to the FARDC during these operations.

However, the FARDC's performance during these operations paled in comparison to those against the M23, reports of abuses by the army once again surfaced, cooperation between the government and the mission deteriorated, and the UN was often left out of operational planning.[205] The mission's assertive and proactive posture was also not sustained. During operations, FIB troops were said to 'lack motivation' and, according to senior UN officials, the quality of forces fielded following the first rotation deteriorated significantly. Troops were described as 'more risk-averse' and, at times, 'unwilling to follow orders' and undertake 'protection-related activities' in volatile areas.[206] In the Secretary-General's 2014 Strategic Assessment of the mission, he reported to the Council that they were underperforming, failing to 'operate at the optimal level'.[207]

What is more, the mission's new proactive strategy and more assertive mandate had little impact on the posture of the rest of the mission, the traditional peacekeeping units—which were now referred to as the framework forces. Some officials even went so far as to claim that these forces became more, not less passive, after the arrival of the FIB.[208] In his report, the Secretary-General characterized MONUSCO as 'mainly static and passive'.[209] He described how peacekeepers continued to limit 'patrolling activities to daylight hours only' and how on 'several occasions' UN forces had failed to 'conduct patrols to the most vulnerable areas' or respond to threat alerts.[210] In one particularly harrowing incident, which took place on 6 June 2014, thirty-three civilians were massacred around the village of Mutarule (South Kivu), 9 km from the nearest UN base. Residents repeatedly called MONUSCO during the attack, using mobile phones given to them by peacekeepers following an attack the previous year. The Pakistani forces stationed in the area did not intervene to stop the killing, however, and only visited Mutarule two days after the massacre.[211]

Contestation: Fragmentation of the Force

How should we understand the mission's posture during this final phase? The FIB's robust assault on the M23, but lacklustre performance in subsequent operations against other armed groups? What explains the passivity of the framework forces?

The deployment of the FIB and defeat of the M23 was the result of a propitious convergence of interests among Kabila's government, regional states, the UN, and the wider donor community. As the M23 became a serious threat, Kabila's allies in the region stepped in to assist the embattled president and to settle their own scores with Kigali.[212] Bilateral relations between Rwanda and both Tanzania and South Africa had soured in recent years, as Kigali was seen to overstep its bounds.[213] According to one diplomat, eradicating the M23 from eastern Congo was a way to put Kagame in his place'.[214]

Consequently, Kabila's allies deployed some of their most capable forces to the FIB, and coordination between contingents and with the FARDC was strong during the operations.

For its part, the UN Secretariat was desperate to turn things around after the fall of Goma. 'We couldn't just let the largest, most expensive peacekeeping mission in the world fail . . . we'd invested too much', as one UN official said to me.[215] Similar to previous periods, broader macro-political dynamics also had an impact on the mission. Deadlock in the Council over Syria as well as new and seemingly intractable crises in South Sudan and CAR, galvanized efforts in Congo. In the words of one official in New York, 'the UN needed a success story, badly'.[216] Senior members of the Secretariat led the negotiations to bring the proposed SADC force 'in house', worked tirelessly with the Council to develop the FIB and, once authorized, maintained close oversight of the force.

What is more, defeating the M23 had become a 'high-level' priority for donors and, in particular, the United States, which took a more critical view of Rwanda than it had previously.[217] Susan Rice, the US ambassador to the UN, who at first resisted the deployment of the force, dropped her opposition in the face of incontrovertible evidence of Rwanda's support to the M23.[218] Russ Feingold, a senior senator and former chairman of the Senate subcommittee on Africa, was appointed US Special Envoy to the region, bringing gravitas to the post. And during the military offensive against the M23, Kagame received calls from US Secretary of State John Kerry, President Obama, and British Prime Minister David Cameron, all urging him not to resupply the militia.[219] Kagame is said to have heeded these warnings, which analysts contend had a decisive impact on the outcome of the operations.

The honeymoon was, however, short-lived. The partnership between the government, region, and wider international community quickly disintegrated following the M23's defeat, as strategic interests clashed. While donors and the mission leadership turned their attention to tackling the FDLR, the government unilaterally announced the start of operations against the ADF—a sign to many of the government's indifference towards the FDLR, a group with whom the FARDC had a history of collusion. In July 2014, anti-FDLR operations were once again stalled when, to the surprise of the UN, the ICGLR and SADC agreed jointly to give FDLR an additional six months to disarm and Tanzania publicly called for negotiations between the FDLR and Rwanda.[220] The UN leadership was adamantly opposed to the delay but had their hands tied as those regional states offering the reprieve were the very same ones that made up the FIB.

In this respect, officials charged that the FIB's lack of momentum and reluctance to forcefully engage groups other than the M23 reflected the strategic and indeed partial interests of those regional states contributing troops to the FIB. This, in turn, divided the mission and engendered contestation. As one official explained: 'Getting rid of the M23 was really their main goal . . . the other armed groups aren't a priority for the FIB countries. And there's very little the mission leadership can do about that.'[221] Some argued that in part explained the deployment of less capable forces by FIB-contributing countries as well as their decrease in motivation during operations against other armed groups. 'Like the mission', the same official lamented 'the FIB is a victim of politics. It is completely politicized.'

As for the rest of the mission, the persistent passivity of the framework forces was hardly surprising, as their frustrations remained unchanged. What is more, India, Pakistan, Bangladesh, and Uruguay, those states contributing the majority of troops to MONUSCO, had strongly resisted the deployment of the FIB during negotiations in New York. They expressed concern over its assertive mandate—the risks involved, including possible retaliation against civilians, as well as the precedent it would set for peacekeeping, more generally.[222] This generated tense relations between contingents and with the leadership who, despite their rousing calls for robust action, failed to motivate the forces.

Alongside this passivity, the broader strategic context was increasingly one of 'déjà vu'.[223] Implementation of the PSCF stalled. Kabila's government had little to no interest in honouring its commitments. With elections forthcoming in 2016, Kabila focused his attention on shoring up his power and engineering a third term presidency in the face of constitutional limitations.[224] The peace process in tatters, the security situation in the east deteriorated and rumours of the M23's remobilization began to circulate. Frustrated by the lack of progress and consumed by other crises, donors disengaged.[225] Both Feingold and Robinson stepped down as special envoys. By 2015, political frictions between Kabila and MONUSCO had reached new levels; government officials accused the UN of 'neo-colonization' and once again called for the mission's draw-down.[226] As one seasoned and particularly frustrated official said to me, 'plus ça change, plus c'est la même chose . . . '[227]

SITES OF CONTESTATION

The analysis of implementation in this chapter has revealed significant contestation over the meaning and appropriateness of assertive impartiality as a norm of peacekeeping in the Congo. This contestation was both a product of and further contributed to disagreements at the macro- and micro-levels.

The Macro-level Politics of Peacekeeping at the Micro-level

As actors interpreted and enacted the norm, the extent of assertive impartiality's ambiguity, the lack of clarity over both the procedural requirements of the norm as well as the expanded *basis for* decision-making was revealed. Whose consent was necessary? How were peacekeepers to reconcile their mandate to support the government with their task of civilian protection? Were peacekeepers supposed to protect civilians first and worry about the potential political implications of such uses of force later? Or were political considerations to take precedence?

These questions were further complicated by the very nature of protection. Peacekeepers might be able to impartially protect civilians in the short-term, but this was not a long-term or sustainable strategy, given the state's role as primary bearer of the duty to provide protection. Was taking action against elements of the state a sound course of action if it risked alienation or even expulsion of the mission? Moreover, what of groups that defined themselves in opposition to and/or in the absence of the state, and claimed to offer protection? Were peacekeepers to use force against them? Ambiguities over what forms of action were to be pursued, when and against whom, were also heightened by considerations of resource scarcity. What could be expected of peacekeepers such as those in Kisangani and Kiwanja when they were inadequately resourced? Did resource constraints change the calculus of which tasks should be prioritized by the mission? Answers to these questions varied significantly and changed over the course of the mission's deployment, as each phase ushered in a new set of political and tactical dynamics.

In addition to revealing ambiguities related to various components of impartiality, macro-level dynamics were magnified by the fact that some of the same actors that contested the norm during institutionalization also raised objections during implementation. During the first phase, for example, the Secretariat reiterated many of the same concerns that it had raised in other peacekeeping contexts. As divisions in the Council dissipated and it became clear that scaling back the mission's mandate was unlikely, the protestations of the Secretariat abated and officials focused their efforts on trying to boost the mission's effectiveness given existing political constraints. By the final phase, the Secretariat had become an active proponent of the more assertive approach.

Contestation at the macro-level also manifested in the behaviour of the TCCs/PCCs. India, Pakistan, Bangladesh, and Uruguay, states that provided the preponderance of forces to Congo, were some of the most vocal critics of assertive impartiality at the macro-level. Initially troops from these countries were willing to use force at considerable risk, as was the case during the Transition and against the CNDP shortly following the elections. However, their robust posture was neither consistent nor sustained. This in part reflected their frustration with the mission—the contradictory directives given to them by the mission leadership, as during the Bukavu crisis, and what they perceived as the lack of strategic vision, particularly following the elections. These concerns and frustrations informed debates over peacekeeping at the macro-level, which also generated their own forms of discontent that, in turn, impacted the mission.[228] Over time, the caveats placed on TCCs deployments were said to become more stringent and risk-averse, and direct communication between forces and their home country increased, entrenching parallel chains of command. This is consistent with other peacekeeping contexts. A recent UN evaluation of eight missions between 2010–13 found a 'persistent pattern' of peacekeeper passivity in which 'force was almost never used'.[229]

The Micro-Level Politics of Peacekeeping in Congo

Understanding how the macro-level politics of peacekeeping impacted practice also requires accounting for those forms of contestation generated during the process of implementation and related to the Congo context. This includes dynamics within the Council and the mission, which, each at times affecting the other, influenced implementation.

Despite Congo's marginal strategic interest to the P5, particularly when compared to countries in the Middle East, decision-making within the Security Council on Great Lakes policy has been subject to significant disagreement. The mission's mandates have been both a reflection and product of this contestation, as well as of the persistent interests of particular members of the Council.

Divisions within the Council over Great Lakes policy were most striking during the first phase of deployment. Acrimonious relations between France and the US–UK hindered peacemaking efforts in the region and meant that states were reluctant to contribute forces. This also in part explains why members of the Council were averse to acknowledging the 'reality gap' inherent in the Lusaka Agreement, the role prescribed for the UN by the signatories, and, indeed, their own mandates for the mission.

While tensions dissipated during the Transition, they never fully disappeared. Until 2013, the US and the UK maintained close relations with Rwanda, and minimized Kigali's support of militias in eastern Congo, focusing instead on the continued presence of the FDLR.[230] And while relations between Kigali and Paris improved, French suspicions of Rwanda lingered. They regarded these militias as the main aggressor, asserting that the FDLR no longer posed a credible threat to Rwanda. Everyone, in other words, had a different villain.

The relationship between member states and the government in Kinshasa also had a considerable impact on implementation. During the Transition, the collective effort of donors played an instrumental role in organizing Congo's landmark elections and ensured that the Transition did not go off the rails at several critical junctures. Similarly, the robust action undertaken by the mission in Ituri was possible in part because Cammaert enjoyed the backing of the Secretariat and the unwavering commitment of the Council. Commenting on the elections and the operations in Ituri, journalist Michael Kavanagh noted that these were important examples 'of what can be done when the international community decides it cannot accept failure'.[231]

The fragmented approach of Congo's Western donors following the elections hampered the mission's ability to adopt a robust posture. While donors briefly came together in 2013 over the M23 crisis, their commitment was not sustained and international coordination over the implementation of the PSCF deteriorated. By 2015, donors had visibly disengaged. What is more, the mission's leverage throughout this period was further undermined by a lack of coordination among the IMF, the World Bank and the UN, the arrival of non-traditional donors such as China,[232] and the increasingly influential role played by Kabila's regional allies.[233]

Council dynamics and donor relations impacted the mission in various ways. They shaped the content of its mandates, the resources made available to the mission, as well as its broader leverage. Moreover, dynamics in the Council also shaped how officials, particularly the political leadership, interpreted their mandate insofar as what the Council mandated was not always an accurate reflection of what it communicated in practice. For example, in Kisangani, sources noted that the military command was acutely aware that any action against the RCD, despite the mission's mandate to protect, would be highly contested within the Council. Similarly, reflecting on the mission posture vis-à-vis the CNDP, one official stated that '[e]ven though the mandate authorized the protection of civilians, the mission's leadership was very sensitive to Council politics and whether action would have "top cover"'.[234]

The mission itself was also mired in contestation. Far from being a homogeneous entity, multi-dimensional peacekeeping missions like that in Congo encompass a diversity of actors with different bureaucratic and operational identities and interests, which in MONUC/MONUSCO's case demonstrably influenced implementation and engendered their own forms of contestation. While disagreements at times reflected the personal biases of individuals, more general patterns also emerged. Two in particular are worth noting.

First, tensions between the military and political command of the mission were visible at various junctures. The senior political leadership, which was based in Kinshasa for most of the mission's deployment, were reluctant to take any action that would risk a possible escalation in hostilities or that would jeopardize consent for the mission and its activities. This reluctance is explained by the close proximity of the leadership to the government and to donors and diplomats based in the capital, and by a desire to project an image of progress back to New York. In contrast, the military command at several junctures, notably including during the Bukavu and Goma crises, called for robust action that was blocked by the political leadership, while at other times they questioned the rationale for operations like *Kimia II* and *Amani Leo*—which were supported by that same leadership.

Second, there was visible disagreement between the field offices and mission headquarters, and specifically between civilian officials working in the Civil Affairs, Political Affairs, and Human Rights Divisions, and the political leadership. The field officers on the frontline saw the consequences of policies set in Kinshasa and by the Council, and were often more compelled to take a critical stance towards the government and to engage armed actors when they believed it was within their capacity and when the adverse effects on the population did not outweigh the benefits, as they argued was the case during *Kimia II* and *Amani Leo*.

Amid this contestation, the mission's political leadership had the greatest degree of influence in determining what decisions were taken and what course of action the mission carried out. In similar fashion to the way the dynamics of contestation played out at the macro-level (Chapter 3), the leadership exercised its dominance in part by controlling the flow of information, filtering out evidence that challenged what it regarded as the course of action worth pursuing, and by impeding access to decision-making forums.

CONCLUSION

The purpose of this chapter has been to examine implementation of the new assertive conception of impartiality in the Congo case. The various forms and sites of contestation illuminated by this chapter's analysis underscore the importance of studying the process of implementation to understand better both the global and local politics of peacekeeping in particular contexts. However, as I have argued, the study of norms must also account for their implications and consequences. To that end, Chapter 5 considers the various effects of *prescribing* an assertive role for peacekeepers in Congo, particularly given the lack of consensus detailed in this chapter. It demonstrates how portraying peace and protection *as* impartial and apolitical—when in fact they are deeply contested—has had consequences for all actors in the Congo case: civilians, armed groups, the Congolese government, and the mission itself. In short, my argument is that losing sight of the 'many-sidedness' of conflict by selectively condemning on moral grounds certain but not all of the participants' words and actions has come at great and grievous cost, particularly for those most vulnerable in this ravaged region.[235]

NOTES

1. Interview with government official, Goma, February 2010.
2. *Human Development Report 2014* (New York: United Nations Development Programme, 2014).
3. This historical overview builds on Chapter 2's discussion of the first UN peace-keeping mission to the Congo (1960–64) as well as that previously deployed to Rwanda (1993–96). For a detailed history of the region, see René Lemarchand, *The Dynamics of Violence in Central Africa* (Philadelphia: University of Pennsylvania Press, 2009); Filip Reyntjens, *The Great African War: Congo and Regional Geopolitics, 1996–2006* (New York: Cambridge University Press, 2009); Jason Stearns, *Dancing in the Glory of Monsters: The Collapse of the Congo and the Great War of Africa* (New York: Public Affairs, 2011); David Van Reybrouck, *Congo: The Epic History of a People* (New York: HarperCollins, 2014).
4. Sarah Kenyon Lischer, 'Collateral Damage: Humanitarian Assistance as a Cause of Conflict', *International Security* 28/1 (2003), 92.
5. Lischer (2003: 101).
6. Fiona Terry, *Condemned to Repeat? The Paradox of Humanitarian Action* (Ithaca: Cornell University Press, 2002), 156.
7. For a detailed account of humanitarian responses in the camps, see Terry (2002: 155–216).
8. United Nations, *Report of the Mapping Exercise Documenting the Most Serious Violations of Human Rights and International Humanitarian Law Committed within the Territory of the Democratic Republic of the Congo between March 1993 and June 2003* (New York: United Nations High Commission for Human Rights, 2010).
9. Gerard Prunier, *Africa's World War: Congo, the Rwandan Genocide, and the Making of a Continental Catastrophe* (New York: Oxford University Press, 2009), 359.
10. Prunier (2009: 155).
11. The AFDL was also backed to a lesser extent by the governments of Ethiopia, Eritrea, Tanzania, and Zimbabwe.
12. In early 1999, a rift between a pro-Kigali and a pro-Kampala wing within the RCD emerged, eventually leading to its split into *RCD-Goma* (RCD-G) and *RCD-Mouvement de Libération* (RCD-ML, initially known as RCD-Kisangani, or RCD-K). In addition, Uganda supported the creation of the *Mouvement de Libération du Congo* (MLC) by Jean-Pierre Bemba to offset to the Rwandan-dominated RCD. See Reyntjens (2009: 243).
13. Prunier (2009: 201–2).
14. Prunier (2009: 257).
15. Stathis Kalyvas, 'The Ontology of "Political Violence": Action and Identity in Civil Wars', *American Political Science Review* 1/3(2003), 479.
16. Lusaka Agreement, 1999, http://peacemaker.un.org/drc-lusaka-agreement99
17. See Philip Winter, *A Sacred Cause: The Inter-Congolese Dialogue 2000–2003* (Edinburgh: Librario, 2012).
18. International Crisis Group (ICG), *Scramble for the Congo: Anatomy of an Ugly War* (Nairobi/Brussels: 2000).

19. ICG (2000: 72). The Lusaka Agreement referred to nine 'negative forces', namely the ex-FAR, ADF, LRA, UNRFN, Interahamwe, FUNA, FDD, WNBF, and UNITA. To monitor the ceasefire prior to the UN's deployment, Lusaka created the Joint Military Commission (JMC), composed of representatives of the various armed groups under a 'neutral' command, appointed by the OAU Chairman. The mandate of the JMC was to establish the location of units at the time of the ceasefire, and verify their disengagement and eventual withdrawal.

20. United Nations, S/RES/1258 (1999).

21. S/RES/1258 (1999).

22. United Nations, S/RES/1279 (1999).

23. United Nations, S/RES/1291 (2000).

24. ICG (2000: 75).

25. United Nations, S/RES/1291 (2000). See United Nations, S/PV 4092.2 (1999), 11.

26. ICG (2000: 66–84).

27. ICG (2000: 66).

28. *Mapping Report* (2010: 307–91).

29. ICG (2000: 72).

30. ICG (2000: 72).

31. Nicholas Stockton, *Humanitarianism Bound: Coherence and Catastrophe in the Congo 1998–2002* (Unpublished study for the Centre for Humanitarian Dialogue, Geneva, 2003), 67; United Nations, S/2000/888 (2000).

32. Unlike his father, Joseph Kabila cultivated ties with the diplomatic community and treated it, as one analyst noted, as 'his powerbase'. Quoted in Stearns (2011: 313).

33. For example, UN helicopters were attacked by the MLC in Equateur and access to areas controlled by the UPDF was also impeded. IRIN, 'UN condemns MLC threat against MONUC', Nairobi, 21 July 2000.

34. Interview with former Congolese military officer, Goma, February 2010.

35. Stockton (2003: 51).

36. Human Rights Watch (HRW), *War Crimes in Kisangani: The Response of Rwandan-backed Rebels to the May 2002 Mutiny* (New York: 2002). Analysis of the Kisangani massacre draws on Emily Paddon, 'Peacekeeping in the Congo: Implementation of the Protection of Civilians Norm', in Alexander Betts and Phil Orchard, *Implementation & World Politics: How International Norms Change Practice* (Oxford: Oxford University Press, 2014), 166–7, reprinted with permission of Oxford University Press.

37. Stockton (2003: 39).

38. Secretary of State Madeleine Albright and Susan Rice, Assistant Secretary of State for Africa, were critical in building this relationship. For both, the Rwandan genocide was 'no abstract event'. Peter Rosenblum, 'Irrational Exuberance: The Clinton Administration in Africa', *Current History* 101/655 (2002). As the US Representative to the UN in 1994, Albright actively obstructed UN intervention to stop the killing; while Rice—at the time a junior official at the National Security Council (NSC)—was derided by colleagues for asking during a meeting what the effect would be on the congressional midterm elections if the administration were to use the word 'genocide' and 'be seen to do nothing'. After the genocide, both Albright

and Rice expressed great remorse and an unwavering resolve to support Rwanda. Quoted in Jason Stearns, 'Rwandan Ghosts', *Foreign Policy*, November 2012.

39. The UK did not have strong historical ties to Rwanda. However, Clare Short, the UK's Secretary of State for International Development, quickly fostered a close personal relationship with Kagame. Between 1997 and 2003, she made frequent trips to Kigali and the two spoke nearly every week on the phone. Clare Short, *The Vaughan Memorial Lecture: The UK and Post-Genocidal Rwanda* (Oxford: Oxford Central Africa Forum, November 2012). For a critical overview of UK policy, see Zoe Marriage, 'Defining Morality: DFID and the Great Lakes', *Third World Quarterly* 27/3 (2006), 477–90.

40. Gordon Cumming, 'The UK and France in the DRC: Making Their Own Peace', in *From Rivalry to Partnership?: New Approaches to the Challenges of Africa*, edited by Tony Chafer and Gordon Cumming (Farnham: Ashgate, 2011), 141.

41. Catherine Gegout, 'The West, Realism and Intervention in the Democratic Republic of Congo (1996–2006)', *International Peacekeeping* 16/2 (2009), 231–44.

42. Interview with senior government official, December 2011.

43. For example, the *Garreton Report*, a UN study on revenge killings during the forced closure of the refugee camps, was cast aside and the follow up investigation delayed ten years until the 2010 mapping report. Roberto Garreton, 'Mission Impossible: The Massacres in Former Zaire', *Le Monde Diplomatique*, December 1997.

44. United Nations, S/2000/128 (2001), para 38, 76; On MONUC's slow deployment, see Virgil Hawkins, 'History Repeating Itself: The DRC and the Security Council', *African Security Review* 12/4 (2003), 47–55.

45. Human Rights Watch (2002).

46. Phone interview with former analyst and senior UN official, March 2010.

47. Phone interview with former analyst and senior UN official, March 2010.

48. United Nations, S/2000/30 (2000), para 67.

49. IRIN, 'DRC: UN responds to HRW criticism over Kisangani massacre', Nairobi, 22 August 2002.

50. United Nations, S/RES/1417 (2002).

51. Jean-Marie Guéhenno, 'On the Challenges and Achievements of Reforming the UN Peace Operations', *International Peacekeeping* 9/2 (2002), 78.

52. The Pretoria Agreement between Rwanda and Congo was signed in July 2002 and the Luanda Agreement between Uganda and Congo in September 2002.

53. The 'one-plus-four' model included: Yerodia Abdoulaye (for Kabila's party/government); Arthur Z'Ahidi Ngoma (for civil society/unarmed opposition); Jean-Pierre Bemba's MLC; and Azarias Ruberwa's RCD-G. The various Mai-Mai militias who signed the peace agreement were not a part of the TG.

54. United Nations, S/2003/566 (2003).

55. Interview with William Swing, former Special Representative of the Secretary-General, MONUC, Geneva, December 2009.

56. The CIAT comprised ambassadors from the five permanent members of the Security Council plus Belgium, Canada, and South Africa (joined later by Angola, Gabon, Mozambique, Nigeria, Zambia, the African Union/African Commission, and European Union/European Commission). In addition to the CIAT, an electoral

assistance unit was created within MONUC; the mission deployed a 'Neutral Force' in Kinshasa to safeguard members of the TG; and lastly, MONUC served as co-chair of the Joint Commission on Security Sector Reform, which worked towards the development of a unified national army and police. See United Nations, S/RES/1493 (2003) and S/RES/1565 (2004).

57. This was still considerably fewer than the 23,900 which the Secretary-General had requested in United Nations, S/2000/566 (2000).
58. MONUC, 'Military Briefing', Goma, 30 March 2005 (Internal).
59. United Nations, S/RES/1565 (2004).
60. United Nations, S/RES/1592 (2005).
61. MONUC, 'Divisional Commander's Operational Directive', Eastern Division, July 2005 (Restricted).
62. Patrick Cammaert, 'A Peacekeeping Commander's Perspective', *The RUSI Journal* 15/3 (2008), 70. Interview with Major General (ret.) Patrick Cammaert, former UN Force Commander for the Eastern Democratic Republic of the Congo, New York, October 2011.
63. Interview with MONUC official, Goma, February 2010.
64. Interview with diplomat, Goma, February 2010.
65. International Crisis Group (ICG), *The Congo's Transition is Failing: Crisis in the Kivus* (Nairobi/Brussels: 2005).
66. International Crisis Group (ICG), *Congo Crisis: Military Intervention in Ituri* (Nairobi/Brussels: 2003), 4. Described as a 'conflict within a conflict', the violence in Ituri was related to, but distinct from, Congo's Second War. See Koen Vlassenroot and Timothy Raeymaekers, 'The Politics of Rebellion and Intervention in Ituri: The Emergence of a New Political Complex?', *African Affairs* 103/412 (2004), 385–412.
67. Interview with Ituri expert, Dan Fahey, Goma, March 2011.
68. See International Crisis Group (ICG), *The Kivus: The Forgotten Crucible of the Congo Conflict* (Nairobi/Brussels: 2003).
69. Prunier (2009: 294).
70. ICG (2005).
71. Cited in Stearns (2011: 246).
72. IRIN, 'MONUC gets tough on foreign armed groups', Bukavu, 22 March 2006.
73. For an overview see Catherine Gegout, 'Causes and Consequences of the EU's Military Intervention', *European Foreign Affairs Review* 10/3 (2005), 427–33.
74. United Nations, S/RES/1565 (2005).
75. Armed groups that were targeted included: the *Forces Armées du Peuple Congolais* (FAPC), *Force de Résistance Patriotique en Ituri* (FRPI), *Front des Nationalistes et Intégrationnistes* (FNI), *Parti pour l'Unité et la Sauvegarde de l'Intégrité du Congo* (PUSIC), *Union des Patriotes Congolais* (UPC), *Front Populaire pour la Démocratie du Congo* (FPDC), and Lord's Resistance Army (LRA). Drawn from MONUC, 'List of Operations conducted since June 2005', Powerpoint 2007 (Internal).
76. Interview with Cammaert, 2011.
77. Interview with Cammaert, 2011. Cited in Paddon (2014: 168), reprinted with permission of Oxford University Press.
78. MONUC, *Civil Affairs Special Report*, 28 June 2006 (Internal).

79. Cammaert (2008).
80. Jason Stearns, 'The Cat's Cradle of Congolese Politics', *World Peace Foundation, Tufts University*, 30 November 2012. Analysis of the Bukavu crisis draws on Paddon (2014: 168–89), reprinted with permission of Oxford University Press.
81. ICG (2005: 6); Human Rights Watch (HRW), *War Crimes in Bukavu* (New York: 2004); MONUC, 'MONUC and the Bukavu Crisis 2004', Best Practices Unit, Department of Peacekeeping Operations, New York, March 2005, (Restricted), reprinted with the permission of the United Nations. (Henceforth, *'Bukavu Report'*).
82. *Bukavu Report* (2005: 6).
83. Reported estimates on the number of MONUC forces in Bukavu tend to be quite higher (for example, the International Crisis Group cites 600 troops and Human Rights Watch cites 700) than those of military deployed in Bukavu at the time who estimate 400 troops.
84. HRW (2004).
85. Human Rights Watch (HRW), *Civilians Attacked in North Kivu* (New York: 2005).
86. In Ituri the main players (UPDF, MLC, and RCD-K/ML) had largely withdrawn by early 2005 and remaining armed groups were not central to the peace process, thereby limiting the risks of peacekeeping action. As a senior MONUC official explained: 'Dealing with the Ituri rebels was feasible because they were of secondary importance. The same thing would never have been possible in the Kivus. There was no Rwandan involvement in Ituri and the parties MONUC was using force against were not critical for the Transition. In the Kivus they were.' Interview with senior UN official, Kinshasa, February 2011.
87. Stefaan Smis and Theodore Trefon, 'Congo: Waiting for Godot', *Review of African Political Economy* 30/98 (2003), 671.
88. MONUC, 'Briefing Presentation', 4 December 2004 (Internal); MONUC, 'Briefing Presentation', 21 December 2004 (Internal).
89. Interview with MONUC official, Kinshasa, February 2011.
90. Other instances of peacekeeper passivity were underpinned by a similar rationale, including the massacre of over fifty civilians by the RCD in Walungu (South Kivu) in April 2003. When a UN official based in Bukavu sought clarification from a senior official in Kinshasa as to what should be the response in Walungu given MONUC's mandate to protect civilians, the official was instructed that the mission could 'not attack an armed group that was about to become a member of the transition . . . I was basically told to swallow fifty deaths for the sake of "peace"'. Interview with former UN official, Nairobi, November 2011.
91. Interview with senior UN official, Kinshasa, February 2011.
92. The Head of Office was alleged to have openly supported Serufuli during his election campaign. And thus, 'it was no wonder' as one official charged 'that the RCD wasn't held to account'. Interview with senior UN official, Kinshasa, February 2011.
93. Interview with UN official, Goma, April 2011.
94. Interview with senior UN official, Goma, January 2009; Interview with military officer, September 2011.
95. *Bukavu Report* (2005: 14).

96. *Bukavu Report* (2005: 6).
97. *Bukavu Report* (2005: 15).
98. *Bukavu Report* (2005: 19).
99. *Bukavu Report* (2005: 18).
100. Interview with former MONUC official, September 2011.
101. According to the *Bukavu Report*: 'If based solely on reports received from MONUC HQ, New York would have been under the impression that the transitional process was healthy and moving forward' (2005: 12).
102. *Bukavu Report* (2005: 19).
103. *Bukavu Report* (2005: 18).
104. *Bukavu Report* (2005: 10).
105. *Bukavu Report* (2005: 16).
106. Interview with Swing, 2009.
107. Interview with NGO official, London, July 2011.
108. Interview with senior UN official, Kinshasa, February 2011.
109. Reuters, 'After Violent Decades, Congo Finally Installs an Elected Leader', 7 December 2006.
110. Reuters (2006).
111. United Nations, S/2007/156 (2007).
112. This included the introduction of the integrated mission concept to coordinate the various agencies under the 'one UN' umbrella. Other reforms included: the common humanitarian funds, the cluster approach, the first country-level Good Humanitarian Donor Initiative, and the establishment of provincial OCHA offices.
113. Interview with senior UN official, New York, June 2011.
114. Interview with senior UN official, New York, June 2011.
115. Interview with MONUC official, Goma, December 2008.
116. Interview with senior UN official, Kinshasa, February 2011.
117. Interview with UN official, Goma, March 2011.
118. Interview with UN official, Goma, March 2011.
119. United Nations, S/RES/1794 (2007).
120. MONUC, 'Force Directive, No. 132', 2008 (Internal).
121. Kabila failed to obtain an absolute majority and a run-off election was held in early 2007. For an account of government abuses during this period, see Human Rights Watch (HRW), *We Will Crush You: The Restriction of Political Space in the Democratic Republic of Congo* (New York: 2008), 3–4; MONUC, 'Report on Election Violence', Human Rights Division, 2008 (Internal).
122. HRW (2008: 3).
123. Herbert Weiss, 'The DRC Crisis' (New York: Panel at Columbia University, March 2010).
124. Ruberwa, the RCD candidate, come fourth in the presidential election, with only 1.7 per cent of the vote. No Tutsi were elected to the North Kivu provincial assembly and only one to the National Assembly, who was not an RCD candidate.
125. International Crisis Group (ICG), *Congo: Bringing Peace to North Kivu* (Nairobi/Brussels: 2007).

126. Jason Stearns, *North Kivu: The Background to Conflict in North Kivu Province of Eastern Congo* (London: Rift Valley Institute, 2012), 30.

127. United Nations, *Mission Report: Military Component Evaluation–United Nations Organization Mission in the Democratic Republic of the Congo (MONUC)* (New York, 19–29 April 2008, Internal), 6.

128. Human Rights Watch (HRW), *Killings in Kiwanja: The UN's Inability to Protect Civilians* (New York: 2008).

129. Interview with senior MONUC official, Goma, January 2010.

130. Alex Perry, 'The man who would be (Congo's) king', *Time World*, 27 November 2008.

131. HRW (2008); United Nations, *Consolidated Report on Investigations Conducted by the United Nations Joint Human Rights Office (UNJHRO) into Grave Human Rights Abuses Committed in Kiwanja, North Kivu, in November 2008* (September 2009).

132. Interview with resident of Kiwanja, February 2010.

133. Interview with senior UN official, New York, March 2010.

134. ICG (2007: 25).

135. Interview with senior UN official, New York, June 2011.

136. Shortly after the elections, China entered into a $6 billion infrastructure for resource accord with Congo, making it China's largest deal on the continent.

137. Human Rights Watch (HRW), *Renewed Crisis in North Kivu* (New York: 2007), 78.

138. Interview with UN official in Goma, January 2011.

139. Interview with senior UN official, Kinshasa, February 2011.

140. For example, two former UN officials recounted their frustration over the visit of Jendayi Frazer, US Assistant Secretary of State for African Affairs, to Goma days after the crisis. Frazer was given a full briefing, during which MONUC's military command provided a detailed account of Rwanda's support to CNDP as well as its direct involvement during the crisis, including attacks by Rwandan military units on Congolese territory. Hours later, at a press conference in Kigali, Frazer stated: 'the United States government has no evidence that Rwanda supports the rebel CNDP of Major General Laurent Nkunda' (Frank Kagabo, '"Rwanda not in Congo" says Frazer', *The New Times*, 2 November 2008). For the mission's military command, Frazer's remarks were 'a slap in the face', particularly given what they had just been through. For others, her statement was 'ridiculous, but hardly surprising'. Interviews with MONUC officials, Goma, January 2009.

141. Interview with senior UN official, New York, June 2011.

142. Interview with senior UN official, New York, June 2011.

143. Interview with former MONUC official, December 2012.

144. Interview with senior MONUC official, Goma, January 2010.

145. Agence France-Presse, 'Lack of troops, "schizophrenic" mandate hamper UN in DR Congo', 12 November 2008.

146. Interview with government official, Goma, January 2010.

147. HRW (2008: 24).

148. Julie Reynaert, 'MONUC/MONUSCO and Civilian Protection in the Kivus', *IPIS*, 2011, 17.

149. Interview with MONUC official, Goma, January 2009.

150. Interview with MONUC official, Goma, January 2009. Africa Confidential, 'More Policing of Peacekeepers. Indian soldiers are being accused of not knowing where their loyalties lie', 6 November 2008.
151. Interview with former UN official, Goma, January 2010.
152. HRW (2008: 3); United Nations, UNJHRO (September 2009: 2–3); Holt and Taylor (2009: 281–3).
153. Interview with former MONUC official, December 2012.
154. Interview with former MONUC official, December 2012.
155. Interview with diplomat, Goma, February 2010.
156. Interview with senior UN official, New York, October 2011.
157. United Nations, S/RES/1856 (2008), 4 (emphasis added).
158. Interview with senior UN official, Goma, January 2009.
159. Interview with senior UN official, Kinshasa, February 2011.
160. Interview with diplomat, Goma, February 2010.
161. Interview with government official, Goma, February 2010. See also United Nations, S/2009/603 (2009), *Final Report of the Group of Experts on the Democratic Republic of the Congo*; International Crisis Group (ICG), *Congo: Five Priorities for a Peacebuilding Strategy* (Nairobi/Brussels: 2009).
162. The mission tried to be involved in the operations. It established a Joint Operations Command (JOC) with the goal of bringing together MONUC, FARDC, and RPA to oversee the operations. However, JOC quickly became referred to as 'JOKE' and was within a week renamed the 'liaison centre' for information sharing, as it became clear that the FARDC and RPA were not in the least interested in joint planning.
163. Interview with government official, Goma, January 2010.
164. Interview with senior UN official, Kinshasa, February 2011.
165. The overall and long-term impact of the operations is less clear, as the FDLR regrouped in a number of locations in the Kivus, and continued to recruit new fighters to replace the defectors. See United Nations, S/2010/596 (2010), *Final Report of the Group of Experts on the Democratic Republic of the Congo*.
166. United Nations, A/HRC/14/24/Add.3 (1 June 2010, advance unedited version), 1.
167. HRW (2009: 85).
168. Interview with UN official, Goma, January 2010.
169. Jason Stearns, *PARECO: Land, Local Strongmen and the Roots of Militia Politics in North Kivu* (London: Rift Valley Institute, 2012).
170. This section draws on Paddon (2014: 172–3), reprinted with permission of Oxford University Press.
171. United Nations, S/RES/1856 (2009).
172. Interview with senior UN official, Kinshasa, February 2011.
173. MONUC, 'Protection Impact of Umoja Wetu', Powerpoint Presentation, 28 February 2009 (Internal); MONUC, 'Summary of Protection Issues Associated with the Coalition Operations against FDLR and Fast-tracked FARDC Integration Process', Civil Affairs Section, 20 February 2009 (Internal).
174. The OLA recommended that MONUC 'establish conditions for respecting international humanitarian law, as required by its mandate, before it began to

support the operations'. The OLA advice also clarified that if the FARDC did violate international law, MONUC would need to take a range of measures, including, if the violations were 'widespread or serious', to end its 'participation in the operation as a whole'. Cited in United Nations, A/HRC/14/24/Add.3 (2010), 11.

175. MONUC, 'Evaluation of the Impact of Kimia II by MONUC-NK Substantive Sections', 6 June 2009 (Internal); MONUC, 'Kimia II: Implications for the Protection of Civilians', Powerpoint Presentation for the Visit of SRSG Alan Doss, 7 June 2009 (Internal).

176. Interview with UN official, Goma, April 2011.

177. Interview with MONUC official, Goma, January 2010.

178. Interview with military officer, Goma, December 2009.

179. Interview with military officer, Goma, December 2009.

180. Oxfam, *Waking the Devil: The Impact of Forced Disarmament on Civilians in the Kivus* (Oxford: Oxfam International, 2009).

181. MONUC, 'Operating Guidelines', viewed by author in Goma, January 2010 (Restricted). The 'conditionality policy' became the basis for the development of the United Nations, A/67/775 (2013), *Human Rights Due Diligence Policy on United Nations Support to Non-United Nations Security Forces*.

182. Interview with senior UN official, New York, June 2011.

183. United Nations, S/2010/596 (2010). The mission had little control over material assistance (e.g., rations could be diverted), FARDC deployment and redeployments (e.g., which commander was sent where) and enforcement of punitive measures against FARDC forces when abuses were detected. These issues persisted. In the words of a peacekeeper: 'The HRDDP is very aspirational. The force just doesn't have the capacity to match the intent.' Interview with military officer, Goma, June 2015.

184. Stephanie McCrummen, 'Abusive Congolese colonel got aid', *Washington Post*, 9 March 2010.

185. McCrummen (2010).

186. Katrina Manson, 'Exclusive: Congo war indictee says directs U.N.-backed ops', *Reuters*, 6 October 2010.

187. Agence France-Presse, 'Kinshasa wants UN mission to start pull out from June: official', 3 March 2010.

188. Emily Paddon and Guillaume Lacaille, *Stabilizing the Congo* (University of Oxford, Refugee Studies Centre Policy Brief, 8, December 2011); ICG, *Eastern Congo: Why Stabilisation Failed* (Nairobi/Brussels: October 2012).

189. Interview with Guéhenno, New York, March 2010.

190. Jason Stearns, *From CNDP to M23: The Evolution of an Armed Movement in Eastern Congo* (London: Rift Valley Institute, 2012).

191. HRW, *DR Congo: War Crimes by M23, Congolese Army. Response to Crisis in the East Should Emphasize Justice* (New York: February 2013).

192. The UN took the position that MONUSCO could not use force to stop the M23 advance because FARDC had fled. However, others have argued that given its PoC mandate it was well within its authority to use force to defend the city. See United Nations, Office of Internal Oversight Services, A/68/787 (2014), 15.

193. Rosie DiManno, 'In Congo, UN troops prove useless again', *The Star*, 21 November 2012; Robyn Dixon, 'U.N. force in Congo, MONUSCO, criticized as ineffective', *Los Angeles Times*, 22 December 2012; Jessica Hatcher and Alex Perry, 'Defining peacekeeping downward: the U.N. debacle in eastern Congo', *TIME Magazine*, 26 November 2012.

194. ICG, *Congo: Ending the Status Quo* (Nairobi/Brussels: December 2014), 3.

195. Separate talks were held between the M23 and the government under the auspices of the International Conference on the Great Lakes Region (ICGLR). They ended with the signing of the Nairobi declarations on 12 December 2013. Implementation of the declarations has been slow, with significant blockages. For details, see ICG (2014: 10).

196. United Nations, 'Framework of Hope: The Peace, Security and Cooperation Framework for the Democratic Republic of Congo and the Region', Office of the Special Envoy of the Secretary-General for the Great Lakes Region of Africa, 2013.

197. United Nations, S/RES/2098 (2013), 7–8. The mandate was subsequently renewed without significant modification in United Nations, S/RES/2147 (2014) and S/RES/2211 (2015).

198. Interview with senior UN official, Goma, June 2015.

199. MONUSCO, 'A New Approach To Protection of Civilians (PoC)', Powerpoint Presentation, MONUSCO FC, SMG-P, 7 September 2013.

200. MONUSCO, 'Mission Concept: Peace it! Together on the Journey to Lasting Peace in the Democratic Republic of Congo', 2013, para 32. During 'shape', the mission was to build an understanding of the armed groups, fixing and isolating them; the FIB supported by FARDC would then 'clear' an area of armed groups; FARDC supported by regular peacekeeping units would proceed to 'hold' it; and the government with support from the UN would then focus on long-term activities to 'build' the area and restore state authority.

201. Statement of SRSG Martin Kobler to the Security Council, 'Building on the momentum', 14 March 2014.

202. UN News Centre, 'UN mission sets up security zone in eastern DR Congo, gives rebels 48 hour ultimatum', July 30, 2013.

203. In one such instance, which has become something of a local legend, a South African sniper is said to have 'taken out' a member of the M23 at a range of 2,125 m, making it one of the longest distance combat sniper shots in military history. Darren Olivier, 'The FIB Goes to War', *African Defence Review*, 29 August 2013, http://www.africandefence.net/the-fib-goes-to-war/

204. Interview with senior UN official, Goma, June 2015.

205. ICG (2014: 7).

206. Interviews with senior UN military staff, Goma, June 2015.

207. United Nations, S/2014/957 (2014), 18; Hugo de Vries, *Going around in Circles: The Challenges of Peacekeeping and Stabilization in the Democratic Republic of the Congo* (The Hague: Clingendael Institute, July 2015).

208. Interviews with civilian and military UN personnel, Goma, June 2015.

209. United Nations, S/2014/957 (2014), 18.

210. S/2014/957 (2014), 18.

211. HRW, *DR Congo: Army, UN Failed to Stop Massacre* (New York: 2014). Similarly, in October 2014 peacekeepers did not respond forcefully during a series of attacks by the ADF in Beni (North Kivu), which killed over 200 civilians. Interview with UN official, Goma, June 2015; ICG (2014: 7).
212. Kabila's government has fostered close bilateral relations with SADC states in recent years. See ICG (2014).
213. Tensions between South Africa and Rwanda developed over the assassination of Rwandan dissident ex-General Nyamwasa in 2010 in South Africa. Tanzania has an even more fraught relationship with Rwanda, exacerbated in recent years by Tanzanian official statements which recognize the grievances of the FDLR. ICG (2014: 13–15).
214. Interview with diplomat, Goma, June 2015.
215. Interview with UN official, New York, October 2014.
216. Interview with UN official, New York, October 2014.
217. Steven Lee Myers, 'Ex-senator Feingold chosen as Special Envoy to African region', *New York Times*, 18 June 2013.
218. James Verini, 'Should the United Nations Wage War to Keep Peace?', Special report in *National Geographic*, 27 March 2014.
219. Verini (2014).
220. 'Second Joint ICGLR-SADC Ministerial Meeting', Communiqué, Luanda, 2 July 2014. Inflaming regional tensions, the Tanzanian foreign ministry described the FDLR as 'freedom fighters from Rwanda settled in DRC'. 'SADC/ICGLR Ministerial meeting', press release, Ministry of Foreign Affairs and International Cooperation, Dar es Salaam, 3 July 2014.
221. Interview with senior UN official, Goma, June 2015.
222. Indrani Bagchi, 'India warns peacekeeping troops in DR Congo of M23 retaliatory strikes', *Times of India*, 28 August 2013; United Nations Security Council '"Intervention Brigade" authorized as Security Council grants mandate renewal for United Nations mission in Democratic Republic of Congo', meetings coverage, New York, 28 March 2013 http://www.un.org/press/en/2013/sc10964.doc.htm. See also, Isobelle Jacques, *Promoting effective international peace operations in increasingly complex environments: Conference report*, WP1336 (Wilton Park, 15–17 June 2014), 5; Verini (2014); De Vries (2015: 40).
223. ICG (2014).
224. Sarah M. Kazadi and Rebecca Sesny, 'Congolese see no end to president's final term', *New York Times*, 8 August 2015; Kenneth Roth and Ida Sawyer, 'Joseph Kabila Forever: The dangers of an extended presidency in the Democratic Republic of the Congo', *Foreign Policy*, 28 July 2015.
225. Stephen Weissman, et al., 'Absent in Central Africa: How the United States Risks Reigniting Chaos in Congo', *Foreign Affairs*, 8 June 2015.
226. James Butty, 'Congo official: DRC will not accept UN "neocolonization"', *Voice of America*, 29 March 2015.
227. Interview with UN official, Goma, June 2015.
228. In 2011, India withdrew its four remaining Mi-35 attack helicopters from MONUSCO. In addition to voicing concerns over the direction in which the mission was heading, Manjeev Singh Puri, India's Deputy Ambassador to the

UN, reiterated objections made previously at the macro-level. Specifically, he underlined the need for 'more consultations' with TCCs and a more equitable distribution of the costs of peacekeeping. 'India withdrawing helicopters from UN's Congo mission', *The Hindu Times,* 16 June 2011; Colum Lynch, 'India's withdrawal of helicopters from Congo points to wider trend', *The Washington Post,* 14 June 2011. Similarly in 2012, the Indian Ambassador to the UN expressed great concern about the mission's assertive mandate. 'There are those that are completely aghast that the Security Council has provided this kind of mandate', he exclaimed. 'We have to be careful about where this is going. The U.N. charter never talks about going in and being a participant.' Quoted in Christopher Rhoads, 'Peacekeepers at war', *The Wall Street Journal,* 23 June 2012.

229. A/68/787 (2014).

230. For example, as Ambassador to the UN under the Obama administration, Susan Rice used American influence within the organization to 'dial down' criticisms of Rwanda and thwart France's pleas for a more punitive approach towards Kagame's government. In 2010, Rice attempted to block the release of the UN mapping report, which, among its many findings, implicated Rwanda in the massacre of thousands of Hutus in the mid-1990s. According to Stearns, senior officials involved with the report asserted that Rice 'didn't see how opening up old wounds would help'. In 2012, Rice attempted to block publication of the UN Panel of Experts' report detailing abuses committed by the M23 and allegedly removed language from a resolution citing Rwanda's and Uganda's well-documented support of the group. In 2013, Rice dropped her objections to the creation of the FIB after she was shown detailed evidence of Rwanda's support for the M23. Stearns, *Foreign* Policy (2012); Colum Lynch, 'How Rice dialed down the pressure on Rwanda', *Turtle Bay,* 3 December 2012; Verini (2014).

231. Michael Kavanagh, 'A Review of Severine Autesserre's "The Trouble with the Congo"', *African Security Review* 20/2 (2011), 90.

232. As a political affairs officer deployed in eastern Congo said to me: 'It is difficult for [the mission] and member states who share a similar vision to say that assistance is conditional, tied to human-rights performance and better vetting of the army, when China just comes along and gives $6 billion without asking any questions.' Interview, Goma, February 2010.

233. Reuters, 'African rivalries weaken U.N. hand against rebels in Congo', 22 October 2014; ICG (2014).

234. Interview with senior UN official, New York, July 2011.

235. Patricia Owens, *Between War and Politics: International Relations and the Thought of Hannah Arendt* (Oxford: Oxford University Press, 2007), 42.

5

The Effects of Assertive Impartiality
in the Congo

On the evening of 29 September 2009, the UN Mission in the Congo (MONUC) sent gunship helicopters to fire on the *Alliance Patriotique pour un Congo Libre et Souverain* (APCLS), a local Hunde militia group based in Masisi, North Kivu.[1] Four civilians were reported to have died in the attack. The peacekeepers were acting in support of the Congolese army, the *Forces Armées de la République Démocratique du Congo* (FARDC). The FARDC claimed that the APCLS had launched an offensive the previous day, killing civilians. In actual fact, however, the FARDC was attempting to cover its tracks, and MONUC forces, on the basis of faulty information, made a serious error in judgment. The day before, FARDC had kidnapped twenty women and girls on their way to buy school supplies at the market. The civilians were held captive and gang-raped by the army. The APCLS had attacked the FARDC in order to release the hostages. As the army retreated, five people were killed trying to escape. In the wake of MONUC's assault, the APCLS lambasted the UN as an aggressor, and denied peacekeepers and humanitarians access to the volatile region.

How, in this sort of situation, does a peacekeeping force know whom to attack? How does one assess, in advance, the likely fallout from such action, from so-called 'assertive impartiality'? How untangle its skein of consequence?

This chapter builds on the analysis of contestation in the previous chapter to examine the effects and unintended consequences of the assertive conception of impartiality as operationalized in Congo. The process of norm implementation, as the UN's assertive action in Masisi illustrates, may impact actors in very different ways. For some, it entails costs. For others, it furnishes benefits. Consequently, the actual or expected behaviour generated by the implementation of a norm may influence the decision-making of actors, compelling them to act in ways they otherwise would not have. During this process, a norm may engender effects and consequences unforeseen by policymakers or those tasked with implementation, and contrary to their original intent. Civilians caught in the line of fire during the mission's attack, and those subsequently prevented from receiving assistance, were imperilled, not protected, by the actions of peacekeepers. And the UN, in this instance, acted against precisely the wrong party.

It is because norms are not unalloyed that it is important to account for their effects. This is a necessary step before value judgments regarding their desirability can or should be made. In other words, before exalting the purposes of contemporary peacekeeping, we must assess their effects now, in this world, as they occur in contexts like Congo. It is only then that practitioners and scholars alike can consider how the harmful effects of a norm can be mitigated.

The chapter proceeds in five substantive sections. In the first four sections, I elucidate the effects and consequences of the norm on four specific sets of actors: civilians, armed groups, the state, and the UN mission. While the discussion is broken down according to actor, the analysis highlights how the effects of the assertive conception of impartiality were often inter-related with implications for multiple actors. In the final section, I evaluate whether my findings confirm or reject the substantive objections about assertive impartiality raised by troop-contributing countries and the Secretariat during the process of norm institutionalization (Chapter 3). In so doing, I examine the level of congruence between contestation at the macro-level—at the United Nations in New York—and the effects of assertive impartiality at the micro-level—on the conflict-torn terrain of Congo. In addition, I consider whether the analysis of peacekeeping practice in Congo reveals other effects of significance unforeseen by actors at the global level. The concluding chapter explores the relevance of my overall findings for other cases in which peacekeepers are deployed.

CIVILIANS

To begin, I examine the direct effects of the mission's assertive mandate on civilian security. This is a germane starting point insofar as concern for civilian protection was what initially instigated the reconceptualization of impartiality. I explain why civilians came to believe that peacekeepers would deter and respond to attacks against them, and take measures to eliminate or restrict the activities of spoilers. Furthermore, I demonstrate how these expectations informed the decision-making of civilians and, in certain instances, adversely affected their security.

Expectations of Peacekeepers

The deployment of a UN mission, as the *Brahimi Report* cautioned, invariably generates expectations among the population that peacekeepers will protect those at risk. Several factors, however, meant that expectations of the mission in Congo were prodigiously high. First, to many Congolese, it simply looked the part. Compared to the shambolic and marauding Congolese army, from 2003 onwards the mission was a seemingly capable and robust force. It had the accoutrements of a modern, professional military, including an arsenal of heavy weaponry, tanks, armoured personnel carriers, attack helicopters, and a fleet of aircraft that in 2005 surpassed all commercial rivals to become Africa's largest airline for a period in time.[2] While UN officials bemoaned what they regarded as the mission's inadequate resourcing, the magnitude and profile of the UN's operational footprint in Congo nonetheless engendered perceptions and expectations among the population that peacekeepers could and would take action. As a Congolese woman in Goma told me: 'They are strong and we are weak.'

Second, expectations of robust peacekeeping in Congo were heightened because the mission's explicit mandate *was* to protect civilians and ensure peace/political processes, and this was regularly communicated to the population. In official speeches, public outreach campaigns, and media reports, the mission disseminated information about its role and activities.[3] Moreover, at several crisis points, UN officials made public pronouncements in which they explicitly promised protection and robust action. In the lead up to the Bukavu crisis, the head of MONUC's office in Bukavu gave assurances in the local media that peacekeepers would enforce a weapons-free zone in the city, and informed the public that additional troops were being flown in as back-up.[4] Similarly, both before and during the 2008 North Kivu crisis, officials pledged to defend Goma, Sake, Masisi, and Rutshuru, and reiterated the mission's mandate to protect civilians—despite admitting in private that the force lacked the capacity to do so.[5] More recently, in 2012, as the M23 rebellion escalated, MONUSCO repeatedly vowed that it would 'not let key towns fall'.[6] These proclamations intensified beliefs that peacekeepers would take action. And yet, in each instance, the mission reneged on the commitments it had made.

Third, and closely related, civilian expectations were magnified in areas where the mission carried out dedicated protection activities and directly engaged with the population on protection issues. Communities were instructed to alert blue helmets to imminent danger through early-warning cells and local protection committees, which were established by the mission as early as 2005, implying that peacekeepers would respond to such warnings.[7] Later, through Joint Protection Teams (JPTs) and Community Liaison Advisors (CLAs), UN officials met with the local population, collected information and conducted vulnerability assessments which were then used to develop recommendations such as the deployment of new operational bases or increased patrols in high-risk areas.[8] In an effort to manage expectations, JPT staff and CLAs explained the mission's mandate, including the constraints they faced, which might impede assistance.[9] These caveats, however, were often lost on civilians as they answered questions about the sources of their insecurity. As one senior official, lamenting the challenges of moderating expectations, stated:

> There is no way of nuancing the word protection. The man in the street, the woman in the street—let alone the woman in the bush—knows what it feels like to be protected and not protected. And if you're going to say that the primary purpose of this mission is protection, you cannot blame people for having a very fundamental and simple understanding of that. Nuances don't matter outside the Council . . . It doesn't count whether or not the mandate is hedged with caveats or people are made to be aware of this. If you say you are there to protect, then that's what they hear. That's what they believe.[10]

Lastly, precedent—instances when peacekeepers actually *did* use force to protect civilians and confront spoilers—heightened expectations. As the previous chapter described, from 2005–06, peacekeepers launched a series of aggressive operations that successfully demobilized thousands of militia in Ituri and the Kivus who posed a threat to the population. Similarly, in 2006 blue helmets gunned down over 150 of Nkunda's men during an advance by the *Congrès National pour la Défense du Peuple* (CNDP) on Goma. And, in 2013, the mission's offensive use of air assets and the Force Intervention Brigade's (FIB) artillery and mortar units played a critical role in defeating the M23. Such shows of force invariably led some to believe that peacekeepers would continue to assume a robust posture for the duration of their deployment. As a woman in Kiwanja told me: '[T]he blue helmets defended Goma and attacked the CNDP at Sake. We assumed they would do the same in Kiwanja . . . Are we any different? Are we not people too?'[11] The woman's two sons were among those killed when the CNDP took control of Kiwanja in 2008. They were shot in the head just a kilometre from the UN base.

Decision-making, Information, and Unintended Consequences

Beyond providing some nebulous hope of protection, expectations that peacekeepers would engage in robust action informed the decision-making of civilians and led them to act in ways they otherwise would not have. This observation is premised on the assertion that civilians are not merely passive victims; their responses to violence and the threat of violence are neither random nor irrational. A growing body of ethnographic research substantiates this assertion, and usefully accounts for civilian agency in conflict settings.[12]

As in other contexts, individuals and communities in Congo developed strategies to avoid, defy, and resist violence.[13] These strategies were informed by previous experience, local knowledge, and networks. When people believed that peacekeepers would protect them and combat spoilers, this factored into their decision-making and risk calculation. In some instances, it emboldened them to take even greater risks. For example, instead of fleeing to areas of possible safety, people remained in place. Others travelled in insecure conditions to areas where peacekeepers were located and knocked on the gates of the UN compound. Some came forward to tell UN officials about how they had been attacked and shared sensitive information about threats they faced. When protection was forthcoming or justice was administered, taking such risks was worthwhile. When it was not, the risks were often all the more grave. Acting on the assumption that robust action would be forthcoming, civilians naturally became even more vulnerable when peacekeepers failed to fulfil their stated purpose or acted in ways that were incommensurate with what was expected of them.

The unintended consequences for civilian security were particularly pronounced in the context of the mission's dedicated protection activities. While the JPTs were widely touted as an innovation and effective protection tool both inside and outside the mission, their record was decidedly more mixed. In some instances, particularly in the first few years of their deployment, the actions of the JPTs exacerbated the threats faced by civilians. These concerns were detailed in a confidential evaluation report written by the Civil Affairs Section (CAS) in 2009.[14] The report recounted how the presence of JPTs created expectations among host communities that could not always be met and maintained that, in several cases, key recommendations of the JPTs could not be implemented.[15]

More damning, however, was the report's finding that those individuals who provided the JPTs with 'crucial information' were 'often targeted by FDLR, FARDC or other armed groups or their intelligence services after the departures of the team'.[16] Such targeting was partly the result of information leaks.[17] As one UN official closely involved recalled:

> The JPT sitreps [situation reports] were used as mission propaganda—as evidence of good practice. They were often leaked and got passed around the UN. This had negative effects on security...There were several instances where CNDP got a hold of the JPT sitreps...CNDP commanders wrote targeted rebuttals to the internal reports. In one case, a senior CNDP, having read the report, called the participants and told them to be careful. If we had known that [they would be] leaked we would have written them differently.[18]

In November 2010—nearly two years after the JPTs were formalized—the mission tightened its protocol on information sharing and wider circulation of the reports ceased. Moreover, steps were taken to strengthen pre-deployment training and human-rights expertise in the teams. Despite these improvements, considerable challenges remained; in particular, UN officials continued to lament the difficulties of mobilizing timely responses to JPT recommendations.[19]

The CLAs and local protection committees encountered similar challenges. Expectations were raised within communities who were led to believe that the presence of a CLA and the formation of a committee offered a 'direct line' of communication to peacekeepers in times of crisis.[20] But warnings to the mission of impending threats or violence that was underway were sometimes met with stony silence. In the case of Mutarule, discussed in the previous chapter, members of the community repeatedly called MONUSCO during a massacre in 2014. They used mobile phones given to them by peacekeepers following an attack the previous year, in which eight civilians were killed. The mission however made no attempt to intervene and stop the killing.[21]

The mission's repeated failures to meet expectations, in some instances further imperilling civilians by its very presence, have left behind a legacy of distrust and discontent among many Congolese. In response to the question 'Who protects you?' a recent study conducted jointly by Harvard researchers and UNDP found that fewer than 1 per cent of those surveyed were willing to volunteer the UN.[22] When asked specifically what the mission could do to improve security, the most popular response was 'leave'.[23] Similarly, a 2014 opinion poll carried out by the McCain Institute in partnership with the CREDDA Institute of ULPGL University Goma, found that 71 per cent of North Kivu residents 'opposed' MONUSCO, with 59 per cent 'strongly' opposing the mission.[24] Such perceptions have both contributed to and are evidence of the mission's marginalization over time, as I explain below. However, before considering the multifarious effects on the mission itself, I first examine the ways in which the assertive conception of impartiality affected armed groups and the state. Here, too, the consequences for civilians were dire.

ARMED GROUPS

For armed groups (AGs) seeking a continuation of conflict and/or a more favourable peace than that which peacekeepers were tasked with enforcing, the assertive role prescribed for the mission was a potential obstacle with considerable political, strategic, and legal consequences. In Congo, as elsewhere, AGs deemed a threat to civilians or accused of spoiling could be attacked by peacekeepers, excluded from peace or political processes, sanctioned by the Security Council or, worse, handed over to the International Criminal Court (ICC). With the balance of power in flux, action against one group could be seen as tipping the balance in favour of another.

Given these stakes, AGs in Congo actively sought to reduce their uncertainty about the mission and how it was likely to carry out its mandate. AGs observed the mission, gathered intelligence on its operational modalities and capacities, and tested the resolve of peacekeepers. 'At some points', observed one senior UN official, 'it seemed that the protagonists knew our policies better than we did . . . [They] were paying far more attention to MONUC than MONUC was paying to them.'[25] In addition, AGs were attuned to political dynamics within the mission and the Security Council that engendered contestation and influenced implementation of the mandate.

AGs used this knowledge in pursuit of their aims and to avert attacks by peacekeepers. Indeed, this sort of strategizing was in play from the mission's inception. As the previous chapter explained, signatories to the Lusaka Agreement deliberately prescribed a role for the UN that was impracticable. They exploited bitter divisions between Anglophone and Francophone interests within the Security and, throughout the first phase of its deployment, actively obstructed the mission from implementing its mandate.

As the political landscape shifted and the resources necessary for a robust approach increased during the Transition, the strategies and tactics of AGs followed suit. To diminish the likelihood of a robust response, AG offensives were planned during troop rotations and shortly after peacekeepers were deployed. AGs surmised that as blue helmets got their bearings and familiarized themselves with the context, they would be reluctant to use force. Similarly, AGs congregated and carried out attacks deep in the bush in areas where peacekeepers were absent, lacked access, or were unlikely to venture. On this last point, Raymond Debelle, an expert on the region, highlights how the *Forces Démocratiques Delibération du Rwanda* (FDLR) capitalized on enmities *between* troop-contributing countries in setting up their base camp on the border between North and South Kivu in 2010.[26] With Indian peacekeepers dominant in North Kivu, and with South Kivu under the remit of Pakistani forces, according to Debelle, the FDLR command had counted on the fact that communication and cooperation between the two contingents was likely to be poor and that blue helmets on each side of the border would be reluctant to cross for fear of igniting a larger conflagration.

In addition to these tactical effects, the normative agenda underpinning the mission mandates had a considerable impact on AGs and provided them with a useful propaganda tool. The discourse of civilian protection and 'spoiling' was coopted and instrumentalized by certain groups in an effort to increase their own legitimacy and/or to delegitimize other actors for strategic ends. As I explain below, exactly how particular groups manipulated this discourse reflected their status as either a domestic or foreign AG, and, related, their future political prospects in the Congo.

Self-Legitimization Strategies of the AGs

Many of the domestic AGs that the mission confronted in Congo had taken up arms with the professed aim of protecting the population from foreign aggression, the iniquities of an unlawful and predatory state, or the precariousness of the state being absent altogether. This is not a new phenomenon. Eastern Congo has a long history of defence militias, often referred to as Mai-Mai, who are rooted in the local community and reflect local customs.[27] To some, they are 'the real freedom fighters in Congo'.[28]

While self-defence and community protection was the modus operandi for these and other groups independent of the mission and its aims, the deployment of peacekeepers as well as the involvement of other international actors such as the ICC cast a spotlight on protection issues in Congo and altered the playing field for those actors seeking to capture and maintain the moral highground. The drive to self-legitimate was important in that it influenced the standing of an AG vis-à-vis the mission, and thus how it was received by peacekeepers. It also carried weight with the group's support base and shaped its prospects for wider and more enduring political recognition.

In this context, numerous armed groups, including the CNDP, M23, APCLS, and various Mai-Mai militias, explicitly used PoC language as an integral part of their communications strategy.[29] Protection concerns figured prominently in their manifestos and memoranda, and were emphasized in discussions with international organizations and the media.[30] They informed the ways in which militia fought and how their actions were represented and relayed to external actors. Charges of human-rights abuses were vehemently denounced. Bodies, both literal and metaphorical, were hidden. And in some instances, access for international actors was blocked in response to charges of AG violations or in order to avert the collection of evidence.

Moreover, efforts were made to cover up alliances with miscreant forces or to distance themselves from particular individuals considered by the international community to be particularly beyond the pale. Sources assert, for example, that in addition to being retaliation for the MONUC attack in September 2009, the APCLS's blockade of access to the UN and humanitarians was partly motivated by a concern that international actors, were they to deploy, might uncover the group's links to the FDLR. This exposure, they feared, would tarnish their legitimacy and scupper any future political deal.[31] In interviews, members of the APCLS vehemently denied affiliation with the FDLR and emphasized their respect for human rights as defenders of the Hunde.[32] Similarly, the prominent role of Bosco Ntaganda, an ICC-indicted war criminal, and Colonel Innocent Zimurinda, who was subject to UN sanctions, within the CNDP and then the M23, was a divisive issue. Senior commanders such as Colonel Sultani Makenga, who also had records of egregious human-rights abuse, actively denied fighting alongside Ntaganda and others, in an attempt to portray themselves as more compliant with international law and to diminish the potential for guilt by association.[33]

AGs also turned the tables on the mission in an effort to legitimize themselves. They claimed a right to exist and argued that their actions were legitimate given the poor performance of peacekeepers in protecting civilians and ensuring security more broadly as well as the mission's perceived partiality. In meetings with UN officials, the CNDP, for example, regularly used protection as a rationale for their actions and a justification for not withdrawing from particular areas. They derided the capabilities of the mission and criticized the historic failure of the international community to uphold human rights. Recalling the UN's earlier involvement in the camps in eastern Zaire, they charged that the international community had a track record of sheltering those who had committed grave human-rights violations.[34]

In this respect, the mission's partnership with the FARDC provided the most fertile ground for critique, not least because many AGs defined themselves against Kabila's regime and Congo's feeble institutions. In an attempt to self-legitimate, groups such as the M23 highlighted human-rights violations by the FARDC and portrayed the UN as complicit.[35] And in the context of battle, some even contrasted the means by which they waged warfare with those of the national army, emphasizing, for example, how their use of 'light weapons' carried less risk of civilian casualties than the FARDC's use of tanks, helicopters, and mortars.[36]

Delegitimization Strategies of the AGs

Self-legitimization was not, however, a viable option for all the armed groups in Congo. Several AGs in Ituri, as well as the FDLR, Lord's Resistance Army (LRA), and Allied Democratic Forces (ADF), were seen by international actors to be particularly abhorrent. They were regularly cast as outlaws, and were subject to Security Council sanctions and national and international criminal investigation.[37] Moreover, given the marginalization of these actors and the fact that several of them were foreign armed groups (FAGs), they had few long-term political prospects in Congo. Therefore, instead of using the normative discourse of protection to bolster their legitimacy, these actors pointed to instances of failure to protect as a means of delegitimizing others and, in particular, the mission. The disastrous consequence of such a strategy was an increase in the intensity of direct and intentional violence against civilians. This was particularly the case with FAGs.

While certain foreign armed groups such as the FDLR and ADF had units, which, after years in Congo became enmeshed in host communities, their history was overwhelmingly one of predation on and brutality towards the local population. Pressure to demobilize, and attacks on their positions by UN peacekeepers and FARDC, frequently resulted in vicious retaliation against civilians within local or nearby communities. Scholars Kristof Titeca and Koen Vlassenroot, for example, recount how a massive joint FARDC–MONUC military offensive against ADF in December 2005 precipitated an increase in 'pillages, taxes, and acts of violence by ADF recruits' against civilians, and that 'several suspected MONUC informants [were] killed'.[38] Similarly, that same year, when Pakistani peacekeepers stepped up operations against the FDLR in Walungu territory (South Kivu) and organized an alert system in villages to warn them of imminent attacks, FDLR responded with brutal retribution on the population. In one such incidence, the militia hacked eighteen villagers to death, mutilated eleven others and held fifty more as hostages. 'The message was clear: if you attack us, it will be the civilians who pay.'[39] Time and time again they backed up that message.

In 2009, the retaliatory practices of the FDLR turned into a deliberate strategy of targeting civilians as a form of warfare. Under *Kimia II*, the FARDC and MONUC attempted to dismantle the FDLR by simultaneously cutting off the group's revenue sources—namely, their access to natural resources and economic centres—and by putting pressure on units to demobilize. As desertions mounted, the senior FDLR command in Europe issued an order to all units instructing them to deliberately target civilians, hospitals, and health centres. A clear violation of international law, the directive explicitly stated that the aim was to create a humanitarian catastrophe that would put pressure on the international community to both halt operations against them and compel the international community to urge Kigali to negotiate with them.[40]

The directive was highly controversial within the group. FDLR in South Kivu were particularly reluctant to carry out the order. Unlike North Kivu units, those in South Kivu had rarely been subject to rotation and had thus established better links with the local population.[41] Internal opposition notwithstanding, the humanitarian consequences of the operations and of FDLR's targeting were catastrophic. In the first nine months of *Kimia II*, the FDLR deliberately killed at least 701 civilians. As Human Rights Watch reported, '[m]any people were chopped to death by machete or hoe. Some were shot. Others were burned to death in their homes'.[42] The perverse logic underpinning FDLR strategy was based on MONUC and the international community's sensitivity to the issue of protection. The aim, as one FDLR ex-combatant explained to me, was to destabilize the mission and weaken its resolve by 'hitting them where it hurts . . . The international community doesn't want us to kill civilians. It makes them look bad'.[43] In sum, instrumentalized as a strategy of legitimization of self and delegitimization of others, the goal of protection in some instances actually created greater risks for civilians and deepened perceptions of the mission's partiality.

THE STATE

The robust mandate prescribed for peacekeepers in Congo also had a marked effect on Kabila's government and the state institutions from which he attempted to wrest control. The moral judgments embedded in the new conception of impartiality meant that the state's ability to protect its citizens and maintain security was opened up to outside scrutiny, and became a benchmark of its legitimacy. At the same time, however, as a sovereign entity Kabila's regime enjoyed privileged status. It remained the primary duty bearer and, among the other powers it exercised, granted access to external actors. As gatekeeper, the state was not so easily passed over by the mission and other international actors.

In this context, ambiguity over the relationship between consent and the assertive conception of impartiality was particularly acute in the post-Transition period, raising questions about the basis for and limits to the authority of peacekeepers vis-à-vis the state. Kabila, like his father, exploited this unresolved tension and actively manipulated the mission and its robust mandate in a bid to shore up and centralize his power. As criticisms of the government's venality and brutality mounted, Kabila played the sovereignty card to constrain the mission and used the government's apparent weakness to blackmail the UN into sustaining it on his terms. Following the 2006 elections, Kabila made himself less available to international donors. One diplomat recalls how, as an indication of this new imperviousness, the president switched his telephone number without warning: 'No one could get a hold of him. For a time, people literally could not reach him, causing panic in the diplomatic community.'[44] Moreover, senior UN officials recount how Kabila has made it clear on numerous occasions that 'if the mission [isn't] willing to throw its complete and unquestionable support behind the government and the FARDC in particular, than it better leave'.[45]

Waging War on Behalf of the State

Throughout the mission's deployment, peacekeepers supported the FARDC in operations to protect civilians and extend the authority of the state. However, following the Transition period the mission became increasingly militarized and emptied of its political content. This was a deliberate strategy of Kabila, who saw the UN force as an appendage to further his own interests. The mission was called upon for material, logistical, and fire support in military operations conducted jointly with FARDC although not based on credible peace agreements. The purposes of multiple agendas at play in these operations were often so shrouded in mystery that the mission was left in the dark about them.

In 2009, for example, the mission provided logistical and material backing to the FARDC to suppress a growing rebellion against Kabila in the province of Equateur, an opposition stronghold.[46] UN support, which proved decisive to *Opération Confiance à l'Ouest*'s success,[47] was offered despite the fact that the mission had little knowledge about what the conflict in Equateur was actually about.[48] Similarly, in the east, peacekeepers backed the FARDC against numerous groups that challenged Kabila's authority, overseeing and enforcing agreements—most notably, but not exclusively, the 23 March Agreement which was based on back-room deals—brokered by the government, the full contents of which the mission was not privy to. Or, as was the case with the FIB-supported operations, agreements such as the 2013 Peace, Security, and Cooperation Framework, for which the government had no intention of fulfilling its commitments. In the context of these operations, critics charged that the mission furthered a multitude of nefarious interests, and enabled Kabila's regime to avoid having to deal with the consequences of its own mistakes and shortcomings.

For many within the government and FARDC, however, the UN's involvement in these operations fell short of what was expected, and assistance provided by peacekeepers was often derided as inadequate.[49] They demanded more of the mission, wanting peacekeepers to not only *support* them in operation but also actively wage war *on their behalf*—particularly when the army was unable or unwilling to do so. During combat, the FARDC regularly retreated, abandoned its positions and fled, leaving peacekeepers to hold the fort. Members of FARDC employed various tactical manoeuvres in active combat to draw the UN into fighting on their side, in such a way that peacekeepers would bear the brunt of retaliatory attacks.[50] Government troops positioned their tanks next to, or behind, positions held by UN forces, with the goal that when whatever militia returned fire on the FARDC, the peacekeepers would be provoked into responding, and government legions could either retreat or seek cover behind the UN.[51] In some instances, as human rights groups documented, these tactics went so far as to constitute war crimes. This was the case during the 2008 Goma crisis, when, on several occasions, the FARDC deliberately installed their post next to civilians clustered at a UN base, using them as 'human shields'.[52]

When the mission refused to play along with such tactics, proved unwilling to meet the FARDC's demands, or was critical of the army and its abuses, the government turned on the UN. For example, during the 2008 Goma crisis, the Congolese Minister of Defence and the Minister of the Interior reportedly 'warned MONUC officials that if it did not engage the CNDP more robustly, they would set the population on the peacekeepers'.[53] These were not idle threats. Throughout the crisis, in various parts of North Kivu, the population targeted peacekeepers. Representatives of the local authorities, incited by the FARDC, threw rocks, erected barricades and confronted peacekeepers with arms, and on numerous occasions members of the national army fired directly at UN forces.[54]

More recently, in November 2014, the government expelled Scott Campbell, the UN's top human rights official in the country, following publication of a

UN report accusing the Congolese police of executions during *Opération Likofi*, a government crackdown on gangs in Kinshasa.[55] Months later, the government once again lashed out at the mission following the UN's withdrawal of support to the FARDC for anti-FDLR operations, after it was announced that the operations would be led by two 'red-listed' Generals.[56] President Kabila summoned SRSG Kobler as well as twenty foreign ambassadors and publicly reprimanded them for interfering in what he charged were sovereign matters.[57]

The Mission as Scapegoat

The government's designs to use the mission's robust mandate to bring about its desired ends were also accompanied by rampant scapegoating. Peacekeepers were condemned for the government's own inadequacies in the latter's attempt to evade responsibility. 'When something went wrong' as SRSG Swing remembers, 'the mission was often blamed... there was lots of scapegoating'.[58] In this respect, the expectations raised by the mission's ambitious mandate were used against it by the state. Failure to protect the Congolese became the failure of peacekeepers, and not of the state for which in actual fact, the provision of protection was a primary responsibility. 'The mission', as one UN official describes, 'became a vector for the people's frustrations.'[59]

To deflect criticisms and shift the blame, Congolese officials drew on historical grievances and the popular view that it was ultimately the mission's job to create peace in the country.[60] The polemical statement of the Congo's permanent representative to the UN, in response to charges of FARDC ill-discipline, provides just one such example. Instead of crediting or constructively engaging with such criticisms, he proclaimed that:

> [t]he United Nations should be driven by a desire to succeed, if only this once, where it sadly failed almost half a century ago, allowing the country to fall into unspeakable chaos. The macabre memories of those violent years are still fresh in the minds of the Congolese people. Today again, the supposed lack of discipline of some elements of the Congolese army seems to be a pretext for the same actors who take pleasure in turning the knife in the wound to perpetuate the misery of the Congolese people.[61]

What is more, UN officials lament how at various junctures the mission's self-flagellation actively played into such views, giving further ammunition to those critical of the UN's past and present involvement in the Congo. As one official explains: 'When the mission comes out and beats its breast and says "we failed, we failed" or we don't have enough of this or we don't have enough of that, it reinforces the notion that this is really *our* job—that it really is the UN's job to bring stability to Congo ... to protect civilians ... It lets the government off the hook.'[62]

The mission could arguably never fulfil the state-like responsibilities it adopted and its attempts to do so, given the UN's history in the region, would never have been seen as legitimate by all. But those attempts were politically expedient for Kabila's regime. For the mission, as I describe below, its failures dealt an even greater blow to its legitimacy. As one senior official states, 'protection was a brickbat that the Council handed the Congolese to beat the mission with ... It was never going to be able to protect everyone everywhere. [And thus] it was always going to be criticized ... It was always going to be partial'.[63]

THE MISSION

The assertive role prescribed for UN peacekeepers in Congo had a number of significant unintended consequences for MONUC/MONUSCO, that is, for the individuals employed by the UN as part of the mission and the mission as a collective entity.

Mission Fragmentation

The judgments, which peacekeepers claimed as impartial, were in fact far from uniform. Who was a 'spoiler' and what constituted 'spoiling activity' was subject to considerable disagreement, with officials within the mission contesting what was an appropriate and impartial response. As the previous chapter described, such divergent interpretations generated acrimonious relations between UN officials both civilian and military and at various levels. Tensions were particularly acute at the field level and for those troop-contributing and police-contributing countries (TCCs/PCCs) on the frontline. Confusion and contestation were pervasive. When peacekeepers responded in ways incommensurate with what others within the mission expected of them, they were censured. In some instances, their courses of action that brought opprobrium merely magnified larger debates at play within the mission and in New York. This was particularly the case during *Kimia II* and *Amani Leo* when peacekeepers partnered with the FARDC to conduct military operations.

An incident that took place in the broader context of ongoing *Amani Leo* operations illustrates these tensions as well as the confusion of peacekeepers. In 2010, peacekeepers providing an escort to several humanitarian workers were stopped at gunpoint by the FARDC (ex-CNDP) on the outskirts of Muhanga IDP camp near Kitshanga in Masisi. The government soldiers instructed the peacekeepers to leave the camp area, which they did, effectively abandoning the humanitarians. With the blue helmets out of sight, FARDC entered the humanitarian vehicles, robbed the staff, and forced them to drive into the camp, which FARDC soldiers then looted.[64] Despite the mission's Chapter VII mandate to protect civilians, particularly vulnerable populations such as IDPs and humanitarian personnel, one UN official, when pressed, flatly stated that 'We can't fire on the FARDC', as these were the very same forces that they were mandated to work with.[65] The mission's apparent impotence caused outrage among officials at the daily situation meeting in which the incident was reported, and an investigation was launched. Later, in Kitchanga, the South African peacekeepers involved in the incident expressed their uncertainty as to what they should have done differently.[66]

Some officials assert that such ambiguity and confusion contributed to more pervasive peacekeeping inaction over the long run—what one official described as a 'palpable atmosphere of apathy' among the traditional troop-contributing countries.[67] According to various sources, the framework forces felt marginalized from decision-making, resented having to support such an inept force as the FARDC and criticized the absence of strategic direction for the mission by the civilian leadership.[68] As frustrations mounted, officials contend that contingents were more inclined to consult their superiors in their respective capitals than their UN superiors. Not wanting their forces to be killed and increasingly reluctant to endorse robust operations, superiors advised their contingents not to pursue life-endangering action and placed stringent caveats on the terms of their deployment. The arrival of the FIB, which several of the main troop-contributing countries resisted, further contributed to the passivity of their forces and exacerbated divisions within the mission. The framework forces were said to 'pass the buck' to the FIB, claiming, inaccurately, that robust action to protect was now the latter's responsibility. Despite the SRSG's proclamation that MONUSCO operate as 'one force, one mission, one mandate', the UN's presence in Congo arguably became more, not less, fragmented over time.

Reputation, Information, and Security

In addition to tensions within the mission, other actors developed expectations of the mission in relation to its robust mandate. When peacekeepers fell short of fulfilling these expectations and civilians suffered—or worse, were killed—criticism rained down on the mission. In some instances, the Congolese took to the street and raged against the mission on the radio and in print media. Massive public demonstrations occurred at various junctures throughout its history, including following the mission's passivity in Kisangani (2002), Bukavu (2004), Kiwanja (2008), and Goma (2012).[69]

The Bukavu crisis, in particular, provoked a groundswell of public protest and violence across the country. UN staff received death threats, and in South Kivu, civil-society groups demanded the departure of the SRSG, whom they condemned for the 'balkanization of the Congo'.[70] Millions of dollars of UN property were destroyed. Indeed, the fallout was so great that it prompted a radical overhaul of the organization's security protocol. The mission's headquarters in the capital, which had once been relatively open and approachable, inconspicuous in the city's downtown quarter, became 'Fortress Kinshasa' with concrete blast walls, reinforced wire sandbags, and security checkpoints.[71]

Just as the mission was criticized for inaction, so too was it censured for assuming a robust posture. It was damned when it acted and damned when it did not. During both the Transition and post-Transition period, the mission's support to FARDC during military operations gave rise to perceptions that the UN was distinctly partial and, according to some, 'in the enemy's camp'.[72] As a result, some communities were hesitant to cooperate with the mission, both because of its links to the FARDC and for fear of reprisals, as discussed above. On several occasions, the UN was denied access to communities, including in the aforementioned case of the APCLS. Civil-society groups mounted significant opposition to several operations and in some places called for the UN's withdrawal. NGOs issued petition letters and the ICRC released an unprecedented statement categorizing the mission as party to the conflict, thereby eroding its protected status under international humanitarian law (IHL).[73]

Decreased cooperation with the population, as well as other actors, limited the information available to UN officials, which further hindered its ability to be impartial. Without sufficient knowledge of what was going on in particular areas, the mission was constrained in developing policy and programmes. This had numerous effects on the mission's activities, including its ability to fulfil its protection mandate by investigating human-rights violations and engaging with armed groups to ensure better compliance with IHL. In 2010, UN Special Rapporteur Philip Alston charged that 'As a party to the conflict, [the mission's] real or perceived ability to independently and effectively investigate allegations of abuses by its FARDC counterparts or by its own forces is compromised.'[74]

The mission's perceived partiality also had an impact on its security. In some instances, hostility towards the mission resulted in attacks on UN bases and the deliberate targeting of peacekeepers and UN officials. Most of these episodes involved armed groups that the mission was engaged in military operations against, and in particular those not party to the peace or political process that the UN was tasked with supporting. The greatest number of peacekeeping deaths resulting from what DPKO categorizes as 'malicious' acts occurred during the mission's most robust phase (2005–07).[75] In early 2005, for example, as operations in Ituri intensified, nine Bangladeshi peacekeepers were killed in an ambush by the *Front des Nationalistes Intégrationnistes* (FNI)—the victims were stripped and their bodies mutilated. A year later, eight Guatemalan peacekeepers were killed and five were wounded during an attack on the LRA in Garamba national park.[76] These attacks deepened tensions at the macro-level in New York, as traditional TCCs became increasingly wary of robust action given their potential, and all too human, consequences.

Political Leverage and the Mission's Marginalization

Perceptions of partiality, and diminished access to information in turn affected the UN's ability to act as a political arbiter, as an honest broker of peace. The mission's acceptance as an unbiased actor was called into question from its very inception, given interests in the Security Council and the historical role of both the UN as well as particular member states within the region. Yet despite these challenges the mission managed, at certain key moments during the Transition period and through what one official described as 'political ju-jitsu', to exert considerable leverage through the *Comité International d'Accompagnement de la Transition* (CIAT) and to play a critical role as mediator. Opportunity and capacity for the mission to play such a role, however, quickly evaporated following the 2006 election. A combination of donor disunity and Kabila's imperviousness to any form of political engagement by outside actors greatly diminished the mission's leverage, and relegated the UN to the sidelines. This occurred at the local level as well as at the national and regional level, where the UN was increasingly marginalized from those forums where political deals were brokered.

Moreover, the mission's political marginalization and fear of being further marginalized compelled its senior leadership and the Council to pursue policies that resulted in precisely what they had feared, and compromised the mission's standing even more. For example, many of the people I interviewed insisted that the mission's willingness to support the FARDC during *Kimia II* and *Amani Leo* was in part out of fear that the government would further cast the mission aside. As the UN had been completely left out of the negotiations leading to the rapprochement between Kigali and Kinshasa, and its involvement during *Umoja Wetu* had all but been blocked, the joint operations were seen as an opportunity to 'get back into the game'.[77] 'The mission', as one senior official offered, 'constructed its participation . . . to be relevant'.[78] Similarly, the mission's support to the FARDC in Equateur—an operation that, as I described above, had questionable purposes—was leveraged to try and gain a seat at the table in the East.[79] Again, concerns of being relegated to the sidelines led the mission's leadership to adopt an ill-informed and potentially compromising position.

The most damning testament to the mission's marginalization and diminished influence came, however, on 11 July 2012. At the close of the emergency session of the International Conference on the Great Lakes Region (ICGLR) on the renewed crisis in the Kivus, regional member states called for the 'immediate establishment of a neutral International Force to eradicate M23, FDLR and all other Negative Forces in Eastern DRC and patrol and secure the Border Zones'.[80] After thirteen years, and billions upon billions of dollars spent, MONUSCO was not so much as even mentioned.

While the UN eventually managed to bring the proposed force 'in house', within the MONUSCO structure, the FIB did little to bolster the UN's leverage, comprised as it was of troops from Kabila's regional allies. Implementation of the Peace, Security, and Cooperation Framework (PSCF) and, particularly those institutional reforms critical to Congo's long-term stability, fell by the wayside as military operations took precedence, yielding little after the M23's defeat. By early 2015, the PSCF was seen by most to be defunct. Relations between the UN and the government were at an all time low. And, as one diplomat said to me, the mission was once again, 'scrambling... desperately looking for ways to show it is still relevant'.[81]

CONCLUSION

The effects of assertive impartiality detailed in the four preceding sections confirm the reservations and concerns raised by actors at the macro-level. As Chapter 3 detailed, these included the perils of engendering false hope and high expectations among civilians, as well as the potential that failure by blue helmets to deliver on their more ambitious mandates would blunt the instrument of peacekeeping itself.

Crucially, the Congo case also reveals several consequences which were unforeseen by actors at the global level. In this respect, the co-optation and instrumentalization of assertive impartiality by armed groups and the state, as distinct from the mission, were particularly salient. Whether as an attempt to bolster their standing and to self-legitimate, or as a tool of delegitimization, these responses negatively affected the mission and those endangered civilians in whose name it justified its continued presence. Moreover, while officials foresaw that the more assertive role prescribed for peacekeepers had the potential to diminish their credibility if expectations were unmet, this critique did not extend to the ways in which it could be self-limiting, placing constraints on whom peacekeepers could engage with and the types of activities they could pursue.

Having highlighted the direct consequences of assertive impartiality and their linkages with contestation at the macro level, I conclude by taking a step back to examine whether the substantive objections put forward were warranted in practice.

The End-State

Assertive impartiality is premised on a particular conception of violence as moral collapse, a circumstance in which a perpetrator or spoiler threatens weak and innocent civilians or victims. The Congo case problematizes this core assumption and its attendant distinctions, which, in practice, repeatedly broke down. Drawing on deep-seated grievances, past victims became present-day perpetrators. The line between combatant and civilian was often ambiguous. Armed groups rarely spoke in unison, and competing factions and splinters emerged.

Unsurprisingly, as a result of these blurred lines, the legitimacy of particular armed groups and individuals, and the actions they took, were subject to vehement contestation within the mission and the Security Council. Who was a 'spoiler' and what constituted 'spoiling activity' were subjective and fluid concepts, and were influenced by a number of ideational and material factors, by past personal experiences as well as institutional realities. But even as these differences became manifest during implementation, they failed to prompt a reassessment of these distinctions or lead to an approach that really engaged with the complex motivations and dynamics behind the violence in Congo.

For much of the mission's deployment, France saw Rwanda as perpetrator, whereas Britain and America saw it as victim. The Council as a collective body, including those dissenting members, nonetheless continued to authorize mandates to protect civilians. In this respect, just as assertive impartiality and the robust role prescribed for peacekeepers was politically expedient for armed groups and, in particular, Kabila's regime, so too did it serve a purpose for members of the Security Council and those senior officials tasked with implementation. In the absence of consensus over a real strategy to resolve Congo's conflicts, and a willingness by member states to commit the necessary political capital and resources, assertive impartiality offered the appearance of constructive and active engagement. Ambitious mandates that aimed to save lives projected an image of consensus that covered up political divisions. In other words, protection was an objective over which only a semblance of agreement need be reached—the details could be worked out later. To paraphrase Guéhenno, being able to espouse assertive impartiality transformed what were highly political and divisive issues—peace and the kind of government desired by various actors—into a largely technical problem.[82] Peacekeepers could support the state and yet still claim to be impartial by pointing to the due diligence policy and the various programs (e.g., SSR, rule of law) aimed at improving the state's ability to protect.

However, given this contestation and in the absence of meaningful political engagement, attempts to reform the Congolese state while simultaneously supporting it have ultimately proved futile. Ambiguities over impartiality's relationship to consent were exploited by Kabila's regime to its advantage, and the leverage of those tasked with implementation was weakened by donor disunity, disagreements within the mission, and the rising influence of regional actors. There was no clear way forward. As one official asked: 'how do you build state capacity? How do you develop an ability to protect civilians in a state that isn't interested in taking on that responsibility, where there is no meaningful political opposition to compel the government into taking on that responsibility, and where the international community doesn't really care most of the time?'[83]

Confronted with this problem, the mission continued to pursue the competing and incompatible tasks of protecting both civilians and the sovereignty of the very government whose agents were at times threatening them. Sovereignty was not overturned, as some at the macro-level feared it might. Rather, the status quo was maintained. If anything, Kabila's regime, which became synonymous with the state, was made more, not less, powerful. The result was that the very processes arguably needed for change that would render the government more accountable were impeded. Indeed, for all the mission's emphasis on impartially upholding rights—human rights, children's rights, gender rights—political rights were given short shrift in Congo. As one senior official, looking back on his time in Congo and on the mission's role, cautioned: '[peacekeepers] must understand that they may be standing in the way of violent but legitimate resistance to oppression . . . Peacekeeping missions may end up usurping the role of the people to stand as external guarantor of state behaviour'.[84] By taking sides myopically, with compromising factors and without deeper political understanding, the UN lost its way in Congo, in many instances hurting the very people on whose behalf it claimed to act impartially.

NOTES

1. Interviews with several UN officials, Goma, February 2010 and April 2011; interview with senior UN official, Kinshasa, February 2011; interview with members of the APCLS, Goma, April 2011. The incident was not widely discussed within the mission and received no press coverage.
2. United Nations, *United Nations Peace Operations Year in Review 2005*, February 2006, http://www.un.org/en/peacekeeping/resources/publications.shtml
3. Radio Okapi, in particular, has served as a critical mouthpiece for the UN with its nation-wide coverage and twenty-four-hour-a-day broadcasting. Established in 2002 by the mission and the Foundation Hirondelle, it is the most ambitious radio operation in the UN's history. See Michelle Betz 'Radio as Peacebuilder: A Case

Study of Radio Okapi in the Democratic Republic of Congo', *The Great Lakes Research Journal* 1 (2004), 38–50. The mission also publishes brochures about its mandate and *Echo de la MONUSCO*, a monthly magazine that chronicles its activities (available at http://monusco.unmissions.org/Default.aspx?tabid=11355).

4. MONUC, 'MONUC and the Bukavu Crisis 2004', Best Practices Unit, Department of Peacekeeping Operations, New York, March 2005, (Restricted), reprinted with the permission of the United Nations, 14.

5. Xan Rice, 'Panic grips Congo as rebels advance on town of Goma', *The Guardian*, 30 October 2008; Human Rights Watch (HRW), *Killings in Kiwanja: The UN's Inability to Protect Civilians* (New York: 2008); interview with diplomat, Goma, February 2010.

6. Voice of America, 'Peacekeepers vow to protect eastern Congo city From rebels', Kinshasa, 10 July 2012.

7. Joshua Marks, 'The Pitfalls of Action and Inaction: Civilian Protection in MONUC's Peacekeeping Operations', *African Security Review* 16/3 (2007): 78.

8. The JPTs existed during the Transition as an informal ad hoc mechanism; they were standardized in 2008 following the Kiwanja massacres. JPTs were composed of staff members with relevant expertise from a cross-range of departments from within the mission; namely, Civil Affairs, Child Protection, Human Rights, and Political Affairs. JPT missions lasted roughly a week and teams were often sent to remote areas. In 2009, the mission developed a network of Community Liaison Interpreters (CLIs), later renamed Community Liaison Advisors (CLAs). The CLAs were staffed primarily by Congolese nationals and, unlike the temporary deployments of the JPTs, they constituted a more permanent presence in the field. Their primary objective was to notify the mission of impending threats with a long-term view of strengthening communication between the mission and the population. For an overview of PoC tools in Congo see Julie Reynaert, 'MONUC/MONUSCO and Civilian Protection in the Kivus', *IPIS*, 2011; MONUSCO, *PoC Handbook: Practical Protection for Civilians Handbook for Peacekeepers*, Protection Working Group, Kinshasa, 2013.

9. Interview with MONUSCO official, Goma, April 2011. MONUSCO's *Protection of Civilians Handbook* (2013) instructs peacekeepers to '[i]nform civilians on the measures put in place to ensure their protection' when they are close to conflict zones, and '[a]lways provide objective information on the security situation and potential threats to civilians'.

10. Interview with former MONUC official, New York, July 2011.

11. Interview with resident, Kiwanja, January 2010.

12. Several ethnographic studies detail civilian coping strategies in conflict, including the creative ways in which people seek to reconfigure their livelihoods in times of war. See for example: Carolyn Nordstrom, *A Different Kind of War Story* (Philadelphia: University of Philadelphia Press, 1997); Danny Hoffmann, 'The City as Barracks: Freetown, Monrovia, and the Organization of Violence in Postcolonial African Cities', *Cultural Anthropology* 22/3 (2007), 400–28. Other studies elucidate how civilians, far from being passive victims, manoeuvre to secure access to humanitarian aid and resources. See for example: Liisa Malkki, 'Speechless Emissaries: Refugees, Humanitarianism, and Dehistoricization', *Cultural Anthropology*

11/3 (1996), 377–404; Erin Baines and Emily Paddon, '"This is How We Survived": Civilian Agency and Humanitarian Protection', *Security Dialogue* 43/3 (2012), 231–47.

13. Interviews with numerous NGO officials, Masisi Center, Kitchanga, Rutshuru, Lubero, and Goma, 2009–11. See also Katherine Haver, *Self-Protection in Conflict: Community Strategies for Keeping Safe in the Democratic Republic of Congo* (Oxford: Oxfam International, 2009); Aditi Gorur, *Community Self-Protection Strategies: How Peacekeepers Can Help or Harm* (Washington: Stimson Center, 2013); Marijke Deleu, *Secure Insecurity: The Continuing Abuse of Civilians in Eastern DRC as the State Extends its Control* (Oxford: Oxfam International, 2015).

14. MONUC, 'A Preliminary Assessment of the Impact of the Joint Protection Teams', Civil Affairs Section, October 2009 (Internal). (Henceforth *JPT Assessment* 2009).

15. *JPT Assessment* (2009).

16. *JPT Assessment* (2009). Quoted in United Nations, 'Lessons Learned: Report on the Joint Protection Team (JPT) Mechanism in MONUSCO. Strengths, Challenges, and Considerations for Replicating JPTs in Other Missions' (New York: DPKO/DFS-OHCHR, 2013), 24, reprinted with the permission of the United Nations.

17. *JPT Assessment* (2009). The report also cited a number of institutional challenges confronted by the JPTs. These included: staffing constraints, security, communication, vehicles, and air transportation.

18. Interview with MONUSCO official, Goma, April 2011.

19. Interview with MONUSCO officials, Goma, June 2015. See also, United Nations, 'Lessons Learned: Report on the Joint Protection Team (JPT) Mechanism in MONUSCO', 2013.

20. Interview with MONUSCO official, Goma, April 2011.

21. Human Rights Watch, *DR Congo: Army, UN Failed to Stop Massacre* (New York: July 2014).

22. By contrast, one in three respondents said 'nobody', or 'God' protected them (32 per cent). The 'national army' or 'FARDC' (20 per cent), 'police' (18 per cent), and the 'community' itself (13 per cent) were also mentioned. The study was based on a random sampling of 5,166 adults in North Kivu and South Kivu, and the district of Ituri. Patrick Vinck and Phuong Pham, *Searching for Lasting Peace: Population-Based Survey on Perceptions and Attitudes about Peace, Security and Justice in Eastern Democratic Republic of the Congo* (Cambridge: Harvard Humanitarian Initiative, Harvard School of Public Health and United Nations Development Programme, 2014), 49–50.

23. On average 28 per cent of respondents said MONUSCO should 'leave' to improve security. That number rose to over 50 per cent in some conflict-affected territories. Vinck and Pham (2014: 49).

24. For details of the poll, see Jason Stearns, 'Poll: How the people of North Kivu feel about their government, elections, and the international community', *Congo Siasa* blog, http://congosiasa.blogspot.com/2015/06/poll-how-people-of-north-kivu-feel.html, 17 June 2015.

25. The same official recounted how he received 'reliable reports from [FDLR] defectors that their senior commanders had conducted an intelligence evaluation

of the entire region and had prepared detailed assessments of the likely response of MONUC...' Philip Lancaster, 'Muddled Thoughts on a Muddled Topic: A Discussion of Child Soldiers, Human Rights and Peacekeeping', University of Victoria, 22 January 2009 (unpublished), 10; Philip Lancaster, 'End-of-Assignment Report', Chief DDR/RR, MONUC, 6 October 2008 (Internal). General Baril made similar observations in his 2008 report.

26. Raymond Debelle, 'FDLR', Presentation at MONUSCO Forward HQ, Goma, April 2011.

27. Koen Vlassenroot, 'Violence et constitution de milices dans l'Est du Congo: le cas des Mayi-Mayi', *L'Afrique des Grands Lacs: Annuaire 2001–2* (Paris: l'Harmattan, 2002), 115–52.

28. Interview with MONUC official, Goma, 2009.

29. Interviews with numerous NGO officials, Goma and Bukavu, March 2011, June 2015. See also, Arthur Boutellis, *In the DRC Communications War, Rebels Learn PoC Language* (New York: International Peace Institute, Global Observatory, July 2012).

30. See, for example, CNDP, *Cahier de Charges du Congrès National Pour la Défense du Peuple* (Bwiza, 14 October 2006); CNDP, *Communiqué de Presse sur les 'Massacres' à Kiwanja* (Bwiza, 19 November 2008); Human Rights Watch, *DR Congo: War Crimes by M23, Congolese Army* (New York: 2013); Local Voices Project, 'Armed Militias in Masisi: A Case Study of the People's Alliance for Free and Sovereign Congo (APCLS)', http://www.localvoicesproject.com/issue-01/armed-militias-in-masisi/; James Verini, 'Should the United Nations Wage War to Keep Peace?', Special report in *National Geographic*, 27 March 2014.

31. Interview with NGO official, Goma, February 2010.

32. Interview with members of the APCLS, Goma, April 2011.

33. Jason Stearns, *Strongman of the Eastern DRC: A Profile of General Bosco Ntaganda* (London: Rift Valley Institute, 2013).

34. MONUC, 'Protection Analysis', Civil Affairs Section, Goma, 06 December 2008 (Internal). Interviews with NGO staff, Goma, April 2011.

35. See, for example, 'Open letter from M23 political leader Bertrand Bisimwa's to Ban Ki-moon', 027/Pres-M23/2013, 22 May 2013; Mmanaledi Mataboge, 'DRC's M23: 'We didn't start the war', *Mail & Guardian*, 4 September 2013.

36. Boutellis (2012).

37. See the final reports of the UN Group of Experts for details of sanctions and judicial charges: United Nations, S/2010/596 (2010); S/2011/738 (2011); S/2012/348 (2012); S/2014/42 (2014).

38. Kristof Titeca and Koen Vlassenroot, 'Rebels Without Borders in the Rwenzori Borderland? A Biography of the Allied Democratic Forces', *Journal of Eastern African Studies* 6/1 (2012), 163. See *The Final Report of the UN Group of Experts* (United Nations, S/2015/19) for an overview of recent abuses committed by the ADF in the context of *Opération Sukola I*, an FARDC, MONUSCO-supported, offensive against the group, launched in January 2014.

39. Marks (2007: 77).

40. FDLR, *Order to all Forces Combattantes Abacunguzi (FOCA) Units*, the military wing of the FDLR, March 2009 (Unpublished, in author's possession). Interviews with ex-combatants, Matobo Reorientation Camp, Rwanda, February 2010.

41. Interview with ex-combatant, Matobo Reorientation Camp, Rwanda, February 2010. Written correspondence with Raymond Debelle, former member of the UN Group of Experts, January 2010.

42. Human Rights Watch, *You Will Be Punished: Attacks on Civilians in Eastern Congo* (New York: 2009), 6.

43. Interviews with ex-combatants, Matobo Reorientation Camp, Rwanda, February 2010.

44. Interview with senior UN Official, New York, June 2011.

45. Interview with senior UN Official, New York, June 2011. Interviews with UN official, Goma, June 2015.

46. MONUC, 'Force Commander Visit to Gemena 10 Dec 2009: After Action Report', Interoffice Memorandum, 11 December 2009 (Internal).

47. Eyewitness accounts describe how MONUC's support was critical to the FARDC's success in forcing the militia to 'back down' from Gemena, the provincial capital, to Dongo. Interview with official, Goma, January 2010.

48. MONUC, 'Incidents of Violence in the area of Dongo, Equateur Province', *Joint Mission Analysis Cell* (JMAC), 3 December 2009 (Restricted). Jason Stearns, former Chair of the UN Group of Experts, wrote: 'The situation still remains shrouded in mystery, even the internal MONUC reports don't shed a great deal of light on the matter.' See 'The mystery of Dongo', *Congo Siasa* blog, http://congosiasa.blogspot.com/2010/01/mystery-of-dongo.html, 6 January 2010.

49. The FIB's support to the FARDC during offensive operations against the M23 in 2013 is a notable exception. Government officials were said to have praised the support given by the UN. However, in 2014, tensions between MONUSCO and the government occurred once again over operations against the ADF and FDLR.

50. Interviews with military officials, Goma, January 2009 and February 2010.

51. BBC World, 'DR Congo army "used aid as bait"', 6 November 2009.

52. HRW (2008: 35).

53. HRW (2008: 22).

54. Interviews with government officials and senior MONUC official, Goma, January 2010; interviews with members of the *Barza Inter-Communautaire* (local leadership council), Rutshuru territory, February 2010.

55. Aaron Ross, 'Congo expels top U.N. official after report on police abuses', *Reuters*, 16 October 2014.

56. Malcolm Beith, 'Congo rejects UN stance on general in anti-rebel offensive', *Bloomberg*, 5 February 2015.

57. *Point de Presse du Ministre de la communication et medias*, Porte-parole du Gouvernement, 16 February 2015.

58. Interview with Ambassador William Swing, former Special Representative of the Secretary-General, MONUC, Geneva, December 2009.

59. Interview with MONUSCO official, Goma, June 2015.

60. Interview with senior MONUC official, Kinshasa, February 2010.

61. United Nations, S/PV.6253 (2009).

62. Interview with senior UN official, New York, July 2011.

63. Interview with senior UN official, New York, July 2011.

64. The incident took place on 15 January 2010 and was reported at the internal MONUC morning briefing on 18 January 2010. In addition to this incident, on several occasions I witnessed MONUC forces interacting with FARDC forces who were at the time using forced civilian labour in contravention of the mandate and in violation of IHL. Each time, MONUC forces failed to intervene to assist the civilians.

65. Interview with military officer, Goma, February 2010.

66. Interview with military officer, UN company operating base in Kitchanga, January 2010.

67. Interview with MONUC official, Goma, March 2011.

68. Interview with senior MONUC official, Kinshasa, February 2010. Interview with former MONUC official, Oxford, December 2012. Similar statements were made about the brigades during interviews conducted in Goma, June 2015.

69. IRIN, 'UN responds to HRW criticism over Kisangani massacre', Nairobi, 22 August 2002; Marc Lacey, '2 die in Congo demonstrations, as protesters storm U.N. sites', *New York Times,* 4 June 2004; Joe Bavier, 'Villagers stone UN investigators in eastern Congo', *Reuters,* 29 May 2007; *Congo News Agency,* 'Thousands protest M23 capture of Goma, turn on government and UN', 21 November 2012.

70. Interview with Congolese activist, Goma, February 2011.

71. Interview with NGO official, London, July 2011.

72. Interview with NGO official, Goma, February 2011.

73. Human Rights Watch and the Congo Advocacy Coalition (84 local and international NGOs), *DR Congo: Civilian Cost of Military Operations is Unacceptable* (New York: 13 October 2009); Aurelie Ponthieu, Christoph Vogel, Katharine Derderian, 'Without Precedent or Prejudice? UNSC Resolution 2098 and its Potential Implications for Humanitarian Space in Eastern Congo and Beyond', *Journal of Humanitarian Assistance* (2014). ICRC, *Letter Addressed to the UN Special Representative of the Secretary-General Alan Doss 'ICRC's Concerns about the Humanitarian Consequences of Ongoing Military Operations in the DRC and MONUC's Related Obligations under IHL'* (Kinshasa: 25 June 2010) (Unpublished). See also, Scott Sheeran and Stephanie Case, *The Intervention Brigade: Legal Issues for the UN in the Democratic Republic of the Congo* (New York: International Peace Institute, 2014).

74. A/HRC/14/24/Add.3 [Advance unedited version] (2010). *Report of the Special Rapporteur on Extrajudicial, Summary or Arbitrary Executions,* 12.

75. United Nations, 'Fatalities by Year, Mission and Incident Type', Department of Peacekeeping Operations. Available at http://www.un.org/en/peacekeeping/resources/statistics/fatalities.shtml

76. Phone interview with senior UN official, August 2010. See also Bryan Mealer, *All Things Must Fight to Live: Stories of War and Deliverance in Congo* (New York: Bloomsbury Press, 2008), 64.

77. Interview with military officer, Goma, February 2010.

78. Interview with senior NGO official, Goma, January 2010.

79. Interview with senior UN official, Goma, February 2010. Interview with senior UN official, Kinshasa, February 2011.

80. International Conference on the Great Lakes Region, *Report of the Regional Inter-Ministerial Extraordinary Meeting on the security situation in Eastern DRC* (Addis Ababa, Ethiopia, 11th July 2012).

81. Interview with diplomat, Goma, June 2015.

82. Interview with Guéhenno, 2011.

83. Interview with senior UN official in Goma, January 2010.

84. Philip Lancaster, 'Muddled Thoughts on a Muddled Topic: A Discussion of Child Soldiers, Human Rights and Peacekeeping', University of Victoria, 22 January 2009 (unpublished), 4.

6

The Politics of Taking Sides

Following the end of the Cold War, as international actors became more heavily engaged in conflicts within states where consent was more tenuous, they confronted difficult questions about their position as third parties, about the basis for their own authority, and about how to adjudicate between local competing claimants of authority. Could international officials remain above the fray when groups turned on each other? How were they to decide with whom to coordinate and work in places where social divisions ran deep and authority was virulently contested? Whose consent, if any, was necessary for their presence? Was impartiality irrelevant, invalid, or obsolete in such contexts? If peacekeeping, indeed the United Nations (UN) itself was to remain relevant, answers to these questions were needed.

But impartiality was not jettisoned. Instead, it was reconceptualized in what represents a radical shift in the very nature and substance of peacekeeping, and in the UN's role as guarantor of international peace and security. Claims to impartial authority were no longer to be based exclusively on terms to which all parties consent. Instead, they were to become premised on a more ambitious and expansive set of human-rights-related norms, around which consensus was now presumed. No longer were blue helmets to be considered impartial mediators whose judgments are based on terms set by those parties directly consenting to mediation, but instead as more assertive agents, akin to police officers that enforce the law and 'penalize infractions'.[1]

This more assertive conception of impartiality, as called for in the *Brahimi Report* in 2000 and made manifest in Security Council practice, has persisted. In June 2015, nearly fifteen years since the last major review of peacekeeping, Secretary-General Ban Ki-moon released *Uniting Our Strengths for Peace*, the much-anticipated report of the High-Level Independent Panel on UN Peace Operations. It reiterated Brahimi's vision and called for a 'progressive interpretation' of peacekeeping's core principles. 'Impartiality', the panel argued, 'should be judged by its determination to respond even-handedly to the actions of different parties based not on who has acted but by the nature of their actions. Missions should protect civilians, irrespective of the origin of the threat.'[2]

This book has analysed this transformation and its implications. It has reframed impartiality as a composite norm and explored political dynamics surrounding this change at the macro-level (UN headquarters), the micro-level (specifically the Congo case) and at their nexus. In doing so, it has sought to provide conceptual clarity on impartiality as a norm of peacekeeping, a norm that, having 'stood the test of time', is often confused in the minds of practitioners and scholars alike.[3]

What, then, is the relevance of this change for other contemporary peace operations beyond the Congo? What might it imply for the future of the UN more broadly? What are its implications for theory and practice? By way of conclusion, I will recapitulate my main argument and then explore these broader questions.

A CRISIS IN PEACEKEEPING AND THE FUTURE OF THE UN

Claims to assertive impartiality, it must be said, have a certain intuitive appeal. They are powerful and purposive. For those working at the hard edge of human misery, they offer seemingly simple and clear accounts of right and wrong, good and evil. They differentiate victim from perpetrator, they assign innocence and guilt, and, far from being bloodless, abstract statements of principle, they compel action. All this makes them difficult to argue with. That civilians should be protected seems a notion that is uncontestably worthy. Who could possibly disagree?

But claims to assertive impartiality must be considered as only that—claims. Far from being universal or absolute, impartial judgments are, as I have demonstrated throughout this book, socially bound. They are *intruths*— valid, true, and good only insofar as the *basis for* judgment reflects shared purposes and resonates with social values.

Addressing the question of how impartiality has been understood as a norm of peacekeeping at both the macro-organizational level and the micro-level has revealed a dearth of consensus over the norm itself, as well as the purposes of contemporary peacekeeping and the actions involved. Although most UN member states and local actors readily use the same vocabulary and largely agree that impartiality must remain a bedrock norm, significant differences and divergent understandings persist as to what keeping peace 'impartially' does, can, and should mean. Rather than *intruths*—relative, contingent, and, arguably, 'real'—judgments rendered by the assertive conception of the norm have become *extruths*, which is to say, claims to authority based on idealized notions of the universal and apolitical

Such claims, however, belie the complex political realities of the world we actually live in. Conflicts of values are, as Isaiah Berlin declared, 'an intrinsic, irremovable part of human life'. They are, as he said, the 'essence of . . . what we are'.[4] While Berlin was writing in the context of the Cold War, his words are no less true today. Conflicts of values are visible at the domestic level in many Western democracies where, given the inherent diversity of the societies they are expected to serve and, indeed, represent, established institutions of impartial authority such as the police, judiciary and civil service are increasingly under strain. This is even more the case in the volatile contexts into which peacekeepers are deployed and, more broadly, in the international realm. The Soviet Union's collapse did not mark the 'end of history' as Francis Fukuyama and others proclaimed.[5] Nor did it signal the beginning of a 'new world order'.[6] While we are more interconnected than ever, with human suffering more visible and 'real', the prevalence of pressing global issues has not produced a monolithic global politics. 'The world', as Jean-Marie Guéhenno writes, 'is just too heterogeneous to be unified by a single conversation' around human rights or anything else for that matter.[7] The contestation over assertive impartiality presented in this book evinces this plurality of contending perspectives and values at multiple levels. Judgments and actions by peacekeepers based on notions of human rights cannot therefore but be regarded as partial—as a matter of taking sides.

It is in this context that this book has addressed a second question: what are the effects of impartiality being a contested norm? My analysis here has focused on Congo, the site of the largest and most costly peacekeeping mission in UN history, one which has become the paradigm case of more assertive approaches to peacekeeping. In doing so, I have drawn linkages between the broader, macro-level forms of contestation during the institutionalization of impartiality, and the implementation of the norm in this particular case.

The Congo case reveals how ambiguities over the dominant conception of impartiality—the result of prior disagreements—became problematic in practice, as actors interpreted and enacted the norm in a process mired in its own forms of contestation related to the historical, social, and political dynamics of that particular place. The sources and sites of contestation were many, with long and deep roots in history—the killing of Lumumba under the UN's watch, decades of Western backing of Mobutu, the failure of peacekeepers to halt the Rwandan genocide or to deal with its consequences in eastern Zaire, as well as the West's more recent favouritism of Kigali. The violence of the present day is often deeply political and polyvalent, sewn into the very fabric of this history. As a result, the binary distinctions inherent to assertive impartiality—victim/perpetrator, innocent/criminal—did not hold up in practice and actually divided all those engaged.

This led to inconsistencies and variations in the decisions and actions of UN officials associated with the mission on the ground. Civilians were protected in some instances and not in others. Certain armed groups incurred the wrath of the blue helmets, while others, unopposed by the mission, augmented their power. For fear of the mission being marginalized or thrown out, officials proved unwilling to use force to confront widespread abuses committed by parties connected to the state. Other effects flowed from these discrepancies as well. Indeed, in order to fully grasp the politics of peacekeeping and its implications, we cannot limit ourselves to looking at the inconsistencies in practice, but must examine the sources that are situated, in a sense, upstream. In other words, it is not just a matter of whether the norm is or is not implemented. What happens both before and afterwards is critical. The policies of international actors do not exist in a vacuum.

The variations in peacekeeper responses in Congo had significant unintended consequences. The robust role prescribed for peacekeepers raised expectations when it came to implementation, and created varying incentives among local actors, related to the specific circumstances in which they found themselves. In doing so, it encouraged particular actions that would not have occurred had their roles been conceived, understood, and enacted differently. As Chapter 5 recounted, in some instances, simply by stating its purpose as one of impartial protection, the mission had the perverse effect of endangering civilians, as armed groups deliberately attacked civilians to undermine it. In this way, the discourse associated with the assertive conception of the norm proved to be a powerful and subversive tool used by local actors both to legitimize themselves and de-legitimize others, including, crucially, the mission itself.

Over time, the UN's authority was eviscerated—a development worsened by the fact that the Security Council's response to policy failure in Congo, time and time again, was to scale up the mission's mandated 'robustness'. This, in turn, only further tarnished its credibility and claims to impartial authority, assertive or otherwise. That its assertive role should in fact be contestable—a core implication of this book—has not prompted the Council to consider changing course in Congo, nor, arguably, elsewhere.

Indeed, the perils and pitfalls seen in Congo are jarringly visible in other contexts where blue helmets are deployed.[8] A few examples serve as illustration and point to this deeper crisis in UN peacekeeping. The UN Mission in the Republic of South Sudan (UNMISS), which began with high hopes following the country's independence in 2011, but which was based on the false assumption that the government was a willing and compliant partner, has similarly struggled to balance its statebuilding functions with its responsibility to protect civilians. The close relations of senior UN officials with organs of the state meant that they failed to heed early warning signs of an impending political crisis and, given their compromised position, proved unable to do anything to halt the violence.[9] Since the country's implosion into civil war, the mission's role has been confined to sheltering civilians on UN bases, a situation which most argue is untenable over the long-run. The UN's access has been greatly curtailed. It is regularly accused of being partial to both the government and rebel opposition forces. What little leverage the mission may once have had has altogether evaporated. Similarly, in Darfur, a mission that many argue was 'set up to fail', the UN has effectively been neutered, excoriated for its passivity and for covering up abuses by all sides.[10] Furthermore, in both contexts, as in Congo, the UN has been marginalized politically, its diplomatic function sidelined in peacemaking efforts, eclipsed by regional actors and organizations.[11]

But why have these calamitous failures not impeded the Security Council from continuing to authorize robust operations? And what are the implications for the future of peacekeeping and the UN? The fact that peacekeeping is something of a hydra-headed institution means, as I explained in Chapter 3, that no single actor is forced, let alone able, to assume the complete costs, political and otherwise, of a UN collective decision. This partializing of burdens greatly increases the likelihood of 'political evasion' and posturing.[12] Those member states that have greatest influence in determining policy and those that authorize mission mandates are rarely the same states that field forces.

What is more, the very nature of assertive impartiality and the contexts into which blue helmets are deployed make it difficult for those who claim such authority to change course. Once members of the Council or peacekeepers proclaim that the UN's primary role is to protect civilians, it becomes difficult, no matter what the circumstances or prospects for success, to go back on their word, particularly in contexts where forces have already deployed and where fears of renewed chaos following possible withdrawal loom large. Here, the typically high tone of peacekeeping language often plays a part. As Adam Branch and others have argued, action justified in a language of crisis, as an urgent response to rights abuses, however ambiguous, militates against further deliberation. Any contestation or hesitation amidst appeals for action runs the risk of being condemned as immoral, and complicit in the suffering.[13]

While these dynamics suggest that assertive peacekeeping is likely to endure, albeit with its persistent problems, the ramifications are potentially larger. They raise fundamental questions about the UN's future role as guarantor of international peace and security. Although the UN has always been involved in human-rights advocacy to some degree, that has never been trumpeted as the institution's overarching purpose. Now, with the declaration of 'Human Rights Up Front', it is. The risk is that by adopting an uncompromising moral line that condemns particular actors or groups, UN officials will find it increasingly difficult to retreat from such firm denunciations and engage in negotiations with these same actors. In other words, the imperative to protect may compromise another imperative that for a generation defined UN diplomacy as well as peacekeeping: namely, to treat both sides as equal.

Consequently, access and the political side-deals that many believe are essential to the resolution of conflict and which reduce civilian imperilment may be harder to justify, and the prospects for an inclusive settlement may wither.

Moreover, the difficulties inherent in the UN's practice of holding all actors to the same standards risk further undermining the institution. As a recent study conducted by a group of international scholars concluded, '[w]hen side-taking cannot be justified by virtue of acceptable behaviour, it becomes arbitrary in the eyes of the world, and the political purpose of engagement is easily seen as hypocritical and painted as part of some conspiracy theory'.[14] Given that the legitimacy of the UN derives both from whether it is seen to reflect and promote shared values, as well as from the degree to which it is actually effective, this does not bode well for the institution itself.

These constraints and the existence of such demonstrable contingency and contestability in the formulation and implementation of any 'impartial' role, suggest that the UN's future is likely to be in the less visible function that the institution plays. Ultimately, its most useful role may not be to adjudge participants as malefactors or victims, but rather to reflect and, in the deepest sense of the word, to 'mediate' among the real-world contradictions, vagaries, and inconsistencies of its member states. In other words, to represent the gap between rhetoric and reality, stated ambition and actual practice, however troubling that may be for those civilians in whose name peacekeepers and the UN now claim to act.

To fully appreciate these implications, however, requires an approach to studying and engaging with impartiality that recognizes its inherently political and contested nature. In raising these questions and by acknowledging these challenges, my aim is not to discredit peacekeeping or to suggest that the UN should stop engaging in the protection of human rights. I do not think we should abandon either impartiality or peacekeeping. Controversy is a sure sign, arguably, of relevance. What it underscores is the need for a different approach, one that is based on a careful and deliberate strategy that is both principled *and* pragmatic.

In the remainder of the Conclusion I summarize this book's more specific contribution to the academic literature as well as possible avenues for future research, both theoretical and empirical.

THE STUDY OF PEACEKEEPING AND ASSERTIVE LIBERAL INTERNATIONALISM

The intention of the present study has been to further existing research on peacekeeping, which until recently has been reluctant to investigate and analyse peacekeeping as an inherently political and contested phenomenon. It has sought to underscore the value of a holistic understanding of peacekeeping as a multi-level and dynamic process. It affirms the necessity of accounting for the history, culture, and politics of those contexts into which peacekeepers are deployed, as well as of the UN and particular member states within such contexts. This study also demonstrates the importance of examining the effects of contestation on a range of actors, including on peacekeeping missions themselves, which, as I have described, must be understood as political entities, comprised of individuals and groups with diverse interests and identities. To overlook these dynamics, as scholars overwhelmingly have done, limits what insights they can offer about peacekeeping, its relationship to the UN, and its role more broadly within international relations.

To this end, the contributions of this book could be amplified and refined by the examination of additional case studies, as well as the practices associated more broadly with assertive liberal internationalism. In what follows, I discuss several of this book's core findings and the ways in which they provide a jumping-off point for further study. I then explain this book's specific contribution to the study of norms in International Relations.

Understanding Impartiality

Despite impartiality's ubiquity in both policy and scholarly discourse, the norm is insufficiently studied and largely misunderstood. Impartiality is widely invoked but rarely accompanied by rigorous conceptual analysis or detailed empirical investigation of how it has operated and continues to operate in practice. This book fills a gap simply by vivisecting the norm, and by charting its evolution in UN peacekeeping. In doing so, the disaggregation of impartiality into its composite parts—the so-called 'structure of impartiality'—provides a framework for future analysis both by scholars and practitioners of peacekeeping, as well as other institutions. Indeed, similar claims to impartial authority and the more compulsory and coercive practices they engender in peacekeeping have, as Chapter 2 details, arisen in other areas of international engagement, including international criminal prosecution and humanitarian assistance, areas that may now be seen as susceptible to similar critique and reconfiguration of purpose.

In this vein, those areas of ambiguity detailed in Chapter 2, which concern the relationship between peacekeeping and other institutions, and which raise issues over impartiality, would prove a profitable second area of further research. In this respect, regional and sub-regional peacekeeping arrangements, including their relationship to UN-led missions and broader implications for the institution's authority, are particularly worthy of scholarly attention, not least because of DPKO's strong commitment to building and strengthening external partnerships, and the growing prevalence of such arrangements in the field.

African states have increasingly become willing to deploy forces and lead broader crisis management processes on their own continent. What is more, in recent years they have emerged as proponents of robust peacekeeping. They are not shy of using force. From an impartiality perspective, the very characteristics that make these actors suited to rapid and robust response often make their lack of bias—whether real or perceived—all the more questionable. As the involvement of regional actors in the FIB in Congo illustrates, neighbours often have their own political agendas, which play out through operations and may impact UN peacekeepers deployed alongside or following such arrangements. Furthermore, the sustainability of such operations is far from guaranteed.

Research on impartiality as a norm of humanitarian practice and international criminal justice would also be of significant value if it were broadened to other institutions and practices, especially where, as described in Chapter 3, there is emphasis on strengthening and deepening cooperation and integration between these actors and peacekeeping missions. While the actors not directly charged with peacekeeping all claim to act impartially, their activities and short-term objectives differ markedly, as may the degree of consent with which they operate. In the Congo case, for example, the UN's decision to undertake joint operations with the FARDC both during *Kimia II* and against the M23 created deep fissures both within the mission and between it and members of the humanitarian community operating in the east of the country. NGOs protested that their access to and acceptance by local communities was greatly diminished because they were tarred with the same brush and were seen to be taking sides. The challenges associated with such perceptions were particularly prominent for UN agencies, operating under the same institutional umbrella as the mission. The adoption of 'Human Rights Up Front' potentially magnifies these issues within the UN beyond the area of peacekeeping. What is the future of OCHA within a UN system that prioritizes speaking out against abuses, when doing so may alienate parties and jeopardize access to vulnerable populations?

Similar tensions come to the fore in the area of international criminal justice. The ICC's involvement in Congo and, in particular, its indictment of General Ntaganda Bosco had a considerable impact on how local actors engaged with the mission and on the credibility of the UN's claims to impartiality. Particularly damning in this respect was the revelation that Bosco was deputy coordinator of the operations that the mission was jointly conducting with the FARDC. The ICC's involvement in Congo, as in other contexts, also has ramifications for humanitarians and particularly for UN agencies, which, like peacekeeping missions, are bound by the ICC/UN Relationship Agreement. If requested, they are thus required to provide information and possible testimony for war crimes investigations. How UN agencies and humanitarian organizations respond to such requests, given the risks that collaboration and cooperation may pose to their own impartiality and the safety of beneficiaries, is an area of research worthy of further exploration.

Institutional Dynamics

This book's examination of how the ambiguities associated with assertive impartiality reflect and engender further contestation underlines the necessity of studying the institutional politics of peacekeeping, as well as of other institutions associated with assertive liberal internationalism. The various sites and sources of contestation uncovered in this book illustrate the importance of disaggregating both the UN and its peacekeeping missions in order to analyse decision-making pathways and processes, and the relative power of and roles assumed by particular actors. Several findings related to both institutionalization and implementation are particularly salient.

Macro-level Dynamics

At the macro-level, this book sheds light on the Secretariat's engagement with peacekeeping in the new millennium. Chapters 3 and 4 described how the Secretariat has shifted from a more sceptical and cautious engagement with assertive impartiality during the initial phases of institutionalization, to a more active role as 'entrepreneur' and 'advocate' of the norm in recent years. This has been clearest in Ban Ki-moon's emergence as one of the most vocal proponents of an assertive approach, calling, among other things, for the Responsibility to Protect to be streamlined through peace operations, and strongly advocating 'Human Rights Up Front'. The change in approach suggests, as I have argued, that the establishment of institutional precedent was of particular concern to the body, but that once established, the Secretariat has increasingly opted to work within, rather than critically to question, the parameters of policy set by the Security Council. This change is of considerable significance given the contestation illuminated in this book, and the fact that impartiality remains a core norm of the Secretariat, enshrined in its very code of conduct. What, then, is to be the role and function of the Secretariat in a more assertively liberal international order, one that, given broader geopolitical shifts, is likely to be even more contested in the years to come? Should the Secretariat advance and advocate a particular normative agenda for the UN, when doing so may be viewed as deeply partial by some of its members? How much consensus is enough to be representative? How should competing interpretations and normative visions be balanced?

The identification of the NAM as a critic of assertive impartiality also offers opportunities for further research. There has been a dearth of scholarship on the politics within and surrounding the NAM in the post-Cold War era, particularly with respect to peacekeeping. Moreover, when scholars do engage the subject, they have tended to speak of a homogeneous global South, especially on issues related to peace and security. The variation of perspectives within the NAM and the global South more broadly, and the increasing role played by regional organizations, challenges this dichotomization and underscores the need for a more nuanced analysis of UN politics in this area.[15] Specifically, further analysis would be beneficial to identify the factors driving such variance, and whether these can be generalized to other policy areas. As Roland Paris asks, how will intensifying geopolitical competition and the increasing participation in peacekeeping of rising powers, including the so-called BRICS countries: Brazil, Russia, India, China, and South Africa, shape the form and character of peace operations, given that, as this book has demonstrated, they have historically reflected broader power politics?[16] What are the implications for the UN's authority? And how are these changes likely to play out in and across different institutional bodies?

Finally, this book offers insights into the Security Council's role as an important, if not *the* most important, actor in determining the content of peacekeeping policy. Chapter 3 asserts that the P5 have demonstrated a modicum of cooperation with regards to peacekeeping in the new millennium, visible in the prevalence of robust mission mandates containing prescriptions for PoC. Rather than demonstrating true consensus among the P5, the pattern of mandating robust operations has, as this book has shown, reflected and will probably continue to reflect political dynamics within the Council, which often relate to issues other than peacekeeping. These dynamics affect where peacekeepers are and are not deployed, as well as the contents of their mandates, including when and against whom force is authorized. Understanding these political dynamics is therefore necessary to comprehend the policies and practices of peacekeeping, as well as other areas of engagement. Crucially, the contestation inherent in and occasioned by these practices, and the inconsistencies that result, may have long-term consequences for the legitimacy of peacekeeping and the UN, including the Security Council. What authority does the Council command if members from the global South are no longer willing to offer up troops or to do so only, as was the case with the FIB in Congo, when it advances partisan agendas? Or if parties decide that the potential costs of UN engagement outweigh the benefits, and so turn to other institutions to address issues related to international peace and security?

Micro-level Dynamics

These questions regarding macro-level dynamics are inextricably linked to the micro-level dynamics, which this book has also brought to light. In this respect, the in-depth study of MONUC/MONUSCO offers several findings that would be strengthened by comparative analysis with other cases of peacekeeping, with potential insights for international practices other than peacekeeping.

Specifically, I have identified several sites of contestation that reflected more consistent differences in interpretations of impartiality among certain actors. These were: tensions between the political leadership and military command of the mission; tensions between the mission leadership based in the capital and officials stationed at field offices in the east of the country; and finally, tensions between the civilian component of the mission and the TCCs/PPCs. Interviews highlighted several factors to explain this variation, including divergent professional cultures and priorities; location and proximity of these actors to the host state, civilians, and armed groups; and issues related to resourcing as well as to policy coherence. These factors, as I have shown, were often inseparable from macro-level contestation: the tasks assigned to peacekeepers and issues of burden sharing; when and what resources are made available; and whether and how a mission forms part of larger donor engagement strategies. Preliminary research into other missions suggests, as I have discussed, that many of the same factors that shaped implementation in the Congo case hold true in other contexts of multi-dimensional peacekeeping. However, further investigation is warranted.

These dynamics take on added significance given the push towards both formal and informal cooperative arrangements between peacekeeping missions and other actors. As peacekeeping practices continue to expand to include a broader set of actors, accounting for these institutional dynamics and potential sites of norm contestation will become ever more crucial.

Local Actors and the Importance of Context

Lastly, the findings of this book underscore the importance of context in the study of peacekeeping and beyond. While research into institutional dynamics may provide a more nuanced understanding of missions and the politics of more assertive forms of engagement, they will never fully be able to account for how mandates translate on the ground. Implementation will invariably be contingent, shaped by the specificities of context, including, crucially, how local actors perceive and engage with peacekeepers during that process.

Until recently, the influence and agency of local actors has received scant attention from scholars interested in peacekeeping and in other international institutions. This oversight is problematic given that the more invasive forms of intervention now pursued by peacekeepers and other international actors are such that these parties are often deeply embedded within host societies and must work closely with local actors. What is more, these deeper and more invasive forms of intervention have a marked and lasting effect on the places in which international actors operate.

In this respect, the findings of Chapter 5 are particularly salient and should give cause for further research. How do civilians understand protection? What are the civilian determinants of security—that is, what does 'being safe' mean in specific contexts? What strategies do people adopt to avoid violence and protect themselves? And how do these strategies change in the presence of peacekeepers? What factors influence civilian expectations? And what factors determine whether international efforts undermine or bolster local protection practices? While practitioners and research analysts are increasingly attuned to such questions, in-depth research in this area is nascent.[17]

Closely related are the various ways in which armed actors may instrumentalize and co-opt the discourse and practices associated with robust mandates and assertive liberal internationalism more broadly. Here, the delegitimization and self-legitimization tactics these actors adopt are particularly worthy of further investigation, not least given their broader relevance for other international participants in a conflict. What factors influence these strategies? Do they change over time? How are they shaped by internal group dynamics and, more broadly, by the relationship between armed groups and civilian populations?

All of these questions, into which this book has provided insight, are fruitful areas for further research. They are crucial to understanding the politics—both local and global—of peacekeeping and assertive liberal internationalism.

The Study of Norms

Aside from insight into the politics and practices of peacekeeping, the analysis of impartiality presented here contributes to the further refinement of the study of norms in International Relations. It attests to the importance of understanding norms not as static and simple but as dynamic and complex ideational structures. It demonstrates how an account of both institutionalization and implementation is vital to the analysis of a norm's development. And it makes the case for studying contestation as an ongoing part of a norm's natural evolution.

First, this book contributes to existing scholarship by developing and introducing the 'composite norm', which, as Chapter 1 detailed, provides analytical purchase for the study of other norms. Specifically, the disaggregation of the norm into its mutable and immutable components allows for a more nuanced conceptual analysis such as is presented in Chapter 2. It also enables the study of changes in a norm's content both in and across historical periods. This was of particular advantage in that it provided a framework to examine alterations in the norm's content within the Congo case, as MONUC/MONUSCO's mandate evolved significantly over the duration of its deployment.

More fundamentally, the finer analysis enabled by the composite norm is necessary to study contestation and move beyond the binary conception of norms that has been so pervasive in constructivist theorizing. It shows that instead of simply rejecting or accepting a given norm, actors have been able to resist particular elements of the norm and, at times, put forward their own interpretations of these elements during both the processes of institutionalization and implementation. This observation was particularly valuable in elucidating impartiality's ambiguity—the tension between elements of the norm and other norms, and the various ways in which the lack of precision during institutionalization (which itself was driven by contestation) had significant implications for implementation.

The second principal contribution of this book is to illustrate the importance of treating norm institutionalization and implementation as dynamic and inter-related—indeed, often inseparable—processes. Institutionalization is important, but does not signal the end of contestation, as many constructivists would suggest. Assertive impartiality was and continues to be hotly contested despite its institutionalization at the end of the 1990s. Similarly, this book demonstrates how, if scholars are to account meaningfully for contestation and the way in which norms are actually enacted, in many instances implementation cannot be studied in isolation from institutionalization. As Chapter 4 revealed, contestation during institutionalization may carry over into implementation in various ways, including in the ambiguities surrounding a norm that is institutionally embedded. The form and substance of contestation in both processes may be inextricably linked in ways that are critical to understanding the effects and implications of impartiality, as well as other norms.

What is more, the unintended consequences of assertive impartiality and the questions it raises regarding the potential moral hazards associated with particular norms make the study of implementation vital. Even seemingly laudable norms such as impartiality are not unalloyed. The process of implementation may occasion new sources of violence, repression, and social exclusion. As others within the discipline have recently argued, such serious consequences demand that scholars reflect more than they have done on the normative assumptions that either implicitly or explicitly guide their research, and their decisions as to how, where, and what norms are studied.[18] Simply put, the scope and gravity of its effects call for greater consideration of the 'normativity' of norms research and the ethics of constructivism as an approach to the study of international relations.

Finally, the methodological analysis employed in this book is part of the embryonic ethnographic turn in IR. Each of the above theoretical findings highlights and affirms the benefits of conducting in-depth research at various levels to study norms and their effects, and, in particular, the vital importance of ground-level experience and observation. However, as scholars of International Relations are increasingly drawn to ethnographic methods to study the norms, institutions, and practices associated with international peace and security, the challenges, ethical questions and, indeed, the potential for unintended consequences implicit in such research warrant greater consideration. How close is too close? When does participant observation risk becoming partisan observation? What obligations and duties do researchers incur when they study vulnerable populations up close?

CONCLUSION

A core contention of this book is that the change in the dominant conception of impartiality as a norm of peacekeeping is an integral part of the emergence in the new millennium of a more assertive liberal internationalism. The present analysis offers valuable insights for and affirms the necessity of further research on the institutions associated with this broader change, which also lay claim to impartial authority—an authority which this book has argued is likely to be even more contested in the years to come. However, if scholars are to advance more than a fragmentary and partial understanding of such norms as impartiality, of the practices associated with these institutions, and, indeed, of the social construction of international relations more broadly, they require a wider, more encompassing set of perspectives.

In this respect, it is crucial to keep in mind that impartiality implies, in Rosanvallon's words, 'vigilance and an active presence in the world, a determination to represent social reality as faithfully as possible'.[19] Far from being a consequence of detachment, of being set apart from society, impartiality, as Rosanvallon argues, is the result of 'reflective immersion'.[20] Arendt maintained that this entails broadening one's own thinking in order to take account of the thinking of others, thereby working towards a greater level of generality.[21] It was through such a practice that Arendt concluded that 'judging was one, if not the most, important activity in which this sharing-the-world-with-others comes to pass'.[22]

Perhaps all that can be hoped for in any collective enlarging of perspective, any bringing into being of a condition that is truly 'sharing-the-world-with-others', is that both individuals and institutions, most especially the United Nations, seek to cultivate a certain degree of humility and honesty about their—our—limitations. An idealized yet simultaneously practical and prudent conception of impartiality, one which discriminates but is less quick to judge, would see people and states as they actually are, not as how they would like to be seen, or how we would like to see them. And it would recognize, by virtue of groups with conflicting interests and values living in this world together, that impartiality is necessarily and inextricably political—but, for all that, no less worthy.

NOTES

1. United Nations, *United Nations Peacekeeping Operations: Principles and Guidelines* (New York: Department of Peacekeeping Operations, 2008), 33.
2. United Nations, *Uniting Our Strengths for Peace: Politics, Partnership and People* (New York: Report of the High-Level Independent Panel on Peace Operations, 2015). Specifically, the report states: 'Impartiality is not the same as neutrality or equal treatment of all parties in all cases for all time, when in some cases local parties consist not of moral equals but of obvious aggressors and victims. Impartiality must mean adherence to the principles of the Charter and to the objectives of a mission mandate that is rooted in these Charter principles' (2015: 32).
3. Ian Johnstone, 'Dilemmas of Robust Peace Operations' in *Robust Peacekeeping: The Politics of Force* (New York: Center for International Cooperation, 2009).
4. Isaiah Berlin, *Liberty: Incorporating 'Four Essays on Liberty'*, edited by Henry Hardy (Oxford: Oxford University Press, 2002), 213.
5. Francis Fukuyama, 'The end of history?', *The National Interest* (1989), 3–18.
6. President George Bush, *Address Before a Joint Session of the Congress on the Cessation of the Persian Gulf Conflict*, 6 March 1991.
7. Jean-Marie Guéhenno, *Fog of Peace: A Memoir of International Peacekeeping in the 21st Century* (Washington: Brookings Institution Press, 2015), 316.
8. Sudarsan Raghavan, 'Record number of U.N. peacekeepers fails to stop African wars', *Washington Post*, 3 January 2014.
9. Jort Hemmer, *'We are Laying the Groundwork for Our Own Failure': The UN Mission in South Sudan and its Civilian Protection Strategy: An Early Assessment* (The Hague: Clingendael Institute, January 2013); Lauren Hutton, *Prolonging the Agony of UNMISS. The Implementation Challenges of a New Mandate During a Civil War* (The Hague: Clingendael Institute, 2014).
10. Colum Lynch, 'A Mission That was Set up to Fail', *Foreign Policy*, 8 April 2014, part 3. Lynch's in-depth three-part investigation of the UN's debacle in Darfur concluded that the peacekeeping mission had been 'bullied by government security forces and rebels, stymied by American and Western neglect, and left without the weapons necessary to fight in a region where more peacekeepers have been killed than in any other U.N. mission in the world'.
11. Chester Crocker, Fen Osler Hampson, and Pamela Aall, 'A Global Security Vacuum Half-filled: Regional Organizations, Hybrid Groups and Security Management', *International Peacekeeping* 21/1 (2014), 1–19; Peter Wallensteen and Anders Bjurner, eds., *Regional Organizations and Peacemaking: Challengers to the UN?* (Abingdon: Routledge, 2014).

12. Philip Cunliffe, *Legions of Peace: UN Peacekeepers from the Global South* (New York: Hurst & Co., 2014), 223.

13. Adam Branch, 'Against Humanitarian Impunity: Rethinking Responsibility for Displacement and Disaster in Northern Uganda', *Journal of Intervention and Statebuilding* 2/2 (2008), 168. See also, Bronwyn Leebaw, 'The Politics of Impartial Activism: Humanitarianism and Human Rights,' *Perspectives on Politics* 5/2 (2007), 223–39.

14. Thorsten Benner, et al. *Effective and Responsible Protection from Atrocity Crimes: Toward Global Action* (Berlin: Global Public Policy Institute, draft, March 2015).

15. Practitioners and scholars have recently begun to explore these issues. See Mateja Peter, *Emerging Power and Peace Operations: An Agenda for Research* (Oslo: Norwegian Institute of International Affairs, October 2014); Jair Van Derlijn and Xenia Avezov. *The Future Peace Operations Landscape: Voices from Stakeholders around the Globe* (Stockholm: SIPRI, 2015).

16. Roland Paris, 'The Geopolitics of Peace Operations: A Research Agenda', *International Peacekeeping* 21/4 (2014), 501–8.

17. See, for example, the Stimson Centre's *Civilians in Conflict* project, http://www.stimson.org/research-pages/civilians-in-conflict/

18. See, for example, the collection of essays in Richard Price, ed., *Moral Limit and Possibility in World Politics* (Cambridge: Cambridge University Press, 2008).

19. Pierre Rosanvallon, *Democratic Legitimacy: Impartiality, Reflexivity, Proximity* (Princeton: Princeton University Press, 2011), 89.

20. Rosanvallon (2011: 89).

21. Hannah Arendt, *Lectures on Kant's Political Philosophy* (Chicago: University of Chicago Press, 1982: 42).

22. Hannah Arendt, *Between Past and Future: Six Exercises in Political Thought* (New York: Viking Press, 1961), 221.

References

Abi-Saab, Georges. *The United Nations Operation in the Congo 1960–1965* (Oxford: Oxford University Press, 1978).

Abtahi, Hirad, Odo Ogwuma and Rebecca Young. 'The Composition of Judicial Benches, Disqualification and Excusal of Judges at the International Criminal Court: A Survey', *Journal of International Criminal Justice* 11/2 (2013), 379–98.

Acharya, Amitav. 'How Ideas Spread: Whose Norms Matter? Norm Localization and Institutional Change in Asian Regionalism', *International Organization* 58/2 (2004), 239–75.

Acharya, Amitav. 'Norm Subsidiarity and Regional Orders: Sovereignty, Regionalism, and Rule Making in the Third World', *International Studies Quarterly* 55/1 (2011), 95–123.

Adebajo, Adekeye. *UN Peacekeeping in Africa: From the Suez Crisis to the Sudan Conflicts* (Boulder: Lynne Rienner Publishers, 2011).

Africa Confidential. 'More policing of peacekeepers. Indian soldiers are being accused of not knowing where their loyalties lie', 6 November 2008.

Agence France-Presse. 'Lack of troops, "schizophrenic" mandate hamper UN in DR Congo', 12 November 2008.

Agence France-Presse. 'Kinshasa wants UN mission to start pull out from June: official', 3 March 2010.

Ahmed, Salman, Paul Keating and Ugo Solinas. 'Shaping the Future of UN Peace Operations: Is there a Doctrine in the House?', *Cambridge Review of International Affairs* 20/1 (2007), 11–28.

Aksu, Esref. *The United Nations, Intra-State Peacekeeping and Normative Change* (Manchester: Manchester University Press, 2003).

Alter, Karen and Sophie Meunier. 'The Politics of International Regime Complexity', *Perspectives on Politics* 7/1 (2009), 13–24.

Anderson, Mary. *Do No Harm: How Aid can Support Peace—or War* (Boulder: Lynne Rienner, 1998).

Andreas, Peter. *Blue Helmets and Black Markets: The Business of Survival in the Siege of Sarajevo* (Ithaca: Cornell University Press, 2008).

Annan, Kofi with Nader Mousavizadeh. *Interventions: A Life in War and Peace* (New York: The Penguin Press, 2012).

Applbaum, Arthur Isak. 'Culture, Identity, and Legitimacy', in *Governance in a Globalizing World*, edited by Joseph Nye and John Donohue (Washington, DC: Brookings Institution Press, 2000).

Arendt, Hannah. *Between Past and Future: Six Exercises in Political Thought* (New York: Viking Press, 1961).

Arendt, Hannah. *Lectures on Kant's Political Philosophy* (Chicago: University of Chicago Press, 1982).

Autesserre, Séverine. *The Trouble with the Congo: Local Violence and the Failure of International Peace Building* (New York: Cambridge University Press, 2010).

Autesserre, Séverine. 'Going Micro: Emerging and Future Peacekeeping Research', *International Peacekeeping* 21/4 (2014), 492–500.

Autesserre, Séverine. *Peaceland: Conflict Resolution and the Everyday Politics of International Intervention* (New York: Cambridge University Press, 2014).

Ayangafac, Chrysantus. *Resolving the Chadian Political Epilepsy: An Assessment of Intervention Efforts* (South Africa: ISS, 2009).

Bagchi, Indrani. 'India warns peacekeeping troops in DR Congo of M23 retaliatory strikes', *Times of India*, 28 August 2013.

Bah, Sarjoh A. and Bruce Jones. *Peace Operations Partnerships: Lessons and Issues from Coordination to Hybrid Arrangements* (New York: Center on International Cooperation, May 2008).

Baines, Erin and Emily Paddon. '"This is How we Survived": Civilian Agency and Humanitarian Protection', *Security Dialogue* 43/3 (2012), 231–47.

Barkin, Samuel. *Realist Constructivism: Rethinking International Relations Theory* (Cambridge: Cambridge University Press, 2010).

Barnett, Michael. *Eyewitness to a Genocide: The United Nations and Rwanda* (Ithaca: Cornell University Press, 2002).

Barnett, Michael and Martha Finnemore. *Rules for the World: International Organizations in Global Politics* (Ithaca: Cornell University Press, 2004).

Barnett, Michael and Thomas Weiss (eds.). *Humanitarianism in Question: Politics, Power, Ethics* (Ithaca: Cornell University Press, 2008).

Barry, Brian. *Justice as Impartiality* (Oxford: Oxford University Press, 1995).

Bavier, Joe. 'Villagers stone UN investigators in eastern Congo', Reuters, 29 May 2007.

BBC World. 'DR Congo army "used aid as bait"', 6 November 2009.

Beith, Malcolm. 'Congo rejects UN stance on general in anti-rebel offensive', *Bloomberg*, 5 February 2015.

Bellamy, Alex and Paul Williams. 'The West and Contemporary Peace Operations', *Journal of Peace Research* 46/1 (2009), 39–57.

Bellamy, Alex and Paul Williams. 'The New Politics of Protection? Côte d'Ivoire, Libya and the Responsibility to Protect', *International Affairs* 87/4 (2011), 825–50.

Bellamy, Alex and Paul Williams. *Broadening the Base of United Nations Troop- and Police Contributing Countries* (New York: International Peace Institute, 2012).

Bellamy, Alex and Paul Williams (eds.). *Providing Peacekeepers: The Politics, Challenges, and Future of United Nations Peacekeeping Contributions* (Oxford: Oxford University Press, 2013).

Benner, Thorsten et al. *Effective and Responsible Protection from Atrocity Crimes: Toward Global Action* (Berlin: Global Public Policy Institute, 2015).

Bentham, Jeremy. *Rationale of Judicial Evidence Vol. VI.* (1843).

Berdal, Mats. 'The UN after Iraq', *Survival* 46/3 (2004), 83–101.

Berdal, Mats. 'The Security Council and Peacekeeping', in *The United Nations Security Council and War: The Evolution of Thought and Practice since 1945*, edited by Vaughan Lowe, Adam Roberts, Jennifer Welsh, and Dominik Zaum (Oxford: Oxford University Press, 2008).

Berdal, Mats. *Building Peace after War* (Abingdon: Routledge, 2009).

Berdal, Mats and David Malone. *Greed and Grievance: Economic Agendas in Civil Wars* (Boulder: Lynne Rienner, 2000).

Berlin, Isaiah. *Liberty: Incorporating 'Four Essays on Liberty'*, edited by Henry Hardy (Oxford: Oxford University Press, 2002).

Betts, Alexander and Phil Orchard. *Implementation and World Politics: How International Norms Change Practice* (Oxford: Oxford University Press, 2014).

Betts, Richard. 'The Delusion of Impartial Intervention', *Foreign Affairs* 73/20 (1994), 20–33.

Betz, Michelle. 'Radio as Peacebuilder: A Case Study of Radio Okapi in the Democratic Republic of Congo', *The Great Lakes Research Journal* 1 (2004), 38–50.

Bevir, Mark. 'Introduction: Interpretive Methods', in *Interpretive Political Science, Volume 2*, edited by Mark Bevir (London: Sage, 2010).

Blokker, Niels and Nico Schrijver (eds.). *The Security Council and the Use of Force: Theory and Reality—A Need for Change?* (Leiden: Martinus Nijhoff, 2005).

Blum, Gabriella. 'The Individualization of War: From War to Policy in the Regulation of Armed Conflicts', in *Law and War*, edited by Austin Sarat, Lawrence Douglas, and Martha Merrill Umphrey (Stanford: Stanford University Press, 2014), 48–83.

Boulden, Jane. 'Mandates Matter: An Exploration of Impartiality in United Nations Operations', *Global Governance* 11/2 (2005), 147–60.

Boulden, Jane. 'Double Standards, Distance and Disengagement: Collective Legitimization in the Post-Cold War Security Council', *Security Dialogue* 37/3 (2006), 409–23.

Boutellis, Arthur. *In the DRC Communications War, Rebels Learn PoC Language* (New York: International Peace Institute, Global Observatory, July 2012).

Bowett, D. *United Nations Forces: A Legal Study of United Nations Practice* (London: Stevens & Sons, 1964).

Branch, Adam. 'Against Humanitarian Impunity: Rethinking Responsibility for Displacement and Disaster in Northern Uganda', *Journal of Intervention and Statebuilding* 2/2 (2008), 151–73.

Breakey, Hugh et al. *Enhancing Protection Capacity: Policy Guide to the Responsibility to Protect and the Protection of Civilians in Armed Conflicts* (Queensland, Australia: Institute for Ethics, Governance and Law, Griffith University, 2012).

Buchanan, Allen. 'Political Legitimacy and Democracy', *Ethics* 112/4 (2002), 689–719.

Buchanan, Allen and Robert Keohane. 'The Legitimacy of Global Governance Institutions', *Ethics and International Affairs* 20/4 (2006), 405–37.

Buergenthal, Thomas. 'The Normative and Institutional Evolution of International Human Rights', *Human Rights Quarterly* 19/4 (1997), 703–23.

Bull, Hedley. *The Anarchical Society: A Study of Order in World Politics*, 2nd ed. (New York: Columbia University Press, 1977).

Bush, George. *Address Before a Joint Session of the Congress on the Cessation of the Persian Gulf Conflict*, Washington, DC, 6 March 1991.

Butty, James. 'Congo official: DRC will not accept UN "neocolonization"', *Voice of America*, 29 March 2015.

Cammaert, Patrick. 'A Peacekeeping Commander's Perspective', *The RUSI Journal* 153/3 (2008), 68–71.

Carr, Edward H. *Twenty Years' Crisis, 1919–1939* (New York: Harper and Row, 1946).

Cass, Loren. 'Norm Entrapment and Preference Change: The Evolution of the European Union position on International Emissions Trading', *Global Environmental Politics* 5/2 (2005), 38–60.

Cassese, Antonio. 'Self-Determination', in *The Oxford Companion to Politics of the World*, edited by Joel Krieger (New York: Oxford University Press, 1993).

Chappuis, Fairlie and Aditi Gorur. *Reconciling Security Sector Reform and the Protection of Civilians in Peacekeeping Contexts* (Washington DC: Stimson Center, 2015).

Chayes, Antonia and Abram Chayes. *The New Sovereignty* (Cambridge: Harvard University Press, 1995).

Checkel, Jeffrey. 'Norms, Institutions, and National Identity in Contemporary Europe', *International Studies Quarterly* 43/1 (1999), 83–114.

Chopra, Jarat, John Mackinlay, and Larry Minear. *Report on the Cambodian Peace Process* (Oslo: Norwegian Institute of International Affairs, 1993).

Claude, Inis. 'Collective Legitimization as a Political Function of the United Nations', *International Organization* 20/3 (1966), 367–79.

CNDP. *Cahier de Charges du Congrès National Pour la Défense du Peuple* (Bwiza: 14 October 2006).

CNDP. *Communiqué de Presse sur les 'Massacres' à Kiwanja* (Bwiza, 19 November 2008).

Coleman, Katharina P. 'Token Troop Contributions to United Nations Peacekeeping Operations', in *Providing Peacekeepers: the Politics, Challenges, and Future of United Nations Peacekeeping Contributions*, edited by Alex J. Bellamy and Paul D. Williams (Oxford: Oxford University Press, 2013).

Coleman, Katharina P. 'The Political Economy of UN Peacekeeping: Incentivizing Effective Participation', *Providing for Peacekeeping Thematic Study No. 7* (New York: International Peace Institute, May 2014).

Commission of Inquiry by Mr Mahoux and Mr Verhofstadt, *Belgian Senate Report* (Brussels: 1997). Available at http://www.senate.be/english/rwanda

Congo News Agency. 'Thousands protest M23 capture of Goma, turn on government and UN', 21 November 2012.

Contessi, Nicola. 'Multilateralism, Intervention and Norm Contestation: China's Stance on Darfur in the UN Security Council', *Security Dialogue* 41/3 (2010), 333–44.

Convergne, Elodie and Michael Synder. *Geospatial Technology as a Conflict Prevention and Management Tool in UN Peacekeeping* (New York: International Peace Institute, March 2015).

Cortell, Andrew and James Davis. 'Understanding the Domestic Impact of International Norms: A Research Agenda', *International Studies Review* 2/1 (2000), 65–87.

Council of Europe. *Guidelines on the Protection of Civilians in CSDP Missions and Operations* (Brussels: Council of Europe, 2010).

Cox, Arthur. *Prospects for Peacekeeping* (Washington, DC: The Brookings Institution, 1967).

Crawford, Neta. *Argument and Change in World Politics: Ethics, Decolonization, and Humanitarian Intervention* (Cambridge: Cambridge University Press, 2002).

Crocker, Chester, Fen Osler Hampson, and Pamela Aall. 'A Global Security Vacuum Half-filled: Regional Organizations, Hybrid Groups and Security Management', *International Peacekeeping* 21/1 (2014), 1–19.

Cronin, Bruce. 'International Consensus and the Changing Legal Authority of the UN Security Council', in *The UN Security Council and the Politics of International Authority*, edited by Bruce Cronin and Ian Hurd (London: Routledge, 2008), 57–79.

Cronin, Bruce and Ian Hurd (eds.). *The UN Security Council and the Politics of International Authority* (London: Routledge, 2008).

Cumming, Gordon. 'Burying the Hatchet? Britain and France in the Democratic Republic of Congo', *The Journal of Modern African Studies* 49 (2011), 547–73.

Cumming, Gordon. 'The UK and France in the DRC: Making Their Own Peace', in *From Rivalry to Partnership?: New Approaches to the Challenges of Africa*, edited by Tony Chafer and Gordon Cumming (Farnham: Ashgate, 2011).

Cunliffe, Philip. 'The Politics of Global Governance in UN Peacekeeping', *International Peacekeeping* 16/3 (2009), 323–36.

Cunliffe, Philip. *Legions of Peace: UN Peacekeepers from the Global South* (New York: Hurst & Co. Publishers, 2014).

Dallaire, Roméo. *Shake Hands with the Devil: The Failure of Humanity in Rwanda* (New York: Carroll & Graff Publishers, 2003).

Daniel, Donald and Bradd Hayes. *Coercive Inducement and the Containment of International Crisis* (Washington: USIP Press, 1999).

Darcy, James. *Human Rights and Humanitarian Action: A Review of the Issues* (London: Humanitarian Policy Group, Overseas Development Institute, 2004).

De Vries, Hugo. *Going around in Circles: The Challenges of Peacekeeping and Stabilization in the Democratic Republic of the Congo* (The Hague: Clingendael Institute, July 2015).

Debelle, Raymond. 'FDLR', presentation at MONUSCO forward HQ, April 2011.

Deere, Carolyn. *The Implementation Game: The Trips Agreement and the Global Politics of Intellectual Property Reform in Developing Countries* (New York: Oxford University Press: 2009).

Deleu, Marijke. *Secure Insecurity: The Continuing Abuse of Civilians in Eastern DRC as the State Extends its Control* (Oxfam International, Briefing Paper 202, March 2015).

DiManno, Rosie. 'In Congo, UN troops prove useless again', *The Star*, 21 November 2012.

Dixon, Robyn. 'U.N. force in Congo, MONUSCO, criticized as ineffective', *Los Angeles Times*, 22 December 2012.

Donald, Dominick. 'Neutral is not Impartial: The Confusing Legacy of Traditional Peace Operations', *Armed Forces and Society* 29/3 (2003), 415–48.

Donald, Dominick. *Active Impartiality: A Survival System for 'Grey Area' Peace Support Operations* (London: King's College London. Department of War Studies, 2006).

Doyle, Michael, Ian Johnstone and Robert Orr. *Keeping the Peace: Multidimensional UN Operations in Cambodia and El Salvador* (Cambridge: Cambridge University Press, 1997).

Durch, William and Michelle Ker. *Police in UN Peacekeeping: Improving Selection, Recruitment and Deployment* (New York: International Peace Institute, 2013).

Durch, William et al. *The Brahimi Report and the Future of UN Peace Operations* (Washington: Stimson Center, 2003).

Dworkin, Ronald. *Taking Rights Seriously* (Boston: Harvard University Press, 1977).

Eckstein, Harry. 'Case Study and Theory in Political Science', in *Handbook of Political Science*, edited by Fred Greenstein and Nelson Polsby (Reading: Addison Wesley, 1975), 94–137.

Ellis, Howard. *The Origin Structure & Working of the League of Nations* (London: George Allen & Unwin, 1928).

Enzensberger, Hans Magnus. *Civil Wars: From LA to Bosnia* (New York: The New Press, 1994).

Epstein, Lee and Jack Knight. *The Choices Justices Make* (Washington, DC: CQ Press, 1998).

Erskine, Toni. 'Blood on the UN's Hands? Assigning Duties and Apportioning Blame to an Intergovernmental Organisation', *Global Society* 18/1 (2004), 21–42.

Evans, Gareth. 'Responsibility While Protecting', *Project Syndicate*, 27 January 2012.

Fabian, Larry. *Soldiers Without Enemies: Preparing the United Nations for Peacekeeping* (Washington, DC: Brookings Institution Press, 1971).

FDLR. *Order to all Forces Combattantes Abacunguzi (FOCA) Units*, the military wing of the FDLR, March 2009 (Unpublished).

Fenton, Neil. *Understanding the UN Security Council: Coercion or Consent?* (London: Ashgate, 2004).

Ferraro, Tristan. 'The Applicability and Application of International Humanitarian Law to Multinational Forces', in special edition on multinational operations, *International Review of the Red Cross* 95, No. 891–2 (2013).

Ferris, Elizabeth. *The Politics of Protection: The Limits of Humanitarian Action* (Washington, DC: Brookings Institution Press, 2011).

Findlay, Trevor. *Use of Force in UN Peace Operations* (Oxford: Oxford University Press, 2002).

Finnemore, Martha. *The Purpose of Intervention: Changing Beliefs about the Use of Force* (Ithaca: Cornell University Press, 2003).

Finnemore, Martha and Kathryn Sikkink. 'International Norm Dynamics and Political Change', *International Organization* 52/4 (Autumn 1998), 887–917.

Foreign Relations of the United States (FRUS), 1958–1960: Africa (Washington, DC: US Government Printing Office, 1992).

Forsythe, David. *The Internationalization of Human Rights* (Lexington: Lexington Books, 1991).

Forsythe, David. *Human Rights in International Relations* (Cambridge: Cambridge University Press, 2012).

Fortna, Virginia. *Does Peacekeeping Work? Shaping Belligerents' Choices after Civil War* (Princeton: Princeton University Press, 2008).

Fox, Fiona. 'New Humanitarianism: Does it Provide a Moral Banner for the 21st Century?', *Disasters* 25/4 (2001), 275–89.

Franck, Thomas. *The Structure of Impartiality. Examining the Riddle of One Law in a Fragmented World* (New York: The MacMillan Company, 1968).

Franck, Thomas. *The Power of Legitimacy Among Nations* (New York: Oxford University Press, 1990).

Franck, Thomas. *Recourse to Force* (Cambridge: Cambridge University Press, 2002).

French Ministry of Defence. *Principles for the Employment of the Armed Forces under UN Auspices* (Paris, 1995).

Friis, Karsten. 'Peacekeeping and Counter-insurgency: Two of a Kind?', *International Peacekeeping* 17/1 (2010), 49–66.

Frontline: The Triumph of Evil. PBS television broadcast, 1999. Transcript available at http://www.pbs.org/wgbh/pages/frontline/shows/evil/interviews/marchal.html

Fukuyama, Francis. 'The end of history?', *The National Interest* (1989), 3–18.

Garreton, Roberto. 'Mission impossible: the massacres in former Zaire', *Le Monde Diplomatique*, December 1997.

Gegout, Catherine. 'Causes and Consequences of the EU's Military Intervention', *European Foreign Affairs Review* 10/3 (2005), 427–33.

Gegout, Catherine. 'The West, Realism and Intervention in the Democratic Republic of Congo (1996–2006)', *International Peacekeeping* 16/2 (2009), 231–44.

George, Alexander and Andrew Bennett. *Case Studies and Theory Development in the Social Sciences* (Cambridge: MIT Press, 2005).

Gert, Bernard. *Morality: Its Nature and Justification*, 2nd ed. (Oxford: Oxford University Press, 2005).

Geyh, Charles. 'The Dimensions of Judicial Impartiality', *Florida Law Review* 65/2 (2014), 493–551.

Gibbs, David. 'The United Nations, International Peacekeeping and the Questions of "Impartiality": Revisiting the Congo Operation of 1960', *The Journal of Modern African Studies* 38/3 (2000), 359–82.

Gilmour, Andrew. 'The Future of Human Rights: A View from the United Nations', *Ethics & International Affairs* 28/2 (2014), 239–50.

Goddard, Stacie and Daniel Nexon. 'Paradigm Lost? Reassessing Theory of International Politics', *European Journal of International Relations* 11/1 (2005), 9–61.

Goldstein, Judith and Robert Keohane (eds.). *Ideas & Foreign Policy: Beliefs, Institutions, and Political Change* (Ithaca: Cornell University Press, 1993).

Goldstein, Judith, Miles Kahler, Robert Keohane, and Anne-Marie Slaughter. 'Introduction: Legalization and World Politics', *International Organization* 54/3 (2000), 385–99.

Gorur, Aditi. *Community Self-Protection Strategies: How Peacekeepers Can Help or Harm* (Washington, DC: Stimson Center, 2013).

Gowan, Richard. 'The Tragedy of 21st Century U.N. Peacekeeping', *World Politics Review* 19 (May 2010).

Gowan, Richard. 'Floating Down the River of History: Ban Ki-moon and Peacekeeping, 2007–2011', *Global Governance* 17/4 (2011), 399–416.

Gowan, Richard. 'Yes, Ban Ki- moon is America's Poodle. And no, that's not a good thing', *Politico Magazine*, 22 January 2014, http://www.politico.com/magazine/story/2014/01/ban-ki-moon-united-nations-united-states-102491

Grady, Kate. 'Sexual Exploitation and Abuse by UN Peacekeepers: A Threat to Impartiality', *International Peacekeeping* 17/2 (2010), 215–28.

Gray, Christine. 'Peacekeeping after the Brahimi Report: Is There a Crisis of Credibility for the UN?', *Journal of Conflict and Security Law* 6/2 (2001), 267–88.

Gray, Christine. *International Law and the Use of Force*, 3rd ed. (Oxford: Oxford University Press, 2008).

Greenhill, Kelly and Solomon Major. 'The Perils of Profiling: Civil War Spoilers and the Collapse of Intrastate Peace Accords', *International Security* 31/3 (2007), 7–40.

Griffith, John. *The Politics of the Judiciary*, 5th ed. (London: Harper Collins, 1997).

Guéhenno, Jean-Marie. 'On the Challenges and Achievements of Reforming UN Peace Operations', *International Peacekeeping* 9/2 (2002), 69–80.

Guéhenno, Jean-Marie. Address to the Challenges Project, London, March 2005, http://www.un.org/en/peacekeeping/articles/article000000.htm

Guéhenno, Jean-Marie. *Fog of Peace: A Memoir of International Peacekeeping in the 21st Century* (Washington: Brookings Institution Press, 2015).

Guidelines for the Protection of Civilians in AU Peace Operations (Addis Ababa: African Union, 2013).

Hammarskjöld, Dag. 'The Uses of Private Diplomacy', in *The Servant of Peace: A Selection of the Speeches and Statements of Dag Hammarskjöld*, edited by Wilder Foote (London: The Bodley Head, 1962).

Hammarskjöld, Dag. *To Speak for the World: Speeches and Statements by Dag Hammarskjöld, Secretary-General of the United Nations 1953–1961* (Stockholm: Atlantis, 2005).

Hammond, Grant. *Judicial Recusal: Principles, Process and Problems* (Oxford: Hart Publishing, 2009).

Hanrahan, Michael. 'The United Nations Special Committee on Peacekeeping Operations: From 1965 to 2005', in *International Peacekeeping: The Yearbook of International Peace Operations* (Leiden: Brill, 2007), 29–45.

Hasegawa, Yuka. 'The United Nations Assistance Mission in Afghanistan: Impartiality in New UN Peace Operations', *Journal of Intervention and Statebuilding* 2/2 (2008), 209–26.

Hatcher, Jessica and Alex Perry. 'Defining peacekeeping downward: the U.N. debacle in Eastern Congo', *TIME Magazine*, 26 November 2012.

Haver, Katherine. *Self-Protection in Conflict: Community Strategies for Keeping Safe in the Democratic Republic of Congo* (Oxford: Oxfam International, 2009).

Hawkins, Virgil. 'History Repeating Itself: The DRC and the Security Council', *African Security Review* 12/4 (2003), 47–55.

Hegel, Georg. *Philosophy of Right*, translated by T.M. Knox (Oxford: Clarendon Press, 1952).

Hemmer, Jort. *'We are Laying the Groundwork for Our Own Failure': The UN Mission in South Sudan and its Civilian Protection Strategy: An Early Assessment* (The Hague: Clingendael Institute, January 2013).

Higgins, Rosalyn. *United Nations Peacekeeping 1946–1967. Documents and Commentary* (Oxford: Oxford University Press, 1980).

Hirono, Miwa and Marc Lanteigne. 'Introduction: China and UN Peacekeeping', *International Peacekeeping* 18/3 (2011), 243–56.

Hirsch, John and Robert Oakley. *Somalia and Operation Restore Hope: Reflections on Peacemaking and Peacekeeping* (Washington, DC: United States Institute of Peace Press, 1995).

Hofferberth, Matthias and Christian Weber. 'Lost in Translation: A Critique of Constructivist Norm Research', *Journal of International Relations and Development* 18/1 (2015), 75–103.

Hoffmann, Danny. 'The City as Barracks: Freetown, Monrovia, and the Organization of Violence in Postcolonial African Cities', *Cultural Anthropology* 22/3 (2007), 400–28.

Hoffmann, Stanley. 'The Crisis of Liberal Internationalism', *Foreign Policy* 98 (1995), 159–77.

Holsti, Kalevi. *The State, War, and the State of War* (Cambridge: Cambridge University Press, 1996).

References

223

Holt, Victoria and Glyn Taylor. *Protecting Civilians in the Context of UN Peacekeeping Operations: Successes, Setbacks and Remaining Challenges* (New York: United Nations, 2009).

Hopgood, Stephen. *Keepers of the Flame* (Ithaca: Cornell University Press, 2007).

Hopgood, Stephen. *The Endtimes of Human Rights.* (Ithaca: Cornell University Press, 2013).

Howard, Lise Morje. *UN Peacekeeping in Civil Wars* (Cambridge: Cambridge University Press, 2008).

Hughes, Anne. 'Impartiality and the UN Observation Group in Lebanon, 1958', *International Peacekeeping* 9/4 (2004), 1–20.

Hulton, Susan. 'Council Working Methods and Procedures', in *The UN Security Council: From the Cold War to the 21st Century,* edited by David Malone (Boulder, CO: Lynne Rienner, 2004).

Human Rights Watch. *War Crimes in Kisangani: The Response of Rwandan-backed Rebels to the May 2002 Mutiny* (New York: 2002).

Human Rights Watch. *War Crimes in Bukavu* (New York: 2004).

Human Rights Watch. *Civilians Attacked in North Kivu* (New York: 2005).

Human Rights Watch. *Renewed Crisis in North Kivu* (New York: 2007).

Human Rights Watch. *Killings in Kiwanja: The UN's Inability to Protect Civilians* (New York: 2008).

Human Rights Watch. *We Will Crush You: The Restriction of Political Space in the Democratic Republic of Congo* (New York: 2008).

Human Rights Watch. *DR Congo: Brutal Rapes by Rebels and Army* (New York: 2009).

Human Rights Watch. *DR Congo: Civilian Cost of Military Operations is Unacceptable* (New York: 2009).

Human Rights Watch. *You Will Be Punished: Attacks on Civilians in Eastern Congo* (New York: 2009).

Human Rights Watch. *Always on the Run: The Vicious Cycle of Displacement in Eastern Congo* (New York: 2010).

Human Rights Watch. *DR Congo: War Crimes by M23, Congolese Army. Response to Crisis in the East Should Emphasize Justice* (New York: 2013).

Human Rights Watch. *DR Congo: Army, UN Failed to Stop Massacre* (New York: 2014).

Humphreys, Adam. 'The Heuristic Application of Explanatory Theories in International Relations', *European Journal of International Relations* 17/2 (2011), 257–77.

Hunt, Charles and Alex Bellamy. 'Mainstreaming the Responsibility to Protect in Peace Operations', *Civil Wars* 13/1 (2011), 1–20.

Hurd, Ian. 'Legitimacy, Power, and the Symbolic Life of the UN Security Council', *Global Governance* 8/1 (2002).

Hurd, Ian. 'The Strategic Use of Liberal Internationalism: Libya and the UN Sanctions, 1992–2003', *International Organization* 59/3 (2005).

Hurd, Ian. *After Anarchy: Legitimacy and Power in the United Nations Security Council* (Princeton: Princeton University Press, 2007).

Hurrell, Andrew. 'Norms and Ethics in International Relations', in *Handbook of International Relations,* edited by Walter Carlsnaes, Thomas Risse-Kappen, and Beth Simmons (London: Sage, 2002), 137–54.

Hurrell, Andrew and Terry MacDonald. 'Norms and Ethics in International Relations', in *Handbook of International Relations*, edited by Walter Carlsnaes, Thomas Risse-Kappen, and Beth Simmons (London: Sage, 2012).

Hutton, Lauren. *Prolonging the Agony of UNMISS: The Implementation Challenges of a New Mandate During a Civil War* (The Hague: Clingendael Institute, 2014).

IASC. *IASC Operational Guidelines: On the Protection of Persons in Situations of Natural Disasters*, The Brookings–Bern project on Internal Displacement, 2011.

Ignatieff, Michael. *The Warrior's Honor: Ethnic War and the Modern Conscience* (New York: Henry Holt & Co., 1998).

International Commission on Intervention and State Sovereignty (ICISS). *The Responsibility to Protect: Research, Bibliography, Background. Supplementary Volume* (Ottawa: International Development Research Council, 2001).

International Committee of the Red Cross. *Geneva Conventions: Article 3 (I), (a)–(d)* (Geneva: 1949).

International Committee of the Red Cross. *Professional Standards for Protection Work: Carried out by Humanitarian and Human Rights Actors in Armed Conflict and Other Situations of Violence* (Geneva: 2009).

International Committee of the Red Cross. *Letter Addressed to the UN Special Representative of the Secretary-General Alan Doss 'ICRC's Concerns about the Humanitarian Consequences of Ongoing Military Operations in the DRC and MONUC's Related Obligations under IHL.* (Kinshasa: Unpublished, 2010).

International Conference on the Great Lakes Region. *Report of the Regional Inter-Ministerial Extraordinary Meeting on the security situation in Eastern DRC* (Addis Ababa: Ethiopia, 11 July 2012).

International Court of Justice. *Certain Expenses of the United Nations* (Article 17, Paragraph 2, of the Charter*)*, Advisory Opinion (1962).

International Crisis Group. *Congo at War: A Briefing on the Internal and External Players in the Central African Conflict* (Nairobi/Brussels: 1998).

International Crisis Group. *Scramble for the Congo: Anatomy of an Ugly War* (Nairobi/Brussels: 2000).

International Crisis Group. *Uganda and Rwanda: Friends or Enemies?* (Nairobi/Brussels: 2000).

International Crisis Group. *From Kabila to Kabila: Prospects for Peace in the Congo* (Nairobi/Brussels: 2001).

International Crisis Group. *Congo Crisis: Military Intervention in Ituri* (Nairobi/Brussels: 2003).

International Crisis Group. *The Kivus: The Forgotten Crucible of the Congo Conflict* (Nairobi/Brussels: 2003).

International Crisis Group. *The Congo's Transition is Failing: Crisis in the Kivus* (Nairobi/Brussels: 2005).

International Crisis Group. *Congo: Bringing Peace to North Kivu* (Nairobi/Brussels: 2007).

International Crisis Group. *Mortality in the Democratic Republic of Congo: An Ongoing Crisis.* (Nairobi/Brussels: 2007).

International Crisis Group. *Congo: Five Priorities for a Peacebuilding Strategy* (Nairobi/Brussels: 2009).

International Crisis Group. *Congo: No Stability in Kivu despite a Rapprochement with Rwanda Africa* (Nairobi/Brussels: 2010).

International Crisis Group. *Eastern Congo: Why Stabilisation Failed* (Nairobi/Brussels: 2012).

International Crisis Group. *Congo: Ending the Status Quo* (Nairobi/Brussels: 2014).

International Peace Academy. *Peacekeeper's Handbook* (Oxford: Pergamon Press, 1984).

IRIN. 'DRC: UN condemns MLC threat against MONUC', Nairobi, 21 July 2000.

IRIN. 'DRC: Rebels expel three UN officials from the east', Nairobi, 3 June 2002.

IRIN. 'DRC: UN rapporteur to probe recent Kisangani violence', Nairobi, 12 June 2002.

IRIN. 'UN responds to HRW criticism over Kisangani massacre', Nairobi, 22 August 2002.

IRIN. 'UN envoy gives militiamen ultimatum to disarm', Kinshasa, 14 March 2005.

IRIN. 'MONUC gets tough on foreign armed groups', Bukavu, 22 March 2006.

Jacques, Isobelle. *Promoting effective international peace operations in increasingly complex environments: Conference report*, WP1336 (Wilton Park, 15–17 June 2014).

James, Alan. 'The United Nations, Peace-keeping, and Nonalignment', in *The Non-aligned and the United Nations*, edited by M.S. Rajan, V.S. Mani, and C.S.R. Murthy (New York: Oceana, 1987).

James, Alan. *Peacekeeping in International Politics* (London: Macmillan, 1990).

Johnstone, Ian. 'Dilemmas of Robust Peace Operations', in *Robust Peacekeeping: The Politics of Force* (New York: Center for International Cooperation, 2009).

Johnstone, Ian. 'Managing Consent in Contemporary Peacekeeping Operations', *International Peacekeeping* 18/2 (2011), 168–82.

Jollimore, Troy. 'Impartiality', in *The Stanford Encyclopedia of Philosophy* (Spring 2014 edition), edited by Edward N. Zalta, http://plato.stanford.edu/cgi-bin/encyclopedia/archinfo.cgi?entry=impartiality

Julius, Anthony. 'Human rights: the new secular religion', *Guardian* 19 April 2010.

Kagabo, Frank. '"Rwanda not in Congo" says US's Frazer', *The New Times*, 2 November 2008.

Kaldor, Mary. 'A Cosmopolitan Response to New Wars', *Peace Review* 8/4 (1996), 505–14.

Kaldor, Mary. *New and Old Wars: Organized Violence in a Global Era*, 2nd ed. (Cambridge: Polity Press, 2006).

Kalyvas, Stathis. '"New" and "Old" Civil Wars: A Valid Distinction?', *World Politics* 54/1 (2001), 99–118.

Kalyvas, Stathis. 'The Ontology of "Political Violence": Action and Identity in Civil Wars', *American Political Science Review* 1/3 (2003), 475–94.

Kaplan, Robert. *Balkan Ghosts: A Journey Through History* (New York: Vintage, 1994).

Karlsrud, John. 'The UN at War', *Third World Quarterly* 36/1 (2015), 40–54.

Karlsrud, John and Randi Solhjell. 'An Honourable Exit for MINURCAT?', *NUPI Policy Brief* 3 (2010).

Katzenstein, Peter. 'Coping with Terrorism: Norms and Internal Security in Germany and Japan', in *Ideas & Foreign Policy: Beliefs, Institutions, and Political Change*, edited by J. Goldstein and R.O Keohane (Ithaca: Cornell University Press, 1996), 265–95.

Kavanagh, Michael. 'A Review of Séverine Autesserre's "The Trouble with the Congo"', *African Security Review* 20/2 (2011), 86–93.

Kazadi, Sarah M. and Rebecca Sesny. 'Congolese see no end to president's final term', *New York Times,* 8 August 2015.

Kenneth, Roth and Ida Sawyer. 'Joseph Kabila Forever: The dangers of an extended presidency in the Democratic Republic of the Congo', *Foreign Policy,* 28 July 2015.

Keohane, Robert and David Victor. 'The Regime Complex for Climate Change', *The Harvard Project on International Climate Agreements* (Cambridge: Harvard University, 2010).

Klotz, Audie. 'Can We Speak a Common Language?', in *Constructing International Relations: The Next Generation,* edited by K.M. Fierke and K.E. Jorgensen (Armonk: M.E. Sharpe, 2001), 223–35.

Krasner, Stephen. *Sovereignty: Organized Hypocrisy* (Princeton: Princeton University Press, 1999).

Kratochwil, Friedrich. 'How Do Norms Matter?', in *The Role of Law in International Politics: Essays in International Relations and International Law,* edited by Michael Byers (Oxford: Oxford University Press, 2000), 35–68.

Kratochwil, Friedrich and John Gerard Ruggie. 'International Organization: A State of the Art on an Art of the State', *International Organization* 40/04 (1986), 753–75.

Krisch, Nico. 'The Decay of Consent: International Law in an Age of Global Public Goods', *American Journal of International Law* 108/1 (2014), 1–40.

Kroslak, Daniela. *The Role of France in the Rwandan Genocide* (London: Hurst & Co., 2007).

Lacey, Marc. '2 die in Congo demonstrations, as protesters storm U.N. sites', *The New York Times,* 4 June 2004.

Lacey, Marc. 'U.N. forces using tougher sanctions to secure peace', *The New York Times,* 23 May 2005.

Lancaster, Philip. 'End-of-Assignment Report', Chief DDR/RR, MONUC, 6 October 2008 (Internal).

Lancaster, Philip. 'Muddled Thoughts on a Muddled Topic: A Discussion of Child Soldiers, Human Rights and Peacekeeping', University of Victoria, 22 January 2009 (unpublished).

Larsen, Kjetil Mujezinović. *The Human Rights Treaty Obligations of Peacekeepers* (Cambridge: Cambridge University Press, 2012).

Leader, Nicholas. 'Proliferating Principles, or How to Sup with the Devil Without Getting Eaten', *The International Journal of Human Rights* 2/4 (1998), 1–27.

Lebor, Adam. *'Complicity with Evil.' The United Nations in the Age of Modern Genocide* (New Haven: Yale University Press, 2007).

Leebaw, Bronwyn. 'The Politics of Impartial Activism: Humanitarianism and Human Rights', *Perspectives on Politics* 5/2 (2007), 223–39.

Legro, Jeffrey. 'Which Norms Matter? Revisiting the "Failure" of Internationalism', *International Organization* 51/1 (1997), 31–63.

Legvold, Robert. 'The Revolution in Soviet Foreign Policy', *Foreign Affairs* 68/1 (1988), 82–98.

Lemarchand, René. *The Dynamics of Violence in Central Africa* (Philadelphia: University of Pennsylvania Press, 2009).

Levine, Daniel. 'Peacekeeper Impartiality: Standards, Processes, and Operations', *Journal of International Peacekeeping* 15/3–4 (2011), 3–4.

Lischer, Sarah Kenyon. 'Collateral Damage: Humanitarian Assistance as a Cause of Conflict', *International Security* 28/1 (2003), 79–109.

Local Voices Project. 'Armed Militias in Masisi: A Case Study of the People's Alliance for Free and Sovereign Congo (APCLS)', http://www.localvoicesproject.com/issue-01/armed-militias-in-masisi

Louis, William Roger. *Ends of British Imperialism: The Scramble for Empire, Suez, and Decolonization* (London: IB Tauris & Co., 2007).

Lucy, William. 'The Possibility of Impartiality', *Oxford Journal of Legal Studies* 25/1 (2005), 3–31.

Lusaka Agreement, 1999, http://peacemaker.un.org/drc-lusaka-agreement99

Luttwak, Edward. 'Give War a Chance', *Foreign Affairs* 78/4 (1999), 36–44.

Lynch, Colum. 'India's withdrawal of helicopters from Congo points to wider trend', *Washington Post*, 14 June 2011.

Lynch, Colum. 'How Rice dialed down the pressure on Rwanda', *Turtle Bay*, 3 December 2012.

Lynch, Colum. 'The Blue Helmet Caste System', *Foreign Policy*, 11 April 2013.

Lynch, Colum. 'A Mission That was Set up to Fail', *Foreign Policy*, 8 April 2014.

MacFarlane, Neil and Yuen Foong Khong. *Human Security and the United Nations* (Bloomington: Indiana University Press, 2006).

Macqueen, Norrie. *Peacekeeping and the International System* (Abingdon: Routledge, 2006).

Macqueen, Norrie. *United Nations Peacekeeping in Africa since 1960* (Abingdon: Routledge, 2014).

McCrummen, Stephanie. 'Abusive Congolese colonel got aid', *Washington Post*, 9 March 2010.

Malkki, Liisa. 'Speechless Emissaries: Refugees, Humanitarianism, and Dehistoricization', *Cultural Anthropology* 11/3 (1996), 377–404.

Manson, Katrina. 'Exclusive: Congo war indictee says directs U.N.-backed ops', *Reuters*, 6 October 2010.

Marks, Joshua. 'The Pitfalls of Action and Inaction: Civilian Protection in MONUC's Peacekeeping Operations', *African Security Review* 16/3 (2007).

Marriage, Zoe. 'Defining Morality: DFID and the Great Lakes', *Third World Quarterly* 27/3 (2006), 477–90.

Mataboge, Mmanaledi. 'DRC's M23: "We didn't start the war"', *Mail & Guardian*, 4 September 2013.

Mazower, Mark. *No Enchanted Palace: The End of Empire and the Ideological Origins of the United Nations* (Princeton: Princeton University Press, 2009).

Mealer, Bryan. *All Things Must Fight to Live: Stories of War and Deliverance in Congo* (New York: Bloomsbury Press, 2008).

Mendus, Susan. *Impartiality in Moral and Political Philosophy* (Oxford: Oxford University Press, 2002).

Mendus, Susan. 'Impartiality', in *The Oxford Handbook of Political Theory*, edited by John S. Dryzek, Bonnie Honig and Anne Phillips (Oxford: Oxford University Press, 2000).

Meron, Theodor. 'Judicial Independence and Impartiality in International Criminal Tribunals', *AJIL* 99/2 (2005), 359–60.

Merrills, J.G. *International Dispute Settlement*, 5th ed. (Cambridge: Cambridge University Press, 2011).

Metcalfe, Victoria, Alison Giffen and Samir Elhawary. *UN Integration and Humanitarian Space: An Independent Study Commissioned by the UN Integration Steering Group* (London: Humanitarian Policy Group, Overseas Development Institute, 2011).

Melzer, Nils. *Interpretive Guidance on the Notion of Direct Participation in Hostilities Under International Humanitarian Law* (Geneva: ICRC, May 2009).

Mill, John Stuart. 'Utilitarianism', in *On Liberty and Utilitarianism* (Knopf: Everyman's Library, Vol. 81, 1992).

Minow, Martha. 'Stripped Down Like a Runner or Enriched by Experience: Bias and Impartiality of Judges and Jurors', *William and Mary Law Review* 33/4 (1992).

MONUC. 'Briefing Presentation', 4 December 2004 (Internal)

MONUC. 'Briefing Presentation', 21 December 2004 (Internal).

MONUC. 'OP DJUGU–III', Eastern Command, Powerpoint Presentation, March 2005 (Internal).

MONUC. 'MONUC and the Bukavu Crisis 2004', Best Practices Unit, Department of Peacekeeping Operations, New York, March 2005 (Restricted).

MONUC. 'Military Briefing', Goma, 30 March 2005 (Internal).

MONUC. 'Divisional Commander's Initial Campaign Plan for Operations in DRC East', 4 April 2005 (Restricted).

MONUC. 'Divisional Commander's Operational Directive', Eastern Division, July 2005 (Restricted).

MONUC. *Civil Affairs Special Report*, 28 June 2006 (Internal).

MONUC. 'List of Operations Conducted Since June 2005', Powerpoint 2007 (Internal).

MONUC. 'Force Directive, No. 132', 2008 (Internal).

MONUC. 'Report on Election Violence', Human Rights Division, 2008 (Internal).

MONUC. 'Protection Analysis', Civil Affairs Section, Goma, 6 December 2008 (Internal).

MONUC. 'Summary of Protection Issues Associated with the Coalition Operations against FDLR and Fast-tracked FARDC Integration Process', Civil Affairs Section, 20 February 2009 (Internal).

MONUC. 'Protection Impact of Umoja Wetu', Powerpoint Presentation, 28 February 2009 (Internal).

MONUC. 'Evaluation of the Impact of Kimia II by MONUC-NK Substantive Sections', 6 June 2009 (Internal).

MONUC. 'Kimia II–Implications for the Protection of Civilians', Powerpoint Presentation for the Visit of SRSG Alan Doss, 7 June 2009 (Internal).

MONUC. 'A Preliminary Assessment of the Impact of the Joint Protection Teams', Civil Affairs Section, October 2009 (Internal).

MONUC. 'Incidents of Violence in the Area of Dongo, Equateur Province', Joint Mission Analysis Cell (JMAC), 3 December 2009 (Restricted).

MONUC. 'Force Commander Visit to Gemena 10 December 2009: After Action Report', Interoffice Memorandum, 11 December 2009 (Internal).

MONUC. 'Operating Guidelines', viewed by author in Goma, January 2010 (Restricted).

MONUSCO. 'A New Approach To Protection of Civilians (PoC)', Powerpoint Presentation, MONUSCO FC, SMG-P, 7 September 2013 (Internal).

MONUSCO. 'Mission Concept: Peace it! Together on the Journey to Lasting Peace in the Democratic Republic of Congo', 2013.

MONUSCO. *PoC Handbook: Practical protection for civilians handbook for peacekeepers*, Protection Working Group, Kinshasa, 2013.

Myers, Steven Lee. 'Ex-senator Feingold chosen as Special Envoy to African region', *New York Times*, 18 June 2013.

Nagel, Thomas. *Equality and Partiality* (Oxford: Oxford University Press, 1990).

Nathan, Andrew. 'How human rights became our ideology', *New Republic*, 16 November 2012.

NATO. *Bi-MNC Directive for NATO Doctrine for Peace Support Operations* (Brussels: 1998).

New York Times. 'The well-fed dead in Bosnia', 15 July 1992.

Newman, Edward and Oliver Richmond. *Challenges to Peacebuilding: Managing Spoilers During Conflict Resolution* (New York: United Nations University Press, 2006).

Nicholas, Herbert. 'UN Peace Forces and the Changing Globe: The Lessons of Suez and Congo', *International Organization* 17/2 (1963), 321–37.

Non-Aligned Movement. *The Jakarta Message: A Call for Collective Action and the Democratization of International Relations*. Tenth Conference of Heads of State or Government of Non-aligned Countries (Jakarta: 6 September 1992).

Non-Aligned Movement. *Final Document of the Sixteenth Conference of Heads of State or Government of Non-Aligned Nations* (Tehran: 31 August 2012).

Nordstrom, Carolyn. *A Different Kind of War Story* (Philadelphia: University of Philadelphia Press, 1997).

Nzongola-Ntalaja, Georges. *The Congo from Leopold to Kabila: A People' s History* (London: Zed Books, 2002).

Nzongola-Ntalaja, Georges. 'Patrice Lumumba: the Most Important Assassination of the 20th Century', *The Guardian*, 17 January 2011.

O'Brien, Conor Cruise with Feliks Topolski. *The United Nations: Sacred Drama* (New York: Simon and Schuster, 1968).

Olivier, Darren. 'The FIB Goes to War', *African Defence Review*, 29 August 2013, http://www.africandefence.net/the-fib-goes-to-war

Onuf, Nicholas. *World of Our Making: Rules and Rule in Social Theory and International Relations* (Columbia: University of South Carolina Press, 1989).

'Open letter from M23 political leader Bertrand Bisimwa's to Ban Ki-moon', 027/Pres-M23/2013, 22 May 2013.

Orford, Anne. *International Authority and the Responsibility to Protect* (New York: Cambridge University Press, 2011).

Owens, Patricia. *Between War and Politics: International Relations and the Thought of Hannah Arendt* (Oxford: Oxford University Press, 2007).

Oxfam. *Self-Protection in Conflict: Community strategies for keeping safe in the Democratic Republic of Congo* (Oxford: Oxfam International, 2009)

Oxfam. *Waking the Devil: The Impact of Forced Disarmament on Civilians in the Kivus* (Oxford: Oxfam International, 2009).

Paddon, Emily. 'Partnering for Peace: Implications and Dilemmas', *International Peacekeeping* 18/5 (2011), 516–33.

Paddon, Emily. 'Peacekeeping in the Congo: Implementation of the Protection of Civilians Norm', in Alexander Betts and Phil Orchard, *Implementation & World Politics: How International Norms Change Practice* (Oxford: Oxford University Press, 2014), 160–78.

Paddon, Emily and Guillaume Lacaille. *Stabilizing the Congo* (University of Oxford, Refugee Studies Centre Policy Brief, 8, December 2011).

Paris, Roland. 'Peace-building and the Limits of Liberal Internationalism', *International Security* 22/2 (1997), 54–89.

Paris, Roland. 'Broadening the Study of Peace Operations', *International Studies Review* 2/3 (2000), 27–44.

Paris, Roland. 'International Peacebuilding and the "Mission Civilisatrice"', *Review of International Studies* 28/4 (2002), 637–56.

Paris, Roland. *At War's End: Building Peace after Civil Conflict* (Cambridge: Cambridge University Press, 2004).

Paris, Roland. 'The Geopolitics of Peace Operations: A Research Agenda', *International Peacekeeping* 21/4 (2014), 501–8.

Pattison, James. 'Humanitarian Intervention and a Cosmopolitan UN Force', *Journal of International Political Theory* 4/1 (2008), 126–45.

Percy, Sarah. *Mercenaries: The History of a Norm in International Relations* (Oxford: Oxford University Press, 2007).

Perry, Alex. 'The man who would be (Congo's) king', *Time World*, 27 November 2008.

Peter, Mateja. *Emerging Power and Peace Operations: An Agenda for Research* (Oslo: Norwegian Institute of International Affairs, October 2014).

Pictet, Jean. *The Fundamental Principles of the Red Cross* (Geneva: Henry Dunant Institute, 1979).

Point de Presse du Ministre de la communication et medias, Porte-parole du Gouvernement, 16 February 2015.

Polgreen, Lydia. 'A massacre in Congo, despite nearby support', *The New York Times*, 11 December 2008.

Ponthieu, Aurelie, Christoph Vogel and Katharine Derderian. 'Without Precedent or Prejudice? UNSC Resolution 2098 and its Potential Implications for Humanitarian Space in Eastern Congo and Beyond', *Journal of Humanitarian Assistance*, 21 January 2014, https://sites.tufts.edu/jha/archives/2032

Posner, Eric A. *The Twilight of Human Rights Law* (Oxford: Oxford University Press, 2014).

Power, Samantha. *A Problem from Hell: America and the Age of Genocide* (New York: Basic Books, 2002).

Price, Richard. *Chemical Weapons Taboo* (Ithaca: Cornell University Press, 1997).

Price, Richard (ed.). *Moral Limit and Possibility in World Politics* (Cambridge: Cambridge University Press, 2008).

Prunier, Gerard. *Africa's World War: Congo, the Rwandan Genocide, and the Making of a Continental Catastrophe* (New York: Oxford University Press, 2009).

Pugh, Michael (ed.). *UN, Peace and Force* (London: Frank Cass, 1997).

Pugh, Michael. 'Peacekeeping and Critical Theory', *International Peacekeeping* 11/1 (2004), 39–58.

Raban, Ofer. *Modern Legal Theory and Judicial Impartiality* (London: Routledge, 2012).

Raghavan, Sudarsan. 'Record number of U.N. peacekeepers fails to stop African wars', *Washington Post*, 3 January 2014.

Rawls, John. 'Two Concepts of Rules', *The Philosophical Review* 55 (1955), 3–32.

Rawls, John. 'Justice as Fairness: Political not Metaphysical', *Philosophy and Public Affairs* 14/3 (Summer 1985), 223–51.

Reuters. 'A massacre in Congo, despite nearby support', 4 March 2005.

Reuters. 'After violent decades, Congo finally installs an elected leader', 7 December 2006.

Reuters. 'African rivalries weaken U.N. hand against rebels in Congo', 22 October 2014.

Review Conference on the Rome Statue of the International Criminal Court (ICC). Kampala: 2010, http://www.iccnow.org/?mod=review

Reynaert, Julie. 'MONUC/MONUSCO and Civilian Protection in the Kivus', *IPIS*, 2011.

Reyntjens, Filip. *The Great African War: Congo and Regional Geo Politics, 1996–2006* (New York: Cambridge University Press, 2009).

Rhoads, Christopher. 'Peacekeepers at war', *The Wall Street Journal*, 23 June 2012.

Rice, Xan. 'Panic grips Congo as rebels advance on town of Goma', *The Guardian*, 30 October 2008.

Richmond, Oliver. 'Critical Research Agendas for Peace: The Missing Link in the Study of International Relations', *Alternatives: Global, Local, Political* 32/2 (April–June 2007), 247–74.

Rieff, David. *A Bed for the Night: Humanitarianism in Crisis* (New York: Simon & Schuster, 2002).

Risse, Thomas. '"Let's Argue!" Communicative Action in World Politics', *International Organization* 54/1 (2000), 1–39.

Risse, Thomas, Stephen Ropp, and Kathryn Sikkink (eds.). *The Power of Human Rights: International Norms and Domestic Change* (Cambridge: Cambridge University Press, 1999).

Roberts, Adam. 'The United Nations and International Security', *Survival* 35/2 (1993), 3–30.

Roberts, Adam. 'The Crisis in UN Peacekeeping', *Survival* 36/3 (1994), 93–120.

Roberts, Adam. 'From San Francisco to Sarajevo: The UN and the Use of Force', *Survival* 37/4 (1995), 7–29.

Roberts, Adam. 'Proposals for UN Standing Forces: A Critical History', in *The United Nations Security Council and War: The Evolution of Thought and Practice since 1945*, edited by Vaughan Lowe, Adam Roberts, Jennifer Welsh, and Dominik Zaum (Oxford: Oxford University Press, 2008), 99–129.

Roberts, Adam and Benedict Kingsbury (eds.). *United Nations Divided World: The UN's Role in International Relations*, 2nd ed. (Oxford: Oxford University Press, 1993).

Roberts, Adam and Dominik Zaum. *Selective Security: War and the United Nations Security Council Since 1945* (Abingdon: Routledge, 2008).

Roberts, David. 'More Honoured in the Breech: Consent and Impartiality in the Cambodian Peacekeeping Operation', *International Peacekeeping* 4/1 (1997), 1–25.

Romano, Cesare. 'The Shift from the Consensual to the Compulsory Paradigm in International Adjudication: Elements for a Theory of Consent', *New York University Journal of International Law and Politics* 39 (2006), 791–866.

Romano, Cesare, Karen Alter, and Yuval Shany (eds.). *The Oxford Handbook of International Adjudication* (Oxford: Oxford University Press, 2013).

Rome Statute of the International Criminal Court, 1998, https://www.icc-cpi.int/nr/rdonlyres/ea9aeff7-5752-4f84-be94-0a655eb30e16/0/rome_statute_english.pdf

Rosanvallon, Pierre. *Democratic Legitimacy: Impartiality, Reflexivity, Proximity* (Princeton: Princeton University Press, 2011).

Rosenblum, Peter. 'Irrational Exuberance: the Clinton Administration in Africa', *Current History* 101/655 (2002), 195–202.

Ross, Aaron. 'Congo expels top U.N. official after report on police abuses', *Reuters*, 16 October 2014.

Rothstein, Bo and Jan Teorell. 'What is Quality of Government? A Theory of Impartial Government Institutions', *Governance* 2/2 (2008), 165–90.

Rubinstein, Robert. 'Intervention and Culture: An Anthropological Approach to Peace Operations', *Security Dialogue* 36/4 (2005), 527–44.

Ruggie, John. *Constructing the World Polity: Essays on International Institutionalization* (London and New York: Routledge, 1998).

Schabas, William. *An Introduction to the International Criminal Court* (Cambridge: Cambridge University Press, 2011).

Scharpf, Fritz. *Governing Europe: Effective and Democratic?* (Oxford: Oxford University Press, 1999).

Schimmelfennig, Frank. 'The Community Trap: Liberal Norms, Rhetorical Action, and the Eastern Enlargement of the European Union', *International Organization* 55/1 (2001), 47–80.

Shaw, Mark and Walter Kemp. 'Spotting the Spoilers: A Guide to Analyzing Organized Crime', *International Peace Institute Policy Papers* (New York: 2012).

Shaw, Martin. *The New Western Way of War: Risk-transfer War and its Crisis in Iraq* (Cambridge: Polity Press, 2005).

Sheeran, Scott and Stephanie Case. *The Intervention Brigade: Legal Issues for the UN in the Democratic Republic of the Congo* (New York: International Peace Institute, 2014).

Short, Clare. *The Vaughan Memorial Lecture: The UK and Post-Genocidal Rwanda* (Oxford: Oxford Central Africa Forum, November 2012).

Sikkink, Kathryn. *The Justice Cascade: How Human Rights Prosecutions Are Changing World Politics* (New York: Norton, 2011).

Simons, Marlise. 'Dutch peacekeepers are found responsible for deaths', *New York Times*, 6 September 2013.

Sloan, James. *The Militarisation of Peacekeeping in the 21st Century* (Portland: Hart, 2011).

Smis, Stefaan and Theodore Trefon. 'Congo: Waiting for Godot', *Review of African Political Economy* 30/98 (2003), 671–8.

Statement by Ambassador Peter Wilson, Deputy Permanent Representative of the UK Mission to the UN, to the Security Council Open Debate on Protection of Civilians, 12 February 2014. Speech available at http://www.gov.uk/government/speeches/protecting-civilians-transcends-politics

Statement by Mr Mohammed Adeep, Honorable Member of Parliament and Member of the Indian Delegation, on Agenda Item 53: Comprehensive Review of the Whole Question of Peacekeeping Operations in all their Aspects, 30 October 2013, https://papersmart.unmeetings.org/media2/703760/item-53-india.pdf

Statement of SRSG Martin Kobler to the Security Council, 'Building on the momentum', 14 March 2014.

Stearns, Jason. 'The mystery of Dongo', *Congo Siasa* blog, http://congosiasa.blogspot.com/2010/01/mystery-of-dongo.html, 6 January 2010.

Stearns, Jason. *Dancing in the Glory of Monsters: The Collapse of the Congo and the Great War of Africa* (New York: Public Affairs, 2011).

Stearns, Jason. 'The Cat's Cradle of Congolese Politics', *World Peace Foundation: Tufts University*, 30 November 2012.

Stearns, Jason. *From CNDP to M23: The Evolution of an Armed Movement in Eastern Congo* (London: Rift Valley Institute, 2012).

Stearns, Jason. *North Kivu: The Background to Conflict in North Kivu Province of Eastern Congo* (London: Rift Valley Institute, 2012).

Stearns, Jason. *PARECO: Land, Local Strongmen and the Roots of Militia Politics in North Kivu* (London: Rift Valley Institute, 2012).

Stearns, Jason. 'Rwandan Ghosts', *Foreign Policy*, November 2012.

Stearns, Jason. *Strongman of the Eastern DRC: A Profile of General Bosco Ntaganda* (London: Rift Valley Institute, 2013).

Stearns, Jason. 'Poll: How the people of North Kivu feel about their government, elections, and the international community', *Congo Siasa* blog, http://congosiasa.blogspot.com/2015/06/poll-how-people-of-north-kivu-feel.html, 17 June 2015.

Stedman, Stephen. 'Consent, Neutrality, and Impartiality in the Tower of Babel and on the Frontlines: United Nations Peacekeeping in the 1990s', in *Managing Arms in Peace Process: The Issues, Disarmament and Conflict Resolution Project* (New York: UNIDIR, 1996).

Stedman, Stephen. 'Spoiler Problems in Peace Processes', *International Security* 22/2 (1997), 5–53.

Stockton, Nicholas. *Humanitarianism Bound: Coherence and Catastrophe in the Congo 1998–2002* (Unpublished study for the Centre for Humanitarian Dialogue, Geneva, 2003).

Suganami, Hidemi. 'Narrative Explanation and International Relations: Back to the Basics', *Millennium: Journal of International Studies* 37/2 (2008), 327–56.

Swaak-Goldman, Olivia. 'Peacekeeping operations and the International Criminal Court: presentation at the International Institute for International Law', Sanremo, Italy, 6 September 2008, http://tableronde08.blogspot.co.uk/2008/03/peacekeeping-operations-and.html

Tannenwald, Nina. *The Nuclear Taboo: the United States and the Non-Use of Nuclear Weapons since 1945* (Cambridge: Cambridge University Press, 2007).

Tardy, Thierry. 'A Critique of Robust Peacekeeping in Contemporary Peace Operations', *International Peacekeeping* 18/2 (2011), 152–67.

Tardy, Thierry. 'For a Renewed Consensus on UN Peacekeeping Operations', Paper presented at *GCSP Geneva Papers: Conference Series* 23 (New York: 16–17 June 2011).

Tardy, Thierry. 'Emerging Powers and Peacekeeping: an Unlikely Normative Clash' (Geneva: GCSP Policy Paper, 2012/13).

Taylor, Charles. 'Neutrality in the University', in *Neutrality and Impartiality: The University and Political Commitment*, edited by Alan Montefiore (Cambridge: Cambridge University Press, 1975).

Teitel, Ruti. *Humanity's Law* (Oxford: Oxford University Press, 2011).

Terry, Fiona. *Condemned to Repeat? The Paradox of Humanitarian Action* (Ithaca: Cornell University Press, 2002).

Thakur, Ramesh. 'From Peacekeeping to Peace Enforcement: The UN Operation in Somalia', *The Journal of Modern African Studies* 32/3 (1994), 387–410.

Tharoor, Shashi. 'Should UN Peacekeeping Go "Back to the Basics?"', *Survival* 37/4 (Winter 1995–6), 52–65.

The Hindu Times. 'India withdrawing helicopters from U.N.'s Congo mission,' 16 June 2011.

The Individualization of War Project, European University Institute, http://iow.eui.eu.

The McCain Institute and Howard G. Buffett Foundation. *North Kivu Public Opinion Survey* (Unpublished draft 2014).

Titeca, Kristof and Koen Vlassenroot. 'Rebels Without Borders in the Rwenzori Borderland? A Biography of the Allied Democratic Forces', *Journal of Eastern African Studies* 6/1 (2012), 154–76.

Traub, James. *The Best Intentions: Kofi Annan and the UN in an Era of American World Power* (New York: Farrar, Straus and Giroux, 2006).

Tsagourias, Nicholas. 'Consent, Neutrality/Impartiality and the Use of Force in Peacekeeping: Their Constitutional Dimension', *Journal of Conflict and Security Law* 11/3 (2006), 465–82.

Tully, James. 'The Unfreedom of the Moderns in Comparison to Their Ideals of Constitutional Democracy', *The Modern Law Review* 65/2 (2002), 204–28.

UK Ministry of Defence. *Peace Support Operations: Joint Warfare Publication 3–50 Joint Warfare Publication* (London, 1997).

UN News Centre. 'UN mission sets up security zone in eastern DR Congo, gives rebels 48 hour ultimatum', 30 July 2013.

United Nations. *Charter of the United Nations* (1945), http://www.un.org/en/documents/charter/index.shtml

United Nations. *Privileges and Immunities of the United Nations,* A/RES/22 A(I) (1946).

United Nations. *'Uniting for Peace' Resolution,* A/377 A (1950).

United Nations. *Aide-memoire on the Basis for the Presence and Functioning of the United Nations Emergency Force in Egypt,* A/3375 (1956).

United Nations. *Creation of an Emergency International United Nations Force to Secure the Cessation of Hostilities in the Suez Canal,* A/RES/998 (1956).

United Nations. *Calling for the Withdrawal of Forces in the Suez Crisis,* A/RES/1002 (1956).

United Nations. *Establishment of a United Nations Command for the Emergency Force,* A/RES/1000 (1956).

United Nations. *First Emergency Session,* A/562 A (1956).

United Nations. *Report of the Secretary-General on Basic Points for the Presence and Functioning in Egypt of the United Nations Emergency Force,* A/3302 (1956).

United Nations. *Summary study of the Experience Derived from the Establishment of the United Nations Emergency Force,* A/3943 (1958).

United Nations. *Cable from the President and the Prime Minister of Congo to the Secretary-General,* S/4382 (1960).

United Nations. *Introduction to the Annual Report of the Secretary-General of the Work of the Organization, 16 June 1959–15 June 1960,* A/4390/Add.1 (1960).

United Nations. *Letter of 9 September 1960 from First Deputy Foreign Minister of USSR,* S/4497 (1960).

United Nations. *UNSC Resolution on the Congo Question,* S/RES/143 (1960).

United Nations. *UNSC Resolution on the Congo Question,* S/RES/161 (1961).

United Nations. *UNSC Resolution on the Congo Question,* S/RES/169 (1961).

United Nations. *Note by the Secretary-General Concerning Certain Aspects of the Function and Operation of the UN Peacekeeping Force in Cyprus,* S/5653 (1964).

United Nations. *Report by the Secretary-General on the United Nations Operation in Cyprus,* S/5950 (1964).

United Nations. *Report of the Special Committee on the Principles of International Law Concerning Friendly Relations and Co-operation Among States,* A/5746 (1964).

United Nations. *Comprehensive Review of the Whole Question of Peacekeeping Operations in all their Aspects,* A/RES/2006 (XIX) (1965).

United Nations. *Report of the Secretary-General in Pursuance of General Assembly Resolution 1123 (XI),* A/3512 (1972).

United Nations. *Report of the Secretary-General on the Implementation of the Security Council Resolution,* S/11052/Rev.1 (1973).

United Nations. *Report of the Special Committee on Peace-keeping Operations, 11th Report of the Working Group, Draft Formulae for Articles of Agreed Guidelines for United Nations Peace-keeping Operations,* A/32/394/AnnII/App.I (1977).

United Nations. *Comprehensive Review of the Whole Question of Peace-Keeping Operations in All Their Aspects: Model Status-of-Forces Agreement for Peace-Keeping Operations,* A/45/594 (1990).

United Nations. *Arms Embargo in Yugoslavia,* S/RES/713 (1991).

United Nations. *An Agenda for Peace: Preventive Diplomacy and Related Matters,* A/47/277-S/24111 (1992).

United Nations. *Note by the President of the Security Council,* S/23500 (1992).

United Nations. *Condemning Attacks on UNOSOM II,* S/RES/837 (1993).

United Nations. *Report of the Secretary-General on Rwanda,* S/1994/728 (1994).

United Nations. *Supplement to an Agenda for Peace: Position Paper of the Secretary-General on the Occasion of the Fiftieth Anniversary of the United Nations,* A/50/60-S/1995/1 (1995).

United Nations. 'Former Yugoslavia - UNPROFOR' (New York: Department of Public Information, 1996), http://www.un.org/en/peacekeeping/missions/past/unprof_b.htm

United Nations. *The Establishment of UNAMSIL*, S/RES/1270 (1999).

United Nations. *On the Protection of Civilians in Armed Conflict*, A/RES/1265 (1999).

United Nations. *Report of the Secretary-General on the Protection of Civilians in Armed Conflict*, S/1999/957 (1999).

United Nations. *Report of the Secretary-General pursuant to General Assembly Resolution 53/35: The Fall of Srebrenica*, A/54/549 (1999).

United Nations. 'Secretary-General says Peacekeeping can no Longer be Seen in Isolation' (Dublin: Address of SG Kofi Annan to the National University of Ireland, 1999), Press Release SG/SM/6870.

United Nations. 'Speech by the Secretary-General' (Washington, DC: Address of SG Kofi Annan at Georgetown University, 1999), Press Release SG/SM/6870.

United Nations. *Comprehensive Review of the Whole Question of Peacekeeping Operations in All their Aspects*, A/54/839 (2000).

United Nations. *Comprehensive Review of the Whole Question of Peacekeeping Operations in All their Aspects*, A/RES/55/135 (2000).

United Nations. *Fourth Report of the Secretary-General on the United Nations Organization Mission in the Democratic Republic of the Congo*, S/2000/888 (2000).

United Nations. *No Exit without Strategies*, Statement by Mr Kamalesh Sharma, 15 November 2000, http://www.un.int/india/ind420.htm

United Nations. *Report of the Panel on United Nations Peace Operations*. A/55/305-S/2000/809 (2000).

United Nations. *Report of the Secretary-General on the Implementation of the Recommendations of the Special Committee on Peacekeeping Operations*, A/54/670 (2000).

United Nations. *Report of the Secretary-General on the United Nations Organization Mission in the Democratic Republic of the Congo*, S/2000/30 (2000).

United Nations. *The Situation Concerning Sierra Leone*, S/RES/1313 (2000).

United Nations. *Third Report of the Secretary-General on the United Nations Organization Mission in the Democratic Republic of the Congo*, S/2000/566 (2000).

United Nations. *United Nations Millennium Declaration*, A/RES/55/2 (2000).

United Nations. 'United Nations Peacekeeping: A Changing Landscape' (Ottawa: Address of DSG Louise Fréchette to the Canadian Institute of International Affairs and the United Nations Association of Canada, 2000), Press Release DSG/SM/96.

United Nations. S/PV.4194 (2000).

United Nations. S/PV.4257 (2001).

United Nations. S/PV.4143.1 (2002).

United Nations. *Handbook on United Nations Multidimensional Peacekeeping Operations* (New York: Department of Peacekeeping Operations, 2003).

United Nations. *Second Special Report of the Secretary-General on the United Nations Organization Mission in the Democratic Republic of the Congo*, S/2003/566 (2003).

United Nations. *The Situation Concerning the Democratic Republic of the Congo*, S/RES/1493 (2003).

United Nations. *Relationship Agreement Between the United Nations and the International Criminal Court*, A/58/874 (2004).

United Nations. *The Situation Concerning the Democratic Republic of the Congo*, S/RES/1565 (2004).

United Nations. *2005 World Summit Outcome*, A/60/2005 (2005).

United Nations. *A Comprehensive Strategy to Eliminate Future Sexual Exploitation and Abuse in United Nations Peacekeeping Operations*, A/59/710 (2005).

United Nations. *The Situation Concerning the Democratic Republic of the Congo*, S/RES/1592 (2005).

United Nations. *The Situation Concerning the Democratic Republic of the Congo*, S/RES/1596 (2005).

United Nations. 'Background Note', *Workshop on Fundamental Principles of UN Peacekeeping. Stockholm, 26–28 September 2006* (New York: Department of Peacekeeping Operations, 2006).

United Nations. *United Nations Peace Operations Year in Review 2005*, February 2006, http://www.un.org/en/peacekeeping/resources/publications.shtml

United Nations. *The Situation Concerning the Democratic Republic of the Congo*, S/RES/1794 (2007).

United Nations. *Twenty-third Report of the Secretary-General on the United Nations Organization Mission in the Democratic Republic of the Congo*, S/2007/156 (2007).

United Nations. *Mission Report: Military Component Evaluation—United Nations Organization Mission in the Democratic Republic of the Congo (MONUC)* (New York, 19–29 April 2008, Internal).

United Nations. *The Situation Concerning the Democratic Republic of the Congo*, S/RES/1856 (2008).

United Nations. *United Nations Peacekeeping Operations: Principles and Guidelines* (New York: Department of Peacekeeping Operations, 2008).

United Nations. *Consolidated Report on Investigations Conducted by the United Nations Joint Human Rights office (UNJHRO) into Grave Human Rights Abuses Committed in Kiwanja, North Kivu, in November 2008.* (September 2009).

United Nations. *Final Report of the Group of Experts on the Democratic Republic of the Congo*, S/2009/603 (2009).

United Nations. *A New Partnership Agenda: Charting A New Horizon for UN Peacekeeping* (New York: Department of Peacekeeping Operations and Department of Field Support, 2009).

United Nations. *Operations Year in Review 2009* (New York: 2009) http://www.un.org/en/peacekeeping/resources/publications.shtml

United Nations. *Report of the Special Committee on Peacekeeping Operations and its Working Group at the 2009 Substantive Session*, A/63/19 (2009).

United Nations. *Report of the Secretary General on Implementing the Responsibility to Protect*, A/63/677 (2009).

United Nations. S/PV.6253 (2009).

United Nations. *Draft Concept Note on Robust Peacekeeping* (New York: Department of Peacekeeping Operations, 2010).

United Nations. *Final Report of the Group of Experts on the Democratic Republic of the Congo*, S/2010/596 (2010).

United Nations. *Peacekeeping: Looking into the Future.* Speech made by Ambassador Hardeep Singh Puri, *Permanent Mission of India to the United Nation*, 23 February 2010.

United Nations. *Report of the Mapping Exercise Documenting the Most Serious Violations of Human Rights and International Humanitarian Law Committed within the*

Territory of the Democratic Republic of the Congo between March 1993 and June 2003 (New York: United Nations High Commission for Human Rights, 2010).

United Nations. *Report of the Special Committee on Peacekeeping Operations 2010 Substantive Session*, A/64/19 (2010).

United Nations. *Report of the Special Rapporteur on Extrajudicial, Summary or Arbitrary Executions*, A/HRC/14/24/Add.3 [Advance unedited version] (2010).

United Nations. 'UN Standards of Conduct' (New York: Department of Field Support, Information and Communications Technology Division, 2010) http://cdu.unlb.org/UNStandardsofConduct/CodeofConduct.aspx

United Nations. *Final Report of the Group of Experts on the Democratic Republic of the Congo*, S/2011/738 (2011).

United Nations. *Report of the Secretary-General: Implementation of the Recommendations of the Special Committee on Peacekeeping Operations*, A/65/680 (2011).

United Nations. S/PV.6531 (2011).

United Nations. *Addendum to Interim Report of the Group of Experts on the Democratic Republic of the Congo*, S/2012/348/Add. 1 (2012).

United Nations. *Interim Report of the Group of Experts on the Democratic Republic of the Congo*, S/2012/348 (2012).

United Nations. *Report of the Secretary-General's Internal Review Panel on United Nations Action in Sri Lanka*, November 2012.

United Nations. *On United Nations Peacekeeping Operations*, S/RES/2086 (2013).

United Nations. SP/6917 (2013).

United Nations. S/PV.6513 (2013).

United Nations. S/PV.6916 (2013).

United Nations. S/PV.6917 (2013).

United Nations. *Rights Up Front: A Plan of Action to Strengthen the UN's Role in Protecting People in Crises. Follow-up to the Report of the Secretary-General's Internal Review Panel on UN Action in Sri Lanka*, 9 July 2013.

United Nations. *The Situation Concerning the Democratic Republic of the Congo*, S/RES/2098 (2013).

United Nations. 'Security Council "Intervention Brigade" Authorized as Security Council Grants Mandate Renewal for United Nations Mission in Democratic Republic of Congo', meetings coverage, New York, 28 March 2013.

United Nations. 'Framework of Hope: The Peace, Security and Cooperation Framework for the Democratic Republic of Congo and the Region', Office of the Special Envoy of the Secretary-General for the Great Lakes Region of Africa, 2013.

United Nations. 'Middle East – UNEF I: Background', http://www.un.org/en/peacekeeping/missions/past/unef1backgr2.html

United Nations. 'History of the United Nations' (2013) http://www.un.org/en/aboutun/history/index.shtml

United Nations. 'Lessons Learned: Report on the Joint Protection Team (JPT) Mechanism in MONUSCO. Strengths, Challenges, and Considerations for Replicating JPTs in Other Missions' (New York: DPKO/DFS-OHCHR, 2013).

United Nations. *Human Rights Due Diligence Policy on United Nations Support to Non-United Nations Security Forces*, A/67/775 (2013).

United Nations. *Evaluation of the Implementation and Results of Protection of Civilians Mandates in United Nations Peacekeeping Operations: Report of the Office of Internal Oversight Services* (*OIOS Report*) A/68/787 (2014).

United Nations. *Human Development Report 2014* (New York: United Nations Development Programme, 2014).

United Nations. *No 'Nobler Goal or Greater Sacrifice' than Peacekeepers' Decision to Leave Home to 'Serve the Cause of Peace, Security and Justice'*, GA/SPD/568 (2014).

United Nations. *Report of the Secretary-General on the United Nations Organization Stabilization Mission in the Democratic Republic of the Congo*, S/2014/957 (2014).

United Nations. *Report of the Secretary-General on the United Nations Organization Stabilization Mission in the Democratic Republic of the Congo*, S/2014/957 (2014).

United Nations. *The Situation Concerning the Democratic Republic of the Congo*, S/RES/2147 (2014).

United Nations. *The Final Report of the UN Group of Experts*, S/2015/19 (2015).

United Nations. *The Situation Concerning the Democratic Republic of the Congo*, S/RES/2211 (2015).

United Nations. *DPKO/DFS Policy on the Protection of Civilians in United Nations Peacekeeping* (2015).

United Nations. *Uniting Our Strengths for Peace: Politics, Partnership and People* (New York: Report of the High-Level Independent Panel on Peace Operations, 2015).

United Nations. *Peacekeeping Factsheet: 31 October 2015* (New York: Department of Peacekeeping Operations) http://www.un.org/en/peacekeeping/resources/statistics/factsheet.shtml

United Nations. *Standards of Conduct: We are United Nations Peacekeeping Personnel*, https://cdu.unlb.org/UNStandardsofConduct/WeAreUnitedNationsPeacekeepingPersonnel.aspx

Urquhart, Brian. 'International Peace and Security: Thoughts on the Twentieth Anniversary of Dag Hammarskjold's Death', *Foreign Affairs* (Fall 1981).

Urquhart, Brian. *Hammarskjöld* (New York: W.W. Norton & Company, 1994).

Van Derlijn, Jair and Xenia Avezov. *The Future Peace Operations Landscape: Voices from Stakeholders around the Globe* (Stockholm: SIPRI, 2015).

Van Reybrouck, David. *Congo: The Epic History of a People* (New York: HarperCollins, 2014).

Verdirame, Guglielmo. *The UN and Human Rights: Who Guards the Guardians?* (Cambridge: Cambridge University Press, 2011).

Verini, James. 'Should the United Nations Wage War to Keep Peace?', Special report in *National Geographic*, 27 March 2014.

Vincent, R.J. *Nonintervention and International Order* (Princeton: Princeton University Press, 1974).

Vinck, Patrick and Phuong Pham. *Searching for Lasting Peace: Population-Based Survey on Perceptions and Attitudes about Peace, Security and Justice in Eastern Democratic Republic of the Congo* (Cambridge: Harvard Humanitarian Initiative, Harvard School of Public Health and United Nations Development Programme, 2014).

Vlassenroot, Koen. 'Violence et constitution de milices dans l'Est du Congo: le cas des Mayi-Mayi', in *L'Afrique des Grands Lacs: Annuaire 2001–2* (Paris: l'Harmattan, 2002, 115–52).

Vlassenroot, Koen and Timothy Raeymaekers. 'The Politics of Rebellion and Intervention in Ituri: The Emergence of a New Political Complex?', *African Affairs* 103/412 (2004), 385–412.

Voeten, Erik. 'The Impartiality of International Judges: Evidence from the European Court of Human Rights', *American Political Science Review* 102/4 (2008), 417–32.

Vohra, Shyla. 'Impartiality in United Nations Peace-Keeping', *Leiden Journal of International Law* 9/1 (1996), 63–85.

Voice of America. 'Peacekeepers vow to protect eastern Congo city from rebels', Kinshasa, 10 July 2012.

Wallensteen, Peter and Anders Bjurner, eds., *Regional Organizations and Peacemaking: Challengers to the UN?* (Abingdon: Routledge, 2014).

Weinlich, Silke. '(Re) generating Peacekeeping Authority: The Brahimi Process', *Journal of Intervention and Statebuilding* 6/3 (2012), 257–77.

Weiss, Herbert. 'DRC Crisis' (New York: Panel at Columbia University, March 2010).

Weiss, Thomas and Meryl Kessler. 'Moscow's UN policy', *Foreign Policy* 79 (1990), 94–112.

Weiss, Thomas, Tatiana Carayannis and Richard Jolly. 'The "Third" United Nations', *Global Governance* 15/1 (2009), 123–42.

Weissman, Stephen et al., 'Absent in Central Africa. How the United States Risks Reigniting Chaos in Congo', *Foreign Affairs*, 8 June 2015.

Weller, Marc (ed.). *The Oxford Handbook of the Use of Force in International Law* (Oxford: Oxford University Press, 2015).

Welsh, Jennifer and Dominik Zaum. 'Legitimation and the United Nations Security Council', in *Legitimating International Organizations*, Dominik Zaum (ed.) (Oxford: Oxford University Press, 2013).

Western, Jon and Joshua Goldstein. 'Humanitarian Intervention Comes of Age: Lessons from Somalia to Libya', *Foreign Affairs* 90/6 (2011), 48–59.

Whalan, Jeni. *How Peace Operations Work: Power, Legitimacy and Effectiveness* (Oxford: Oxford University Press, 2013).

Wheeler, Nicholas. *Saving Strangers: Humanitarian Intervention in International Society* (Oxford: Oxford University Press, 2002).

Wiener, Antje. 'The Dual Quality of Norms and Governance beyond the State: Sociological and Normative Approaches to "Interaction"', *Critical Review of International Social and Political Philosophy* 10/1 (2007), 47–69.

Wiener, Antje. *The Invisible Constitution of Politics. Contested Norms and International Encounters* (Cambridge: Cambridge University Press, 2008).

Wills, Siobhán. *Protecting Civilians: The Obligations of Peacekeepers* (Oxford: Oxford University Press, 2009).

Winter, Philip. *A Sacred Cause: The Inter-Congolese Dialogue 2000–2003* (Edinburgh: Librario, 2012).

Woodhouse, Tom and Oliver Ramsbotham. 'Cosmopolitan Peacekeeping and the Globalization of Security', *International Peacekeeping* 12/2 (2005), 139–56.

Yamashita, Hikaru. '"Impartial" Use of Force in United Nations Peacekeeping', *International Peacekeeping* 15/5 (2008), 615–30.

Zaum, Dominik. *The Sovereignty Paradox: The Norms and Politics of International Statebuilding* (Oxford: Oxford University Press, 2007).

Zaum, Dominik. 'The Uniting for Peace Resolution', in *The United Nations Security Council and War: The Evolution of Thought and Practice since 1945*, edited by Vaughan Lowe, Adam Roberts, Jennifer M. Welsh, and Dominik Zaum (Oxford: Oxford University Press, 2008).

Zaum, Dominik (ed.). *Legitimating International Organizations* (Oxford: Oxford University Press, 2013).

Index